THE FEDERAL
COURTS
AS A
POLITICAL SYSTEM

0

Harper's American Political Behavior Series,
Under the Consulting Editorship of DAVID J. DANELSKI

HARPER & ROW, PUBLISHERS

New York, Hagerstown, San Francisco, London

THE FEDERAL COURTS AS A POLITICAL SYSTEM

Second Edition

SHELDON GOLDMAN

University of Massachusetts

THOMAS P. JAHNIGE

Late, Smith College

Sponsoring Editor: Dale Tharp
Project Editor: Richard T. Viggiano
Production Supervisor: Will C. Jomarrón
Compositor: American Book–Stratford Press, Inc.
Printer and Binder: The Murray Printing Company
Art Studio: Soho Studio

THE FEDERAL COURTS AS A POLITICAL SYSTEM, Second Edition
Copyright © 1976 by Sheldon Goldman. Copyright © 1971 by Sheldon Goldman and Thomas P. Jahnige.

Library of Congress Cataloging in Publication Data

Goldman, Sheldon.
  The Federal courts as a political system.

  (Harper's American political behavior series)
  Includes bibliographical references and index.
  1. Courts—United States. 2. Law and politics.
I. Jahnige, Thomas P., joint author. II. Title.
KF8700.Z9G63 1976   347'.73'202   75-26782
ISBN 0-06-042382-X

In memory of Thomas P. Jahnige (1938–1973)
and for
his wife Molly and children Kathy and Paul

CONTENTS

PREFACE

PLANNING for this edition began shortly before Tom Jahnige's untimely death from Hodgkin's disease. Tom was enthused about undertaking a second edition, because we were both gratified with the response of colleagues and students alike concerning the usefulness of the first edition. I have sought to carry through the general points Tom and I agreed would provide the basis for this edition. In particular, the systems framework as we originally utilized it has been retained, but of course many new materials have been incorporated that have been published or became available since the first edition. Original empirical analyses have also been brought up to date. New sections (such as the one on legal services lawyers and the one on criminal sentencing) have been added where appropriate, to take into account the latest developments concerning the federal judicial system, as well as the research topics that have been the focus of increased scholarly attention since the first edition.

There are many people to thank. First and foremost, David Danelski has been a constant source of encouragement and a fount of excellent suggestions. He was for Tom and remains for me a treasured friend and colleague. There are numerous scholars in the field without whose research contributions this book could not have been written. A glance at the index should indicate some measure of my indebtedness to them. In particular, I would like to thank Professor Jerry Goldman for providing most helpful data, comments, and suggestions concerning Chapter Four and for leading me to some of the excellent studies published by the Federal Judicial Center. James McCafferty of the Administrative Office of the U.S. Courts was specially helpful in providing the immensely useful maps and reports prepared by the Administrative Office. Professor Jonathan Casper read the entire manuscript and offered valuable advice. None of these colleagues and institutions are to be held responsible for the use to which I put their materials and advice. Molly Jahnige did a superb job of typing the manuscript, and her help in meeting manuscript deadlines and in proofreading was in the spirit of collaborator rather than typist. Ms. Sandra Bloomfield did a marvelous job of copyediting, and the folks at Harper & Row, especially Dick Viggiano and Ron Taylor, showered attention on the manuscript beyond my expectations thereby making this publishing experience most satisfying. Finally, I must acknowledge the support (both positive diffuse and positive specific) of my wife Marcia and my children Ellen, Jeremy, and Sara. They are to be thanked (or blamed) for allowing me to get this edition out of my system.

SHELDON GOLDMAN
September 1975

PREFACE TO THE FIRST EDITION

I N this text we seek to demonstrate the workings of the federal courts as a political system within the context of the larger American political system. Systems analysis as developed by David Easton and adapted for our concerns provides the conceptual framework.

To write a relatively brief introductory work imposes severe limits. The subject matter is so vast that sins of omission (and perhaps commission) will be evident in the pages ahead and for that we must assume full responsibility. Nevertheless, we have attempted to integrate a large body of material concerning the federal judicial process and its political context so that an otherwise unrelated torrent of data and analysis will hopefully make some sense to the beginning student. It is our hope that, rather than provide obscure jargon, systems concepts as developed here can help to sharpen the student's analytical abilities.

We would be less than candid if we did not acknowledge that systems analysis has recently been subjected to severe scrutiny by some in the discipline. Although the major issues raised are discussed in the final chapter, it is perhaps useful at the outset to emphasize that we believe the principal virtues of the framework are its organizing and heuristic qualities. *At best*, judicial systems analysis is one step toward the development of an empirical theory of courts and judicial behavior.

We have a special debt to Professor David J. Danelski for his encouragement and advice. His constructive suggestions were invariably pertinent and surely whatever merit this book possesses must be attributed in large measure to him. Numerous other scholars contributed more indirectly to this enterprise. We hope their invaluable contributions are recognized by the footnote citations. Many others deserve our thanks and public acknowledgment. Mrs. Donna Deery and Mrs. Virginia Goodrich provided expert typing services. Some of the original empirical analyses were undertaken with the aid of grants from the University of Massachusetts (faculty research, growth, and computer time grants) and the Social Science Research Council to Sheldon Goldman. Smith College generously provided Thomas Jahnige with a semester's leave in which to work on this book. The *Rutgers–Camden Law Journal, Jurimetrics Journal,* and *Polity* have allowed us to draw upon our articles which have appeared in their publications.

Once again, our wives patiently endured our affair with textbook writing and to them we affectionately dedicate this book.

THOMAS P. JAHNIGE
SHELDON GOLDMAN

THE FEDERAL
COURTS
AS A
POLITICAL SYSTEM

ONE
INTRODUCTION

O VER the last four decades, an increased commitment to empirical investigation has been apparent among the practitioners of political science. In more recent years, they as well as other social scientists have also been developing general theories, models, or frameworks with which to examine the subject matter of their respective disciplines. One such general framework that has been widely used by political scientists is *political systems analysis*.[1] In this book systems analysis as developed by David Easton[2] is used to examine the federal judicial process.[3]

[1] See William C. Mitchell, "Political Systems," *International Encyclopedia of the Social Sciences*, 15 (1968), 473–479.

[2] Easton first developed political systems analysis in "An Approach to the Analysis of Political Systems," *World Politics*, 9 (1957), 383–400. His most extensive formulations upon which this book is based were contained in *A Framework for Political Analysis* (Englewood Cliffs, N.J.: Prentice-Hall, 1965) and *A Systems Analysis of Political Life* (New York: Wiley, 1965). Easton responded to his critics in "Systems Analysis and Its Classical Critics," *Political Science Reviewer*, 3 (1973), 269–301, and in "Systems Analysis in Politics and Its Critics," in H. J. Johnson (ed.), *Political Theory* (Dordrecht, The Netherlands: Reidel, 1973).

[3] Alternative political systems analyses of the state and/or federal judiciaries (some of which borrow in part from Eastonian analysis) include: S. Sidney Ulmer, "Homeostatic Tendencies in the United States Supreme Court," in S. Sidney Ulmer (ed.), *Introductory Readings in Political Behavior* (Skokie, Ill.: Rand McNally, 1961), pp. 167–188; James Herndon, "The Role of the Judiciary in State Political Systems: Some Explorations," in Glendon Schubert (ed.), *Judicial Behavior: A Reader in Theory and Research* (Skokie, Ill.: Rand McNally, 1964), pp. 153–161; Walter Murphy, *Elements of Judicial Strategy* (Chicago: University of Chicago Press, 1964), pp. 31–36; Glendon Schubert, *Judicial Policy-Making* (Glenview, Ill.: Scott, Foresman,

A system, according to Easton, is "any set of variables regardless of the degree of interrelationship among them."[4] In practice, political scientists are interested in political systems in which the basic unit interactions are highly dependent upon and interrelated with one another and which as a set exhibit *boundary-maintaining* characteristics. This means that those involved in the interactions behave in such a manner as to strive to maintain the system's integrity and cohesion.[5]

Every political system exists within and is affected by the physical, biological, social, economic, and cultural environments (all of which may also be analyzed from a systems approach). What distinguishes a political system from these environments is that its interactions deal with the authoritative allocation of values for a society;[6] that is, a political system is concerned with deciding in the name of society who within that society gets what, when, where, and how.[7]

1965; revised edition, 1974); Jay Sigler, *An Introduction to the Legal System* (Homewood, Ill.: Dorsey, 1968); Joel B. Grossman, "A Model for Judicial Policy Analysis: The Supreme Court and the Sit-In Cases," in Joel B. Grossman and Joseph Tanenhaus (eds.), *Frontiers of Judicial Research* (New York: Wiley, 1969), pp. 405–460; Joel B. Grossman and Austin Sarat, "Political Culture and Judicial Research," *Washington University Law Quarterly* (1971), 177–207; Daryl R. Fair, "A Framework for Analyzing the Elements of Stability in Judicial Policy-Making," *Rutgers-Camden Law Journal*, 3 (1972), 395–409; Henry R. Glick and Kenneth N. Vines, *State Court Systems* (Englewood Cliffs, N.J.: Prentice-Hall, 1973); Charles H. Sheldon, *The American Judicial Process: Models and Approaches* (New York: Dodd, Mead, 1974). Also see Thomas P. Jahnige and Sheldon Goldman (eds.), *The Federal Judicial System: Readings in Process and Behavior* (New York: Holt, Rinehart and Winston, 1968), for an earlier and less complete adaptation of Eastonian analysis than now presented. A discussion of the major analyses published during the 1960s and how they differ from Eastonian analysis as used here can be found in Sheldon Goldman and Thomas P. Jahnige, "Systems Analysis and Judicial Systems: Potential and Limitations," *Polity*, 3 (1971), 334–359. It should be noted that in this book the subject of military justice is not treated. Rather the focus is exclusively on the principal federal civilian courts. Various aspects of military justice, however, are investigated in S. Sidney Ulmer, *Military Justice and the Right to Counsel* (Lexington: University Press of Kentucky, 1970); Paul Lermack, "Summary and Special Courts-Martial," Ph.D. dissertation, University of Minnesota, 1972; Joseph W. Bishop, Jr., *Justice under Fire: A Study of Military Law* (New York: Charterhouse, 1974).

[4] Easton, *A Systems Analysis of Political Life*, p. 21.

[5] Easton discusses this in *A Framework for Political Analysis*, pp. 25, 36.

[6] *Ibid.*, p. 50.

[7] This is a paraphrase of Harold Lasswell's famous definition. See his *Politics: Who Gets What, When, How* (Cleveland: Meridian Books, World, 1958). For an alternative and broader view of politics see Harry Eckstein, "Authority Patterns: A Structural

Those who do the interacting are considered to be the *politically relevant members* of the system. They are, in Easton's words, "those members of a system who count, . . . who share in the effective power of the system."[8] Some of them are considered in systems terminology to be the *authorities,* that is, those occupants of systemic roles who exercise discretion and influence in making decisions for allocating such valued things as wealth, power, prestige, and ideals. The system's *regime rules* specify the manner by which the authorities may allocate those values.

Political systems are *open systems.* They are thus constantly subject to stresses or disturbances that emanate from the environment. If the system is to persist, these disintegrative forces must be defused. In other words, these disturbances must be confronted and processed if the system's authorities are to maintain their ability to allocate values for the society and to induce most members of the system to accept those allocations as binding. How the system handles such disturbances shapes the nature of its particular political system. To understand how a system persists means discovering how the system deals with and reduces stress.

Constantly entering the system are *demands* for particular authoritative allocations of values. At the same time, the system's politically relevant members hold certain views reflecting their satisfaction or dissatisfaction with the system. These attitudes can be specific in relation to past allocations (in systems terminology this is called *specific* support) or more general or diffuse views of the system (called *diffuse* support). The demands and the two types of support are a major *input* to the system.

The authorities in their institutional roles confront, evaluate, reshape, and process this input. This decision-making stage is called *conversion* (or the conversion of inputs into systemic responses). The decisions that are made are *output* of the system. The output's subsequent impact generates behavioral responses that are communicated or fed back (*feedback*) to the system as new input.

These are the basic Eastonian political systems concepts that provide the organizational framework for examining the structure, process, and behavior of the federal courts.

Basis for Political Inquiry," *American Political Science Review,* 67 (1973), 1142–1161. Cf. Fred M. Frohock, "Notes on the Concept of Politics: Weber, Easton, Strauss," *Journal of Politics,* 36 (1974), 379–408.

[8] Easton, *A Systems Analysis of Political Life,* p. 22.

THE FEDERAL COURTS AS A POLITICAL SYSTEM

The federal judicial system[9] can be conceptualized as encompassing all interactions in American society concerning the authoritative allocation of values involving the judicial authorities of the federal courts. Courts primarily allocate values by deciding cases and issuing rules of procedure and other court orders. The authorities of the system include judges, jurors, administrative and supporting court personnel, and private attorneys as well as attorneys for the federal government whose practice takes them before the federal courts. Litigants and witnesses are not considered authorities because their behavior is not governed by any unique role considerations other than such general cultural injunctions as "tell the truth," nor do they make authoritative decisions for the system. Rather, they are considered politically relevant sources and carriers of demands and information. Members of the general public are also considered politically relevant when aware of the operation of the system and act (or can be expected to act) in response to its output. The same is true of interest groups and the mass media. The federal judicial system's regime rules include the formal laws, rules, and procedures followed and applied by the authorities in processing demands and various legal and judicial cultural concepts such as judicial neutrality, adherence to precedent, and lawyer advocacy. Figure 1.1 illustrates the interrelationship of the principal systems concepts in the federal judicial system.[10]

Input

The federal judicial system is embedded in an environment that includes the various physical, biological, social, economic, cultural, and, of course, political systems. The political environment contains all other political systems within the United States including Congress,

[9] It should be recognized that the federal judicial (or court) system can also be conceptualized as a subsystem of the larger American political system and for certain purposes it is more useful to so treat it.

[10] The diagram is a simplification of reality. It is applicable to cases that begin in the district courts and are appealed to the appeals courts and then to the Supreme Court. Certain demands in the form of litigation can take other routes not illustrated by the diagram. For example, some cases of special constitutional significance are heard by three-judge district courts and then are appealed to the Supreme Court, thus bypassing the appeals courts. Most federal agency appeals bypass the district courts and go directly to the appeals courts. Appeals from the highest state courts are demands made exclusively on the Supreme Court.

Figure 1.1 The federal judicial system

the fifty state judicial systems, the fifty state legislative systems, and the federal and state executive-bureaucratic systems. These systems are constantly subjected to the changing material and psychic conditions of the members populating them. Such conditions generate needs, wants, resentments, and expectations to which the federal judicial system as an open system is subject. They are transmitted to the courts as demands principally through litigation. As with all political systems, both the form and content of acceptable demands may be limited by two types of mechanisms that regulate the flow of demands: regime rules and gatekeeping.

Regime rules control the flow of demands by inhibiting many wants from being converted into demands in the first place. Within the federal judicial system such regime rules are subsumed in concepts such as *jurisdiction* (whether the court under federal and constitutional law has the authority to adjudicate the matter), *standing to sue* (a variety of rules to determine whether the court will recognize the litigant and the matter brought to court, for example, is there a genuine case or controversy in which the litigant is personally involved?), and *justiciability* (for example, if the court has jurisdiction and the litigant has standing, is the matter suitable for resolution by the judicial branch? Is there a remedy that is appropriate for the court to administer? Or is the matter better resolved by the political branches of government?). Regime rules not only regulate demand flow at the point of introduction of litigation into the system, but they may limit the extent to which a demand will be treated by the system. Certain formal and informal rules and processes result in settlement without trial of most litigation in the federal system. Other rules and processes operate to regulate demand input at the appellate stage.

The second major mechanism limiting demand flow is what Easton calls "gatekeeping."[11] Gatekeepers are those situated at the boundary of the system and at various points within it who reduce the number of demands or modify their content. Judges and particularly attorneys (both public and private) perform this function for the federal system by, for example, encouraging guilty pleas and out-of-court settlements.

Support (both specific and diffuse) is another key input for the federal judicial system. A major source of stress on the system can be a decline of favorable attitudes on the part of the politically relevant members of the system concerning particular policy outputs and/or the general functioning of the system. High levels of unfavorable specific or diffuse attitudes are thought to be related to difficulties in obtaining compliance with the system's output. Because the federal courts have no independent enforcement machinery to compel compliance, coercion, when it is needed, must be supplied by executive officials. At the very least, therefore, the federal judicial system requires a minimum level of positive support among these officials to be able to function.

By definition, demands and support as inputs link the system to the different kinds of disturbances that originate in the environment. Disturbances that stem exclusively from *within* the system, however, can be separately considered as "withinputs." According to Easton, withinputs are "those demands formed through experiences and activities [of those in the system when acting] in strictly political roles."[12] Demands and other inputs of positive or negative support on the part of the lower federal courts toward the Supreme Court, as well as the reverse, can be considered a type of judicial system withinput. Various intrasystemic structures, such as judicial councils and conferences, can also generate as well as process withinput.

[11] Easton, *A Systems Analysis of Political Life,* pp. 87–96, 133–137.
[12] *Ibid.,* p. 55.

Conversion

Conversion, it will be recalled, is the decision-making-by-the-authorities stage. A complete portrait of conversion in the federal judicial system would include an analysis of jury decision making as well as decision making by all other authorities in the system (including private and government attorneys, law clerks, and administrative court personnel) as they exercise discretion and influence judicial output by virtue of the decisions they make within the system. Since judges, however, are the primary authorities of the federal judicial system, our focus shall be on them and judicial conversion.

Output

Judicial outputs involve both the workings of the federal judicial system, such as the rules concerning the processing of criminal and civil cases, and the transactions between the judicial system and its political and other environments (the latter being responsible for most of the business of the federal courts). *Authoritative outputs* are the binding rulings resolving particular cases, judicially articulated rules of procedure, and court orders. *Associated outputs* include the written justification for the rulings as well as public and private activity related in any way to the judge's official position.

Feedback

The outputs return "to haunt the system"[13] by stimulating behavioral responses by members of the political system. These responses are fed back to the authorities (this is called "information feedback") through various formal and informal channels. The impact, existence of compliance or noncompliance, or changes in the level and kind of support, or attempts to limit the authorities and redefine the boundaries of the system, are all communicated to the judicial authorities through these channels. A major formal channel of feedback for the federal judicial system consists of the new demands (cases) fed into the system in response to past decisions. Another obvious form of feedback is in the appointment of new judges to the Supreme Court and the lower federal courts. Easton assumes that the authorities are responsive to feedback in order to minimize discontent or satisfy

[13] *Ibid.*, p. 29.

grievances that arose over the initial outputs. Indeed, Easton categorically states that "without feedback and the capacity to respond to it, no system could survive for long, except by accident."[14]

These and other systems concepts shall be examined more thoroughly in subsequent chapters, and their utility for understanding the federal judicial process will be demonstrated. However, at this point it is helpful for purposes of illustration to use the basic systems approach for an interpretation of two key events concerning the Supreme Court. The first event involves the federal judiciary's handling of federal and state economic regulation cases during the 1930s. The second concerns the transformation of the Warren Court into the Nixon Court.

THE HUGHES COURT AND THE SWITCH OF 1937

From the 1880s well into the 1930s, the Supreme Court adopted and promoted a policy of economic laissez-faire by which the Court generally questioned the constitutionality of state and federal economic regulation.[15] By maintaining the old conservative economic doctrines during the difficult years of the Great Depression, the Court was clearly out of step with the times, needs, and wants of the country. Finally after the 1936 presidential election, President Roosevelt presented a court reform plan to Congress that would have potentially increased the membership of the Supreme Court to a maximum of fifteen members (the plan was popularly referred to as Roosevelt's "court-packing" plan).

Several months later an unusual judicial event occurred. The Supreme Court suddenly began sustaining the constitutionality of state and federal economic regulation. This switch was most dramatically signaled by a change in the voting behavior of Justice Owen Roberts. Early in 1936 Roberts had voted with Justices Van Devanter, McReynolds, Sutherland, and Butler to form a 5–4 majority striking down New York State's minimum wage law (*Morehead* v. *New York*

---

[14] *Ibid.*, p. 32.

[15] This is recounted in Robert G. McCloskey, *The American Supreme Court* (Chicago: University of Chicago Press, 1960). Also see the description of the 1937 "revolution" in Loren P. Beth, *Politics, the Constitution and the Supreme Court* (New York: Harper & Row, 1962), pp. 111.–130. But cf. Martin Shapiro and Douglas S. Hobbs, *The Politics of Constitutional Law* (Cambridge, Mass.: Winthrop, 1974), pp. 90–94, 143–153.

ex rel. Tipaldo[16]). However, after the election of 1936, Roberts joined Chief Justice Hughes and Justices Cardozo, Brandeis, and Stone to uphold a Washington State minimum wage law indistinguishable from the New York law (the case was *West Coast Hotel* v. *Parrish*[17]). This was the turning point. The Court's new liberal attitude toward government economic regulation found expression in case after case thereafter. This profound change on the part of Justice Roberts became known, in light of the Roosevelt court-packing plan, as the switch-in-time-that-saved-nine.[18] How can the systems framework interpret these momentous events?

At the outset we can consider the judicial authorities on the Hughes Court. The justices differed markedly in their political, economic, social, and jurisprudential attitudes. Four justices (Van Devanter, McReynolds, Sutherland, and Butler) can perhaps be best described as reactionaries in that they were simply not attuned to the political, economic, and social realities of twentieth-century America. Three justices (Cardozo, Brandeis, and Stone) were liberals in that they recognized the need of government to be able to confront the grave economic crisis and to be able to manage the economy of the nation. Justice Roberts was somewhat more moderate than the reactionaries, and Chief Justice Hughes was somewhat to the left of him. As Chief Justice, Hughes was entitled (when he voted with the majority) to make the assignment as to who would write the Court's opinion. Hughes was vitally concerned with who spoke for the Court on what issue, and this meant that he liked to be on the winning side so that he could exercise his opinion-assignment power.[19] Apparently he

[16] 298 U.S. 587 (1936).

[17] 300 U.S. 379 (1937).

[18] But cf. Roberts's explanation of his behavior in Felix Frankfurter, "Mr. Justice Roberts," *University of Pennsylvania Law Review*, 104 (1955), 313–316.

[19] David J. Danelski, "The Assignment of the Court's Opinion by the Chief Justice," paper read at the Midwest Conference of Political Scientists, Annual Meeting, 1960, pp. 18–22. Perhaps the classic example of a Chief Justice dominating opinion assignment was John Marshall's voting with the majority even when he disagreed with it so that he could write the Court's opinion. See John Schmidhauser, *The Supreme Court: Its Politics, Personalities and Procedures* (New York: Holt, Rinehart and Winston, 1960), pp. 110–114. In general, see David W. Rohde, "Policy Goals, Strategic Choice and Majority Opinion Assignments in the United States Supreme Court," *Midwest Journal of Political Science*, 16 (1972), 652–682; Gregory James Rathjen, "Policy Goals, Strategic Choice, and Majority Opinion Assignment in the U.S. Supreme Court: A Replication," *American Journal of Political Science*, 18 (1974), 713–724.

tried to make antigovernment decisions less provocative by assigning the opinion either to Justice Roberts, one of the more diplomatic nonliberals, or to a liberal if one happened to be voting with the majority.[20] We can interpret Hughes's behavior as Chief Justice as attempting to favorably influence diffuse if not specific support.

The political and nonpolitical environments must also be considered. The country was in the midst of the most devastating economic depression in our history. A frighteningly large proportion of the nation was unemployed and destitute. The economic and social environments were the source of profound disturbances that were translated into demands presented to all levels of government for immediate relief measures and programs that would reverse the Depression. The political, social, and economic environments ultimately were the source of demands on the Hughes Court to sustain the constitutionality of New Deal legislation.

The Court's antipathy toward economic and social welfare legislation to ameliorate the harsh effects of the Depression produced a great variety of activity within the environment as the economy continued to falter, as social and political unrest increased, and as unemployment continued high and wages remained low. Within the law schools and the universities, criticism of Court policies was severe. Politicians gained office and popularity by supporting views of economic regulation that the Court had ruled unconstitutional. There was talk about amending the Constitution. Congress and the state legislatures passed new economic regulations after the old ones had been declared invalid. Finally the presidential court-packing plan was introduced, which public opinion polls initially showed to be favorably received by a majority in the country.

As an open system these facts were fed back to the Court. The widespread denunciation of the Court by politicians and the press, the Gallup polls that indicated that a large majority of Americans opposed the Court's policies, Roosevelt's landslide victory in 1936 and his subsequent court reform plan were negative feedback of the

[20] David J. Danelski, "The Influence of the Chief Justice in the Decisional Process of the Supreme Court," in Jahnige and Goldman (eds.), *Federal Judicial System,* pp. 157–158. It should also be noted that there was probably another motive for Hughes's voting with the majority. If Hughes would have been a fourth member of a minority, he could avoid a 5–4 decision by going along with the majority and thereby give greater weight to the majority's decision and opinion.

most profound sort. More formally, new litigation was the principal conveyor of feedback.

The loss of both specific and diffuse support, the demands from the President and Congress, the fact that its decisions produced more stress on the Court rather than less, the fact that the ability of the Court to allocate values authoritatively and to have those allocations accepted as binding was seriously threatened, all meant that the Court *had* to adjust its output if it was to retain its integrity as a system. Something had to give if the federal judicial system was to persist. And it did. Output changed and the Court abandoned its restrictive economic policies. That it was Roberts (and also Hughes) who were vehicles of the change is largely irrelevant from a systems viewpoint. The change in output could even have been brought about through the more "normal" mechanism of appointment (as will be seen shortly with our second example). The point is that the federal judiciary as an open system is subjected to this feedback. Its future policy outputs are ultimately influenced by the impact of previous outputs and subsequent feedback.

FROM THE WARREN COURT TO THE NIXON COURT

Just as the pre-1937 Court was generally committed to laissez-faire economic values and was activist in promoting them, the Warren Court was committed to civil libertarian values and was activist on their behalf. The pre-1937 Court generally had the backing of the political right and the opposition of the political left, while the Warren Court generally derived its backing and opposition from exactly the opposite sources. The output of the pre-1937 Court did not adequately respond to negative feedback, but rather served to increase stress on the system. The ability of the system to persist was so threatened that a change in output was inevitable. It would seem that there also are parallels with the Warren Court.

Over the years the Warren Court accumulated a host of vigorous opponents. The landmark desegregation decisions, the reapportionment decisions, decisions concerning prayers in the public schools, obscenity, the rights of alleged subversives, and most importantly the rights of criminal defendants stimulated an opposition that substantially reduced positive support for the Court among the general public and government officials.[21] Feedback was increasingly negative and for the most part output was unresponsive. A high point for the opponents of Warren Court policies occurred in June, 1968, with the fight over the nomination of Justice Fortas to succeed Chief Justice Warren (who had previously announced his intention to retire). Fortas became the scapegoat for the liberal Court, and both were subjected to fierce verbal attacks during the Senate filibuster over the nomination. When the Senate failed to invoke cloture to end the filibuster, Justice Fortas asked President Johnson to withdraw his nomination because of his desire to put a stop to (in his words) "destructive and extreme assaults upon the Court."[22]

Subsequently in the 1968 presidential campaign the Supreme Court became a major issue (just as its rulings were in the 1936 campaign). Two presidential candidates, Nixon and Wallace, attacked the Court for its civil libertarian policies, in particular those relating to the rights of criminal defendants. Both anti-Court candidates received a combined total of 57 percent of the popular vote and one became President. Then in a move strikingly similar to Roosevelt's court-packing stratagem, the Nixon Administration moved against Justice Fortas who, because of the earlier controversy, was one of the more vulnerable Warren Court liberals. The end result was the creation of a vacancy on the Court that, along with the vacancy of the Chief Justice slot, permitted President Nixon to appoint two justices who would (and did) bring about a turnaround on the Court particularly concerning the issue of the rights of criminal defendants.[23] How the Nixon Administration brought about the Fortas resignation is of interest.[24]

[21] Supporting data and citations are presented in Chapters 4 and 7. Also see Fred P. Graham, *The Self-Inflicted Wound* (New York: Macmillan, 1970).

[22] *New York Times*, October 3, 1968, p. 42.

[23] These points are explored in later chapters. Also see James F. Simon, *In His Own Image: The Supreme Court in Richard Nixon's America* (New York: McKay, 1973) and Leonard W. Levy, *Against the Law: The Nixon Court and Criminal Justice* (New York: Harper & Row, 1974).

[24] Although there is much behind-the-scenes detail of which we know little, in light of the sordid, illegal, and unethical modus operandi of the Nixonians that is now a matter of public record (see, e.g., the 1973 Senate Watergate Committee Hearings and the 1974 Impeachment Proceedings of the House Judiciary Committee), it is now plausible to interpret the actions of the Nixonians described in the text as having their genesis in what would later be known as a political enemies strategy.

In the May 5, 1969, issue of *Life* magazine, an article appeared containing serious allegations and insinuations of improper behavior on the part of Justice Fortas.[25] These same charges had been dismissed six months earlier by the previous Democratic Administration's Attorney General (Ramsey Clark) as without merit.[26] However, within a two-week period, the Republican Nixon Administration successfully exerted pressure on liberal Democrat Justice Fortas to resign from the Court. During that period the Justice Department initiated a federal grand jury investigation into charges against Fortas's old law firm (a move that questioned the integrity of the firm and, by implication, Fortas);[27] the Justice Department vigorously investigated the allegations and subpoenaed personal letters and papers of financier Louis Wolfson with whom Fortas allegedly was improperly involved;[28] Attorney General John Mitchell hinted to the press that the Justice Department had uncovered "far more serious" (but unspecified) wrongdoings that would become public unless Fortas resigned;[29] conservative Republican congressmen announced their intention of instituting impeachment proceedings against Fortas if he did not resign immediately;[30] and Attorney General Mitchell met with Chief Justice Warren reportedly to brief him on the matter and to enlist his aid in persuading Fortas to resign.[31]

For a different view of these events see Robert Shogan, *A Question of Judgement: The Fortas Case and the Struggle for the Supreme Court* (Indianapolis: Bobbs-Merrill, 1972).

25 William Lambert, "The Justice . . . and the Stock Manipulator," *Life*, May 5, 1969, pp. 32–37. One of Lambert's sources in the White House was the later-to-be-convicted Watergate conspirator E. Howard Hunt who let Lambert see and copy forged State Department cables that, if published, would have damaged the reputation of the Kennedy Administration. Lambert did not use this particular material. See J. Anthony Lukas, "Watergate: The Story So Far," *New York Times Magazine*, July 22, 1973, p. 14.

26 *New York Times*, May 15, 1969, p. 28.

27 *Congressional Quarterly*, May 9, 1969, p. 674. Also see *New York Times*, May 8, 1969, p. 34.

28 *New York Times*, May 18, 1969, p. 1.

29 *New York Times*, May 12, 1969, p. 35.

30 *New York Times*, May 8, 1969, p. 34. Also see *New York Times*, May 12, 1969, p. 1.

31 *New York Times*, May 13, 1969, p. 23; *Congressional Quarterly*, May 16, 1969, pp. 705–709.

The low level of support for the Court seems in part responsible for the fact that few came to Fortas's defense. Although the public record contained no shred of evidence that Justice Fortas ever interceded on behalf of or took part in any legal, administrative, or judicial matter concerning Wolfson or his associates, the pressure was too great and Fortas resigned well aware that impeachment proceedings would further damage the Court's prestige as well as his own.[32] Shortly thereafter another liberal, Justice Douglas, accused the Administration of also trying to force him off the bench. At the time nothing came of Douglas's charges or his fears,[33] but some months later he was subjected to a renewed attempt to force him off the Court—an attempt led by then–Republican House Leader Gerald R. Ford.[34]

The most successful form of feedback calculated to change output is the appointment of new justices. Within the first six months of holding office, President Nixon not only had an opportunity to appoint a new associate justice, but also had the chief justiceship position to fill. To the latter post he appointed Warren Burger, a strong opponent of the Court's libertarian views concerning various rights of criminal defendants, and as associate justice he first nominated an economic and political conservative from South Carolina, Chief Judge (of the U.S. Court of Appeals for the Fourth Circuit) Clement Haynsworth. Haynsworth's nomination was opposed by labor and civil rights groups as well as by those who accused Haynsworth of judicial insensitivities perhaps even more serious than those that forced Fortas's resignation because they involved allegations concerning Haynsworth's voting behavior as an appeals court judge.[35] President Nixon nevertheless strongly supported Haynsworth and frankly admitted to newspaper reporters that "the Court needs balance, . . . a man who is conservative."[36] The Senate defeated the Haynsworth

[32] New York Times, May 16, 1969, p. 1.

[33] New York Times, May 27, 1969, p. 34.

[34] See New York Times, November 8, 1969, p. 1; Congressional Quarterly, April 17, 1970, p. 1045; Milton Viorst, "Bill Douglas Has Never Stopped Fighting the Bullies of Yakima," New York Times Magazine, June 14, 1970, p. 52.

[35] New York Times, October 21, 1969, p. 35. See Edward N. Beiser, "The Haynsworth Affair Reconsidered: The Significance of Conflicting Perceptions of the Judicial Role," Vanderbilt Law Review, 23 (1970), 263–291.

[36] Congressional Quarterly, October 24, 1969, p. 2103.

nomination and also the subsequent nomination of another southern conservative, G. Harrold Carswell. However, the President eventually succeeded in placing on the Court Judge Harry Blackmun, a conservative midwestern federal court of appeals judge.[37] In early autumn, 1971, Justices Black and Harlan, both in ill health, retired and President Nixon filled the vacancies with two more conservatives, a southerner and former American Bar Association president, Lewis Powell, and a Justice Department official, William Rehnquist.

The transformation of the liberal Warren Court to the more conservative Nixon Court, although not as dramatic[38] as the switch-in-time of 1937, nevertheless is what could be expected from adopting the systems approach. Something *had* to give. Support for the Court was at a low ebb among the general public and among key government officials. Instead of reducing stress, output was contributing to it. Although systems analysis could not predict the form that change would take nor precisely when it would occur, the approach nevertheless alerted us to the variables that inevitably precede change.

WHY USE THE SYSTEMS APPROACH?

The previous examples briefly considered two well-known judicial events from a broad systems perspective. At the very minimum, systems analysis extends our view. It allows us to consider interactions and processes that otherwise might be ignored. The systems framework imposes a logic on political institutions, actors, and events. It provides concepts with which to organize large and diverse accumulations of data. Systems analysis is simple enough for the beginning student to comprehend despite lack of familiarity with the statistical

---

[37] *Congressional Quarterly*, April 17, 1970, p. 1044. The preceding account, of course, is an oversimplification of the events that occurred in the Senate. A full appreciation of the dramatic events of the doomed Haynsworth-Carswell nominations would have to take into account the Senate as a system including its relationship to the President. See Joel B. Grossman and Stephen Wasby, "Haynsworth and Parker: History Does Live Again," *South Carolina Law Review*, 23 (1971), 345–359.

[38] Note that for some justices the transformation apparently *has* been dramatic. For example, in a dissent, Justice Stewart castigated the majority in Mitchell v. W. T. Grant Company [94 S. Ct. 1895 (1974) at 1914] with his observation that "A basic change in law upon a ground no firmer than a change in our membership invites the popular misconception that this institution is little different from the two political branches of the Government."

and mathematical techniques of the social sciences, yet at the same time studies using such techniques can be placed and discussed within the systems framework. Systems analysis, then, can provide useful organizing concepts and can serve as a helpful heuristic device. Despite several limitations of the framework,[39] it will undoubtedly help to illuminate the intricate workings and interrelations of the federal judicial system.

---

[39] A discussion of some limitations of the framework can be found in Goldman and Jahnige, "Systems Analysis and Judicial Systems: Potential and Limitations."

TWO
REGIME RULES: SYSTEMIC ORGANIZATION, PROCEDURES, AND NORMS

THE federal judicial system, like every political system, is characterized by a complex of rules and concepts prescribing the process by which decisions are made by the authorities. These rules and concepts are the system's *regime rules*. Many are formally stated in statutes and judicial rules or are written in the U.S. Constitution. Others exist as commonly held beliefs as to "how things should be done" and how the authorities should behave. Together they go far in determining the roles and powers of the system's various authorities, its organization, and its procedures.

Regime rules give the system much of its surface stability and continuity. Individual lawyers, jurors, and judges continuously enter and leave the system. Yet most of the rules and norms relating to structure, procedure, and roles remain beyond even a complete change of personnel. Although regime rules do change over time, the changes—such as with criminal or civil procedure or the development of the appeals courts—have tended to be slow and moderate. Major rules concerning judicial and legal roles have changed very little in the last century and a half.

Here we are concerned with the system's formal structure, in particular, its links to the state judicial systems, its internal structures, and how the system formally processes demand input. This is followed by a consideration of the roles systemic authorities are expected to play in processing cases with attention to such legal cultural norms as judicial impartiality, lawyer advocacy, and *stare decisis* (the rule of adherence to precedent). The chapter concludes with a view of the federal judicial system as a bureaucratic organization. Using Max Weber's ideal type of bureaucracy, we look at the extent to which the structure of the federal judiciary approximates this model. This is of interest because Weber and later students of bureaucracy have suggested that inherent in bureaucratic organization are certain limits as to how authorities behave and make decisions as well as the kind of decisions made.

THE FEDERAL AND STATE JUDICIAL SYSTEMS: DIFFERENCES, OVERLAP, AND LINKS

In addition to the federal judicial system, each state and the Commonwealth of Puerto Rico has its own system. The total number of state and local courts in the United States in 1971 was 16,460.[1] Although there is no official compilation as to how many civil and criminal cases are started within the entire country each year, it doubtless runs into the many millions. Of these, in fiscal 1974, for example, only a little over 140,000 were commenced within the federal district courts.[2] Not only is the federal system small in comparison to the full range of judicial activity, but it is also small in comparison with many individual state systems. For example, there are over twice as many full-time judges in the New York State judicial system as there are in the entire federal system. Each year large state court systems such as New York's dispose of a vastly greater number of civil and criminal cases (and are much more expensive to run) than the federal system. Most common crimes and most private wrongs leading to civil suits fall under the jurisdiction of state courts alone. State law and judicial proceedings generally affect the day-to-day life of the average citizen more directly than do their federal counterparts.

The courts of each state judicial system are totally independent of the courts of every other state system. Although Article IV, Section I,

[1] *National Survey of Court Organization, 1971* (Washington, D.C.: U.S. Department of Justice, Law Enforcement Assistance Administration, June, 1972), p. 1.

[2] *Annual Report of the Director, Administrative Office of the United States Courts, 1974*, Tables C-1 and D-1. The Report is hereafter cited as *Report, U.S. Courts, 1974*. Note that the fiscal year refers to the twelve-month period and year ending June 30. Fiscal 1974 thus began July 1, 1973, and ended June 30, 1974. For a broad cross-cultural consideration of litigation and the role of courts, see Austin Sarat and Joel B. Grossman, "Courts and Conflict Resolution: Problems in the Mobilization of Adjudication," *American Political Science Review*, 69 (1975), in press.

of the Constitution declares that "Full Faith and Credit shall be given in each State to the public acts, Records, and judicial Proceedings of every other State," this is a very minimal demand. Normally the courts of different nations follow much this same procedure in litigation. A commercial contract made in England, for example, will generally be viewed as valid by the courts of France.

The relationship of state courts and law to federal courts and law is much more complex. For some purposes state courts serve as an alternative to the federal courts. By congressional statute state courts have exclusive jurisdiction over civil suits between citizens of different states (these are called "diversity" cases) where the amount sued for is less than $10,000 and concurrent jurisdiction with the federal courts in diversity cases involving larger amounts (that is, the suit may be tried in either a state or a federal court, the option resting with the litigants). In many other cases, even of the most local variety, questions of federal law must be taken into account. In civil suits, when state courts try cases that raise federal questions, the substantive law is federal although the procedural law is state. In criminal cases, procedure is also affected by federal constitutional interpretations. State judges are bound by oath to follow federally announced constitutional rights concerning, for example, interrogation, right to counsel, use of tainted evidence, voluntariness of confession, jury selection, and right of appeal regardless of what state statutes, state judicial interpretations, or state constitutional provisions may say. Failure on the part of a state's courts to interpret properly and to comply with any question of federal law may eventually result in having the judgment overturned by a federal court.

Since 1938 federal courts are similarly called upon to interpret and enforce state law in diversity cases.[3] They are supposed to follow state judicial interpretations of state law. The relationship between the federal courts and the state courts is not symmetrical, however. While state court proceedings can be reviewed by the federal judiciary to oversee proper implementation of federal law, federal court proceedings cannot be reviewed by the state judiciaries. Thus, the state courts have no way of supervising how the federal courts deal with state law.

Once the site of trial is established and the case has been tried, all

---

[3] Between 1842 and 1938, federal courts disregarded state law and instead developed and applied national norms. See Swift v. Tyson, 16 Pet. 1 (1842). Erie R. Co. v. Tompkins, 304 U.S. 64 (1938), reverted to the pre-1842 practice of using state law.

appeals must remain within the same court system. A case can never be appealed from the courts of one state to those of another. Under some circumstances (to be discussed in a moment), a state case can be appealed to the federal system, but never, no matter what the substantive law involved, can a case be appealed from a federal to a state court.

In a criminal case a defendant can only be brought to trial in a court of the government whose law was broken.[4] Thus, a New Jersey court cannot try a man for committing a crime in New York even if the man is apprehended in New Jersey. If the crime was a state crime, he can only be tried in a court of the State of New York. Therefore, New York authorities must request extradition from New Jersey. If the crime was a federal offense, he can only be tried in a federal court. Although the courts of each government have exclusive original jurisdiction over their own criminal cases, the federal courts are increasingly exercising a supervisory role over state criminal procedures.

Compliance of state judges to federal law is encouraged by procedures for review by state and federal courts. Failure by a trial judge to give proper weight and interpretation to a validly raised federal question normally opens the case to appellate review within the state's own court system where the claim may be aired. Failure of the state appellate courts, either out of ignorance or defiance, to demand compliance with the federal law can result in one of two different forms of federal judicial intervention.

The oldest, most obvious, and best-known of these is appellate review by the United States Supreme Court. This is available for both state civil and criminal cases. (With civil cases it is the only way a state proceeding may be reviewed by a federal court.) The Supreme Court's rulings are binding both for the jurisdictional (Is the claim pressed

---

4 There is an exception to this usually categorically stated rule. Under a civil rights law passed in 1866, two grounds were given for removal of state criminal cases to the federal courts prior to trial. These are (1) cases involving federal officials charged with crimes when performing their duties (this is to prevent state harassment of federal officials involved in investigations or law enforcement), and (2) cases where the defendant can point to a specific state law, constitutional provision, or judicial interpretation that would "predictably" deprive him of his equal civil rights. Particularly in the mid-1960s petitions for removal to the federal district courts increased dramatically. See Georgia v. Rachel, 384 U.S. 780 and City of Greenwood v. Peacock, 384 U.S. 808 (1966), for Supreme Court interpretation of the second ground particularly. Also see Johnson v. Mississippi, 95 S.Ct. 1591 (1975).

truly federal?) and the substantive (What does federal law require?) questions. The Supreme Court reviews relatively few state cases and does not extensively supervise state court proceedings. Indeed, with civil cases there are still large areas of state judicial activity and substantive law beyond the reaches of federal judicial power.

The second method by which a state court proceeding may be reviewed by the federal judiciary has much broader implications for obtaining compliance. It concerns only criminal cases in which the defendant is found guilty and placed in jail. Such a prisoner may institute a *habeas corpus* action before a U.S. district court on the ground that his conviction was characterized by a violation of the Constitution. Extensive use of this federal *habeas corpus* relief stems from a 1963 Supreme Court decision.[5] Traditionally it was used only for challenging the unlawful detention of a prisoner by executive officials—as when military authorities arrest and hold civilians when civil courts are in operation or police hold a captive without pressing charges or turning him over to the courts for trial. Technically in its use involving state prisoners, a federal *habeas corpus* action is a proceeding ordering the jailer to bring the prisoner to court and to indicate the basis for his detention. Its effect, however, is to allow a federal district judge to review state court proceedings to make sure that federal constitutional norms have been followed. Failure by a state to make such a showing results in release of the prisoner or a new trial. In contrast to the difficulties encountered in obtaining Supreme Court review, having a district court consider a state prisoner's *habeas corpus* case is relatively easy. The very status of the petitioner as a prisoner is the chief consideration, although the federal district judge is given the option of refusing to grant the petition if it is shown that the petitioner has deliberately bypassed state remedies. Furthermore, since there are 89 district courts (in the states) and only one Supreme Court, we can readily see why modern federal *habeas corpus* allows for much more extensive surveillance of state criminal proceedings than was traditionally available by Supreme Court review. In the 1960s when the number and impact of federal norms relating to state criminal procedures rapidly grew, the federal judiciary thus

[5] Fay v. Noia, 372 U.S. 391 (1963), removed technical barriers that previously had made it difficult for state prisoners to institute *habeas corpus* actions in federal district courts.

devised a way for greatly increasing its ability to gain compliance.

Although there are overlaps and links, it is nevertheless useful to conceptualize the federal judicial system as distinct from the state judicial systems. One state judiciary has no direct relationships with any other state judiciary. Different states recruit judges by different methods. Interactions of the state judiciaries with the federal judiciary are relatively infrequent. In contrast, the federal courts constitute integrated sets of relationships.

THE INTERNAL STRUCTURE OF THE FEDERAL JUDICIAL SYSTEM

The federal judicial system consists of courts and administrative bodies. The most important courts are the three principal constitutional courts: the U.S. Supreme Court, the 11 U.S. courts of appeals,[6] and 90 of the 94 U.S. district courts.[7] They are called constitutional courts because they are authorized by Article III, the judicial article, of the Constitution. This article protects these judges from diminution in pay and provides for lifetime appointment.

Congress has also created from time to time various other administrative agencies and specialized courts that also perform a judicial or quasi-judicial function. Most of these (e.g., the National Labor Relations Board, the Federal Trade Commission, and the Interstate Commerce Commission) are not considered a part of the judicial branch. Others, such as the Court of Claims, the Court of Customs and Patent Appeals, and the Customs Court, are part of the federal judicial system and are considered constitutional courts. Such courts and agencies together handle many more cases than do the principal constitutional courts. In practically all cases their decisions can be appealed or reviewed by the regular federal courts.

[6] Congress in 1971 created the Temporary Emergency Court of Appeals to have exclusive jurisdiction over constitutional challenges to the Economic Stabilization Act of 1970 (the Nixon Administration's economic program). The statute provided that the court's judgments are reviewable by the Supreme Court. Personnel of the court are drawn from the ranks of active federal judges. Contrary to initial expectations, the court was not flooded with litigation, and in fact it has been little used. See *Reports, U.S. Courts, 1973,* p. II-11.

[7] Eighty-nine U.S. district courts are located within the fifty states. The 90th is the U.S. District Court for the District of Columbia (Washington, D.C.). The remaining four courts are territorial and legislative courts.

Another part of the judicial branch that has rather unique character-istics of jurisdiction and status are the federal district courts and local courts operating in the territories of the Canal Zone, Guam, and the Virgin Islands. There the U.S. district courts exercise jurisdiction over local as well as regular federal cases. These three territorial courts are also unique in other ways. Foremost among them is that the judges of the district courts of the Canal Zone, Guam, and the Virgin Islands are appointed for a set number of years and their salaries are not pro-tected from diminution by Congress. Before 1966 this was also true of another territorial court, the federal District Court of Puerto Rico, but since a 1966 statute its judges have had lifetime tenure. Like the regular district courts it only exercises federal jurisdiction (this was true even before 1966). The territorial courts outside the continental United States along with the Court of Military Appeals and the Tax Court are considered legislative rather than constitutional courts be-cause they are seen as implementing one of the enumerated powers of Congress as stated in Article I of the Constitution. The U.S. District Court for the District of Columbia is the only territorial district court within the continental United States. Before the District of Columbia Court Reorganization Act became law in 1970, the U.S. District Court had both federal and local jurisdiction. Now the District Court handles federal cases leaving the local cases (involving laws only applicable to the District of Columbia) to the local municipal-type lower courts. In 1933, the Supreme Court ruled that both the District Court and the U.S. Court of Appeals for the District of Columbia—both of whose judges can be involuntarily removed only by impeachment and whose judicial salaries cannot be diminished by Congress—are both legis-lative and constitutional courts.[8] The other lower courts in the District of Columbia, on the other hand, are strictly legislative courts. As can be seen, the distinction between a constitutional and a legislative court is of the type that would have delighted those meticulous medieval scholastics who argued about how many angels would fit on the head of a pin.

The courts' administrative bodies are the judicial council and judicial conference of each of the eleven circuits, the Judicial Confer-ence of the United States, the Administrative Office of the United

---

[8] O'Donoghue v. United States, 289 U.S. 516 (1933).

States Courts, and the Federal Judicial Center.[9] Each circuit's judicial council consists of the judges of that circuit's court of appeals. Each council monitors case loads, district judge assignments, and in general supervises its district courts. The councils are authorized by the Administrative Office Act of 1939 to order federal judges within their respective circuits to comply with council policies, or those policies set by the national judicial conference, or indeed those set by Congress. The circuit conferences consist of the district and appeals judges of each circuit and selected members of the federal bar. These annual conferences are to some extent social gatherings, but they also provide communication links within the circuit, between the circuit and the national judicial conference, and between the circuit and the bar.

The Judicial Conference of the United States consists of the chief judges of the appeals courts and one district judge from each circuit. The Chief Justice of the Supreme Court presides over the conference, which serves as the central administrative policy-making organization for the federal judicial system. In addition, the conference and its committees consider and formulate proposed legislation concerning the federal courts (e.g., additional judgeships and court personnel, salaries, budgets, and rules of procedure). The conference's recommendations are transmitted to the appropriate congressional committees.

The Administrative Office of the U.S. Courts assumes responsibility for the more routine administrative matters such as preparation of the budget, supervision of clerical and secretarial personnel as well as probation officers and referees in bankruptcy, staff work for the Judicial Conference, and congressional liaison. The Administrative Office also compiles detailed statistics on the work of the system which are

[9] A detailed analysis of the structure and functions of these administrative bodies can be found in Peter G. Fish, *The Politics of Federal Judicial Administration* (Princeton, N.J.: Princeton University Press, 1973). Note also that for the Supreme Court as well as in each circuit and district, there is a clerk's office that administers the day-to-day operations of their courts. At the circuit level there are also the circuit executive offices and at the Supreme Court level the office of the Administrative Assistant to the Chief Justice of the United States, offices concerned with administrative practices and managerial policies. Also see, in general, Russell Wheeler and Howard R. Whitcomb, *Perspectives on Judicial Administration: Readings in Court Management and the Administration of Justice* (Englewood Cliffs, N.J.: Prentice-Hall, 1976).

published in its annual reports. The Federal Judicial Center has the responsibility for coordinating and planning educational and training programs (such as sentencing institutes, seminars for new district judges[10] and referees in bankruptcy, institutes for probation officers, and the training of the United States magistrates and circuit executives) and for undertaking research into the workings of the system. In 1974 close to 9,400 people were employed in the federal judicial system.[11]

The district courts are the basic points of input. They are the system's main trial courts (the Customs Court and the Tax Court handle trials in their respective spheres; U.S. magistrates located within the districts try minor offenses). In 1974 there were 94 district courts with 400 district judge positions authorized by Congress. In addition, a large number of senior (retired) district judges helped out by sitting as trial judges.[12] Supporting personnel within the districts include law clerks, secretaries, court clerks, probation officers, referees in bankruptcy, and U.S. magistrates (this position replaced the U.S. commissioner post). In fiscal 1974, 103,530 civil cases and 39,754 criminal cases were commenced in them. In the same year they tried 10,972 civil cases and 7,600 criminal cases.[13] The large discrepancy between cases commenced and cases that go to trial is only partly a manifestation of "delay in court." More importantly, it is indicative of how

[10] See Beverly B. Cook, "The Socialization of New Federal Judges: Impact on District Court Business," *Washington University Law Quarterly*, (1971), 253–279.

[11] *Report, U.S. Courts, 1974*, p. III-2.

[12] In fiscal 1973, 80 senior judges sat and many of them handled the normal caseloads assumed by judges in active service. *Report, U.S. Courts, 1973*, p. I-3.

[13] *Report, U.S. Courts, 1974*, Table C-7. Note that some of the cases tried were originally filed before fiscal 1974. Not all cases filed in fiscal 1974 were disposed of in that fiscal year. Of the civil cases that went to trial only 10 percent took five months or less from the time of filing to the completion of trial. Forty percent of the cases took from over five months to sixteen months from filing to the end of trial. Another 40 percent of the cases took from over 16 months to under 42 months, and 10 percent of the cases terminated in fiscal 1974 had taken over three-and-a-half years from the time of filing to the completion of trial. See *Report, U.S. Courts, 1974*, Table C-5. The record for criminal trials was considerably better in fiscal 1974 with half the cases tried by jury having taken under six months from the time of filing to the conclusion of trial and half the cases tried by the judge alone taking about four months and one week, or less. *Report, U.S. Courts, 1974*, Table D-6.

many civil cases are settled out of court and how many criminal cases are disposed of by guilty pleas, usually achieved by a "bargain" between the defendant and the prosecution, or by dismissal.

Each state, the Commonwealth of Puerto Rico, the District of Columbia, Guam, the Virgin Islands, and the Canal Zone has, as is shown in Figure 2.1, at least one district. Texas, California, and New York State have four. The number of judges assigned to each district varies from 1 to 27.[14]

The jurisdiction of the district courts is original only. It includes all federal crimes, federal civil and diversity cases where the amount in controversy exceeds $10,000,[15] admiralty and maritime cases, review and enforcement of actions by certain federal administrative agencies, and various other cases assigned by Congress. (As noted earlier, four territorial district courts also exercise local jurisdiction.) The district courts also perform various administrative and supervisory tasks. These include naturalization of aliens, approval of passport applications, supervision of bankruptcy proceedings, and parole of federal prisoners.

Cases in the district courts are generally tried before a single judge. However, special three-judge district courts whose membership includes at least one circuit court judge may be convened to consider certain special cases. These include petitions for injunctions restraining the enforcement of allegedly unconstitutional laws or administrative orders, orders of the Interstate Commerce Commission, and certain other cases such as civil rights and reapportionment. In fiscal 1974, 249 such courts were convened. Fifty-one concerned review of ICC orders; 171 concerned civil rights issues; 8 concerned reapportionment cases; and 19 concerned review of state or local laws or regulations.[16]

---

[14] A detailed discussion of the district as well as appeals court "constituencies" can be found in Richard Richardson and Kenneth Vines, *The Politics of Federal Courts* (Boston: Little, Brown, 1970), Chap. 3.

[15] The $10,000 minimum amount also applies to every member of a class in a class action suit (brought on behalf of all those similarly situated). See Zahn v. International Paper Co., 94 S. Ct. 505 (1973).

[16] *Report, U.S. Courts, 1974*, p. IX-44. Note that in December, 1974, Congress enacted legislation eliminating the requirement of a three-judge district court to hear appeals from ICC orders. Now, ICC cases are treated the same as cases involving other administrative agencies. They are first heard by a court of appeals, and appeal to the Supreme Court is by certiorari.

Figure 2.1 District and appeals courts' boundaries. (The large numerals indicate the various courts of appeals and the heavy lines represent the jurisdictional boundaries of each circuit. The broken lines represent jurisdictional boundaries of district courts in states having more than one district.)

The losing party in a case tried before a district court has the right to an appeal. Generally these appeals are heard by the court of appeals in whose circuit the district court lies. Under special circumstances, however, appeal may be direct to the Supreme Court. This primarily occurs (1) with cases heard by three-judge district courts; (2) when a federal statute has been declared unconstitutional and the United States appeals the case; and (3) when a case is of great public importance and requires immediate settlement such as the famous Nixon tapes case, which when decided by the Court hastened the collapse of the Nixon presidency.[17]

The eleven U.S. courts of appeals (the circuit boundaries are shown in Figure 2.1) are directly above the district courts in the formal judicial hierarchy. In 1974 there were 97 authorized appeals court judgeships. There were also 42 senior (retired) judges performing substantial judicial service on circuit panels.[18] Appeals court jurisdiction includes all cases tried by the district courts except for those few where appeal is direct to the Supreme Court. These courts also consider cases calling for review or enforcement of actions and orders of many federal independent regulatory agencies, administrative agencies, and departments. The courts of appeals do consider a few original proceedings that all relate to lower court behavior. Supporting personnel include law clerks, secretaries, and court clerks. Each circuit has authorized for it a Circuit Executive to handle administrative matters within the circuit, thereby providing the Chief Judge of each circuit with considerable managerial assistance and expertise.[19] In fiscal 1974, there were 16,436 cases filed in these courts, about

[17] United States v. Nixon, 94 S. Ct. 3090 (1974). Another such expedited case was Youngstown Sheet and Tube Co. v. Sawyer, 343 U.S. 579 (1952), the famous "steel seizure" case that arose when President Truman ordered the Secretary of Commerce to take over the steel mills in order to prevent a union strike that would impair the Korean War effort. For a consideration of various aspects of federal jurisdiction, see Paul M. Bator, Paul J. Mishkin, David L. Shapiro, and Herbert Wechsler, *Hart and Wechsler's The Federal Courts and the Federal System* (Mineola, N.Y.: Foundation Press, 1973).

[18] *Report, U.S. Courts, 1973,* p. I-6.

[19] According to the 1971 legislation that created the positions, each circuit executive is appointed by the Judicial Council and serves at its pleasure. See Robert J. Martineau, "The Federal Circuit Executives: An Initial Report," *Judicature,* 57 (1974), 438–445.

three times as many filings compared to only eleven years earlier. Included were 13,812 appeals from the district courts, 2,205 petitions to review or enforce administrative orders, and 419 original proceedings.[20]

Each court of appeals has from three to fifteen judges. The number is determined by Congress and is supposed to reflect the workload of the circuit.[21] In considering cases, judges normally sit in ad hoc panels of three. Ordinarily, the Chief Judge of the circuit makes the assignments. In controversial cases, all the judges may hear the case *en banc*,[22] but in practice this is exceedingly rare. In fiscal 1974, out of the 5,978 cases in which hearings were held, only 49 were heard *en banc*.[23]

Besides its regular judges, each circuit has designated to it a member of the Supreme Court. Two Supreme Court justices are each assigned to two circuits, the other justices are ordinarily each assigned to one. This is a link to an earlier era before the appeals courts were established as separate intermediate level courts. Then, during recesses of the Court, Supreme Court justices would literally "ride the circuit" and sit as circuit judges. Today, on occasion, justices are called upon to act on petitions for emergency relief.

At the apex of the formal judicial hierarchy is the Supreme Court. The Court is only one court in a system of over 100, and it has only 9 judges out of about 560 in the federal judiciary. It delivers full opinions in relatively few cases. For example, during the 1973–1974 term only 188 cases were so handled, and, if we take into consideration consolidation of some cases, we find that only 157 full opinions of the Court were written. Yet not only is it the most important court in the system, it is undoubtedly the most important court in the nation. The Court exercises *judicial review* over the acts and actions

---

[20] *Report, U.S. Courts, 1974*, Tables B-1, B-3.

[21] *Report, U.S. Courts, 1968*, pp. 49–51, 100. See also *Congressional Record—Senate*, August 25, 1967, pp. 12218–12237. But cf. Richardson and Vines, *Politics of Federal Courts*, pp. 41–45; and Glendon Schubert, *Judicial Policy Making*, rev. ed. (Glenview, Ill.: Scott, Foresman, 1974), pp. 16–23.

[22] See Paul D. Carrington, "Crowded Dockets and the Courts of Appeals: The Threat to the Function of Review and the National Law," *Harvard Law Review*, 82 (1969), 580–585.

[23] *Report, U.S. Courts, 1974*, p. IX-10.

of government and governmental officials at all levels of government. Many of the policies announced by the Court can only be formally changed by constitutional amendment or by the Court itself.

The Court has both original and appellate jurisdiction. Article III of the Constitution, as modified by the Eleventh Amendment, suggests that the Court's original jurisdiction is extensive. It includes cases between two or more states or between the United States and a state; cases involving foreign ambassadors, ministers, consuls, and their staffs; and cases commenced by a state against the citizens of other states or nations. With cases between two or more states and those commenced against foreign diplomatic personnel, the Court has exclusive original jurisdiction. With all of the other cases mentioned, it has concurrent original jurisdiction with the district courts.[24] Thus the Supreme Court takes relatively few cases under its original jurisdiction. In fact, from its establishment through the end of its 1973 term, the Court had adjudicated under its original jurisdiction only 155 cases.[25] The Court is, in other words, primarily a forum for appellate review.

There are presently four methods by which a case is brought before the Court for review. These are certiorari, appeal, certification, and extraordinary writ. Only the first two methods are of any quantitative significance.

After one's case has been considered by a state court of last resort, a U.S. court of appeals, the Court of Claims, or the Court of Customs and Patent Appeals, any disappointed litigant may petition the Supreme Court for a writ of certiorari, which is technically an order to the court whose decision is being challenged to send up the records of the case so that the Supreme Court can make certain that the lower court's decision correctly applied the law. Congress has given the Court complete discretion as to whether or not it will grant the certiorari petition. The writ is issued if at least four justices so vote. In practice, it is granted in only a small proportion of cases brought

[24] 28 USC § 1251. Diplomatic personnel can bring suits in the state courts as well as the federal courts.

[25] Henry J. Abraham, The Judicial Process, third ed., (New York: Oxford, 1975), p. 170. "The Supreme Court, 1973 Term," Harvard Law Review, 88 (1974), p. 277. Note that the term of the Court begins in October and ends in early summer. However, it is referred to by the year in which the term begins; thus the 1973 term began in October, 1973, and ended in July, 1974.

to the Court. In the 1968–1972 period, about 8 percent of lawyer-drafted petitions and under 3 percent of self-drafted petitions (mostly drawn by impoverished prisoners in state and federal prisons) were granted.[26] This, it should be mentioned, was a major decline from the previous five-year period 1963–1967 when about 13 percent of lawyer-drafted petitions and about 4 percent of pauper petitions were granted. In fact, the mix of cases decided on the merits has shifted from one in which certiorari was the route that about two-thirds of these cases had taken to the more recent period when *certiorari* cases have constituted considerably less of a place in that mix. In the 1971 and 1972 terms, only about one-third of the cases decided by the Court on the merits came via certiorari. In the 1973 term, 205 cases decided on the merits (out of a total of 527 so decided) had come to the Court on certiorari.[27]

Under the terms of the Judiciary Act of 1925, certain types of cases are entitled to review by the Supreme Court. This technical right to an appeal exists (1) in cases coming from a state court of last resort when either a federal law or treaty has been held unconstitutional or a state law or provision of a state constitution has been upheld against the challenge that it conflicts with a federal law, treaty, or the U.S. Constitution; (2) in cases from a U.S. court of appeals when either a state law or provision of a state constitution has been ruled unconstitutional; and (3) cases from a court of appeals, a U.S. district court, the Court of Claims, and the Court of Customs and Patent Appeals when a federal law has been held unconstitutional and the United States or one of its agencies, officers, or employees is a party. Appeals can also be made from a three-judge district court and from district court cases involving federal interstate commerce, communications, and antitrust laws. In practice, most appeals either come from state courts or from three-judge district courts.

Although disappointed litigants in the cases just mentioned technically have a right to an appeal, in fact, a "rule of four" similar to that used for certiorari exists. In the 1967–1970 terms, the Court dismissed over 40 percent of appeals filed for "lack of a substantial federal question" or "want of jurisdiction." Just as with certiorari

[26] The percentages were calculated from data presented in "The Supreme Court, 1972 Term," *Harvard Law Review*, 87 (1973), p. 310.

[27] *Harvard Law Review*, 88 (1974), p. 277.

petitions, appeals can be divided into two groups: lawyer-drafted appeals and appeals *in forma pauperis* (literally in the form of a pauper, that is, those appeals by poor litigants, usually prisoners). In the 1969–1972 terms, lawyer-drafted appeals accounted for about 3 out of 4 appeals heard on the merits with the balance accounted for by pauper appeals.[28] Even getting an appeal accepted, however, may not do the appellant much good. Often the Court disposes of it without any oral argument by "affirming" the decision of the "court below."[29] In sum, the members of the Court in deciding whether to take an appeal for an extended consideration of the case appear to treat such appeals much as they do petitions for certiorari. Although there are historical and surface technical differences between the writs, the Court in practice exercises discretion with each. Notably with the Nixon Court in the 1969 term, the trend has appeared for the Court to accept for decision on the merits more appeals and somewhat fewer petitions for certiorari. In the 1971 and 1972 terms about two-thirds of the cases decided on the merits reached the Court as

[28] Statistics on appeals were calculated from data from the *Harvard Law Review* and *Statistical Abstract of the United States, 1973* (Washington, D.C.: U.S. Department of Commerce, 1973), p. 159, Table 259. At this point, a note of caution is in order. We found with almost all the court statistics examined where there was more than one source reporting, there were usually minor and sometimes major discrepancies in the figures. For example, in trying to determine cases filed, cases disposed of, and cases left pending for the Supreme Court's 1966 term, the *Harvard Law Review*, the *Statistical Abstract*, *Law Week*, and *Congressional Quarterly Almanac* were checked. No two agreed on all three figures. In general, for Supreme Court statistics reliance was placed on the *Harvard Law Review's* annual summary; for the lower federal courts the publications of the Administrative Office of the U.S. Courts provided the data. When data were lacking from these two sources other sources were used, in particular the *Statistical Abstract* whose data are supplied by the Administrative Office. Beginning with the 1970 term there have been major changes in the statistics gathered for the Supreme Court which make it impossible to conduct certain types of analyses. The *Harvard Law Review* explained, "The elimination or consolidation of certain categories was mandated by reductions in the statistics prepared by the Office of the Clerk of the Supreme Court" (*Harvard Law Review*, 87 (1973), p. 310). Presumably Chief Justice Warren Burger ordered the change for reasons best known to him.

[29] It should be noted that unlike a denial of certiorari, which supposedly implies no approval or disapproval of lower court behavior, both the decisions to affirm and to dismiss are decisions on the merits of the case. Every year there are a number of appeals that the Court dismisses as improperly brought, but which the Court then treats as petitions for certiorari that are denied. This process makes it clear that the Court is not necessarily giving approval to the lower court decision.

appeals. In the 1973 term about three out of five cases decided on the merits were appeals.[30]

Certification cases arise when the judges of the Court of Claims, a court of appeals, or a district court ask the Supreme Court to rule on questions of law in cases pending in their respective courts for which there is considerable uncertainty. Such cases rarely occur. Even more rare is the taking of a case on an extraordinary writ. Acting on such a writ the Supreme Court can directly intervene into the activities of a trial judge either directing him to perform some act (*mandamus*) or forbidding him from some other act (prohibition). It is not unusual each term for only one or not even any such cases to be accepted.

Less than half of the approximately 450 cases decided each year by the Court on the merits have been subjected to a full hearing, including oral argument (whereby lawyers for both sides have a limited time to argue their case in person before the Court and to be questioned by the justices). About 85 percent of these cases are then disposed of by a detailed opinion of the Court written and signed by one of the majority justices. The remainder of these cases and those for which no oral argument was conducted are typically disposed of by a *per curiam* opinion (a short, unsigned opinion literally "by the Court") or a brief memorandum order such as "dismissed," "affirmed," "vacated," or "reversed and remanded" (i.e., overruled and sent back to the "court below" for final disposition).

As can be seen, the Supreme Court exercises great flexibility in allocating its time and deciding which questions it will treat. In practice the contemporary Court will consider any case that at least four justices, for whatever their reasons, decide they want to hear.

THE JUDICIAL ROLE AND THE JUDICIAL PROCESS

The United States has a regime in which the legitimacy of its policies supposedly rests upon those policies being an expression of popular will. In conflict with this democratic ideal are the federal courts whose primary authorities are appointed for life and are legally held accountable to no one. Individually and collectively these judicial authorities can make national policies that are authoritatively superior to those made by the regime's popularly elected legislative and executive officials.

[30] *Harvard Law Review*, 88 (1974), p. 277.

The presence of a nondemocratic, independent, policy-making judiciary exercising judicial review in an otherwise popularly based government becomes even more difficult to rationalize when it is realized that such an institution is not a necessity of modern government. Other democratic political systems, Great Britain's, for example, manage quite well without a court system that makes constitutional policies. Nor is a constitutional court system a prerequisite for the maintenance of federalism. The Swiss seem to do nicely without one.

Why our judicial system has developed as it has is in part explained by the recognition that historically most Americans, besides advocating popular sovereignty (i.e., "government of the people, by the people, and for the people"), have also wanted a "government of laws, not men." The basic law, traditionally the very symbol of law in America, is the United States Constitution. In the quest for a government bounded by the basic law, the judiciary—an institution whose function is the application of law in the resolution of disputes— became a major institution for making national policies.[31]

In making policy the judiciary's legitimacy rests, at least traditionally, upon its acting judicially. In other words, the historic rationale for allowing judges to pronounce national policies based on constitutional law was that judges were expected to be judge-like. This implies certain standards of faithfulness to law, impartiality, objectivity, and professionalism. Yet, as any student of American history knows, this is only half the story. The basic ideological ethos, perhaps since the election of Jefferson and definitely since the election of Jackson, is profoundly democratic. When over the long run the flow of judicial policy making has systematically run counter to popular needs or popular constitutional interpretations, the legitimacy of those policies has been seriously questioned. A fascinating tension, therefore, surrounds judicial policy making, and this tension is reflected in regime rules related to judicial role playing.

Role[32] conceptions provide the normative framework through

[31] For an explanation of how this process occurred and some of its ramifications, see Alexander Bickel, *The Least Dangerous Branch* (Indianapolis: Bobbs-Merrill, 1962), especially pp. 1–33.

[32] Talcott Parsons, one of the leading social system theorists, sees role at the heart of a social system. See, in particular, Parsons and Edward A. Shils (eds.), *Toward a General Theory of Action* (Cambridge, Mass.: Harvard University Press, 1951); and Parsons, *The Social System* (New York: Free Press, 1951). Perhaps more compre-

which members of a system determine how they should behave when performing systemic duties or functions. They serve as reference points for members in two ways. First, a member's expectations concerning the role he occupies indicates how he should and should not act in various situations. Second, in a similar manner, this same person feels secure in performing those aspects of his role that are based on widely acknowledged regime rules because of the expectation that other members of the system will likewise adhere to the regime rules relating to their roles. This is important since most roles are complementary rather than redundant, for example, the adversary process at trial is conceived of as two opposing advocates and a neutral and impartial judge and jury.

The social and psychological pressures (to say nothing of potential disciplinary actions) involved in directing authorities in a professionally staffed system such as the federal judiciary to follow the regime rules related to their roles are numerous. Members of the legal profession typically have been immersed in an environment of legalism from about the age of twenty on. This legal-cultural environment is created and maintained in law school, through membership in various professional organizations, by intraprofessional contacts, and, of course, for most, through a constant workday world as judge or lawyer. Much of the intent and effect of this process is to indicate to the lawyer and potential lawyer how to think and act when confronted with a legal situation. Generally, the rewards of higher professional attainment and respect are reserved for those who have demonstrated at least surface conformity to such regime rules.

To examine these regime rules as they define the roles played by the major authorities in the processing of litigation, one could turn to the literature of traditional jurisprudence.[33] There are, however, problems with this literature and it must be used with care. First, despite the multitude of efforts to articulate, rationalize, and formu-

---

hensible to the student is William C. Mitchell, *Sociological Analysis and Politics: The Theories of Talcott Parsons* (Englewood Cliffs, N.J.: Prentice-Hall, 1967). Note that role is discussed from the perspective of judicial conversion in Chapter 5.

[33] This literature is immense and has a vast range as to quality, approach, and subject matter. Traditional views of legal and judicial roles and norms are discussed, for example, in Lewis Mayers, *The American Legal System*, rev. ed. (New York: Harper & Row, 1964); Edward H. Levi, *An Introduction to Legal Reasoning* (Chicago: Phoenix Books, 1948); and Henry S. Drinker, *Legal Ethics* (New York: Columbia University Press, 1953).

late judicial system roles into codes of ethics, rarely does full agreement exist as to just what constitutes proper behavior under all circumstances for such authorities as trial and appellate judges, defense lawyers, and prosecutors. Second, this literature has typically been denigrated by many behavioral scientists as camouflaging a reality of personal values, biases, convenient informal relations, and even unethical behavior. Although it is now clear that traditional jurisprudence provides neither an accurate nor complete description of empirical reality, it is also apparent that it does suggest certain regime rules, certain norms that provide the basis for much role playing.

The idealized case of traditional jurisprudence goes through three stages: pretrial, trial, and appeal. Traditional jurisprudence focuses upon trial and appeal as the most important parts of this process. In so doing, it betrays a bias toward the adversary method. There is strong evidence, however, against the primacy of the adversary method in the empirical world of civil litigation and criminal case processing. Typically, in the federal district courts over 90 percent of civil cases are settled out of court before the conclusion of trial, and for over 60 percent of criminal defendants a trial judgment is avoided by a plea of guilty or *nolo contendere,* usually arrived at through bargaining between the prosecution and the defense. With somewhat more than half the remaining criminal defendants, the prosecution drops the charges. Thus, for only about one in six defendants does trial occur.[34] These figures indicate that most cases are not resolved by an adversary process but rather by pretrial negotiations.

Bargaining before trial requires a very different set of roles than does an adversary proceeding. Lawyers familiar with the existing world of settling cases adjust their behavior to meet the functional needs of the system.[35] But to scholars, both traditional and behavioral, and laymen who come upon this situation from the outside, the sense of betrayal is often great.[36] Making the situation more complex, of

[34] These figures are for recent fiscal years. See, for example, *Report, U.S. Courts, 1974,* Tables C-4, D-7.

[35] See Arthur L. Wood, "Professional Ethics among Criminal Lawyers," *Social Problems,* 7 (1959), 70–83; Jerome E. Carlin, *Lawyers' Ethics* (New York: Russell Sage Foundation, 1966).

[36] For a psychological appraisal of litigants' reactions to courtroom justice, see Robert Redmont, "Psychological Discontinuities in the Litigation Process," *Duke Law Journal* (1959), 571–587. For an example of a lawyer-sociologist's disenchant-

course, is the fact that if negotiation does not lead to an out-of-court settlement or a guilty plea, a trial will result and the lawyers will then assume adversary roles. In civil cases even the judge is affected by this role switch. At pretrial he was probably an aggressive arbitrator trying to pressure the litigants to settle.[37] At the trial he becomes a more passive referee.

In the Anglo-American legal tradition, trial is highly formalized combat between two parties. Both the high level of formalization—typified by extremely technical rules concerning, for example, framing of the complaint and the presentation of evidence—and the emphasis on winning gives a trial a sporting atmosphere. This no doubt explains the popularity of courtroom fiction where the trials are more gamelike than is typical.

In the model trial one typically finds the following participants: a judge, two parties or litigants (plaintiff and defendant in a civil suit, prosecutor and defendant in a criminal case), their lawyers, witnesses, and a jury. Traditional theory presumes that the trial will resolve two types of questions: questions of fact and questions of law. It further presumes that these two questions can be both analytically and empirically distinguished.

It is the jury's task to decide on the questions of fact, that is, what happened. In many civil suits, the jury also sets damages by deciding how much the case is worth to the plaintiff. The jurors are not supposed to decide until all the evidence has been presented. In a civil case, the jury decides which side "a preponderance of the evidence" favors. In a criminal case, it decides whether the defendant is guilty "beyond a reasonable doubt." Civil and criminal proceedings are kept separate from each other. This is true even if the same action, for example an assault, leads to both types of trial, a criminal proceeding to bring the perpetrator of the assault to justice and a civil action by the victim to collect damages. A court's verdict of guilty in the criminal case cannot be used as evidence in the civil trial; an

ment with criminal case bargaining, see Abraham S. Blumberg, "The Practice of Law as a Confidence Game: Organizational Cooptation of a Profession," *Law and Society Review*, 1 (1967), 15–39. But see Milton Heumann, "Plea Bargaining Systems and Plea Bargaining Styles: Alternate Patterns of Case Resolution in Criminal Courts," paper delivered at the 1974 Annual Meeting of the A.P.S.A.

[37] See, for example, the account of one federal district judge in J. Skelly Wright, "The Pretrial Conference," *Federal Rules Decisions*, 18 (1962), 141–158.

award of damages in the civil case cannot be used as proof of guilt in the criminal proceeding.

Often when there are no contested facts and the amount of damages is not an issue, the trial is held before a judge only without a jury. This is called a "bench trial." Parenthetically, it should be noted that a jury trial is not mandatory. If both parties agree, the right to a jury trial can be waived and a bench trial held. For various historical reasons, cases in equity, in distinction to cases in law, are always tried before a judge only.

In a bench trial the judge tends to be rather active. Since there are no jurors and often no witnesses, the main participants (judge and opposing counsel) are all professional lawyers. The exchange between bench and bar tends to be spirited and framed in the highly technical language of the law.

In a jury trial the judge is more passive. This is true not only in comparison to a bench trial but also in comparison with trial judges in other Western nations such as Great Britain.[38] In the model jury trial the judge instructs the jury as to the substantive law of the case and also maintains proper procedure and decorum. In the course of the trial the judge is mainly concerned with ruling on matters of procedure. Uncorrected procedural errors may lead to a higher court's reversing or vacating the trial court's judgment.

The law concerning procedure is mainly concerned with what types of physical evidence, testimony, and questioning of witnesses are permissible for establishing the facts of the case. The courtroom professionals, judge and lawyers, are expected to be alert and allow only permissible evidence, since jurors cannot be expected to know what is permissible and what is not. There are tight restrictions on what evidence may be introduced, particularly in criminal trials. For example, coerced confessions, illegally seized evidence, hearsay evidence, and testimony concerning a defendant's past or his prior criminal record are generally forbidden.

The tools available to the judge for maintaining proper procedure and preserving courtroom decorum are many. He may forbid the submission of various forms of evidence or instruct the jurors to disregard

---

[38] Delmar Karlen, *Anglo-American Criminal Justice* (New York: Oxford University Press, 1967), Chap. 8; Fred L. Morrison, *Courts and the Political Process in England* (Beverly Hills, Calif.: Sage, 1973), Chap. 7.

it. He may call a mistrial, thus causing a new trial to be held. He can give a directed verdict to the jury if he finds the evidence in no way can be held to constitute the alleged wrongdoing. Finally, he may discipline counsel or witnesses by citing them for contempt of court.[39] After both sides have completed their presentations, the judge states the law of the case to the jury and spells out the consequences of various findings of fact. The jury makes a collective decision, which in the federal judicial system must be unanimous, unless in civil suits both parties agree to abide by the verdict or finding of a majority of the jurors. A "hung" jury, that is, one where an unanimous decision is not reached, results in a mistrial (but note that under contemporary Supreme Court rulings unanimous juries in the states are not required, thus allowing the states, if they wish, to permit less than unanimous jury verdicts).[40]

After the verdict of the jury is delivered, the judge states it as the judgment of the court and specifies the remedy or sentence, if any. In a civil case in law, the typical remedy that the plaintiff asks for and receives is damages paid in money. In a case in equity a much greater range of remedies is possible. These include among others the *injunction* (a court order instructing the defendant not to do or continue to do some action that would cause irreparable harm to the plaintiff) and the writ of *specific performance* (an order obliging the defendant to abide by the terms of the contract or agreement to sell a specific object or perform a specific service or to specifically do or not to do something). In criminal cases the types of sentences that presently are given are many. They are still centered, however, on the traditional ones of fine, probation, and imprisonment.

Although they are the court's formal decision makers, judge and jury themselves do not unearth evidence. Evidence is presented to them by the opposing lawyers. It is their function to gather documents, physical exhibits, and witnesses for establishing the facts of the case. Similarly, control of errors in both procedure and substantive law, even though requiring rulings from the bench, rests upon objection and argument by the lawyers. Rarely will a judge stop the sub-

[39] Litigants, too, can be disciplined. See Illinois v. Allen, 397 U.S. 337 (1970).

[40] The Supreme Court upheld a Louisiana state law that enabled a nine- out of twelve-person majority to render a jury verdict. See Johnson v. Louisiana, 406 U.S. 356 (1972).

mission of forbidden evidence unless called to do so from the bar. Nor, in actuality does an error in procedure or interpretation of substantive law including judicial precedent generally provide grounds for appeal unless it is objected to within time limits set by the system's procedural rules. Just as courts are not self-starting (that is, they do not go out searching for cases, but depend upon cases being brought to them by a plaintiff or prosecutor), neither are they automatically self-correcting.

Most of the content of the lawyer's role as partisan advocate has already been suggested. However, there are limits to lawyer advocacy. These stem from the lawyer's collateral role as "officer of the court." According to the Canons of Legal Ethics,[41] a lawyer is liable to possible punishment in the form of censure, suspension, disbarment, or contempt if, for example, the lawyer promotes a case that he or she knows is patently spurious or knowingly allows presentation of perjured or deliberately misleading testimony or falsified documents or physical evidence. The canons also require the lawyer to present evidence and precedents even though they may be detrimental to the client's cause, and lawyers are supposed to behave so as to preserve the decorum of the court and the integrity of the judicial process. In practice, however, sanctions are rarely applied to enforce the canons.[42]

Thus far we have outlined almost the full structure of the model trial with hardly mentioning either witnesses or, seemingly the most important participants of all, the private litigants. This is because their parts are very small and the standards of behavior expected from them are minimal. A litigant, for example, once the lawyer has been hired and once the case goes to trial (a decision that can always be averted by an out-of-court settlement in a civil case or a guilty plea in a criminal case) has little else to do. At most the litigant takes the stand to testify (and in criminal cases the defendant has the constitutional right not to do so). There, the only normative demand upon the

[41] The Canons of Legal Ethics and the Canons of Judicial Ethics have been formulated and published by the American Bar Association. Courts have occasionally given them the force of law in disciplining those who violate them. See Drinker, *Legal Ethics.*

[42] See Carlin, *Lawyers' Ethics,* especially Chaps. 6 and 9; F. Raymond Marks and Darlene Cathcart, "Discipline within the Legal Profession: Is It Self-Regulation?" *Illinois Law Forum* (1974), 193–236.

litigant, as with all witnesses, is to tell the truth. Failure to do so may lead to a charge of perjury and subsequent judicial proceedings.

After judgment is entered, the disappointed party (except for the prosecution in a criminal case when there is an acquittal) has to decide whether to appeal. Appellate proceedings are only supposed to be used for correcting legal errors from the trial. The only questions, therefore, are questions of law: substantive, procedural, or both. Despite this conceptualization of appeal, one sometimes finds in the opinions of appellate courts the most surprising "facts" as compared to those ostensibly established during the trial. These "facts" moreover, may be social or economic facts and not necessarily the narrowly construed facts of the case.

Since at appeal there are no facts to determine, there are no witnesses, no displays of physical evidence, and, of course, no jury. The only active participants are the judges and the lawyers. The litigants are usually not even present. Similar to a bench trial, the exchange between bench and bar is often spirited. As at trial, it is the lawyer's role to be a partisan advocate in preparing his brief and during oral argument. In Supreme Court cases, when there are larger implications of the policy at issue, other interested parties are often allowed to join the formal parties through the presentation of *amicus curiae* (friend of the court) briefs.

Like trial judges, appellate judges are expected to be objective articulators of the law. They are expected to adhere to precedent (the rule of *stare decisis*). Since, however, the ostensible reason for appeal is that the trial courts can err, or the precedents are conflicting or ambiguous, the questions considered in the model appeal are those in which there supposedly is some professional doubt as to what is the law. Thus, the typical appellate judge has a greater opportunity than the typical trial judge to be a creative policy maker.

There is no general agreement as to how creative and how broad judicial policy making should be. Those who most feel the tensions of having a nondemocratic policy-making judiciary in a democratic system have generally urged judicial restraint. This means avoiding when possible cases that force policy making or if avoidance is impossible deciding them narrowly. Others, who welcome the opportunity to use the legal tools developed by the judiciary to correct injustice, are judicial activists. They show less reluctance to consider politically controversial issues and to make broad constitutional policies.

Interestingly, there seems to be no consistent ideological orientation associated with either one of these two role conceptions. In the late nineteenth and early twentieth centuries, conservatives were activists, while liberals urged judicial restraint. Today, liberals are generally activists, while conservatives at least pay lip service to restraint.

Appellate court decisions that the judges consider important are usually announced with a full opinion. The Opinion of the Court, among other things, is an appellate court's attempt to show to both members of the legal profession and the general public that the judicial criteria of objectivity, professionalism, and fidelity to the law have been met. If there is a dissenting opinion, its main purpose is to show that the court has erred while attempting to meet these judicial criteria. Typically, both types of opinions contain citations of appropriate precedents, statutes or constitutional provisions, historical materials on legislative intent, and treatises by recognized legal scholars. In recent years the courts have more frequently turned to commentaries and analyses published in law reviews. Even various social science writings have been cited. The purpose of all these citations is to legitimize the decision, to show that the court acted professionally.

THE FEDERAL JUDICIAL SYSTEM AS A BUREAUCRACY

The federal judicial system displays most of the attributes of Max Weber's ideal type of *bureaucracy*.[43] In fact, much of Weber's original description is concerned with governmental organizations exercising judicial or quasi-judicial functions even though he conceived of bureaucracy as a form of organization found in private as well as governmental institutions.

In brief, Weber states that the function of a bureaucratic organization is the administration of law. This consists of the application of technical rules and norms to particular cases. The rules and norms are typically given, or at least not disapproved, by institutions that lie outside and formally above the bureaucratic unit. The authority of the organization's officials is binding only to the extent to which these

[43] *The Theory of Social and Economic Organization*, trans. by A. M. Henderson and Talcott Parsons, (New York: Free Press, 1947), pp. 329–341. See also Martin Shapiro, *The Supreme Court and Administrative Agencies* (New York: Free Press, 1968), for an extensive use of "bureaucratic theory" applied to the Supreme Court.

externally given rules and norms are faithfully and objectively applied. This model in large part is consistent with traditional notions of the federal judiciary's constitutional relationships with the states, Congress, and the President.[44]

This organizational model, however, appears to provide little explanation for the large degree of discretion shown by the federal courts, particularly the Supreme Court, in articulating judicial norms. This is both a function of various aspects of the model which are thus far unstated and a reflection of some unique characteristics of American constitutionalism and the federal judiciary.

No bureaucracy can resolve particular disputes without articulating rules and norms on its own unless the system of law being applied meets the following criteria: (1) each rule or norm is unambiguous; (2) the entire set of rules and norms is detailed and complete; and (3) all the rules and norms are consistent with one another. Obviously the set of rules and norms that the federal courts use for resolving cases does not and, to some degree, cannot meet all these criteria.

No law, no matter how detailed and complete, is unambiguous for all cases. This is especially true in a world of rapid technological and social innovation. The Constitution and many federal statutes such as the Sherman Antitrust Act primarily contain general principles. General principles, however, cannot be used for resolving concrete cases without the presence of interstitial norms and rules. According to Weber, it is some outside institution, Congress, for example, whose task it is to supply these rules through legislation. In fact, neither Congress nor any other institution has done so for all areas.

For example, in *Bibb* v. *Navajo Freight Lines*[45] one finds a situation in which a lack of interstitial rules, though not surprising, proved important. The case concerned truck mudflaps. In the absence of action either by Congress or the Interstate Commerce Commission, two states had passed directly conflicting regulations. Full enforcement of both regulations was seriously hampering the flow of interstate truck transport, a situation inconsistent with the principle of freely flowing domestic trade implicit in the commerce clause of the Constitution. The Supreme Court created a national mudflap regulation in order to

[44] See, for example, Hamilton's view of the Supreme Court in Jacob E. Cooke (ed.), *The Federalist* (New York: World, 1961), *Federalist* No. 78, pp. 521–530.

[45] 359 U.S. 520 (1959).

resolve the dispute. In similar cases the Court has decided the permissible length of railroad trains[46] and the maximum width of motor trucks.[47]

Like all bureaucracies the federal judiciary enforces norms and rules given it by institutions exterior to it *acting in their legal capacities*. But unlike most bureaucracies, the federal judiciary has allocated to itself the function of determining when these institutions (e.g., Congress, the President, administrative agencies, the states) are so acting. This means that the federal courts in articulating rules and norms are involved in more than just interstitial interpretation.

Even though the federal judiciary demonstrates a broader discretion in making the rules and norms that it applies in adjudicating cases than do most bureaucratic organizations, this discretion is exercised in a bureaucratic manner. It is based on the interstitial interpretation of written law in the adjudication of particular concrete cases. The broader and more creative policy-making aspects of this process are carried on most visibly by the highest court in the system, the Supreme Court. But even the Supreme Court operates under limits resulting from its bureaucratic nature. It is not, as both its attackers and apologists have sought to maintain, either a legislature or an ongoing constitutional convention.

Not only does the federal judicial system exhibit the functional attributes of a bureaucratic organization, it also exhibits structural attributes. This should not be surprising since the central core of Weberian analysis is that function and structure are irrevocably bound to each other. Let us compare, therefore, the basic structural attributes of bureaucratic structure with the structure of the federal judicial system.

Bureaucratic organization is characterized by a rigidly prescribed division of labor based upon geography and function. This division of labor concerns both the subunits of the organization and the offices making up each unit. The actions taken by each official and subunit have authority only insofar as their actions lie within the official's or subunit's sphere of competence. Subunits are arranged hierarchically with a right to appeal the decisions of a lower subunit to a higher one. This serves to maintain uniformity in decision making. The main

---

[46] Southern Pacific Co. v. Arizona, 325 U.S. 761 (1945).

[47] South Carolina State Highway Department v. Barnwell Bros., 303 U.S. 177 (1938).

mechanism for achieving uniform decision making, however, is through the technical training of the officials. This is accomplished by selecting officials by appointment only from among those who have demonstrated the proper technical qualifications as certified by education and/or examination. Officials, once appointed, are bound to their office by a salary. In general, officials regard their salary as their primary means of support and treat their offices as life-long careers. The private and official lives of the officials are radically separated. Officials are not to appropriate either the funds or resources of their offices for private use. All official acts and decisions are put formally in writing. These constitute the "files" of the organization.

To belabor the obvious, note how easily Weber's analysis of bureaucracy accounts for the essentials of judicial organization, selection, tenure, formal behavior, and procedure. The organization's basic subunits are its courts. Each has a unique geographical and/or functional jurisdiction. Lower courts are linked to higher courts through appellate review. Judges in particular, but other court officials as well (including lawyers), must meet certain technical qualifications. Selection of permanent court officials is by appointment. Remuneration for the most important of these officials—the judges—is by set income that cannot be diminished. It is of such a scale that it is their primary or sole source of income.[48] Judicial authority extends only to official acts. All official acts are set down as written transcripts, orders, rules, and opinions. The whole system is permeated by rigid rules relating to such matters as jurisdiction, procedure, admissibility of evidence, remedies, and appellate review.

To Weber, the structural characteristics of bureaucracy account for the ability of this mode of organization to rationally carry out its func-

[48] In 1969, judicial salaries were increased to the following yearly salaries: district judge, $40,000; appeals judge, $42,500; associate justice of the Supreme Court, $60,000; the Chief Justice of the Supreme Court, $62,500. With inflation becoming a severe economic problem, the absence of a pay raise to meet the increased cost of living became a sore point for the judiciary by the mid-1970s. See, for example, "More Pay Sought for U.S. Judges," New York Times, March 18, 1974, p. 19; "Judge to Resign: Cites Low Salary," New York Times, June 7, 1974, p. 40; "Travia Resigning as Federal Judge: The 5th to Quit in Last Year," New York Times, October 17, 1974, p. 42. Finally, in 1975, bipartisan-supported legislation was introduced to provide a substantial pay increase to federal judges. Under the bill, district judges will receive $48,000, court of appeals judges $51,000, and justices of the Supreme Court $72,000. The Chief Justice's annual salary under the legislation would be $74,500. See New York Times, April 19, 1975, p. 16.

tion of administration. This rationality is manifested in consistency, efficiency, and impersonality in decision making. To Weber, bureaucracy was a laudable term. But as we know both from popular lore and from works of later sociologists, bureaucracy has some not so laudable, *dysfunctional*[49] aspects. The rigid rules and impersonality of the system exact large temporal, monetary, and psychic costs upon the bureaucracy's clients. Organizational and procedural maintenance become of greater importance to officials than the accomplishment of such formal goals as efficient administration of the law. Rigid adherence to precedent may lead to decisions that are irrelevant or even counterproductive in a society characterized by rapidly changing social mores and a developing technology. For example, judicial economic conservatism in the early 1930s—a conservatism that largely ignored changes in economic patterns and relationships—can in one sense be considered to have been a bureaucratic problem.

Weber's model of bureaucracy also obscures many informal patterns of behavior prevalent in organizational life. This obscurity in itself decreases the suitability of the Weberian ideal type as an explanatory model. Systems analysis, in contrast, suggests the investigation of all systemic interactions both formal and informal. It is these more informal interactional and behavior patterns that will receive the greatest emphasis in the following chapters.

---

[49] "Dysfunctional" refers to aspects of systemic processes and structures that by their operation tend to defeat the achievement of systemic goals. See Robert K. Merton, *Social Theory and Social Structure*, rev. ed. (New York: Free Press, 1957), for a development of the concepts of functional and dysfunctional.

THREE
THE AUTHORITIES: RECRUITMENT, BACKGROUNDS, AND SOME INTERACTION PATTERNS

IN order to appreciate how a political system functions— what values it allocates and why it allocates those values the way it does— some knowledge is needed about the authorities of that system. The previous discussion of regime rules suggested the framework within which the authorities behave. Now we examine the authorities themselves more closely in terms of recruitment, backgrounds, and some patterns of interaction. Because judges of the three principal constitutional courts are the primary authorities for the federal judicial system, we devote much of our attention to them. But we also briefly examine some other authorities within the system, particularly government and private lawyers and jurors.[1]

JUDICIAL RECRUITMENT

A number of questions that deserve answering are raised by the subject of judicial recruitment. How are judges chosen? What kind of people does the selection process favor? What socialization experiences do they have in common? What are the implications of the current recruitment process for the administration of justice?

Judicial selection in the United States is unlike the selection processes of most Western democracies where many of the fictions associated with traditional jurisprudence are more strongly maintained

---

[1] This chapter does not contain a consideration of the police authorities of the federal system. It should be mentioned that while the principal police work is done by the Federal Bureau of Investigation (FBI) there are other federal agencies en-

and being a judge is treated as a distinct profession requiring special-ized judicial training. Here, judicial recruitment is a political process with few formal requirements. Nowhere in the Constitution is there a requirement that one must be a lawyer in order to be appointed to the Supreme Court although, of course, in practice only lawyers have served on the Court. To become a federal judge requires (1) nomina-tion by the President; (2) senatorial confirmation by a simple majority vote; and (3) presidential appointment (i.e., the signing and delivery of the Commission, a routine and presumably nondiscretionary act of the President). Behind stages one and two lie a complex of activities.

The appointment of any one judge is the culmination of a unique series of interrelated events that propel one person and not another toward the nomination. Understanding any one particular nomination requires obtaining access to a myriad of often confidential materials. No one appointment can be adequately explained without study of the unique transactions involved.[2] The discussion of recruitment that follows, however, is a general examination of participants and con-siderations that are thought to be relevant for at least some of the appointees some of the time. First, the focus is on lower court ap-pointments, then on Supreme Court nominations.

Selection of a lower federal court judge typically involves a number

---

gaged in such work. In addition to the FBI, within the Department of Justice there is the Immigration Border Patrol. Within the Department of the Treasury, there is the Bureau of Narcotics, the Secret Service, and units concerned with violations of federal income and other taxes and customs laws. Within the Postal Service, there is the inspector's office with responsibility for investigating postal offenses. On the FBI see the following three works by John T. Elliff: "Aspects of Federal Civil Rights Enforcement: The Justice Department and the FBI, 1939–1964," *Perspectives in American History,* 5 (1971), 605–673; *Crime, Dissent, and the Attorney General: The Justice Department in the 1960's* (Beverly Hills, Calif.: Sage, 1971); "The Politics of Domestic Intelligence Surveillance and Civil Liberties under the Nixon Adminis-tration," paper presented at the 1974 Annual Meeting of the American Political Science Association. Also see Victor S. Navasky, *Kennedy Justice* (New York: Atheneum, 1971), Chaps. 1–3.

Note also that other federal judicial system authorities not discussed in this chap-ter include federal magistrates (who perform minor judicial duties), probation offi-cers (whose presentence reports on convicted criminals may heavily influence the sentence handed down by the judge), and parole board members (who exercise dis-cretion in the granting, denial, or revocation of parole).

[2] For a theoretical discussion of appointment transactions, see David J. Danelski, *A Supreme Court Justice Is Appointed* (New York: Random House, 1964), pp. 145–153.

of different participants. They include: (1) the President; (2) officials in the Justice Department, especially the Attorney General, the Deputy Attorney General and his assistants; (3) the U.S. senators of the President's party from the state where the potential nominee resides; (4) various other political leaders of the President's party, such as congressmen, state party chairmen, governors, national committeemen, and mayors of large cities from the state "receiving" the nomination; (5) those who aspire to federal judgeships (and their supporters among the bar and bench) who campaign for a position by contacting those just mentioned; (6) the members and particularly the Chairman of the American Bar Association's Standing Committee on Federal Judiciary; and (7) the members of the Senate, in particular those serving on the Senate Judiciary Committee.

The Process

The Justice Department maintains files on likely candidates for newly created judgeships and vacant or soon-to-become-vacant lower court judicial positions. In filling a judgeship, Justice officials usually start by considering names proposed by senators and other important party leaders. They may also have their own candidate to promote. The candidates are then informally investigated by an aide to the Deputy Attorney General (in recent years, the Executive Assistant) who typically will contact a wide variety of persons both in and out of government.[3] The names of the leading candidates are then given to the American Bar Association Standing Committee on Federal Judiciary, which since the Eisenhower Administration has investigated and rated those candidates. The ratings currently used are "Exceptionally Well Qualified," "Well Qualified," "Qualified," and "Not Qualified." At the early stages, the Committee gives Justice officials an informal tentative-but-probable rating of the leading contenders. Poor tentative ratings can be used by Justice officials as the basis for dropping candidates from consideration.

A candidate who has the strong backing of his senators and the

[3] The judicial selection process is examined in some detail by Joel B. Grossman, *Lawyers and Judges* (New York: Wiley, 1965); Sheldon Goldman, "Judicial Appointments to the United States Courts of Appeals," *Wisconsin Law Review*, (1967), 186–214; Harold W. Chase, *Federal Judges: The Appointing Process* (Minneapolis: University of Minnesota Press, 1972); Donald D. Jackson, *Judges* (New York: Atheneum, 1974), Chap. 12; Joseph C. Goulden, *The Benchwarmers* (New York: Weybright and Talley, 1974), Chap. 1.

party leaders of his state is assured of nomination and confirmation if he also meets the standards of the Justice Department and the ABA Committee. However, when there is no consensus as to the nominee, Justice officials must engage in extensive negotiations with the senators and/or other party leaders of the President's party. The extent to which Justice officials will defer, in particular, to the wishes of senators depends upon instructions from the President. Presidents Eisenhower and Kennedy let it be known that their Justice Department officials were authorized to negotiate for the best possible nominees. President Johnson, on the other hand, was amenable to having his officials defer to the wishes of Democratic Party senators unless the candidates were clearly unacceptable.[4] President Nixon put his confidence in his Attorney General John Mitchell and Deputy Attorney General (later Attorney General) Richard Kleindienst to handle matters as they saw fit on a case-by-case, senator-by-senator basis.[5]

Prior to the Nixon Administration, the Justice officials would, on the basis of their own and the ABA Committee's investigations, be ready to make the decision as to whom to recommend for a post. The Justice officials typically would informally check with members of the Senate Judiciary Committee to make sure no unexpected difficulties with a nomination would arise. Then, as a virtual last step in the process, the FBI would be instructed to conduct a routine investigation of the candidate. Assuming no unexpectedly adverse information was uncovered, the Attorney General would formally recommend him in a letter to the President. The White House would then announce the nomination and send the appropriate nomination papers to the Senate.

This process and particularly the use of the FBI investigation changed during the Nixon Administration, although the beginnings of the expanded use of the FBI can be traced to the Morrissey nomination fiasco in 1965 (discussed in greater detail shortly) in which some crucial facts about Morrissey's past were discovered by newspaper reporters rather than the FBI. The Morrissey episode convinced Justice officials that the FBI investigation would have to be more thorough to prevent further such embarrassments. But it was not until the Nixon Administration took office that the major changes occurred.

---

[4] Chase, *Federal Judges*, p. 184.

[5] Interview with John Duffner, Executive Assistant to the Deputy Attorney General, August 28, 1974.

In the early days of the Nixon Administration, Justice officials and the ABA Committee agreed that, in order to be seriously considered, each candidate for a judicial slot would be required to complete an extensive questionnaire that would provide a wide variety of personal and professional information about the candidate. Candidates would also be required to sign waivers permitting inspection of all their medical records. Among other matters the questionnaire contains items asking each candidate to list the ten most important cases handled and the names of opposing counsel and the judges before whom the cases came. In the hands of the FBI the completed questionnaire and the medical records waiver have provided the basis for a thorough, more wide-ranging investigation than the routine FBI investigations of the past.

During the Senate's consideration of the ill-fated Carswell nomination to the Supreme Court, newspaper reporters dug from the clipping files of a local newspaper an account of a racist speech that Carswell had once made as a young candidate for public office, and this caught the Justice Department and the FBI by surprise. After Carswell, the FBI would go through the clipping files of the local newspapers in the areas where the candidate had lived as part of the investigation. During the Nixon years the FBI became a major tool for discovering the racial, social, economic, and political views of the candidates. Thus, the information contained in the FBI dossier in the hands of the Justice officials is a powerful resource in the negotiations with senators and even the ABA Committee.[6]

Once a nomination is sent to the Senate, it is given to the Senate Judiciary Committee. Then, as a matter of routine, the Chairman of the Senate Judiciary Committee sends out what are known as the "blue slips." These are forms that officially notify the senators from the nominee's home state that the nomination has been received by the Committee. The form also has space for the senator's reply and, in addition, contains this caveat: "Under a rule of the Committee, unless a reply is received from you within a week from this date, it will be assumed that you have no objection to this nomination."[7]

[6] Ibid. Also cf. Chase, Federal Judges, pp. 23–26, 42–43.

[7] A copy of such a blue slip is contained in the Hearings on the Nomination of Phillip W. Tone to Fill a Vacancy on the United States Court of Appeals for the Seventh Circuit, Subcommittee on Nominations, Senate Judiciary Committee, May 1, 1974 (unpublished hearing). Judge Tone, an Illinois resident and at the time of his nomination a federal district court judge, was sponsored by Charles Percy, the

During closed sessions the Committee determines when and if to hold public hearings. If a senator returns the blue slip indicating that a nomination is personally obnoxious, that will ordinarily result in the nomination's being buried by failure of the Committee to take action. The Committee thus defers to the views of the senators from whose state the vacancy is to be filled, particularly if one or both are of the President's party. If the senators do not object to the nomination, the Committee typically votes to recommend confirmation and sends the nomination to the floor of the Senate. On occasion, opposition is voiced on the Senate floor against a nomination. It is customary, however, for the Senate to vote to confirm a nominee favorably recommended by the Committee. Once the nomination is confirmed, it is sent to the President, and he signs the appointment documents. The judge takes the judicial oath and begins his tenure on the federal bench.

Selection variable: "qualified" appointments

Perhaps the most important constraint on all principal participants in the recruitment process is the now widespread expectation that judicial nominees should be "qualified." Obviously the federal bench is no place for party hacks and incompetents. The problem, however, is how to evaluate a candidate for a judicial post. What makes one person "qualified" and another not? Ostensibly the ABA Committee makes distinctions in its ratings, for example, between "Exceptionally Well Qualified" and "Well Qualified" or between "Qualified" and "Not Qualified" on the basis of age, professional (particularly trial court) experience, reputation, scholarly qualities, and "judicial temperament." But how objective are these criteria and, more important, how objective is the ABA Committee in applying them?

One study of the ABA Committee during the Kennedy Administration revealed that assessments of candidates were primarily made by Wall Street and Bar Association–establishment types.[8] In the past, the organized bar was known to oppose candidates with liberal views. A prominent example of this occurred when the organized bar almost

---

Republican Senator from Illinois. Percy sent back his blue slip with the handwritten reply "Fully approve—rating especially well qualified by ABA" followed by his signature. The other Illinois senator, Democrat Adlai Stevenson, handwrote "No objections" and signed his name.

[8] Grossman, *Lawyers and Judges*, pp. 250–251.

en masse opposed the nomination of liberal Louis Brandeis to the Supreme Court in 1916.[9] By the mid-1960s, however, the American Bar Association seemed to become somewhat less conservative,[10] and, in fact, the ABA Committee in 1968 supported liberal Abe Fortas's nomination to the chief justiceship at a time when conservative criticism of the Supreme Court was at a peak (although the ABA was of no help to Fortas less than a year later when he was, in effect, forced to resign from the bench[11]). Even if the ABA is no longer biased against liberal views and those who hold them[12] and may now be able to more objectively evaluate judicial candidates of different ideological leanings, the question nevertheless remains whether a private

[9] A. L. Todd, *Justice on Trial: The Case of Louis D. Brandeis* (New York: McGraw-Hill, 1964).

[10] For example, the president of the American Bar Association during 1969–1970 was Bernard G. Segal. *The New York Times* published an article about Segal at the time he assumed office that contained the observation that Segal "represents the small group of comparatively liberal and highly successful corporate lawyers who have dominated the organization for the last dozen years, shepherding its philosophy from conservatism to progressivism." The article also noted that Segal "has campaigned arduously in behalf of civil rights." See *New York Times*, August 15, 1969, p. 36. The change in orientation of the ABA was also at least implied by the response of the ABA to President Nixon's request to establish a study group to examine the Federal Trade Commission. The ABA appointed sixteen members who later issued a report attacking the FTC for failure to protect consumers from deceitful and fraudulent practices of businesses. The ABA commission's recommendations were decidedly "liberal" and certainly light-years away from the laissez-faire business orientation of a half-century earlier. See *New York Times*, September 16, 1969, p. 1. In the area of civil liberties, the executive council of the association's Criminal Law Section opposed key provisions of the Nixon Administration's anticrime bills. See *New York Times*, June 25, 1970, p. 32. During the controversy over the legal services program, the ABA came down firmly in favor of the program, which at that time was under attack by conservatives. See *New York Times*, February 13, 1973, p. 11. The ABA at that same meeting voted to support the "exclusionary rule" and to oppose legislation that would permit the introduction in a criminal trial of illegally obtained evidence.

[11] At the request of Republican Senator Williams of Delaware, an ABA committee examined Fortas's relationship with financier Louis Wolfson and expressed the opinion that eight canons of judicial ethics appeared to have been violated. See *New York Times*, May 21, 1969, p. 1.

[12] Cf. John R. Schmidhauser, *The Supreme Court: Its Politics, Personalities, and Procedures* (New York: Holt, Rinehart and Winston, 1961), pp. 6–29; Albert P. Melone, "Lawyers and the Republic: The American Bar Association and Public Policy," Ph.D. dissertation, University of Iowa, 1972; Chase, *Federal Judges*, pp. 157–164.

group should play such a role in recruitment of such important authorities.

Over a decade ago, the ABA Committee's role and political clout in the recruitment process came into prominent view when the Johnson Administration decided to nominate a man considered unqualified by the members of the ABA Committee. In late September, 1965, President Johnson sent to the Senate the nomination of Boston Municipal Court Judge Francis X. Morrissey for a position on the District Court of Massachusetts. Morrissey, an old friend of the Kennedy family, was sponsored by Senator Edward Kennedy. The ABA Committee could barely contain its outrage. A parade of ABA dignitaries testified against Morrissey before the Senate Judiciary Committee. They revealed that Morrissey had obtained his law degree from an unaccredited Georgia diploma mill; in the course of his work at that substandard school he managed to fail four important courses; he also failed his bar examination twice before barely passing it on the third try; he had virtually no legal experience before his appointment as a municipal judge; and his tenure on the bench was, to say the least, undistinguished. In a highly unusual move, Chief Judge Charles Wyzanski of the Federal District Court of Massachusetts wrote to the Senate Judiciary Committee vigorously opposing the nomination. He asserted that Morrissey "has neither the familiarity with the law nor the industry to learn it."[13] Editorial writers throughout the country decried the nomination, one suggesting it was nauseating.[14]

The Chairman of the ABA Committee questioned Morrissey's integrity by testifying that Morrissey, in gaining admission to the Georgia bar, claimed he was a resident of Georgia only to leave shortly thereafter for Boston. Morrissey, in his defense, testified that he had remained in Georgia for about six months after receiving his law degree trying to establish himself. He had thus considered himself a Georgia resident. A few days after Morrissey's testimony, however, a Boston newspaper revealed that during the time that Morrissey claimed he was a Georgia resident, he was a candidate for a seat in the Massachusetts legislature, a fact the FBI investigation on Morrissey failed to reveal!

---

[13] *Washington Post,* September 29, 1965, p. 1, as cited in Chase, *Federal Judges,* p. 174. This account of the Morrissey affair is drawn from Chase, pp. 173–177.

[14] Chase, *Federal Judges,* p. 174.

Although the Massachusetts Bar Association endorsed Morrissey and Senator Edward Kennedy pressed hard for the nomination, the nomination appeared doomed. On October 21, 1965, Kennedy dramatically asked the Senate to send the nomination back to committee, and his colleagues complied. Two weeks later the President withdrew the nomination at Morrissey's request.

Aside from illustrating the activity of the ABA Committee, this episode also demonstrates how difficult it has been in the last decade for a judgeship to be obtained for a person considered by the ABA to be unqualified.[15] However, it should be noted that because of the very extensive FBI investigation, in instances where a candidate was given a marginal rating, the Justice officials could suggest to the ABA Committee Chairman that the information upon which the relatively poor rating was based was inadequate and that the Committee should go back and recheck the candidate, this time contacting different sources. Apparently this was done in a few instances and resulted in better ratings.[16]

Early in his Administration, President Nixon pledged that he would not nominate any person rated "Not Qualified" by the ABA Committee.[17] Thus, the ABA Committee was given a veto in the judicial

---

[15] *Ibid.*, pp. 177–178.

[16] Interview with John Duffner, August 28, 1974. There is obvious subjectivity and imprecision involved in the ratings process despite the ABA Committee's efforts to articulate and apply certain criteria. On occasion the Committee is divided over what rating to give a candidate. For example, in 1963, a Kennedy nominee for a post on the Sixth Circuit, George C. Edwards, Jr., received a "Qualified" rating from a majority of the Committee, with a minority voting "Not Qualified." See Chase, *Federal Judges*, pp. 167–168. Another example, in 1973, is that of the Committee rating of Joseph T. Sneed for a seat on the Ninth Circuit. The ABA Committee Chairman, as is the procedure, sent the Committee report to the Senate Judiciary Committee. The report on Sneed was as follows: "A substantial majority of our Committee is of the opinion that Joseph T. Sneed is *well qualified* for appointment as Judge. . . . A small minority found him *qualified*. However, some of those who voted *well qualified* indicated that they would have found Mr. Sneed *exceptionally well qualified* except for his lack of trial experience." (Italics added.) *Hearings on the Nomination of Joseph T. Sneed to Fill a Vacancy on the United States Court of Appeals for the Ninth Circuit*, Senate Judiciary Committee, August 2, 1973 (unpublished hearing). In general see Chase, *Federal Judges*, Chap. 4; Jackson, *Judges*, pp. 257–269; and Grossman, *Lawyers and Judges*.

[17] *Congressional Quarterly*, August 15, 1969, p. 1484. Note that after the Haynsworth-Carswell defeats, the Administration, in an unprecedented move, agreed to submit the names of the leading candidates for Supreme Court vacancies to the

recruitment process that lasted up to the last days of the Administration. But, during Nixon's last full day in office, he sent to the Senate the nomination of Thomas Meskill, Governor of Connecticut (and former congressman), to fill a vacancy on the prestigious U.S. Court of Appeals for the Second Circuit. Meskill was unanimously rated "Not Qualified" by the ABA Committee. Why Mr. Nixon chose to defy the ABA is unclear. Why the Justice officials bowed to the pressure from Meskill's sponsor, Senator Lowell Weicker, was also unclear.[18] Mes-

---

ABA Committee. Although it was not explicitly stated, the implication was clear that the Administration would not nominate a person to the Supreme Court who received the "Not Qualified" rating. See New York Times, July 28, 1970, p. 1. This new procedure had its first test in the early fall of 1971 when two vacancies caused by the resignations of Justices Black and Harlan were to be filled. The Administration first submitted to the ABA Committee the name of conservative Virginia Congressman Richard H. Poff. At the outset it had been leaked to the press that Poff was under serious consideration and immediately civil rights groups and organized labor mounted a campaign against him. (Poff's voting record in the House over a period of nineteen years included total opposition to civil rights legislation and marked unfriendliness to the position of organized labor.) Before the ABA Committee had an opportunity to conclude their deliberations concerning Poff's candidacy, Poff decided to take himself out of the running. See Congressional Quarterly, October 16, 1971, p. 2129. Within two weeks, the Nixon Administration submitted to the Committee a list of six persons. The White House requested that the Committee focus on two names, the presumed front-runners for the two nominations, Herschel H. Friday (a Little Rock, Arkansas, lawyer and specialist in municipal bond law) and Mildred L. Lillie (a California state appeals court judge). The names of the six surfaced and opposition mounted. The Committee found Lillie unqualified by a vote of 11 to 1, and it split down the middle on a rating for Friday with half the Committee voting Friday not qualified and the other half voting "not opposed." The upshot was that Friday and Lillie were dropped along with the arrangement with the Committee concerning candidates for Supreme Court positions. When President Nixon announced the nominations of Lewis Powell and William Rehnquist for the vacancies on October 21, 1971, it came as a surprise to the ABA Committee as well as to the rest of the nation. See Jackson, Judges, pp. 352–353.

[18] Senator Weicker was clearly not on good terms with the ABA Committee. The New York Times (October 12, 1973, p. 37) suggested that the ABA Committee had found Weicker's candidates for the Second Circuit to be not qualified, while Weicker in turn viewed the Committee and the Second Circuit as "snooty." The impasse between Weicker and the Committee over the Second Circuit vacancy had existed since Judge Joseph Smith's retirement in November, 1971. The judges on the Second Circuit were anxious for the impasse to be broken. Judge Smith, it should be noted, occupied one of the two "Connecticut" seats (in fact, those positions from the time of their creation had been filled only by Connecticut residents) on the nine-member Second Circuit. When Senator Weicker sponsored Governor Meskill to replace Smith, it was no doubt difficult for the Justice officials to dismiss a candidate with such impressive surface credentials. It is also likely that, after his rebuffs

kill's nomination brought out the opposition of leading law professors from the Yale and University of Connecticut law schools,[19] as well as the ire of the editorial writers of *The New York Times*.[20] Yet the ABA was on less firm ground than with the Morrissey nomination because, after all, they were dealing with a former congressman and an incumbent governor. The unwillingness of the ABA Committee to fight as they did in the Morrissey case and their inability to clearly face the issue of whether Meskill had the competence and judicial temperament for a seat on the prestigious Second Circuit was the major reason why the ABA lost the fight.[21] Despite the Meskill episode, it is clear that those who aspire to be serious judicial candidates can be expected to be attuned to the ABA's values and norms of behavior (such as can be identified).

Selection variable: party considerations

As far back as statistics have been gathered, judicial appointments have primarily gone to members of the President's party. In recent administrations at least 90 percent of those appointed have had partisan credentials.[22] By maintaining the importance of partisan con-

---

from the ABA Committee, Weicker was determined to stand firm. We can speculate that by the spring of 1974 Justice officials felt they had no choice but to yield to Weicker. Weicker's prestige with Connecticut Republicans and, of course, Governor Meskill's career were directly on the line. When he agreed to be Weicker's choice, Governor Meskill had taken himself out of running for reelection. In any event, the Meskill nomination was announced and sent to the Senate (the White House evidently had hesitated) on Nixon's last working day in office. Finally, in April, 1975, the three and a half year vacancy on the Second Circuit was filled when Thomas Meskill was confirmed and was sworn into office.

19 *Congressional Quarterly*, September 21, 1974, pp. 2570–2571; *New York Times*, September 15, 1974, p. 22.

20 *New York Times*, September 18, 1974, p. 40.

21 The Committee had based its "Not Qualified" rating ostensibly on Meskill's lack of trial experience. Ironically, the biggest loser was probably the Justice Department, for in bucking the ABA and yielding to senatorial pressures on behalf of a candidate with controversial credentials, the Justice officials undercut one of their dominant themes used in negotiations with senators—the need for high-quality judges on the federal bench. With the Meskill episode in mind, some senators may be more assertive in pushing candidates with controversial qualifications.

22 See Goldman, "Judicial Appointments," pp. 196–199. Also concerning appointments to the U.S. courts of appeals, see *Legislative History of the United States Circuit Courts of Appeals and the Judges Who Served during the Period 1801 through May 1972* (Washington, D.C.: U.S. Senate, Committee on the Judiciary, 92nd Congress, Second Session, 1972), p. 2.

siderations, the administration strengthens the President's party and his position as party leader. Reward of the party faithful who have the other necessary qualifications for judicial office encourages lawyers with judicial ambitions to become politically involved. To depart from the tradition of partisan consideration would invite conflict with senators and other party leaders who expect that partisans will be given first preference.

At the very least, senators and major state and local leaders of the President's party expect to be able to "clear," that is, to approve, all appointments of people from their states or localities. Without such influence a party leader's political standing would be severely undermined. Sometimes the appointment situation can become extraordinarily complex when the senators and other major party leaders support different candidates and threaten not to clear another's choice. The following events are illustrative.

In early January, 1956, Chief Judge Major of the U.S. Court of Appeals for the Seventh Circuit notified President Eisenhower of his intention to retire by the end of the following March. Judge Major came from Illinois. However, there was another Illinois judge on the Court of Appeals. According to the informal tradition of state representation on the appeals courts, it was now Indiana's turn for the appointment. Problems soon arose because the two Republican Senators from Indiana (Capehart and Jenner) could not agree on which candidate to back. Moreover, Indiana Republican Congressman Charles Halleck, high in the Republican House hierarchy, had his own candidate. The Senators, however, agreed on one point. They would not clear Halleck's candidate, Federal District Judge Parkinson, because they believed that Halleck had received more than his fair share of patronage.[23] Senator Capehart, running for reelection in 1956, wanted the appointment to go to John Hastings who also happened to be Chairman of the Citizens Committee for Capehart. Senator Jenner wanted the appointment to go to Lloyd Hartzler.

Robert Grant, a former congressman, cognizant of Halleck's influence with the Eisenhower Administration and anticipating the selection of Judge Parkinson for the appeals post, went to Washington to line up support for the vacancy on the district bench that would

[23] These events and those that are cited in the subsequent two paragraphs in the text are based on reports published by The Chicago Tribune, March 16, 1956, p. 23, and March 15, 1957, p. 17.

occur with Parkinson's elevation. Eight Indiana Republican Congressmen promised Grant their support. Thus, within a short time after Judge Major announced his intention to retire, the three most important Republican leaders in Indiana actively supported three different men for the soon-to-be-vacant seat on the appeals court. In addition, eight congressmen backed a candidate for an anticipated vacancy on the district bench.

Stalemate resulted. Republican Senator Dirksen of Illinois was waiting in the wings with *his* candidate if the Indiana Republicans were unable to "clear" a candidate. Justice Department officials negotiated with the principals, but an impasse existed for over a year. Then apparently accommodation was reached. John Hastings received the appointment to the appeals court. The next appeals court vacancy went to Judge Parkinson. Grant eventually received the district court appointment he so actively sought.

Selection variable: ideological and policy position considerations

It is difficult to pinpoint with precision the extent to which an administration will take into consideration the ideological or policy views of a candidate. There is evidence, however, that such considerations do play a role. A Democratic administration will rarely appoint a Goldwater conservative and a Republican administration will not go out of its way to appoint a Kennedy liberal.

Nixon, prior to his election in 1968, made it perfectly clear that he would appoint judicial conservatives to the Supreme Court, and he implied that they would be appointed to the lower courts as well.[24] The appointment of former Goldwater Campaign Manager Richard Kleindienst as Deputy Attorney General in early 1969 signaled Nixon's intention to carry out his pledge. There is every reason to believe that subsequently Nixon was not disappointed with Kleindienst. For example, in one widely reported instance, a distinguished black attorney and former dean of Howard Law School was rejected by Kleindienst for a post on the Third Circuit because he was "soft on crime."[25] In any event, when running for reelection in 1972, Nixon boasted that

[24] See, for example, *New York Times,* November 3, 1968, p. 1, and January 4, 1970, p. 46. During the 1970 congressional campaign, Nixon made it obvious that this was precisely what he was doing and intended to continue doing. See *New York Times,* October 25, 1970, p. 1.

[25] *Congressional Quarterly,* December 16, 1972, p. 3160.

his appointments to the federal courts made the Constitution "more secure," and he promised to continue to appoint more "strict constructionists."[26]

Examination of Senate Judiciary hearings on Nixon nominees revealed several instances when ideology was explicitly recognized as an important selection consideration. For example, one nominee was introduced by his senator as "a strict constructionist."[27] Another nominee was lauded as one who will practice "judicial restraint."[28] Another, an incumbent state judge, was praised for being "a conservative but perceptive thinker."[29] One observer gave this assessment of the Nixon appointees in an interview with journalist Donald Dale Jackson:

You can't be a federal judge today unless you believe the whole hardnosed line. It's like getting ahead in the FBI—you have to be for the death penalty, you have to regard all the criminal decisions of the Warren Court as wrong. I've never seen such stereotypes. Any background of liberalism or orientation towards the Bill of Rights is a disqualifier. . . . There are some exceptions, where you have liberal Republican senators like Percy or Javits. But if there's no liberal senator, then you get one-hundred-percent law and order.[30]

It should be emphasized, as suggested in this quote, that the involvement of moderate and liberal senators in the appointment process in a number of instances blunted the sharp edge of the Nixon Administration's professed right-wing goals.

A study of behind-the-scenes activity concerning appeals court appointments during the Eisenhower and Kennedy Administrations revealed examples of ideological considerations prominently at work.[31]

[26] New York Times, October 16, 1972, p. 1.

[27] Hearings on the Nomination of Thomas G. Gee to Fill a Vacancy on the United States Court of Appeals for the Fifth Circuit, Subcommittee on Nominations, Senate Judiciary Committee, July 10, 1973 (unpublished hearing), p. 5.

[28] Hearings on the Nomination of D. Dortch Warriner to Fill a Vacancy on the United States District Court, Eastern District of the State of Virginia, Subcommittee on Nominations, Senate Judiciary Committee, May 15, 1974 (unpublished hearing), p. 2.

[29] Hearings on the Nomination of John A. Reed, Jr., to Fill a Vacancy on the United States District Court, Middle District of the State of Florida, Subcommittee on Nominations, Senate Judiciary Committee, July 26, 1973 (unpublished hearing), p. 5.

[30] Jackson, Judges, p. 270.

[31] Goldman, "Judicial Appointments," pp. 203–212. For a different behind-the-scenes view of the Kennedy appointments that focuses on the Southern appointees

One instance during the Kennedy Administration occurred when the two Democratic Senators from Montana, from where the appointee would be chosen, narrowed their list to two men (James Browning and one other) and decided to leave the final selection to the Justice officials. A Washington, D.C., attorney, himself once a member of the Justice Department, wrote a letter to Attorney General Robert Kennedy and succinctly articulated the alternatives faced by the Justice officials. The letter began by noting that the choice of candidates involved Browning and "X."

Assuming that I exaggerate and that these men are actually comparable in competence and judicial temperament, there are I think the intangibles which weigh more heavily in favor of Browning than [X]. I must tread softly here for, by definition, intangibles are hard to weigh. Nonetheless, I submit the trend as toward Browning and against [X]:

First, not only is the Ninth Circuit a weak bench, it is a conservative bench quite out of step with the premises of the New Frontier as almost all of us understand those premises. In the great run of cases it does not matter whether a judge is liberal or conservative if he is a good judge. There are a handful of cases, however,—and, Heaven knows, they always seem to be the important ones!—where the judicial mind can go either way, with probity, with honor, self-discipline and even with precedent. This is where the "liberal" cast of mind (we all know it, few of us can define it) can move this nation forward, just as the conservative mind can and does hold it back. This is intangible truth, but every lawyer knows it as reality! Browning would go forward, [X] would hold back.

Second, the political point of view of a candidate deserves weight when other things are equal, or almost equal. . . . I know of Browning's devotion to the Democratic Party. . . . I personally know that over the years he has contributed vast amounts of time and money to good Democrats. On this point, both of his Senators will strongly attest. . . .

[X] is entitled, as aren't we all, to his convictions and if his convictions in the 1950s happened to be Eisenhower that was not only his privilege, it was his duty. But I also think privilege and duty carry with them the consequences of their acts. I do not think it is unduly partisan of me if I feel a good man cannot and should not live in both worlds.

Browning received the appointment.[32]

---

and the relevance (or irrelevance) of the ideological or policy views of the nominees, see Navasky, *Kennedy Justice*, Chap. 5.

[32] That Browning received the nomination is even more noteworthy because the ABA Committee rated him "Not Qualified." The Kennedy people in the Justice Department, however, viewed the rating as a manifestation of antiliberal bias on the part of those Montana lawyers contacted by the ABA whose views provided the

Supreme court appointments

The three considerations of competence, party, and ideology are all relevant for Supreme Court appointments. Supreme Court nominations in this century have typically gone to respected lawyers and judges of the President's party who share the President's ideological proclivities. Moreover, unlike lower court appointments, Supreme Court appointments have tended to be the personal choice and occasionally a personal friend of the President. Early examples suggesting the interplay of ideology along with party and friendship to the President in Supreme Court appointments include President John Adams's appointment of staunch Federalist John Marshall to the chief justiceship in 1801; Jackson's appointment in 1836 of strong supporter and close cabinet member Roger B. Taney to succeed Marshall; and Grant's appointments in 1871 of William Strong and Joseph Bradley, both supporters of Grant's legal tender policy (significantly, with the votes of these two justices a new Court majority, much to the relief of the Grant Administration, overturned the previous Court's restrictive legal tender policy).

Ideology   President Theodore Roosevelt's correspondence with Massachusetts Senator Henry Cabot Lodge concerning the Supreme Court nomination of Massachusetts Supreme Court Justice Oliver Wendell Holmes further illustrates the importance of ideology. Before nominating Holmes, Roosevelt wrote to Lodge: "I should like to know that Judge Holmes was in entire sympathy with our views, that is, with your views and mine . . . before I would feel justified in supporting him."[33] Years later President Franklin D. Roosevelt took care to appoint economic liberals to the courts.

A more recent description of the saliency of ideology in the appointment of Supreme Court justices is found in a report by journalist James Clayton of a 1963 interview with Attorney General Robert Kennedy about President Kennedy's two appointments to the Supreme Court.

---

basis for the rating. Interestingly, Judge Browning has served well on the bench (this evaluation is based on highly favorable references to Browning in personal interviews with appeals judges and others as well as a reading of a number of his opinions). For another account of Judge Browning's nomination see Grossman, *Lawyers and Judges*, pp. 144–145.

[33] Quoted in Schmidhauser, *Supreme Court*, p. 48. In general, see Henry J. Abraham, *Justices and Presidents* (New York: Oxford University Press, 1974).

Thinking back on the process months later, the Attorney General tilted back in his chair and said: "You wanted someone who generally agreed with you on what role government should play in American life, what role the individual in society should have. You didn't think about how he would vote in a reapportionment case or a criminal case. You wanted someone who, in the long run, you could believe would be doing what you thought was best. You wanted someone who agreed generally with your views of the country." Both he and the President believed that [Byron] White and [Arthur] Goldberg met that test.[34]

President Nixon frankly admitted on several occasions that he was deeply concerned with the policy views of those he appointed to the Supreme Court.[35] His intention to appoint conservatives was apparent with the nominations of Warren Burger, Clement Haynsworth, G. Harrold Carswell, Harry Blackmun, Lewis Powell, and William Rehnquist.

Geographic Representation State or geographic representation is also a consideration for federal court appointments. Under federal law, federal district judges must reside in the districts to which they are appointed. With the courts of appeals, the custom is to appoint an individual from one of the states within the circuit. With the exception of the First Circuit, there are enough positions so that every state can be represented. This is the expectation of senators and party organizations.[36] Geographic representation on the Supreme Court

[34] James E. Clayton, *The Making of Justice: The Supreme Court in Action* (New York: Dutton, 1964), p. 52, as cited in Henry J. Abraham, *The Judicial Process*, 2nd ed. (New York: Oxford University Press, 1968), p. 66. It is of interest to note that White and Goldberg's voting behavior on the Supreme Court diverged. See Joel B. Grossman, "Dissenting Blocs on the Warren Court: A Study in Judicial Role Behavior," *Journal of Politics*, 30 (1968), 1068–1090; Glendon Schubert, *The Judicial Mind Revisited: Psychometric Analysis of Supreme Court Ideology* (New York: Oxford University Press, 1974).

[35] See, e.g., *New York Times*, November 3, 1968, p. 1, November 22, 1969, p. 1; *Congressional Quarterly*, October 24, 1969, p. 2103.

[36] The Ninth Circuit presents a special problem in that one state, California, dominates the circuit in terms of population and volume of litigation. Justice officials have felt that California should have the lion's share of the total number of seats (currently thirteen) and that some of the remaining eight states should forego representation. But this does not sit well with senators and local bar associations. One Republican Senator, Hiram Fong from Hawaii, claimed one of the California seats when a vacancy arose in 1970 after the retirement of Judge Stanley Barnes. Fong was able to get his man Herbert Y. C. Choy on the bench. As of this writing, however, Justice officials have been able to hold off the Alaskans (Alaska is the only one of the nine states that has never been "represented" on the Ninth Circuit).

stems from the nineteenth-century practice of Supreme Court justices riding the circuit and sitting as circuit judges. It was then a matter of convenience to appoint a judge who would ride the circuit of the region in which he resided. Today the general practice appears to be that every major section of the country is "represented" on the Supreme Court. In fact, after the Haynsworth and Carswell defeats, President Nixon attempted to make Southern representation on the Court an issue. In so doing, he frankly admitted the saliency of geographic representation as a consideration in the appointment process.[37] Nixon eventually made good his promise to put a Southerner on the bench with the appointment of the distinguished lawyer and former ABA President Lewis Powell of Virginia.

Religious and Ethnic Considerations Another consideration frequently mentioned is that of religious and ethnic representation, that is, reserving one seat on the Court for each of the nation's principal minority groups. The extent to which religion is actually considered by an administration cannot be conclusively determined. The first Roman Catholic to sit on the Court was Roger B. Taney, a Jackson appointee. However, there is no evidence that Taney's religion was relevant for his appointment. Since 1894, however, with the exception of a seven-year period (1949–1956), there has been at least one member of the Catholic faith on the Court.

The first member of the Jewish religion to serve on the Court was Louis Brandeis, a Wilson appointee. Judging from some of the opposition to Brandeis's nomination, he probably was nominated despite his religious affiliation.[38] From Brandeis's appointment in 1916 until mid-1969 there was at least one member of the Jewish faith sitting on the Court. These justices included Cardozo, Frankfurter, Goldberg, and Fortas. Starting with Cardozo who replaced Holmes, these four justices occupied the same seat; that is, they each succeeded one another. However, after Fortas resigned from the bench in May, 1969, President Nixon's nominees for Fortas's seat were all Protestant (two Southerners and one Midwesterner).

[37] See President Nixon's statement in *The New York Times*, April 10, 1970, p. 14. Note that during the 1970 congressional campaign, Vice-President Agnew pledged that the Administration would place a Southern conservative on the Supreme Court. See *New York Times*, October 27, 1970, p. 1.

[38] See Todd, *Justice on Trial*.

President Johnson's appointment of Thurgood Marshall in 1967 is probably the beginning of Negro representation on the Court. Johnson was well aware of the historic nature of the appointment. In announcing it he stated, "I believe it is the right thing to do, the right time to do it, the right man and the right place."[39]

This seems to suggest that as long as religion and ethnicity remain important to Americans, and there is little evidence that the "melting pot" has substantially lowered their importance thus far,[40] there will be an expectation that each important minority group will have "a seat" on the Court.

Nominations and the Senate   In the nineteenth century, close to one out of three nominations to the Supreme Court met fatal resistance in the Senate.[41] In the twentieth century, the rate has been about one out of nine (with three of the four rejections occurring in the 1968–1970 period). Apparently, with the conspicuous exception of President Nixon, twentieth-century presidents have taken into account probable senatorial reaction when considering candidates for the Supreme Court. At least until the Nixon presidency, it was a common practice for presidents to informally check with members of the Senate Judiciary Committee as well as the leadership of both parties in the Senate. In all likelihood this increased sensitivity to the probable reactions of the Senate and the efforts made by presidents to smooth the way for nominees was responsible for the low rejection rate. Only four nominees in the twentieth century failed to achieve senatorial confirmation: President Hoover's nomination in 1930 of Fourth Circuit Judge John J. Parker; President Johnson's nomination in 1968 of Justice Abe Fortas for the position of Chief Justice;[42] and President

---

[39] As quoted in CQ *Guide to Current American Government, Fall 1967* (Washington, D.C.: Congressional Quarterly, 1967), p. 85.

[40] See, for example, Michael Parenti, "Ethnic Politics and the Persistence of Ethnic Identification," *American Political Science Review*, 61 (1967), 717–727; and Nathan Glazer and Daniel P. Moynihan, *Beyond the Melting Pot* (Cambridge, Mass.: M.I.T. and Harvard University Press, 1963).

[41] *Congressional Quarterly*, November 21, 1969, pp. 2312–2313.

[42] When Justice Fortas was nominated for elevation to the chief justiceship, President Johnson also nominated Fifth Circuit Judge Homer Thornberry to fill the vacancy that would exist upon Fortas's elevation. Since Fortas's nomination was not approved, no vacancy existed and Thornberry's nomination also died.

Nixon's first two nominations for Fortas's vacated seat, Appeals Judges Clement Haynsworth (Fourth Circuit) and G. Harrold Carswell (Fifth Circuit). The first two nominations aroused *unexpectedly* fierce ideological and partisan opposition with severe anti-Court overtones when they were submitted to the Senate.[43]

In conclusion it is prudent to remember that the considerations discussed serve only to narrow the population from which the appointee will be chosen. Through the operation of one or another of these considerations, many potential candidates are eliminated. Still there may be a number of possible candidates. Understanding why one person is selected and not another requires intensive study of the entire complex of events surrounding that particular appointment. The careful student of recruitment will keep this in mind.

JUDICIAL BACKGROUNDS

Who are the people recruited for judicial office? What are their backgrounds? Have they shared the same socialization experiences and if so what are they? These are some of the questions that have interested political scientists particularly because of the evidence suggesting that the values of decision makers influence their decisions and the survey evidence suggesting that certain attitudes and values are associated with backgrounds and experiences.[44] Examined in this section is the extent to which certain backgrounds (which have presumably facilitated the development of certain values) are overrepresented or underrepresented as compared to the population at large.

Family backgrounds

Studies of the family backgrounds of federal judges have revealed that historically high social status and wealth have been greatly over-

[43] President Johnson was particularly disturbed about Republican opposition to the Fortas nomination because he had gone to the trouble of clearing the nomination with Republican Senate Minority Leader Everett Dirksen. See the transcript of the Johnson press conference in *The New York Times*, August 1, 1968, p. 16. The Parker and Fortas nomination fights were won by opponents of the Court. The Haynsworth and Carswell battles were won largely by supporters of the Court. A journalistic account of the Carswell fight can be found in Richard Harris, *Decision* (New York: Dutton, 1971). Also see Joel B. Grossman and Stephen Wasby, "Haynsworth and Parker: History Does Live Again," *South Carolina Law Review*, 23 (1971), 345.

[44] The major public opinion polls regularly break down their surveys by demographic variables such as age, sex, region, religion, income, education level, occupation, and party affiliation.

represented on the federal bench. The leading study of the backgrounds of Supreme Court justices reveals that about 90 percent of the justices came from economically comfortable families and the remainder from humble backgrounds.[45] In the period before the Civil War, the justices came primarily from the landed gentry. After the Civil War until recently, the justices came predominantly from the upper middle class (where the fathers tended to be in one of the professions). This pattern, however, appears to have at least temporarily ended. The Supreme Court of 1968–1969 contained the largest number of justices from humble beginnings ever to sit on the Court at one time. On the Court then were the great-grandson of a slave (and son of a Pullman car steward), the son of a railroad worker, the son of poor Irish immigrants, the son of an impoverished minister who died when the boy was five, and the son of a poor merchant. This perhaps reflected the progress the country has made over the last four decades toward achieving equal opportunity for all.[46]

With the exception of James Wilson (a Federalist) and Earl Warren (a Republican), all of the Supreme Court justices through 1974 with humble backgrounds were Democrats. In all, 28 percent of the justices appointed by Democratic presidents (9 out of 32) were from humble backgrounds, while only about 9 percent of the justices appointed by Republicans (4 out of 45, three of whom were Democrats) were from such backgrounds.[47] This no doubt reflects the difference in the groups to which each party has appealed, a difference that has persisted for almost as long as our parties have been in existence. Further examination of the data lends support to this. The three Democratic appointees with humble backgrounds appointed in the nineteenth century were Jackson or Van Buren appointees. The remaining six were appointed during or since Franklin D. Roosevelt's Administration. All these administrations had vigorously sought support from low-status voters.

The available data concerning lower court judges indicate much the same pattern. At least three-fourths of the Eisenhower appointees

---

[45] Schmidhauser, *Supreme Court*, pp. 31–32.

[46] The Supreme Court of 1974–1975 contained three justices from humble backgrounds. For an analysis of social mobility and opportunity throughout American history, see P. M. G. Harris, "The Social Origins of American Leaders: The Demographic Foundations," *Perspectives in American History*, 3 (1969), 159–344.

[47] This analysis adds the following to Schmidhauser's original list of justices from humble backgrounds: Justices Douglas, Brennan, Goldberg, Fortas, and Marshall.

to the courts of appeals and at least one-half of the Kennedy appointees came from the middle or upper classes. However, close study suggests that the high-status Eisenhower appointees were a cut above the Kennedy appointees (as determined by father's education and occupation). Of a sample of eleven Kennedy appointees personally interviewed, only one reported that his father had completed higher education. Of a sample of sixteen Eisenhower appointees, nine reported that their fathers graduated from either college or a professional school.[48]

Study of other aspects of family background reveals that about two-thirds of all Supreme Court justices came from politically active families and over one-third of the justices were related to prominent judges.[49] The 1974–1975 Supreme Court, however, contained only one justice who fit into these categories. Justice Stewart hails from an old Ohio Republican family, and his father was a judge on the Ohio Supreme Court.

Education

Close to 85 percent of those appointed to the Supreme Court have attended the "best" law schools or (as was typical of legal education in the nineteenth century) had served apprenticeships with prominent lawyers and judges.[50] Findings for the lower court appointments of the Eisenhower and Kennedy Administrations were that about one-third of the judges went to state-supported law schools and the remainder went to private schools.[51] A larger proportion of Eisenhower

[48] Sheldon Goldman, "Politics, Judges, and the Administration of Justice: The Backgrounds, Recruitment, and Decisional Tendencies of the Judges on the United States Courts of Appeals, 1961–1964," Ph.D. dissertation, Harvard University, 1965, pp. 64–67.

[49] Schmidhauser, Supreme Court, p. 34.

[50] John R. Schmidhauser, "The Justices of the Supreme Court: A Collective Portrait," Midwest Journal of Political Science, 3 (1959), Table 8, reprinted in Glendon Schubert (ed.), Judicial Behavior (Skokie, Ill.: Rand McNally, 1964), p. 222.

[51] Sheldon Goldman, "Characteristics of Eisenhower and Kennedy Appointees to the Lower Federal Courts," Western Political Quarterly, 18 (1965), p. 757. Note that Richardson and Vines reported that about six out of ten district judges serving in 1963 had attended law school in the same state in which their district was located. A similar pattern of localism or regionalism was found for appeals judges. They suggested that state and sectional values and viewpoints may thereby be absorbed and represented on the bench. See Richard J. Richardson and Kenneth N. Vines, The Politics of Federal Courts (Boston: Little, Brown, 1970), pp. 70–73.

than Kennedy appointees attended Ivy League law schools.[52] This appeared to reinforce other findings that the Republican Eisenhower appointees tended to come from a higher social class than did the Democratic Kennedy appointees, the assumption being that one had to be fairly well-heeled to be able to attend an Ivy League law school in the 1920s. President Johnson, however, appointed about the same proportion of Ivy League law school graduates as President Eisenhower did (although the proportion of Johnson appointees is slightly less than that of the Nixon appointees[53]).

At first blush this would seem to undermine the class-party argument. However, the situation is probably much more complex. As the applicants to Ivy League schools (including their professional schools) have increased since the mid-1930s, these schools have increasingly considered ability and not just family background or financial status as the basis for admission. Since the average age of the Johnson appointees was 51, this would place their legal education precisely during the period when the Ivy League law schools were undergoing their transformation from aristocracy to meritocracy.[54] Thus the relatively high proportion of Johnson-appointed Ivy Leaguers does not, as it would have in the past, necessarily suggest a preponderance of appointees with upper-middle-class and upper-class origins.

Religious and ethnic background

Close to nine out of ten Supreme Court justices have been affiliated with a Protestant religion, and of these eight out of ten have been identified with what sociologists consider high-status Protestant reli-

[52] The figures are 21.5 percent of the Eisenhower district court appointees as compared to 18.4 percent of the Kennedy district court appointees; 28.8 percent of the Eisenhower appeals court appointees as compared to 19.1 percent of the Kennedy appeals court appointees. From Goldman, "Characteristics of Eisenhower and Kennedy Appointees to the Lower Federal Courts."

[53] The figures are 21.3 percent of the Johnson district court appointees as compared to 21.2 percent of the Nixon district court appointees; 27.5 percent of the Johnson appeals court appointees as compared to 35.6 percent of the Nixon appeals court appointees. See Sheldon Goldman, "Judicial Backgrounds, Recruitment, and the Party Variable: The Case of the Johnson and Nixon Appointees to the United States District and Appeals Courts," *Arizona State Law Journal* (1974), 211–222, for the backgrounds of Johnson and Nixon (first-term) appointees. Data concerning the 1973 and 1974 Nixon appointees came from the sources cited in this article.

[54] A suggestive article is by Christopher Jencks, "Social Stratification and Higher Education," *Harvard Educational Review*, 38 (1968), 277–316, especially the argument on pp. 289–290.

Table 3.1 Religious origins or affiliations of lower federal court judges by the appointing administrations

Administration	Protestant		Catholic		Jewish	
	Number	Percent	Number	Percent	Number	Percent
Combined Harding, Coolidge, and Hoover[a]	170	82.1	8	3.8	8	3.8
Roosevelt[b]	132	67.0	52	26.4	7	3.6
Truman[c]	75	59.1	38	29.9	12	9.4
Eisenhower[d]	133	78.2	27	15.8	10	5.8
Kennedy[e]	73	58.9	38	30.7	13	10.4
Johnson[f]	94	58.0	49	30.2	19	11.7
Nixon[g]	163	72.8	41	18.3	20	8.9

Sources: For appointees from Harding through Truman, Samuel Lubell, *The Future of American Politics* (Garden City, N.Y.: Doubleday, 1956), p. 83. For the Eisenhower and Kennedy appointees, Sheldon Goldman, "Characteristics of Eisenhower and Kennedy Appointees to the Lower Federal Courts," *Western Political Quarterly,* 18 (1965), p. 759. For the Johnson appointees and the Nixon appointees during his first term, Sheldon Goldman, "Judicial Backgrounds, Recruitment, and the 'Party Variable': The Case of the Johnson and Nixon Appointees to the United States District and Appeals Courts," *Arizona State Law Journal* (1974), p. 211. For the remainder of the Nixon appointees, *Who's Who in America,* Senate Judiciary Committee Hearings, and other public sources.

[a] Out of 207 appointments for which religious background of 21 judges was unknown.

[b] Out of 197 appointments of which 6 judges were unrecorded.

[c] Out of 127 appointments of which 2 judges were unrecorded.

[d] Out of 170 appointments to the district and appeals courts. Some estimates of religion made.

[e] Out of 124 appointments to the district and appeals courts. Some estimates of religion made.

[f] Out of 162 appointments to the district and appeals courts. Some estimates of religion made.

[g] Out of 224 appointments to the district and appeals courts through August 8, 1974. Some estimates of religion made.

gions.[55] Low-status Protestants as well as the Catholic and Jewish appointees have typically been Democrats. Tables 3.1 and 3.2 report similar findings for lower court judges. Again it is possible to conclude that differing ethnic and class support given to the major parties is

[55] Schmidhauser, *Supreme Court,* pp. 38–39. Also see Nicholas Jay Demerath, III, *Social Class in American Protestantism* (Skokie, Ill.: Rand McNally, 1965); Garlen Gockel, "Income and Religious Affiliation: A Regression Analysis," *American Journal of Sociology,* 74 (1969), 632–647; Bruce L. Warren, "Socioeconomic Achievement and Religion: The American Case," *Sociological Inquiry,* 40 (1970), 130–155; David Knoke, "Religion, Stratification and Politics: America in the 1960s," *American Journal of Political Science,* 18 (1974), 331–345.

Table 3.2 The religious origins or affiliations of all Democratic and Republican appointees to the federal courts of appeals, 1953–1974

Religion[a]	Republican administration appointees[b]		Democratic administration appointees[c]		1950 U.S. Populace
	Number	Percent	Number	Percent	Percent
Higher social status, Protestant religion	46	51.1	15	24.5	13
Roman Catholic	13	14.4	16	26.2	34
Jewish	7	7.8	7	11.5	6
Lower social status, Protestant religion	11	12.2	18	29.5	42
Other Protestant (unspecified)	12	13.3	5	8.2	
Unknown	1	1.1	—	—	5
Total	90	99.9	61	99.9	100

[a]Religious origins if known, or religious affiliation.
[b]Includes all appeals court appointees of the Eisenhower and Nixon Administrations.
[c]Includes all appeals court appointees of the Kennedy and Johnson Administrations.

reflected in the appointments. The figures also reveal that there is an "overrepresentation" of "higher status" religions on the bench today. It should be kept in mind, however, that it is not uncommon to convert from a low-status Protestant sect to a high-status sect. Undoubtedly this has occurred and is in part responsible for the overrepresentation.

The few black Americans on the federal bench have been primarily appointed by Democratic presidents. President Eisenhower did not name any black Americans to a federal district court or a court of appeals. President Kennedy named four to district courts and one to an appeals court. President Johnson named five to district courts, two to appeals courts, and was responsible for the first appointment of a black American to the Supreme Court. The Republican Nixon Administration returned to the appointment tendencies of past Republican Administrations in that white, middle- or upper-class, high-status Protestants received the bulk of appointments, and the only appointments to blacks on the three principal courts were the six named to the district courts.

Political activism

The political nature of the recruitment process results in many, if not most, federal judges having backgrounds of engaging in political activity prior to ascending the bench. In the 1974–1975 Supreme Court we find that Chief Justice Warren Burger played a key role in the Republican Convention of 1952,[56] Byron White was a campaign strategist and political associate of John F. Kennedy, Potter Stewart was an Ohio Republican Party leader, William Rehnquist was an active supporter of Barry Goldwater during the 1964 presidential campaign, and William O. Douglas was a friend and advisor to Franklin Roosevelt as well as Chairman of the Securities and Exchange Commission. About 75 percent of all appeals court judges serving in 1963 had been politically active in the party that ultimately was responsible for their appointments.[57]

One analysis involved an interview sample of Eisenhower and Kennedy appeals court appointees in which each judge was asked to classify himself as either a strong, moderate, or weak party supporter. Party support was defined in terms of one's sympathy with party traditions, principles, or programs and not political activity. Two-thirds of the Eisenhower appointees classified themselves as "strong Republicans," and all but one of the Kennedy appointees claimed to be "strong Democrats." The strong party supporters were invariably political activists during their pre-judicial careers.[58] An examination of the more prominent partisan activities of district and appeals judges before ascending the bench suggested that at least half the Johnson and Nixon appointees could be classified as prominent partisan activists.[59]

Career experiences

When we turn to major career experiences we find that a substantial portion of Supreme Court justices held high political or legal office or were prominent lawyers or law professors.[60] About 25 percent of all appeals judges serving in 1963 had at some time served with the U.S. Attorney's office, in the Justice Department, or in another legal capacity for the federal government. Over 30 percent of

[56] Julius Duscha, "Chief Justice Burger Asks: 'If It Doesn't Make Good Sense, How Can It Make Good Law?' " New York Times Magazine, October 5, 1969, p. 149.

[57] Goldman, "Politics, Judges, and the Administration of Justice," p. 93.

[58] Ibid., pp. 95–96.

[59] Goldman, "Judicial Backgrounds," pp. 218–219.

[60] Schmidhauser, Supreme Court, pp. 44–47.

the Johnson and over 20 percent of the Nixon district judge appointees held a legal position with the federal government. About 20 percent of both administrations' appeals courts appointees had prior legal experience with the federal government. State and local prosecutorial experience was also prominent in the backgrounds of roughly one out of five judges. Over 40 percent of the Johnson and Nixon appointees had some prosecutorial experience—either federal, state, or local—at some point in their careers. About 36 percent of both Eisenhower and Kennedy district and appeals court appointees had previous judicial experience before their appointments. About 42 percent of the Johnson and 40 percent of the Nixon appointees had previous judicial experience.[61] In fact, only about one-third of the Johnson and Nixon district court appointees and about one-fifth of the appeals court appointees had neither judicial nor prosecutorial experience.[62]

At the time of appointment to the district courts, about half the Eisenhower and Kennedy appointees were in private practice. Significantly, a larger proportion of Democratic Kennedy appointees than Republican Eisenhower appointees were with small law firms.[63]

[61] About one-third of the district judges as compared to about two-thirds of the appeals judges had judicial experience.

[62] If the Southern district court appointees are excluded, the proportion of district court judges without judicial or prosecutorial experience drops to about the same for appeals court appointees. The sensitivity of issues of racial equality in the South and the fact that political life until recently was undertaken in the context of legally and culturally enforced apartheid may provide the key to why the majority of the Southern district court appointees of both the Johnson and Nixon Administrations failed to have judicial or prosecutorial backgrounds. Those most active in Southern political life may have publicly supported the prevailing segregationist political culture thereby possibly injuring their prospects for federal judicial position in later years. See Sheldon Goldman, "Johnson and Nixon Appointees to the Lower Federal Courts: Some Socio-Political Perspectives," *Journal of Politics*, 34 (1972), 940. Note that in general it is reasonable to speculate that Justice officials prefer considering candidates with judicial or prosecutorial experience because such experience means that the candidate has a public track record that can be evaluated. In addition, a prosecutorial background may be favored by Justice officials because such a background is likely to have sensitized one to the problems a prosecutor's office faces and one might be more understanding if not sympathetic to the government's side in criminal prosecutions.

[63] Goldman, "Characteristics of Eisenhower and Kennedy Appointees to the Lower Federal Courts," p. 758. This too suggests that there were class differences in the appointments of both administrations.

About 44 percent of the Johnson district court appointees as compared to about 58 percent of the Nixon district court appointees were in private practice. Once again, a considerably larger proportion of Democratic than Republican district court appointees were from small firms, while close to twice the proportion of Nixon than Johnson appointees were from large law firms. The remainder of all four administrations' appointees were for the most part in either governmental or judicial positions. At the time of appointment to the appeals courts, about 25 percent of the Eisenhower and Kennedy appointees, approximately 30 percent of the Johnson, and 33 percent of the Nixon appointees were in private practice. Again there were proportionately more Republicans than Democrats from large law firms and the opposite finding for small law firms. At least half the appeals courts appointees of all four administrations held judicial positions (mostly federal district court positions), and the balance were primarily in governmental positions.

CONSEQUENCES OF THE RECRUITMENT PROCESS

It is appropriate to consider what difference it makes that we recruit our judicial authorities the way we do, the consequences this has for the larger American political system, and the implications of the recruitment process for the administration of justice.

Consequences for the larger political system

No doubt, as most political scientists argue, the nature of the recruitment process has very important consequences for the American political system. Presidents can and do use their power of judicial appointment to further Administration policy. President Franklin Roosevelt, for example, learned early that the federal judiciary could block important Administration programs. Consequently, he took care to offer judicial appointments to supporters of his New Deal programs. Other presidents have similarly been concerned with the ideological or policy views of their nominees. The recruitment process thus permits party responsibility.

The judiciary, a branch of government not directly responsible to the electorate, can be kept in touch with popular sentiment through the process of political recruitment. Judges chosen by a democratically elected administration can be expected to be in harmony, in a general sense, with the goals and commitments of the administration and to some extent the sentiments of the current majority. It should be apparent, then, that judicial appointments represent an output of the executive and legislative systems. The inputs that are processed to produce the appointment outputs are similar to other inputs produced by the democratically elected branches of government. Feedback from judicial policies becomes part of that input. New demands concerning the direction that judicial policies should take are part of that input. Demands as to the type of judges who should sit on the bench are input to the appointment process. Thus, it is apparent that the political recruitment process not only permits but encourages party responsibility and by so doing provides a potential link between court output and the current political climate.

The recruitment process, by virtue of its responsiveness to partisan considerations, has resulted in a diversity of social, economic, and political outlooks being represented on the federal bench. One wonders whether a recruitment process less politically sensitive would have or could have resulted when it did in the appointment of a black American to the Supreme Court or could have produced the current mix on the lower courts of labor lawyers, corporation lawyers, solo practitioners, Wall Street–type lawyers, members of minority ethnic groups, and old stock Americans. Political recruitment tends to make the judiciary a career with openings for at least some members of all groups and classes within American society.[64]

Women and black Americans are, of course, the most seriously underrepresented on the federal courts. Presumably women and black Americans are now finding the barriers lowered, attitudes changing, and new opportunities to pursue legal careers. They are also much more politically important than ever before. Political

[64] This does not necessarily mean that all groups will take the same advantage of these opportunities. Members of certain groups and classes in society have been at a disadvantage not only in acquiring financial resources necessary for an undergraduate and legal education but also in acquiring the cultural values and attitudes that encourage such an education and the deprivations required in the process of obtaining it. Historically, lower-class Catholics, low-status Protestants particularly of rural background, black Americans, and women to some extent have been least likely to acquire the necessary resources or to have the appropriate supportive values. Of course, women and racial minorities have also historically faced outright discrimination thereby denying them equal opportunity with others to pursue legal and judicial careers. Thus, political judicial recruitment has not resulted in creating a judiciary that mirrors American society.

recruitment may thus soon result in the appointment of a woman to the Supreme Court and over the next decade a significant increase in the number of black Americans and women on the federal bench.

A recruitment process rooted in politics also serves to encourage talented people who aspire to federal judgeships to participate in politics. It is doubtful whether a democratic political system can be viable without providing inducements that encourage capable minds and talents to participate. Whether or not a judgeship is a proper inducement is of course a matter of dispute.

There are, however, less attractive consequences of political recruitment. Spokesmen for the organized bar have argued that, at times, the process is incompatible with the objective of placing the best-qualified people available on the bench. Although there are difficulties in assessing the qualifications of candidates for judicial positions and certainly in determining who is the *best* available, there are certain standards that one could argue are objectively necessary for the successful functioning of the judicial system as well as for the larger American political system. For example, the appointment of incompetents or segregationists or proponents of the views of the John Birch Society or the Weathermen would clearly be dysfunctional for the judicial system and larger political system. In practice, some incompetents and dozens of segregationists have received appointments over recent decades.[65]

It is also noted that the selection process puts the chief litigant (i.e., the Department of Justice) into the position of recruiting the judges before whom its cases will be tried. This may add a pro-government bias to recruitment and give the public the impression that federal judges tend to be more sympathetic to the claims of the government than to those of the citizenry. Furthermore, it is claimed that the public is dissatisfied with the nexus of politics and judicial selection and that *political* selection lessens public confidence in the judicial process. In addition, it has been argued that inevitably a few occasions have arisen under the current process when a nominee has been subjected to public abuse and harassment by senators (e.g., the 1968 hearings and Senate floor debate on the nomination of Justice Fortas to the chief justiceship; the 1969–1970 controversies over the nomina-

[65] See, for example, Navasky, *Kennedy Justice*, Chap. 5 and Goulden, *The Benchwarmers*.

tions of Judges Haynsworth and Carswell). This could well undermine the public's confidence in and support for the courts.

There have been various proposals for altering the recruitment process. Essentially these proposals[66] seek to eliminate partisan considerations and to intensify the influence of the organized bar. They would deemphasize the political participation and party responsibility advantages of the present process and stress bar association participation and responsibility to the norms and values of the highest strata of the legal profession. Some cynics claim that efforts to reform the recruitment process reach a peak during Democratic administrations and a nadir during Republican administrations. The Nixon and Ford Administrations demonstrated little inclination to suggest basic reform of the recruitment process. It is doubtful that senators and the President will voluntarily relinquish their powers.

Consequences for the administration of justice

Available data suggest that federal judges, whatever their party or appointing administration, share much in common. Regardless of their economic and religious origins, those appointed to the federal courts have had a good legal education, have been socialized into the legal profession, and have tended to have governmental legal experience. They tend to be solidly grounded in the middle or upper middle class at the time they become federal judges, and it is not unreasonable to assume that they share the predominant middle-class social, economic, and political values of American society.[67]

Yet there are differences in degree in the results of the recruitment process so that recruitment patterns of Democratic administrations differ from those of Republican administrations. Democratic presidents tend to appoint more judges from humble backgrounds as defined in terms of economic, religious, and ethnic status. The questions that come to mind are: Do these differences produce a distinction (subtle or otherwise) in the decisional patterns of Democratic and Republican judges? Is the administration of justice influenced by the backgrounds of the judges who decide the cases? Are some back-

[66] See the discussion of one such proposal in Sheldon Goldman, "Political Selection of Federal Judges and the Proposal for a Judicial Service Commission," *Judicature*, 52 (October 1968), 94–98.

[67] Cf. Stuart S. Nagel, *The Legal Process from a Behavioral Perspective* (Homewood, Ill.: Dorsey, 1969), pp. 199–218.

ground characteristics and experiences more important than others?

Although the answers to these questions will be considered when we examine judicial conversion, it is appropriate to note here a line of thinking that has won wide acceptance among political scientists:[68] Judges have opportunities to use judicial discretion. As a result they may disagree as to how a case should be decided. They differ because they have different hierarchies of political values and different ways of perceiving and evaluating reality. The differences in backgrounds and experiences may yield the key to why a judge behaves the way he does. Thus it has been widely accepted during the last several decades that the administration of justice—that is, the type of "justice" that is dispensed—is intimately connected with the judges who do the dispensing. It is believed therefore that judicial recruitment has profound consequences for the administration of justice and thus the operation of the federal judicial system.[69]

GOVERNMENT LAWYERS

Of the approximately 355,000 American lawyers in practice close to 19,000 work for the federal government.[70] Many are involved in activities relating to federal litigation. In particular these are lawyers employed by the regulatory agencies and the Department of Justice. The bulk of federal litigation is handled by the Justice Department principally through the Office of Solicitor General, the seven legal subject area divisions of the Justice Department,[71] and the offices of the United States Attorneys.

[68] Perhaps the earliest and best statement of this position is that by Charles G. Haines, "General Observations on the Effects of Personal, Political, and Economic Influences in the Decisions of Judges," Illinois Law Review, 17 (1922), 96–116, reprinted in Schubert (ed.), Judicial Behavior, pp. 40–49.

[69] The empirical testing of the hypotheses suggested by the above argument has produced only some support for the propositions as they have been tested with aggregates of judges in terms of broad backgrounds categories. Studies of individual judges (judicial biographies and single-judge analyses), however, have more persuasively documented the development of attitudes and values in the context of specific background experiences. Chapter 5 contains a discusssion of these points along with some of the relevant evidence.

[70] Bette H. Sikes, Clara N. Carson, and Patricia Gorai (eds.), The 1971 Lawyer Statistical Report (Chicago: American Bar Foundation, 1972), pp. 5, 12.

[71] The divisions are Tax, Civil, Lands, Antitrust, Criminal, Civil Rights, and Internal Security.

The Solicitor General and his staff decide what cases the federal government will appeal from the district courts to the appeals courts and also what cases the government will appeal to the Supreme Court. Cases that raise matters of major importance for the government are personally argued before the Supreme Court by the Solicitor General. Staff members represent the federal government in other cases brought before the Supreme Court in which the government is either a litigant or *amicus curiae*. Typically the Solicitor General or his staff participate in over half the cases the Supreme Court hears on the merits.[72]

Each of the seven Justice Department divisions is led by an Assistant Attorney General and staff lawyers with competence in the specialized legal areas. The divisions supervise the handling of litigation by the U.S. attorneys, or in some major cases may send a staff lawyer to prepare a case before the district court. The divisions handle the appeals to the appeals courts and also assist the Solicitor General's office with appeals to the Supreme Court.

The 94 U.S. attorneys' offices are responsible for most of the prosecutions and much of the other litigation involving the government before the district courts.

It should be apparent that these government lawyers influence to a significant extent the rate of demand input as well as the kind of demands that go into the system. This is a gatekeeping task similar to that performed by judges and private lawyers (more about gatekeeping in the next chapter). Government lawyers are clearly authorities of the federal judicial system in that they occupy decision-making roles that affect the allocation of values. It is therefore appropriate to study them by asking the sort of questions political scientists ask about other authorities: What are their backgrounds and how are they recruited? How do they perceive their roles? What are their relationships with one another and with the other politically relevant members of the system? Why do they make decisions to prosecute or to appeal? How is their behavior associated with their attitudes and values? What are their relationships with the politically relevant members of the larger political system?

[72] See, for example, "The Supreme Court, 1972 Term," *Harvard Law Review*, 87 (1973), 307–309; and "The Supreme Court, 1967 Term," *Harvard Law Review*, 82 (1968), 308–309.

United States attorneys

The position of U.S. Attorney was created by the Judiciary Act of 1789. Today there is one such lawyer in each of the 94 federal judicial districts. Their offices vary in size with some U.S. attorneys having only one assistant U.S. attorney and others, such as those in the large metropolitan areas, having considerably more. (For example, the Southern District of New York in New York City has over 65 assistant U.S. attorneys.) The Attorney General has formal supervision over the U.S. attorneys. He can instruct them to try or not to try a case. He can relieve a U.S. attorney from handling a case and replace him with a Justice Department lawyer, and he can fire any assistant U.S. attorney at any time. The President appoints U.S. attorneys to four-year terms after their nominations have been confirmed by the Senate. They can be reappointed indefinitely or removed by the President at his discretion. Typically, U.S. attorneys are members of the President's party, and this is facilitated by the custom of U.S. attorneys resigning their posts when the opposition party wins the Presidency.

The recruitment of U.S. attorneys has many similarities to judicial recruitment.[73] Screening of candidates is done in the Justice Department (by the Executive Officer for U.S. Attorneys). Senators of the President's party and state and local party leaders recommend people, and senators in particular expect to "clear" all nominations. The most pronounced difference between recruitment of U.S. attorneys and recruitment of federal judges is the absence of any institutionalized participation on the part of the organized bar. Again, similar to judicial recruitment, administrations tend to be interested in the policy views of the candidates. Those appointed tend to have a history of party activism and to be in essential sympathy with the administration.[74] Of course, no particular appointment can be understood without knowledge of the transactions that preceded it.

[73] See the discussion in James Eisenstein, *Politics and the Legal Process* (New York: Harper & Row, 1973), pp. 36–42.

[74] For example, a Nixon appointee to a U.S. Attorney post revealed in an interview: "Obviously this Administration was elected on the basis of certain pledges it made that fell in the legal area. And I believe that it would be incumbent on a U.S. Attorney to attempt—within the limits of the law—to carry out these policies. . . . Other things being equal, since the office has somewhat of a policy-making role which ought to reflect the Administration's policy, those who are appointed [should be] in sympathy with the policies and work to carry them out." *New York Times,* October 12, 1969, p. 62.

Study of the backgrounds of U.S. attorneys suggests that a marked pattern of localism underlies recruitment. Most U.S. attorneys are born in the state in which they serve. A majority have attended college or law school in their home state (but over one-third have received all their schooling without leaving the confines of their state[75]). The recruitment process suggests that those with a local background and extensive local ties have the greatest opportunities for appointment. It is likely that they are closer to the "local" rather than the "cosmopolitan"[76] in attitudes, values, and life style. How this affects, if indeed it does, decisions to prosecute, the conduct of pre-trial negotiations, as well as relationships with others in the system, is difficult to ascertain.[77]

U.S. attorneys are disproportionately drawn from the high-status Protestant denominations[78] with the South having the largest proportion of those affiliated with Protestant denominations and Republican administrations appointing proportionately more Protestants than Democratic administrations (findings similar to those for judicial appointees). Most U.S. attorneys have been active in party politics before their appointments, and most have had prior governmental experience primarily at the public prosecutorial level including the position of assistant U.S. attorney. In recent administrations about one-fourth of the U.S. attorneys have had governmental experience as an assistant U.S. attorney. At the time of appointment, however, most U.S. attorneys are in private practice.

Many U.S. attorneys regard their position as a stepping stone to a federal judgeship. Political scientist James Eisenstein surveyed contemporary U.S. attorneys and found that close to six out of ten indicated that they aspired to a federal judgeship. Many U.S. attorneys

[75] James Eisenstein, "Counsel for the United States: An Empirical Analysis of the Office of United States Attorney," Ph.D. dissertation, Yale University, 1968, Chap. 7, pp. 8, 14, 16, 20.

[76] These terms suggest differences in orientation rather than geographical differences. See Robert K. Merton, "Types of Influentials: The Local and the Cosmopolitan," in Edward C. Banfield (ed.), Urban Government (New York: Free Press, 1961), pp. 390–400.

[77] But see James Eisenstein, "The Federal Prosecutor and His Environment," paper presented at the 1968 Annual Meeting of the American Political Science Association. For an examination of state prosecuting attorneys, see George F. Cole, Politics and the Administration of Justice (Beverly Hills, Calif.: Sage, 1973), Chap. 4.

[78] Eisenstein, "Counsel for the United States," Chap. 7, pp. 2–3.

saw their position as one that enabled them in the course of their work to make contacts with leading members of the bar. Such contact was thought to be able to enhance their professional opportunities when they returned to private practice.[79]

In attempting to understand the relationship between United States attorneys (*USA*), assistant United States attorneys (*AUSA*), and United States district court judges (*USDCJ*), it is necessary to recognize the powers of the judge.[80] The judge decides when cases will be heard and when briefs, motions, and answers must be submitted. The judge is master of the courtroom and can reprimand or punish lawyers, make rulings on the admissibility of evidence, and comment to and charge the jury, and, of course, decide the case. The judge's determination of who wins has the most direct effect on the careers of USAs and AUSAs because their reputations rest on their ability to win criminal and civil cases.

The larger districts contain larger numbers of USDCJs and larger numbers of AUSAs. The proportion of time any given member of the USA's office spends before each judge is less than in a one- or two-judge district. Procedures for scheduling cases and the atmosphere surrounding trials tend to be more formal in the larger districts. In contrast, the small districts, especially those containing only one USDCJ, place the USA at the mercy of the judge. Interaction is frequent and procedures are less formal. The USA frequently becomes intimately acquainted with the judge, and his knowledge of the judge's idiosyncracies affects decisions to prosecute and courtroom strategy.[81]

Interaction is also facilitated by the close physical location of both the judges' offices and the USA's office. Typically both offices are housed in the same building and opportunities for interchange may arise. It is to the advantage of the USA to establish as close a working relationship with the judges as possible. As one AUSA has stated it: "If you have a good relationship, the judge is willing to listen to you present your arguments. He may [eventually rule against you] . . . but at least he's willing to listen to you."[82] Furthermore, a cooperative

[79] *Ibid.*, Chap. 7, pp. 23, 24, 26, 27.

[80] The analysis in this section is drawn from Eisenstein's study, "Counsel for the United States," in particular Chap. 3.

[81] *Ibid.*, p. III-32.

[82] *Ibid.*, p. III-27.

and sympathetic judge will be lenient with the USA's office concerning scheduling of motions, answers, and so forth. During the trial the judge who is on good terms with the USA's office is likely to be considerate in his treatment of government lawyers. A USA also benefits from the frequent informal talks that characterize a close relationship. The judge then tends to be more understanding of the USA's problems and the USA gains insight into the judge's thinking. These talks, of course, provide a USA with an opportunity not ordinarily shared by private attorneys to influence judges. One USA gave an example: "For instance, the judge might say, 'I don't quite get what you were driving at in court the other day.' This gives you an opportunity to explain again in congenial surroundings. This is an opportunity to persuade."[83]

The nature of the relationship between the judge and the USA's office depends also on the judge's conception of his role. Judges have different views as to the propriety of their suggesting to the USA that he prosecute or not prosecute a particular case or type of case or suggesting the form in which cases should be brought to court. Judges have different views as to how they should behave in conducting a trial. For example, personal values can motivate a prosecution-minded judge to intervene when it appears that a defendant he thinks is guilty is about to go free. On the other hand, a judge who feels strongly that it is his duty to see that justice is done will interject his own questions to witnesses or elucidate matters for the jury. Some judges are aloof because they believe it is not their job to tell the USA what cases to prosecute, how to prosecute them, to give critique sessions to AUSAs, or to show favoritism to government lawyers. At the other extreme are judges who feel it is their duty to carefully supervise the behavior of the USAs. An example of this latter relationship is suggested by the following observation of an AUSA.

The judges go beyond themselves in overseeing the office. They don't say we shouldn't bring certain categories of cases anymore. But they are concerned with whether specific cases should be prosecuted. The Chief Judge will be in the U.S. Attorney's office all the time. They'll talk about the status of different cases and the different investigations pending. That's where [the Chief Judge] plays quite an important role. The judges feel like we are working for them to some extent. And we are, but this can go too far.[84]

[83] *Ibid.*, p. III-28.
[84] *Ibid.*, pp. III-58, III-59.

James Eisenstein, however, believes that most judges fall between these two extremes.

In some smaller districts, judges sometimes work closely with the USA. One former USA recalled that:

After the judge had made up his mind, he would tell me how he was going to decide the case. We'd write an opinion for him. We'd do all the work, and he'd just sign it. All our dealings were straight across the board. We handled more damn stuff when we were in there. . . . A lot of the time, the defense attorney would want to know if they entered a plea of guilty, what they might expect. The judge wouldn't tell them directly. But he gave me a pretty good idea and I conveyed it to them. . . . We had such a good relationship that I could discuss this [the length of a sentence] with him. There were no ironclad commitments. This was a gentleman's agreement. But we could do this.[85]

Legal services lawyers

By the mid-1970s about 2,500 lawyers were employed by more than 900 federally funded local legal services offices. These legal services lawyers are engaged in an enterprise vastly different than that engaged in by U.S. attorneys, assistant U.S. attorneys, and other Justice Department and federal agency lawyers. Instead of handling litigation on behalf of the federal government, legal services lawyers handle litigation on behalf of individuals too poor to hire their own attorney. The program originated as part of the Economic Opportunity Act of 1964 (the original "War on Poverty" legislation sponsored by the Johnson Administration), and the Legal Services Division was housed in the Office of Economic Opportunity (OEO). Neighborhood law offices were not initiated by OEO. People in the local community (typically young reform-minded activist lawyers) prepared proposals for the Legal Services Division and those proposals that met certain stated specifications were funded. By 1973 over $70 million was being spent to operate the over-900 legal services offices (of varying sizes) around the country. About a million cases a year were being handled on behalf of poor people who otherwise would be denied access to the state and federal court systems.

The program was controversial from the start. At first legal services lawyers took on criminal cases as well as civil matters, but that aroused the opposition of, among others, the local law enforcement

[85] *Ibid.*, p. III-55.

establishment and the local criminal bar. As a result, in 1967 Congress passed an amendment to the Economic Opportunity Act that forbade neighborhood law offices from handling criminal cases unless there was no other public means to assist the poor criminal defendant. What this has meant in practice is that legal services lawyers have almost exclusively been engaged in civil suits.

But here too there has been continuing controversy because legal services lawyers have been assisting the poor not only with grievances concerning private individuals or businesses but also their grievances involving public officials and agencies. This has meant that the federal government has financed lawsuits against state and local governmental agencies and in some instances against itself as well. Some of these lawsuits have been successful, and as a consequence in some cases governmental agencies have been ordered by courts to spend millions of additional dollars for aid to the poor.[86] Some public officials actively opposed the legal services program, and they were encouraged in 1972 by Vice-President Spiro Agnew who seemed to be speaking for the Nixon Administration when he attacked legal services lawyers for becoming "ideological vigilantes" on behalf of political and social reform.[87]

The legal services program in 1973 appeared to be in trouble as the Nixon Administration was in the process of dismantling OEO. However, the American Bar Association went on record in support of the program as well as favoring higher funding for legal services.[88] For several years, backers of the program had advocated a separate Government Legal Services Corporation, and the Administration publicly favored that device, although it had found fault with some of the provisions of a 1971 bill to establish such a corporation, and Mr. Nixon had vetoed it. When the director of the program was fired in February, 1973, he charged that the Nixon Administration was really trying to kill the program.[89] It took almost a year-and-a-half, but finally in 1974 an independent Legal Services Corporation passed Congress and was

[86] New York Times, July 6, 1972, p. 17. For an overall view of the "war on poverty" legislation and legal services, see Mark R. Arnold, "The Good War That Might Have Been," New York Times Magazine, Sept. 29, 1974, pp. 56–73.

[87] New York Times, February 11, 1973, p. 24.

[88] New York Times, February 13, 1973, p. 11.

[89] New York Times, February 13, 1973, p. 13.

finally signed into law by President Nixon on July 25, just two weeks before he left office. The legislation attempted to meet some of the objections of the opponents of legal services in that it contained numerous restrictions on the political and reform activities of the legal services lawyers and the types of cases the program could handle. (For example, legal services lawyers cannot handle lawsuits aimed at desegregating public schools or facilitating the obtaining of abortions[90]).

It is clear there is much we have to learn about the workings of the neighborhood law offices, their impact on the poor, their impact on the various court systems including the federal judicial system (pumping one million cases into the state and federal systems each year surely has profound consequences for the ability of court systems to regulate demand input), and the relationship of legal services lawyers and law offices with other components of the bar in the local communities.[91]

Other government lawyers

Brief mention should be made of some other government lawyers directly involved in the federal judicial system. For example, in fiscal 1974 there were 72 federal public defenders working in fifteen of the 89 districts in the states. (Each district court has the option of instituting a public defender's office or staying with the traditional method of assigning private counsel to represent indigents; under the Criminal Justice Act funds are available to finance either option[92]). In six other districts community defender organizations operated on sustaining grants approved by the Judicial Conference of the United States. In the District of Columbia, a Public Defender Service has been established and included 41 staff attorneys during fiscal 1974.

[90] For details of the legislation see *Congressional Quarterly*, July 27, 1974, pp. 1981–1982.

[91] But see Harry P. Stumpf, Henry P. Schroerluke, Forrest D. Dill, "The Legal Profession and Legal Services: Explorations in Local Bar Politics," *Law and Society Review*, 6 (1971), 47–67; Harry P. Stumpf, *Community Politics and Legal Services: The Other Side of the Law* (Beverly Hills, Calif.: Sage, 1975); Ted Finman, "OEO Legal Services Programs and the Pursuit of Social Change: The Relationship between Program Ideology and Program Performance," *Wisconsin Law Review* (1971), 1001–1084; Earl Johnson, Jr., *Justice and Reform: The Formative Years of the OEO Legal Services Program* (New York: Basic Books, 1974).

[92] *Annual Report, Administrative Office of the U.S. Courts*, 1974, pp. III-2, IX-94–5.

Each lower federal court judge is entitled to one law clerk. Associate Justices of the Supreme Court receive three, and the Chief Justice has additional aid. The law clerks are selected by the judges from law school graduates. Appointments are typically for one year, and thus there is a constant turnover of clerks. There has been some speculation that the law clerks, presumably by bringing with them the latest thinking of the law schools and the fresh perspective of the young, are in a position to influence the judge and the course of the judge's decision making. There is no hard evidence to definitively support or refute this. At the Supreme Court level, the clerks who brief the petitions for certiorari may have the opportunity to influence the threshold certiorari decisions, but here too our evidence is largely anecdotal and unsystematic.[93] During fiscal 1974 the judges on the U.S. Court of Appeals for the Fourth Circuit experimented with the use of staff attorneys not assigned to any one judge. These attorneys had what would seem to be great potential for influencing the course of decision making by the court in that they would initially review appeals and make recommendations to the judges. However, an extensive study of staff attorneys conducted by two scholars affiliated with the Federal Judicial Center came to the conclusion that the staff attorneys mirrored the policy views of the judges of the circuit and exercised little independent authority of their own.[94] In sum, at this stage of our knowledge we can speculate that law clerks and possibly staff attorneys meet the systems definition of authorities in that they

[93] See "The Decision to Decide" and Nathan Lewin, "Helping the Court with Its Work," in Walter Murphy and C. Herman Pritchett (eds.), *Courts, Judges and Politics,* 2nd ed. (New York: Random House, 1974), pp. 87–94, 497–501. Also see "Judicial Clerkships: A Symposium on the Institution," *Vanderbilt Law Review,* 26 (1973), 1123–1257; J. Harvie Wilkinson, III, *Serving Justice: A Supreme Court Clerk's View* (New York: Charterhouse, 1974). David N. Atkinson in his study of Justice Sherman Minton sent questionnaires to the Justice's former law clerks and he also personally interviewed some of them. Atkinson concluded that Justice Minton considered the law clerks "valuable contributors to the decision-making process" and that the law clerks at times did influence Minton's judicial behavior. David N. Atkinson, "Mr. Justice Minton and the Supreme Court," Ph.D. dissertation, University of Iowa, 1969, p. 127, and pp. 121–124, 162–164. Also note the description of law clerks in Nina Totenberg, "Behind the Marble, Beneath the Robes," *New York Times Magazine,* March 16, 1975, 15, 58–67.

[94] Steven Flanders and Jerry Goldman, "Screening Practices and the Use of Para-Judicial Personnel in a U.S. Court of Appeals," paper presented at the 1974 Annual Meeting of the American Political Science Association.

occupy systemic roles and have at least some (if only minor) influence on the course of the system's policy output. However, we are unable to demonstrate with any precision the extent of their influence.

PRIVATE LAWYERS

It is difficult to determine how many nongovernmental lawyers practice before or participate in the preparation of cases tried in the federal courts. Of greater importance, however, is the kind of private lawyer who practices before the federal courts, in particular the nature and style of practice. It would be useful to be able to present evidence that would indicate what differences (if any) there are in the backgrounds, attitudes, and values of lawyers whose practice takes them primarily before the federal courts as opposed to those whose practice is largely in the local courts. Although such data are unavailable, there are several studies by sociologists of law that have focused on the legal profession. Their findings shed some light on these questions.

Two principal approaches have been used to study the legal profession: the client-group approach and the style-of-practice approach.[95] The client-group approach leads the researcher to examine the segment of the bar that serves a specialized group of clients, for example, business enterprise, interest groups, or criminal defendants. Historically, lawyers for business and property interests have been the principal nongovernment lawyers practicing in the federal courts. This was particularly true during the seventy-year period following the Civil War, when the relationship of government to private enterprise was the subject of constitutional policy making.[96] Today the federal courts are heavily involved in litigation involving government regulation of industry, in particular statutory interpretation and the rulings of regulatory agencies. It is likely that a significant proportion of private lawyers who come before the federal courts represents business and financial concerns and are either "house counsel" (em-

[95] See the discussion in Richard S. Wells, "The Legal Profession and Politics," *Midwest Journal of Political Science*, 8 (1964), 166–190.

[96] See Robert G. McCloskey, *The American Supreme Court* (Chicago: University of Chicago Press, 1960), pp. 101–179.

ployed by the business) or associated with a large law firm.[97] Lawyers representing particular labor unions are also, of course, before the courts in connection with labor litigation.

Another group of lawyers that comes before the federal courts represents interest groups. Included are the staff lawyers and volunteer lawyers of the civil rights and civil liberties organizations[98] and the staff lawyers of business associations and the AFL-CIO. One might speculate that there are differences in the backgrounds and values of lawyers who work, for example, for organized labor, the NAACP, and the Chamber of Commerce.

A segment of the bar that has wide contact with the federal judicial system is the criminal bar. There is some evidence that suggests that criminal lawyers differ from lawyers primarily engaged in civil suits. One study[99] reported that, in contrast to civil lawyers, criminal lawyers tended to be divorced from the business community. They were also found, when compared to civil lawyers, to be more active in political party work, to have more liberal voting preferences, and generally to have a lower status among members of the profession and the community at large. The criminal bar has been described as containing a few high-priced, well-known practitioners who cater to the select few who can afford them, and the private practitioners, legal aid lawyers, and public defenders who handle the bulk of criminal cases. Most private criminal law practitioners earn their living by handling a large volume of business. Most of these private practitioners do little in the way of preparing cases and are more concerned with their own niche

[97] See the data reported in the two studies by Nathan Hakman: "Lobbying the Supreme Court—An Appraisal of 'Political Science Folklore,'" *Fordham Law Review*, 35 (1966), 15–50; "The Supreme Court's Political Environment: The Processing of Noncommercial Litigation," in Joel B. Grossman and Joseph Tanenhaus (eds.), *Frontiers of Judicial Research* (New York: Wiley, 1969), pp. 199–253.

[98] See Jonathan D. Casper, *Lawyers before the Warren Court* (Urbana: University of Illinois Press, 1972) and *The Politics of Civil Liberties* (New York: Harper & Row, 1972). Also see Ann Fagan Ginger (ed.), *The Relevant Lawyers* (New York: Simon and Schuster, 1973); Stuart A. Scheingold, *The Politics of Rights: Lawyers, Public Policy, and Political Change* (New Haven, Conn.: Yale University Press, 1974). The latter two works focus on the new breed of activist lawyers committed to social change and working on their own or with the newer activist groups.

[99] Arthur Lewis Wood, "Informal Relations in the Practice of Criminal Law," *American Journal of Sociology*, 62 (1956), 48–55. Also see Delmar Karlen, *Anglo-American Criminal Justice* (New York: Oxford University Press, 1967), pp. 34–35.

in the social structure of the courthouse than with their clients.[100] Typically, eight out of ten convictions in the federal district courts involve a guilty plea.[101] This suggests that the routine relationships that have been found to exist in local courthouses between criminal lawyers and public prosecutors may also exist in the federal courthouses between defense attorneys and the U.S. Attorney. On the other hand, the widely publicized backlogs in the federal courts suggest that many criminal lawyers are taking advantage of liberalized criminal procedural policies to benefit their clients.[102]

Studies using the style-of-practice approach for the analysis of the legal profession have revealed similar findings. Lawyers who practice the "institutional style" tend to be corporation lawyers whose clients are from the highest economic strata and whose cases frequently take them before the appeals courts and the U.S. Supreme Court. These lawyers handle antitrust, securities, credit financing, tax, and regulatory agency matters. The corporation lawyer is typically drawn from a high-status, white Protestant background and has graduated from a private liberal arts college and a prestigious law school.[103] In contrast,

---

[100] Abraham S. Blumberg, "The Practice of Law as a Confidence Game: Organizational Cooptation of a Profession," *Law and Society Review*, 1 (1967), 15–39. Also see Jonathan D. Casper, *American Criminal Justice: The Defendant's Perspective* (Englewood Cliffs, N.J.: Prentice-Hall, 1972), Chaps. 3, 4; Cole, *Politics*, Chap. 5.

[101] See the discussion of plea bargaining in Chapter 4.

[102] See Paul D. Carrington, "Crowded Dockets and the Courts of Appeals: The Threat to the Function of Review and the National Law," *Harvard Law Review*, 82 (1969), 543–549.

[103] See Erwin O. Smigel, *The Wall Street Lawyer* (New York: Free Press, 1964). The second edition of Smigel's book (Bloomington: Indiana University Press, 1970), however, reports that New York City's largest law firms are undergoing greater "democratization" in that there are increasing openings for Jews and Negroes as well as increasing interest in aiding the poor with their legal problems. In spite of these developments, there is fragmentary evidence that some graduates from the prestige law schools are bypassing a corporation law career, at least temporarily. For example, it was reported that none of the 39 editors of the Harvard Law Review graduating in 1970 planned to enter private practice immediately. They preferred instead to clerk for judges or to work with public or private poverty, social reform, or civil liberties groups (*New York Times*, November 19, 1969, p. 37). A systematic survey of University of Chicago law school graduates revealed no widespread changes in career choices, but did note that the top ranking graduates were more likely than were earlier top graduates to go into legal reform and assistance-type jobs. See Rita J. Simon, Frank Koziol, and Nancy Joslyn, "Have There Been Significant Changes in the Career Aspirations and Occupational Choices of Law School Graduates in the 1960s?" *Law and Society Review*, 8 (1973), 95–108.

---

the lawyers who practice solo or "metropolitan style" are frequently of new American stock, from low-status families, and are graduates of the less prestigious law schools. Their clients are both individuals and small businessmen, and the cases they handle are primarily personal injury, criminal cases, workmen's compensation, divorce, and real estate. There is little contact between the two types of lawyers.[104] The solo practitioners will appear primarily in the city courts, although some will handle criminal cases in the federal courts. The institutional lawyers generally handle the economic cases of large business and financial institutions, and this means that they typically practice before the federal courts.[105]

JURY SELECTION AND BEHAVIOR

Juries are the principal nonprofessional authorities in the judicial process and they share decision making with trial judges. Under the Sixth Amendment to the Constitution, jury trials in federal criminal cases are guaranteed to all who want them. Typically, seven out of ten criminal defendants who plead not guilty choose to exercise this right (rather than have their cases tried by the judge alone).[106] The Seventh Amendment guarantees jury trials for most federal civil cases, but only about one-third of the litigants whose cases come to trial exercise their jury trial option, while the balance have their cases heard and decided only by the judge.

Several studies of both federal and state juries have suggested that there have been wide disparities in the selection of jurors.[107] In the

[104] Jack Ladinsky, "Careers of Lawyers, Law Practice, and Legal Institutions," *American Sociological Review*, 28 (1963), 47–54. Also see Jerome E. Carlin, *Lawyer's Ethics* (New York: Russell Sage Foundation, 1966), pp. 11–40.

[105] A third style of practice (the rural style) is suggested by Wells, "Legal Profession and Politics."

[106] *Statistical Abstract of the United States, 1968* (Washington, D.C.: Government Printing Office, 1968), Table 224, p. 152; *Federal Offenders in United States District Courts 1971* (Washington, D.C.: Administrative Office of the U.S. Courts, 1973), p. 38; *Annual Report, U.S. Courts, 1973*, Table C-7.

[107] See the discussion in Herbert Jacob, *Justice in America*, 2nd ed. (Boston: Little, Brown, 1972), pp. 122–125. Also see Edward N. Beiser, "The Trial Jury: Empirical and Normative Considerations," paper presented at the 1973 Annual Meeting of the American Political Science Association, pp. 1–12, and "Are Juries Representative?" *Judicature*, 57 (1973), 194–199.

South, blacks were grossly underrepresented.[108] In the North as well as the South, juries have consisted disproportionately of white-collar, middle- to upper-class, middle-aged (or older) males.[109] Before 1969 potential federal jurors were chosen individually by a court clerk or jury commissioner at his discretion. The selection procedure in widespread practice was the "key-man" procedure, whereby the person responsible for jury selection solicited names of prospective jurors from "important" people in the community.

The Federal Jury Selection and Service Act of 1968 eliminated the key-man procedure and required that jurors be randomly selected from voter registration lists. The law requires each jury clerk or commissioner to include on his list the names of at least one-half of one percent of the total names on the voter registration lists in his federal district. Each county within the district court must be represented by at least one-half of one percent of the registered voters in that county. All names are randomly picked and potential jurors fill out questionnaires to determine their eligibility. Each federal district has its own jury selection procedure in accord with the broad guidelines of the act. There is evidence that the new procedures for jury selection are changing the makeup of federal juries. For example, it was reported that within a month after the law went into effect in the Southern District of New York, more women, laborers, and nonwhites were serving on federal juries than had served previously.[110]

The behavior of juries is another matter.[111] The major research has been conducted by the lawyers and sociologists associated with the University of Chicago Jury Project.[112] The principal research was re-

[108] See S. Sidney Ulmer, "Supreme Court Behavior in Racial Exclusion Cases: 1935–1960," *American Political Science Review*, 56 (1962), 325–330; Dale W. Broeder, "The Negro in Court," *Duke Law Journal* (1965), 19–31.

[109] See Hans Zeisel, "Dr. Spock and the Case of the Vanishing Woman Juror," *University of Chicago Law Review*, 37 (1969), 1–18; Edwin S. Mills, "A Statistical Profile of Jurors in a United States District Court," *Law and the Social Order*, 1 (1969), 329–339; Beiser, "The Trial Jury."

[110] *New York Times*, January 13, 1969, p. 26.

[111] Technically jury behavior should be studied as the conversion process for this set of authorities within the system. However, since the focus of this book will be on judicial conversion, it is convenient to discuss jury behavior here.

[112] See the bibliography of publications based on that project in Harry S. Kalven and Hans Zeisel, *The American Jury* (Boston: Little, Brown, 1966), pp. 541–545. Cf. Michael H. Walsh, "The American Jury: A Reassessment," *Yale Law Journal*, 79 (1969), 142. For an overview of jury research by others as well as the Chicago re-

ported in *The American Jury*, whose data base consisted of a sample of both federal and state jury trials (the researchers did not distinguish between federal and state juries, nor apparently did they believe such a distinction was relevant for their purposes). The findings were manifold. Perhaps of greatest general interest was the finding that in only about 20 percent of criminal or civil trials did the jury come to a conclusion different from that reached by the judge. In other words, in about four out of five cases both jury and judge were in agreement.[113] Where they differed, the jury in criminal cases tended to be "non–rule minded" and thus more lenient than the judge in their willingness to "move where the equities are."[114] However, no marked directionality in judge-jury disagreements in civil cases was found.[115] The source of judge-jury disagreements was seldom found to be a disagreement over the facts alone, but rather to be either over values alone or as they are inextricably involved with the determination and evaluation of facts.[116]

The Chicago researchers were unable to discern a relationship between the backgrounds of the jurors and their decision making, but the possibility of such relationships was not ruled out.[117] Earlier work by a member of the project had suggested that jurors of German and British ancestry have a greater tendency to favor criminal convictions than those of Negro and Slavic ancestry.[118]

---

searchers, see Howard S. Erlanger, "Jury Research in America: Its Past and Future," *Law and Society Review*, 4 (1970), 345–370. Also see the discussion by Glendon Schubert in *Judicial Policy Making*, rev. ed. (Glenview, Ill.: Scott, Foresman, 1974), pp. 110–113. Also see Stuart Nagel and Lenore Weitzman, "Sex and the Unbiased Jury," *Judicature*, 56 (1972), 108–111; Beiser, "The Trial Jury," pp. 13–30; and Edward N. Beiser and Rene Varrin, "Six-Member Juries in the Federal Courts," *Judicature*, 58 (1975), 424–433.

[113] An extended discussion of these findings appears in Harry Kalven, "The Dignity of the Civil Jury," *Virginia Law Review*, 50 (1964), 1055–1075.

[114] Kalven and Zeisel, *American Jury*, p. 495.

[115] *Ibid.*, pp. 63–64.

[116] *Ibid.*, pp. 116, 469. Also see Dale W. Broeder, "Plaintiff's Family Status as Affecting Jury Behavior: Some Tentative Insights," *Journal of Public Law*, 14 (1965), 131–141. Note the results of a Justice Department study that found the attitudes of jurors responsible for the Government's string of losses in its "political trials." See, *New York Times*, April 19, 1975, p. 15.

[117] Kalven and Zeisel, *American Jury*, pp. 465, 466–468.

[118] Dale W. Broeder, "University of Chicago Jury Project," *Nebraska Law Review*, 38 (1959), 748.

The deliberations of juries have also been of interest and have been studied by simulation[119] and by attempts to reconstruct the deliberations through interviews of jurors.[120] The Chicago researchers interviewed jurors who decided 225 criminal cases in Chicago and Brooklyn and collected other data on jury first ballot voting. They found that unanimity prevailed on the first ballot vote in 31 percent of the cases.[121] Where the vote was evenly split, the final verdict was guilty as often as it was not guilty. In nine out of ten of all other cases, the jury eventually decided in accord with majority sentiment evidenced on the first ballot. Kalven and Zeisel, senior authors of *The American Jury*, emphasized, "with very few exceptions the first ballot decides the outcome of the verdict." This further led them to conclude that "the real decision is often made before the deliberation begins."[122] How do juries manage to achieve consensus? Kalven and Zeisel suggest that the consensus-building process is a combination of "rational persuasion, sheer social pressure, and the psychological mechanism by which individual perceptions undergo change when exposed to group discussion."[123]

---

[119] See Rita James Simon, "Jurors' Evaluation of Expert Psychiatric Testimony," *Ohio State Law Journal*, 21 (1960), 75–95; Stanley Sue and Ronald E. Smith, "How Not to Get a Fair Trial," *Psychology Today*, 7 (May 1974), 86–90.

[120] Kalven and Zeisel, *American Jury*, pp. 482–491.

[121] *Ibid.*, p. 487.

[122] *Ibid.*, p. 488.

[123] *Ibid.*, p. 489.

FOUR
INPUT

AMONG the members of American society are constantly spawned needs, expectations, wants, desires, and conflicts. These "disturbances"[1] are the raw material from which input is produced and injected into a political system. For example, such social systems as families, schools, street gangs, and voluntary associations indoctrinate or socialize maturing members into holding and acting out various beliefs, expectations, and codes of behavior. This produces members of society who are variously law-abiding and law-breaking, timid and aggressive, right-wing chauvinist and left-wing radical, productive and lazy, prudish and prurient, satisfied and dissatisfied, altruistic and selfish. The resulting "disturbances" often (but not always) become input to a political system.

In a similar way, through the workings of the economic system persons are employed as well as not employed, job conditions are found to be desirable as well as undesirable, people are encouraged by advertising to buy good as well as shoddy merchandise, wages and bills are paid as well as not paid, property is accumulated as well as lost, contracts are fulfilled as well as broken, customers are satisfied as well as swindled, and business firms compete fairly as well as unfairly. From this complex of activities, expectations and needs for reform, retribution, relief, and other types of action and inaction also arise. Many of the disturbances are processed without any direct gov-

[1] David Easton, *A Framework for Political Analysis* (Englewood Cliffs, N.J.: Prentice-Hall, 1965), pp. 90–91.

ernmental interference at all. Employees change jobs. Complaining customers have their money returned or otherwise receive satisfaction. Defaulting employers and customers agree to pay what they owe. Thus, in one way or another, a vast number of mutually satisfying (or not so satisfying but still acceptable) accommodations are worked out. Still with the economic system, a vast number of calls for political action are generated by its activities.

One could look at other social processes and systems of behavior and note phenomena similar to those just mentioned. As students of politics our interest, of course, is in those disturbances that eventually become input to a political system. Although our special concern is with the federal judicial system, that system is only one of many (both judicial and nonjudicial) within the larger American political system which receive political input.

Input may be characterized as being of two types: demands and support. *Demands,* in Eastonian analysis are "articulated statements, directed toward the authorities, proposing that some kind of authoritative allocation ought to be undertaken."[2] *Support* refers to the input of satisfaction or dissatisfaction on the part of the system's publics, both elite and mass, regarding the system's operations, structure, and output.

DEMANDS

Demands processed by the federal judicial system are those that satisfy the system's regime rules which specify the form demands must take as well as certain substantive criteria. Although the federal courts are authorized to process a narrow range of administrative tasks (such as the approval of passport applications, naturalization of aliens, parole and probation of those convicted of federal crimes), the principal demands processed by the system are criminal and civil cases and controversies that meet the requirements of jurisdiction and justiciability. In processing both types of demands—administrative but most particularly litigative—there is also a set of formal regime rules relating to procedure that limits what information may be presented in the pressing of a demand.[3]

[2] *Ibid.,* p. 120.

[3] For example, the data that establish the "facts" of a case at the trial level are presented through various physical and documentary evidence (contracts, signed statements, depositions) and through oral examination and cross-examination of witnesses and litigants.

Table 4.1 Administrative demands processed by the federal judicial system during fiscal 1973

Type of demand	Jurisdiction of[a]	Number[b]
Direct administrative functions:		
passport applications	district courts (State Department)	139,356
naturalization petitions	district courts	104,213
Supervisory administrative functions:		
probation and parole	district courts (officers and staff of the Division of Probation)	54,346[c]
Bankruptcy		
cases commenced	district courts (referees in bankruptcy)	173,197
cases appealed	courts of appeals	338
Internal administration:		
collection of statistics, payroll, budgeting, etc.	Administrative Office of the United States Courts	
institutes for court personnel and research leading to recommendations for improvements of administrative practices	Federal Judicial Center	
monitoring caseloads and administrative supervision of lower courts	Judicial Council of each of the 11 Circuits	
discussion of problems within each circuit and recommendations for improvements	Judicial Conference of each of the 11 Circuits	
revision of rules of federal civil and criminal procedure	Supreme Court (Judicial Conference of the United States)	

Source: Administrative Office of the United States Courts, *Annual Report of the Director, 1973* (Washington, D.C.: Government Printing Office, 1974), *passim.*
[a] Institutions or officials in parentheses indicate those doing initial or main processing of demands if other than institution having ultimate authority.
[b] Number of applications, petitions, or cases *filed* in fiscal 1973.
[c] Number of those under supervision of federal probation officers on June 30, 1973.

Administrative demands

Administrative demands encompass certain direct and supervisory bureaucratic tasks as well as those relating to the system's internal administration.[4] The institutions or officials responsible for converting

[4] Note that the review and enforcement of administrative agency orders are not considered as an "administrative" function of the courts. Because of their form, content, and the courts' methods of processing them, such cases are considered litigative demands.

such demands into outputs as well as the number of such demands fed into the system in fiscal year 1973 (July 1, 1972, through June 30, 1973) are presented in Table 4.1.

These various demands are not "cases or controversies" as these terms are strictly used, and all have had the term "administrative" applied to them in one or another sense of that word. Demands concerning passport applications, alien naturalization, internal court administration, and even to some extent parole and probation do not typically present the conflict situation characteristic of litigation. Demands to institute bankruptcy proceedings, on the other hand, frequently do have such adversary characteristics. Yet traditionally these are also considered administrative matters.

Demands for the processing of passport applications and the naturalization of aliens are probably the least judicial of the administrative demands. Although large numbers are involved, they require little judicial time.[5] Bankruptcy as well as parole and probation supervision require somewhat more judicial time.[6] District judges have the responsibility of appointing and supervising referees in bankruptcy as well as supervising parole and probation. However, the main brunt of the work is carried on by others. In fiscal 1973, for example, 201 federal referees in bankruptcy handled bankruptcy matters,[7] and 784 probation officers of the Federal Probation Service prepared presentencing reports and supervised those on probation.[8]

Passport applications, naturalization petitions, bankruptcy petitions, and so forth, reflect political demands generated from the environment that one governmental agency or another must fulfill. On the other hand, demands concerned with the internal administration of the federal judicial system are generated from *within* the system and

---

[5] Passport applications can be made to the clerks of the district courts. Applications are then processed by the State Department. Naturalization proceedings, however, are conducted by federal district judges.

[6] See the observations of Glendon Schubert, *Judicial Policy-Making*, rev. ed. (Glenview, Ill.: Scott, Foresman, 1974), pp. 84–85.

[7] They were assisted by 901 clerks. See *Annual Report of the Director of the Administrative Office of the United States Courts, 1973* (Washington, D.C.: Government Printing Office, 1973), hereafter cited as *Report, U.S. Courts, 1973*, p. VII-3.

[8] They were assisted by 558 clerks. See *Report, U.S. Courts, 1973*, p. VII-3. In fiscal 1974 there was a dramatic jump in the number of probation officers. Some 1,124 were assisted by 744 clerks. *Report, U.S. Courts, 1974*, p. III-2.

can only (and, indeed, must if the system is to operate) be processed *within* that system. These demands are considered in Eastonian analysis to be *withinputs*.[9] The most prosaic of these withinputs are concerned with the day-to-day tasks of the administration of minor court personnel, budgeting, disbursing, and the collection and reporting of court statistics. These demands are primarily handled by the Administrative Office of the U.S. Courts. Demands within the system for efficiency and consistency of behavior by court authorities are dealt with in part by the Federal Judicial Center through its various institutes (for example, sentencing institutes for judges, institutes for referees in bankruptcy) and the research projects it sponsors and undertakes that may yield recommendations for improvements of administrative practices. The management of caseloads in terms of judicial personnel is in the hands of each circuit's judicial council. The councils monitor caseloads, call upon retired judges when the burdens become heavy and request the temporary assignment of judges from other circuits. In one instance, a judicial council prevented a district judge, apparently for a variety of reasons including inefficiency, from handling any cases at all.[10] Problems within each of the circuits are discussed at the annual circuit judicial conferences. Perhaps the most important form of system withinput is handled by the Judicial Conference of the United States, which is officially described as "the governing body for the administration of the Federal judicial system as a whole."[11] By far its most important function is the promulgation and revision of the various rules of federal civil and criminal procedure (by which litigation is processed). The Judicial Conference solicits the views of a wide variety of systemic authorities before making its recommendations. After usually receiving pro forma approval by the Supreme Court, the new rules are transmitted to

[9] Easton, *A Framework for Political Analysis*, pp. 114–115.

[10] That judge, Stephen S. Chandler, challenged the legality of the action, but the Supreme Court denied his motion for relief. See Chandler v. Judicial Council of the Tenth Circuit, 90 S. Ct. 1648 (1970). See the discussion of the Chandler case and, in general, the findings of Beverly Blair Cook, "Perceptions of the Independent Trial Judge Role in the Seventh Circuit," *Law and Society Review*, 6 (1972), 615–629. Concerning Chandler, see Joseph C. Goulden, *The Benchwarmers* (New York: Weybright and Talley, 1974), pp. 206–249.

[11] *U.S. Government Organization Manual, 1969–1970* (Washington, D.C.: Office of the Federal Register, 1969), p. 46.

Congress by the Chief Justice. If Congress does not issue a formal congressional resolution disapproving them within ninety days, the rules have the force of law.[12]

Litigative demands

The litigative input into the federal district courts is split into two formal categories, civil and criminal. As trial courts with original jurisdiction the federal district courts process these demands for the first time.[13] In fiscal 1973, for example, civil cases accounted for 70 percent of the cases filed in the district courts, and their trials consumed over 60 percent of court trial time. Table 4.2 gives an overview of the district courts' civil litigation in terms of cases filed in fiscal 1973.[14] Noted in this table are both the jurisdiction heading under which the cases fall and the nature of the suits.

During the 1950s and most of the 1960s there was a slow but steady rise (about 2 to 3 percent) in the number of civil cases filed each year. A plateau of about 71,000 per year was reached in the fiscal 1966–1968 period. In fiscal 1969, however, there was an 8 percent increase in cases filed. Fiscal 1970 had a 13 percent rise, and in fiscal 1971 there was a 7 percent increase. In fiscal 1972 and 1973 the rate of increase was down to the pre-1966 level of between 2 and 3 percent although fiscal 1974's 5 percent rate might reflect a new round of litigation inflation. By fiscal 1974 there were over 100,000 civil cases filed in federal district courts. The sharp increases in filings in part can be

[12] In 1974 Chief Justice Burger sent to Congress proposed changes in the Federal Rules of Criminal Procedure. These changes included matters with major substantive policy implications covering such areas as admissibility of evidence and plea bargaining. On July 1, 1974, the House of Representatives voted to delay by one year the date for implementation of the new changes. Finally, on June 23, 1975, the House passed a revised version of the Federal Rules of Criminal Procedure that differed in some major respects from the proposed changes sent by the Chief Justice. For a discussion of the new rules as passed by the House, see *Congressional Quarterly*, June 14, 1975, pp. 1231–1232 and June 28, 1975, p. 1361.

[13] But note that the district courts do review previous state and federal court proceedings when they consider petitions for *habeas corpus*.

[14] Note that these figures include those for the special three-judge courts which in recent years have been infrequently convened. In fiscal 1973, for example, 320 cases were heard by three-judge district courts. Included were 52 reviews of orders of the Interstate Commerce Commission, 183 civil rights cases, and 7 reapportionment cases. Under legislation enacted in late 1974, review of orders of the Interstate Commerce Commission no longer is done by the three-judge district courts but rather follows the same route other administrative agency cases take (i.e., first going to the courts of appeals).

Table 4.2 Civil cases commenced in the district courts by basis of jurisdiction and nature of suit, fiscal year, 1973

Nature of suit	Total	Percent	United States cases		Federal question	Private cases	
			Plaintiff	Defendant		Diversity of citizenship	Local jurisdiction
Total cases	*98,560*	*100*	*13,881*	*13,603*	*43,291*	*25,281*	*2,504*
(Percent of total)			(14.1)	(13.8)	(43.9)	(25.7)	(2.5)
Contract actions	*19,468*	*20*	*3,372*	*972*	*4,154*	*10,601*	*369*
Real property	*4,113*	*4*	*2,527*	*313*	*316*	*745*	*212*
Tort actions	*23,105*	*23*	*176*	*1,729*	*6,853*	*13,916*	*431*
Actions under statutes	*49,950*	*51*	*7,756*	*10,550*	*31,566*		*78*
Antitrust	1,206		45	9	1,152		
Bankruptcy trustee suits	514		1	3	510		
Civil rights	7,679		276	712	6,691		
Commerce	3,341		107	107	3,127		
Deportation	271			271			
Prisoner petitions	17,218			4,535	12,664		19
Labor laws	4,861		1,691	81	3,089		
Copyrights, patents, trademarks	2,056		1	30	2,025		
Securities, commodities, and exchanges	1,999		184	11	1,804		
Social Security	2,497			2,497			
Tax suits	1,577		261	1,257			59
Other statutory actions	6,731		5,190	1,037	504		
Other actions	*1,924*	*2*	*50*	*39*	*402*	*19*	*1,414*

Source: Administrative Office of the United States Courts, *Annual Report of the Director, 1973* (Washington, D.C.: Government Printing Office, 1974).

attributed to the petitions filed by state and federal prisoners concerning demands for orders to vacate sentences, issue *habeas corpus*, grant parole, and modify living conditions in prisons and prison regulations.

Between 1966 and 1968, state prisoner petitions increased by one-third and federal prisoner petitions by almost one-fourth. (But, as there were decreases in other case categories, the overall case filings hardly increased.) Between 1969 and 1974, state prisoner petitions increased by 44 percent and federal prisoner petitions by 38 percent (though increases in most of the other case categories affected the overall case filings). The large increase in prisoner petition input is doubtless a feedback effect from Supreme Court decisions dealing with criminal procedure and the availability of federal *habeas corpus* to state prisoners. During the 1966–1968 period civil rights filings increased by one-fourth, but between 1969 and 1974 the number of civil rights cases more than tripled.[15] During the 1966–1974 period, on the other hand, certain areas of civil litigation either remained stable or declined.[16] Thus, in recent years the civil suit input into the district

[15] The overwhelming proportion of civil rights cases were initiated by private parties. Interestingly, the role of the federal government in civil rights litigation shifted from the high point of the Johnson Administration where in fiscal 1967 the Administration was the plaintiff in 56 percent of the civil rights cases in which the federal government was involved to the low point of the Nixon Administration in fiscal 1972 when the Administration was the *defendant* in 80 percent of the cases in which it was a principal party in the suit. The increase in civil rights litigation can most likely be attributed to the activity of legal services offices and the new public-interest lawyers and law firms that sprouted in the late 1960s and early 1970s as well as the expanded activities of the civil rights and civil liberties organizations. By case category, the largest proportion of class action suits filed in the federal courts were those involving civil rights (48 percent of all class action suits filed in fiscal 1974). Class action suits accounted for over 15 percent of all civil rights suits filed in fiscal 1973 and in fiscal 1974. The deep South (the Fifth Circuit) was the site of about 30 percent of all fiscal 1974 class action civil rights suits. Prison reform has been the objective of class action suits against state and local penal institutions brought to the federal courts under the federal civil rights law. See "Why Prisoners Are Looking to Federal Courts," *New York Times*, December 3, 1974, p. 43.

[16] For example, real property filings (most government mortgage foreclosures) were down 14 percent from 1966 to 1973. In fiscal 1966 they accounted for about 7 percent of civil cases commenced and in fiscal 1973 they accounted for 4 percent. But in fiscal 1974 they were close to 5 percent. Government forfeiture and penalty suits between 1966 and 1968 declined markedly by more than 31 percent, but during the 1968–1973 period increased sufficiently so that during fiscal 1973 they were at the 1966 level in absolute numbers of cases (although somewhat less as a proportion of all cases filed due to the major increase in total filings). But in fiscal 1974 there was a one-third drop in the forfeiture and penalty suits filed.

courts has shifted somewhat away from the protection of property rights and toward the protection of civil rights and liberties, although as suggested by Table 4.2, property rights still dominate the civil case dockets.

A typology of the district courts' criminal case input (cases commenced) from fiscal years 1967 to 1974 is presented in Table 4.3. As suggested by the table, this demand input increased through fiscal 1972, but then dropped over 14 percent in fiscal 1973 and another 7 percent (approximately) in 1974. As with civil cases, one can observe important fluctuations in the types of cases filed. Selective service cases increased as the Vietnam War progressed into the late 1960s and early 1970s. With the end of American participation in the war and the end of the draft, prosecutions for selective service violations

Table 4.3 Criminal cases originating in the district courts, by nature of the offense

Nature of offense	Fiscal 1967	Fiscal 1969	Fiscal 1972	Fiscal 1973	Fiscal 1974	Percent of 1974 Total
Total	30,534	33,585	47,043	40,367	37,667	100.0
General offenses:						
Homicide	177	197	309	144	160	0.4
Robbery	1,135	1,570	2,422	1,568	1,556	4.1
Assault	519	594	646	695	710	1.9
Burglary	524	605	357	269	271	0.7
Larceny and theft	2,495	2,758	3,742	3,516	3,565	9.5
Embezzlement	1,399	1,712	1,810	1,571	1,612	4.3
Fraud	2,150	1,531	2,748	3,076	3,073	8.2
Auto theft	4,888	4,139	2,350	1,960	1,790	4.8
Forgery and counterfeiting	3,151	3,113	4,685	4,104	4,360	11.6
Sex offenses	226	224	274	180	189	0.5
Narcotics	2,338	3,458	6,758	8,817	7,374	19.6
Miscellaneous	1,511	2,152	5,066	5,020	6,021	15.9
Special offenses:						
Immigration	3,386	4,107	5,904	2,208	1,921	5.1
Liquor, Internal Revenue	2,443	1,409	1,254	901	641	1.7
Antitrust	16	14	14	20	24	0.1
Civil rights	115	81	91	136	134	0.4
Selective service	1,335	3,305	5,142	3,043	1,008	2.7
Other federal statutes	2,726	2,616	3,471	3,139	3,258	8.6

Source: Administrative Office of the United States Courts, *Annual Report of the Director* (Washington, D.C.: Government Printing Office, 1968–1975).

dropped sharply. Also, immigration law prosecutions reached a peak in fiscal 1972, but sharply declined during the following two years. (This was due, however, to the fact that many of these violations were petty offenses that in 1972 began to be handled by U.S. magistrates rather than district court judges.) There were declines in some other areas as well as is shown in Table 4.3.[17] In contrast we can observe the steady increase through fiscal 1973 in prosecutions of narcotics laws violators (associated with the implementation of the tough enforcement provisions of the Drug Abuse Prevention and Control Act of 1970).[18]

In looking at federal criminal cases one characteristic that should be noted is the relatively low proportion of cases dealing with violent crimes. This is largely due to the nature of federal offenses. With the exception of federal territories and the District of Columbia before fiscal 1972, the federal courts do not have jurisdiction over local crimes, which includes most crimes of violence.

When we examine district court processing of both civil and criminal litigation, we find that few cases are actually resolved by trial. Table 4.4 presents the data for fiscal 1973. Only about 11 percent of the civil cases and about 17 percent of the criminal cases were resolved by trial. In terms only of completed trials in fiscal 1973 from which cases could be appealed, in the district court output pool there

[17] The Director of the Administrative Office of the U.S. Courts noted in the 1973 Annual Report: "The continued downturn of auto theft cases reflects Department of Justice policy to decline prosecution of joy riders and youthful auto thieves and center Federal efforts on prosecuting auto thefts connected with organized crime or multi-theft violations" (*Report, U.S. Courts, 1973*, p. II-57). The Report also contained the observation that the decline in liquor law violations was due to these cases being handled by U.S. magistrates or being turned over to state authorities (p. II-58). It should also be mentioned that under the 1970 Court Reorganization Act for the District of Columbia there was a transfer beginning in part in fiscal 1972 from the federal district court to the "local" Superior Court of all offenses in violation of the District of Columbia Criminal Code except those that were also a violation of the United States Code (and also applicable nationwide). This brought about a dramatic drop in the criminal case input to the federal District Court of the District of Columbia from fiscal 1971 to fiscal 1974. In fiscal 1971, for example, 2,306 criminal cases were begun. But in fiscal 1974 this was cut by almost two-thirds to 835 cases. The biggest drop was in homicide, robbery, burglary, and sex offenses, precisely the areas in which the figures for all district courts nationwide in Table 4.3 indicated a drop for fiscal 1974. Thus in these areas, as in some others, cases were shifted out of the federal courts and were prosecuted elsewhere.

[18] *Report, U.S. Courts, 1973*, p. II-58.

Table 4.4 District court case flow and methods of disposition, fiscal 1973

	Cases pending July 1, 1972	Cases filed fiscal 1973	Terminated fiscal 1973	Cases pending July 1, 1973
Civil	101,032	98,560	98,259	101,333
Criminal	25,438	42,434 (40,367 original proceedings and 2,067 received by transfer)	43,456 (49,649 defendants)	24,416

Methods of Termination

	Number	Percent of total
Civil Cases:		
Trial	10,896	11.1
Without trial	87,363	88.9
Criminal defendants:		
Not convicted	12,388	24.9
Dismissed	10,268	(20.7)
Acquitted after trial	2,120	(4.2)
Convicted:	37,261	75.0
Plea of guilty or *nolo contendere*	30,852	(62.1)
Found guilty at trial	6,409	(12.9)

Source: Administrative Office of the United States Courts, *Annual Report of the Director, 1973* (Washington, D.C.: Government Printing Office, 1974).

were 10,896 civil cases and 6,409 losing criminal defendants. About four out of five civil cases and about two out of three criminal cases were appealed from the district courts to the appeals courts that same fiscal year.[19] In marked contrast, of 180,467 bankruptcy cases termi-

[19] The figures for civil cases may be misleading. Jerry Goldman has persuasively argued that one should consider all appealable decisions of district judges and not just completed trials. Goldman made use of unpublished data collected by the Administrative Office of the U.S. Courts categorized as "contested judgments" and considered those rather than completed trials as representing appealable decisions. On this basis his calculations for fiscal 1970 suggested approximately a one-in-four rate of appeals. See Jerry Goldman, "Federal District Courts and the Appellate Crisis," *Judicature*, 57 (1973), 211–213. If completed trials were used to determine the rate of appeal for fiscal 1970 the rate would be three out of four! Thus the four-out-of-five rate cited for fiscal 1973 (and which also held for fiscal 1974) should *not* be treated as the rate of all appealable civil decisions but only the rate in terms of completed trials. It should be recognized, as Goldman does in his article (p. 211), that the use of Administrative Office contested judgments has drawbacks in that the data are in aggregate form and individual cases are not traced through the system. Thus the figures for appeals for fiscal 1973 may contain cases begun in the district courts in fiscal 1972 or earlier as well as those begun in fiscal 1973. One

nated by the district courts in fiscal 1973, 338 appeals were commenced.

Demand input to the United States courts of appeals not only consists of civil and criminal appeals from the federal district courts, but also of petitions to review or enforce administrative agency orders and a small number of original proceedings. This demand input for fiscal 1973 is shown in Table 4.5. It should be noted that administrative agencies consider many tens of thousands of issues each year, most of which are resolved through informal proceedings. As one observer has noted, "Of the many thousands of formal administrative decisions reached each year, probably only one or two percent are appealed to

Table 4.5 Courts of appeals input by source and nature of case, fiscal 1973

Nature and source of case	Number	Percent of source input	Percent of total
District courts:[a]	*13,329*	*100*	*87*
Civil	8,876	67	(58)
United States cases[b]	1,713	(13)	
Private cases[b]	4,344	(33)	
Prisoner petitions	2,819	(21)	[18]
U.S. cases	991		
Private cases (state prisoners)	1,828		
Criminal	4,453	33	(29)
Administrative agencies:	*1,616*	*100*	*11*
National Labor Relations Board	612	38	(4)
Tax Court of the United States	241	15	(2)
Immigration and Naturalization Service	228	14	(2)
All other	535	33	(3)
Original proceedings	*346*	*100*	*2*
Total	15,291[a]		100

Source: Administrative Office of the United States Courts, *Annual Report of the Director, 1973* (Washington, D.C.: Government Printing Office, 1974).

[a] Excludes 338 bankruptcy appeals from the district courts.

[b] Excludes prisoner petitions.

study that did keep track of cases from the appeals courts to the Supreme Court was conducted by J. Woodford Howard, Jr. See his "Litigation Flow in Three United States Courts of Appeals," *Law and Society Review*, 8 (1973), 33–53. The full report of this research is contained in his Report to the Federal Judicial Center, *The Flow of Litigation in the United States Courts of Appeals for the Second, Fifth, and District of Columbia Circuits*, Research Report No. 3 (Washington, D.C.: Federal Judicial Center, 1973).

the courts."[20] Another point worth noting is that the appeals courts have experienced dramatic increases in their caseload. In just six years (from 1968 to 1974), the number of cases appealed from the district courts increased over 80 percent. Indeed, criminal appeals about doubled over the six-year period, although as indicated in Table 4.5, they accounted for about one-third of the cases appealed from the district courts. However, if the prisoner petition appeals (which increased by about two-thirds over the six years) are added to the criminal cases, one finds that about half of the appeals from the district courts (and over 40 percent of *all* appeals filed in the appeals courts) in fiscal 1974 were comprised of cases raising questions of personal rights and liberties in which the machinery of criminal justice was involved.[21] This is a profound change in demand input as compared to only one or two decades ago when the federal judicial system for the most part processed demands associated with property rights and other economic demands. One can plausibly infer a causal link between the massive social and cultural changes in the 1960s and the generation of new demands concerning personal rights and liberties, particularly when government has invoked the criminal process. It appears that the policy output of the Warren Court played no small part in fostering those changes and awakening people's sensitivities to their individual rights.

Table 4.6 shows how the courts of appeals disposed of their case input during fiscal 1973. About 64 percent of the cases filed during fiscal 1973 were disposed of by formal court decisions after a hearing or formal submission. Of these, about one in six cases involved a reversal of the district court or administrative agency.[22]

---

[20] Martin Shapiro, *The Supreme Court and Administrative Agencies* (New York: Free Press, 1968), p. 262.

[21] Goldman in his study of the "Federal District Courts and the Appellate Crisis" documents what he appropriately calls the "startling" change in criminal appeals (in contrast to the rate of appeal in civil cases which fluctuated between 20 and 24 percent between 1951 and 1970): "In 1951, approximately 14 out of every 100 defendants found guilty after trial appealed their convictions. By 1970, more than half of all defendants found guilty after trial appealed their convictions" (p. 212). As noted earlier this climbed to about two out of three by 1973. Goldman attributes the growth in appeals in part to the Criminal Justice Act of 1964 that began providing funds necessary to permit indigent defendants to enjoy free legal assistance.

[22] In fiscal 1974 only about 51 percent of the cases were disposed of after hearing or submission and of these close to 1 in 5 cases were reversals; a reversal pattern more typical of the 1960s.

Table 4.6   Courts of appeals case input and methods of disposition, fiscal 1973

Cases pending July 1, 1972	Cases filed fiscal 1973	Cases terminated fiscal 1973	Cases pending July 1, 1973
9,939	15,629	15,112	10,456

Methods of Disposition

	Number	Percent
Cases disposed of after hearing or submission:		
Affirmed or granted	7,163	74.5
Dismissed	540	5.6
Reversed	1,693	17.6
Other	222	2.3
Subtotal	9,618	100.0[a]
Without hearing or submission	3,942	
By consolidation	1,552	
Total	15,112	

Source: Administrative Office of the United States Courts, *Annual Report of the Director, 1973* (Washington, D.C.: Government Printing Office, 1974).
[a] Total cases after hearing or submission.

The demand input into the Supreme Court in terms of cases filed has grown steadily in recent years. There were 1,940 cases, for example, filed during the 1960 term. During the 1967 term the number had risen to 3,106 cases. During the 1971 term, 3,643 new cases were filed (though the 1972 term had an extremely small increase of only 106 new case filings over the 1971 total). The 1973 term saw a startling 12 percent increase in filings, bringing the number of cases to the Supreme Court to an historic high: 4,187 new cases.[23] Unlike the other courts in the federal judicial system, the Supreme Court's case input includes a large number of cases from state court systems. In recent years the Court has been spending a good chunk (though not the major portion) of its time on state judicial activities.[24]

[23] *U.S. Law Week*, 43 (1974), 3085.

[24] This is particularly true for state criminal cases. For example, over five times as many state criminal cases were the subject of full written opinions during the 1966–1968 terms than during the 1948–1950 terms. In the 1972 and 1973 terms, about one out of four cases decided with full opinion by the Court either came from the state judicial systems or were *habeas corpus* cases concerning state prisoners. Five years earlier during the Warren Court period over a third of the cases decided with full opinion originated with the state judicial systems.

All cases filed by the Supreme Court are divided into three major categories and placed onto three different dockets. On the Original Docket go cases over which the Court has original jurisdiction. Typically the number of these cases filed is low. (The 1962–1967 term average was four cases per term; the 1971–1973 term average was five.) On the Appellate Docket go (professionally drafted) appeals and petitions for writs of certiorari. Appeals have increased over past terms from 134 in the 1962 term to 352 in the 1970 term. Petitions for certiorari have also risen from 823 in the 1962 term to 1,188 disposed of in the 1970 term. On the Miscellaneous Docket are motions *in forma pauperis* (appeals and petitions for certiorari from impoverished state and federal prisoners) and other applications for leave to file various writs (rehearings, etc.). Among these various cases, prisoner petitions represent the largest number and have been growing dramatically from a 1959–1962 mean of 1,034 to a 1963–1967 mean of 1,480 to a 1971–1973 mean of 2,016. (Note that the number of petitions in the 1973 term was a record 2,118.)

The Supreme Court, unlike the other courts in the system, has been given under the system's regime rules considerable discretion as to how much of this demand input it need accept for formal processing and eventual output in opinions and court orders. Only with cases on the Original Docket is there any generally held expectation that a case filed will receive a formal court resolution. With petitions for certiorari and motions for leave to file writs on the Miscellaneous Docket, acceptance of these demands by the Court is completely discretionary. Such cases are only accepted if four or more judges so desire. Rejection of these case demands need not be, and almost always is not, accompanied by any comment. Even with appeals, a similar "rule of four" operates in making the decision of whether to note probable jurisdiction. Otherwise the case is dismissed with such pro forma and unilluminating notations as dismissed "for lack of jurisdiction" or "want of a substantial federal question." Even many appeals that are not dismissed never go to oral argument, and the decision of the lower court is merely "affirmed" or "reversed" in a summary order. The extent of the Court's discretion in these processes is illustrated in Table 4.7, which shows how the Court disposed of its Appellate Docket input from the 1965 through the 1970 terms.[25] Over the five

[25] At the direction of Chief Justice Burger, the Clerk's office has not provided breakdowns of the docket in terms of appeal and certiorari cases since the 1970 term. Glendon Schubert is convinced that the reason for this is to hide the fact

Table 4.7 Supreme Court disposal of Appellate Docket cases, 1965–1970 terms

Term	1965	1966	1967	1968	1969	1970
Appellate Docket Total	1,172	1,232	1,338	1,288	1,433	1,540
Appeals disposed of	124	156	186	305	312	352
[By dismissal]	[69 55.6%]	[80 51.3%]	[58 31.2%]	[106 34.8%]	[136 43.6%]	[139 39.5%]
Petitions for certiorari disposed of	1,048	1,076	1,152	983	1,121	1,188
[Denied or dismissed]	[914 87.2%]	[955 88.8%]	[986 85.6%]	[882 90.7%]	[1,026 91.5%]	[1,087 91.5%]

Source: Harvard Law Review, vols. 80–85, November, 1966–1971.

terms from 1969 through the 1973 terms, the Court disposed of from about 3,300 to over 3,800 cases per term. Yet the number of cases decided on their merits with more than pro forma consideration averaged only about 360 cases per term, and the number of cases going to oral argument each term ranged from 144 in 1969 to 177 in both the 1971 and 1972 terms. The number disposed of by full opinions, including long *per curiams,* never exceeded 188 in any one term. In these ways the Court handled its input so as to spend substantial judicial time only on those cases with which its members wished to deal.

PREVENTING DEMAND INPUT OVERLOAD

Demand input overload refers to two different empirical conditions: (1) an excessive number of demands each of which may take relatively little time to process, but whose great volume threatens the decision-making capacities of the system; and (2) demands, each of which takes an inordinate amount of time to process. If a political system is faced with processing demand input characterized by either one or both of these two conditions, its limited capacities for decision

that appeals are being handled not too differently than certiorari cases and are not receiving the special attention to which they presumably are entitled under current law. Schubert bases his analysis on the findings contained in *Report of the Study Group on the Case Load of the Supreme Court* (Washington, D.C.: Federal Judicial Center, 1972), which is reprinted in 57 F.R.D. 573 (1972). See the analysis and discussion in Schubert, *Judicial Policy-Making,* rev. ed., pp. 78–83.

making are soon overwhelmed, and thus the system itself is in danger of collapse. Every system can therefore be expected to confront the problem of reducing demand input to that which can be adequately managed.

The federal judiciary, like the various state judiciaries, is subject to numerous demands. This in general seems to reflect the democratic ethic that everyone is entitled to one's day in court. But the federal judiciary has only so many courts and judges with which to process case input. It is appropriate, then, to examine some of the mechanisms by which input is regulated and overload prevented. Eastonian analysis suggests that two mechanisms—cultural and structural—discourage, limit, avoid, or otherwise inhibit demand input.[26]

Regime rules as cultural inhibitors of demand input

The major cultural inhibitors of demand input (considered *cultural* inhibitors because they have grown out of our political and Anglo-American legal culture or traditions) are the formal and informal regime rules that serve to prevent, discourage, or modify the transformation of wants into formally articulated demands (i.e., litigation) calling for authoritative court judgments. They also serve to regulate the processing of litigation and operate at both the trial and appellate court levels. Such federal judicial rules include those concerning jurisdiction, standing to sue, justiciability, court costs, procedure, the role of the jury, and the availability of appellate review. Court costs, the uncertainties of jury behavior, and the complexity of the rules themselves (which makes it necessary to hire counsel or have one appointed by the court), suggest a long process until court judgment and do serve to discourage trials. At the appellate level, consideration of the cost in time and money imposed by the system's rules, special rules concerning the grounds and procedures of appeal, and (particularly as far as the Supreme Court is concerned) rules that give almost total discretion to the judges as to which demands to process further limit the system's demand input.

The system's rules of jurisdiction, standing, and justiciability allow the federal judiciary to avoid certain types of demands. *Jurisdiction*[27]

[26] Easton, *A Framework for Political Analysis,* pp. 122–125.

[27] A definitive discussion of jurisdiction, standing, and justiciability can be found in Edward S. Corwin, *The Constitution of the United States of America: Analysis and Interpretation,* rev. ed. (Washington, D.C.: Government Printing Office, 1964),

refers to whether a particular court has the legal authority to process the demand. Does the subject matter of the demand raise a federal question? Does the demand involve a state, foreign nation, or citizens of different states suing each other? If so, the federal courts have jurisdiction over the matter. If not, the courts will refuse to process the demand on the ground that it is outside their authority. The concept of *standing to sue* refers to those bringing demands to the courts and the criteria they must satisfy. For example, courts will only entertain demands presented within the framework of a case or controversy; that is, the litigation should represent a genuine conflict involving opposing parties personally involved contesting their real interests. If administrative action is challenged, all available administrative channels for reversing that action must have been followed before going to court. Furthermore, any conflict brought to the courts must be *justiciable*, that is, able to be resolved by the courts. Using such a notion of justiciability, the federal courts have, for example, refused to process (1) demands in which the controversial issue involved could not be conclusively determined by a court judgment because final authority was thought to rest or best lie with some other governmental body (the courts call these political question cases); (2) demands in which a court judgment would have no practical effect because of a change in the law, the status of the litigants, or some act of the parties involved that dissolves the controversy (moot cases); and (3) demands in which there is no action that a court can prescribe to right the alleged wrong (lack-of-a-judicial-remedy cases).

Jurisdiction, standing, and justiciability determine whether a dispute will or will not be processed. However, a suit may contain not only the demand to resolve the dispute but the demand to resolve it in a particular manner, such as a special interpretation of the law or Constitution. Here, too, there is wide latitude for the federal courts in processing demands. The courts can determine cases on broad or exceedingly narrow grounds, skirting controversy if they wish and certainly avoiding major constitutional issues.[28] Thus, even when the

---

pp. 597–726. Also see Harold W. Chase and Craig R. Ducat, *Edward S. Corwin's The Constitution and What It Means Today* (Princeton, N.J.: Princeton University Press, 1973), pp. 167–195.

[28] Justice Brandeis discussed this point in his well-known opinion in Ashwander v. T.V.A., 297 U.S. 288 (1936), at 346–347. There he specified the circumstances under which the Court would or would not avoid deciding a case based on an interpretation of the Constitution.

courts agree to process the case, there is no assurance that the case will be decided on the grounds argued by counsel. Of course, whether the system's regime rules will be used to avoid treating specific issues depends largely on the judicial philosophy and policy proclivities of the judges. The proponents of the judicial restraint philosophy urge that the courts avoid issues that can be better decided by the "political branches" of government. An underlying (but not the only) premise of this position is that to do otherwise would produce negative feedback. Activist judges, presumably because they are more concerned with being "right" than popular, have often disregarded the rules and doctrines of restraint. Thus in *Pollock* v. *Farmers' Loan Association*[29] and *Carter* v. *Carter Coal Co.*,[30] "friendly" litigants were able to elicit widesweeping constitutional judgments from the Supreme Court that struck down an early version of the income tax and a major piece of New Deal legislation. In Dred Scott (which also involved "friendly" litigants)[31] the Court in a burst of activism on the slavery issue overturned the Missouri Compromise. In *Baker* v. *Carr*[32] the Court reversed the precedent that had treated malapportionment of state legislatures as a non-justiciable "political question." The regime rules thus have some flexibility and can be used by judges to approach or avoid demands. Knowledge of previous judicial behavior of individual judges can aid in predicting how they will apply the regime rules in regulating demand input.

Kenneth Vines and Richard Richardson offered some insights into how the rules, the policy proclivities of the judges, and the desire of litigants to win, interact in modifying demands at the different stages of trial and appellate review. They analyzed cases that raised civil liberties issues when appealed from the district courts to the Courts of Appeals for the Third, Fifth, and Eighth Circuits during the 1956–1961 period.[33] Of the cases studied, the authors found that only about

[29] 157 U.S. 429 (1895).

[30] 298 U.S. 238 (1936).

[31] 19 How. 393 (1857). See Walker Lewis, *Without Fear or Favor: A Biography of Chief Justice Roger Brooke Taney* (Boston: Houghton-Mifflin, 1965), pp. 384–386.

[32] 369 U.S. 186 (1962).

[33] Richard Richardson and Kenneth N. Vines, "Review, Dissent and the Appellate Process: A Political Interpretation," *Journal of Politics*, 29 (1967), 597–616. A "civil liberties case" was defined as one in which a claim was made under the Bill of Rights, Thirteenth, Fourteenth, and Fifteenth Amendments, or Article I, Section 9 of the Constitution.

one-third had a civil liberties content in the district courts with the remainder not raising such issues. It was the latter cases that were specially examined, and it was found that at trial they were fairly routine cases having such low policy salience that they rarely resulted in a written opinion by the trial judge.

Vines and Richardson described two such cases. *Reyes* v. *United States*[34] was a narcotics case in which the judge realized after sentencing that the sentence he had given was below the statutory minimum. Thus, three days later he recalled the defendant and increased the sentence. The defendant appealed on grounds that his constitutional right to due process had been violated. *Proffer* v. *United States*[35] was a fraud case in which the defendant, a lawyer, waived his right to counsel and represented himself. After conviction the lawyer-defendant appealed on grounds that his constitutional right to counsel had been violated. In both cases the appeal was unsuccessful.

These two cases and undoubtedly the others suggest that the system's rules can generate an issue metamorphosis in litigation. Vines and Richardson suggested that appeal to the circuit courts is also encouraged by their collegial structure, more deliberative atmosphere, and the more cosmopolitan backgrounds of their judges. This presumably makes them more receptive to civil liberties claims than the district courts whose primary decision makers (judge and jury) are often rooted in local political cultures less sensitive to civil liberties claims. By their very complexity, the rules create opportunities for judicial "error" and as such serve to encourage appeals. When alleged errors occur, the almost absolute right to appeal given civil liberties claims and their high policy salience are seized upon as offering a second chance to trial court losers.

It might be further noted that the issue transformation observed here means that the courts of appeals in these cases can be conceived as forums of the first instance. Although the litigants remain the same as at trial, the legal issues and even the salient "facts" have changed. This conceptualization challenges conventional wisdom that conceives of these courts only as filters for demands initially raised and fully aired at trial as determining what are the issues of the case. In systems terms, this means that the courts of appeals often serve as

[34] 262 F.2d 801 (1959).

[35] 288 F.2d 182 (1961).

forums in which new policy demands are put into the system. Thus, in this instance, the rules of the system, rather than inhibiting demand input, help generate it. One should also note that, since passage of the Criminal Justice Act of 1964, indigent criminal defendants are entitled to a cost-free appeal of their convictions. Without the financial burden, appeal may be an attractive option when it would postpone the imposition of imprisonment.[36] Thus the Act of 1964 represented a change in the rules that has resulted in the generation of demand input to the appeals courts. Interestingly, the Supreme Court in a 1974 decision[37] made it clear that indigents are only entitled to free counsel through the first appeal. The opinion of the Court seemed to be openly acknowledging the full implications that a change in the rules may have for demand input.

Gatekeeping

The major structural inhibitors of demand input are the *gatekeepers*.[38] These are systemic authorities who by enforcing regime rules and through discretionary action control demand input. The federal judicial system's gatekeepers include lawyers of potential litigants (including lawyers for interest groups that finance test cases), law enforcement officials, and, of course, the judges. Each has a part in controlling the system's demand input by actions in advising clients, providing funds for litigation, making decisions as to what criminal cases to prosecute, and deciding which cases to accept on grounds of importance, jurisdiction, standing, and justiciability. Without stretching the truth too much it might be observed that lawyers, prosecutors, and judges typically act as if they were engaged in a vast conspiracy aimed at keeping litigants out of court. The effects of this "conspiracy" are most evident at the two levels of the court system (district court and Supreme Court) where authorities have perhaps the greatest discretion for playing their parts as systemic gatekeepers.[39]

[36] This point was suggested by Jerry Goldman in a letter to Sheldon Goldman (September 5, 1974).

[37] Ross v. Moffitt, 94 S. Ct. 2437 (1974). The case was decided by a vote of 6 to 3.

[38] They are considered "structural" because they occupy roles in the judicial structure; that is, they are "built into" the system. See Easton, *A Framework for Political Analysis*, p. 122.

[39] Table 4.6 showed that about one-third of courts of appeals cases in fiscal 1973 were disposed of by consolidation or without hearing or submission. Thus gate-

In fiscal 1974, the district courts terminated 97,633 civil cases. Only 10,972 (about 11 percent) were terminated by trial. In fiscal 1974, 48,014 criminal defendants had their cases disposed of by the district courts. Only 7,335 (about 15 percent) had trials.[40] Thus, as far as the district courts are concerned, "justice without trial" is not only common, it is the norm.[41] How just this justice is and how and why litigants so overwhelmingly forfeit their right to trial are questions now to be considered.

Disposing of Civil Litigation without Trial Some typical statistics concerning the processing of tort cases (i.e., personal injury and personal property damage cases) illustrate how civil cases are settled without trial in the federal courts. Tort cases constituted close to one-fourth of all civil cases filed in the district courts in fiscal 1974, making them the largest single category of cases filed. Of these, only about 14 percent actually went to and completed trial, and of those that did

---

keeping of course occurs at this level in the judicial system. However, the fact that the appeals courts do not have discretionary gatekeeping authority comparable to that held by the Supreme Court has meant that in recent years the problem of demand overflow has been severe. In 1972, Congress created the Commission on Revision of the Federal Appellate System and directed it "to study the present division of the United States into several judicial circuits and to report . . . its recommendations for changes in the geographical boundaries of the circuits as may be most appropriate for the expeditious and effective disposition of judicial business." As quoted in Commission on the Revision of the Federal Court Appellate System, *The Geographical Boundaries of the Several Judicial Circuits: Recommendations for Change* (Washington, D.C.: 1973), p. 2. The Commission recommended that the fifth and ninth circuits each be split into two new circuits.

[40] *Report, U.S. Courts, 1974*, Tables C-1 and 7, D-7, pp. A-12, 36, 58.

[41] It should be noted that, with civil cases, judges adjudicate certain demands without a formal trial but rather by court hearings. The judge's rulings are appealable, for example, with prisoner petitions for the writ of *habeas corpus* or motions to reduce or vacate sentence. Thus while justice-without-trial may be common, justice-without-judicial-adjudication is less frequent. Using unpublished data gathered by the Administrative Office of the U.S. Courts on contested judgments consisting of all actions by judges that are appealable, Jerry Goldman found that for fiscal 1970 some 23 percent (excluding prisoner petitions) resulted in contested judgments. When prisoner petitions were included the figure jumped to 37 percent. This still meant that justice without trial or adjudication was the norm, but it also meant that justice-with-adjudication was at least three-and-a-half times greater than simply justice with trial. Jerry Goldman, unpublished Table One, "Ratio of Contested Judgements to Total Civil Terminations."

only about one out of three was appealed to an appeals court.[42] It is, therefore, apparent that tort claims are resolved with a large degree of finality at the district court level.

In analyzing the dynamics of tort claim processing it is useful to examine the studies of tort cases in the state courts because in general, the law, fact situations, and even the participants (a victim/plaintiff and defendant's insurance company) are much the same in the federal and state courts. In fiscal 1974, for example, of the 24,231 tort cases filed in the district courts, 14,336 (about 60 percent) were diversity of citizenship cases. These differ from those tried in state courts only by the fact that federal procedure was used (although a number of states now use the same procedures) and that the amount of damages sought exceeded $10,000 (as required by federal law).[43]

In New York City during the late 1950s, there were approximately 193,000 accident victims each year who sought to recover damages on the grounds that their accidents were the fault of someone else. These were all potential litigants in personal injury actions, quantitatively the most important field of tort law. Only 40 percent of these potential litigants (about 77,000) even got as far as going to court and filing suits. Gatekeeping was thus under way in a substantial manner even before the courthouse doors were reached. Further gatekeeping is strongly evident at each subsequent step of the litigative process. Only in about 48,000 cases were notes of issue filed, signifying that both plaintiff and defendant were ready for trial; in only about 7,000 cases were trials actually commenced; and, finally, in only about 2,500

[42] In comparison it would appear that about all of the other types of civil cases completing trial in fiscal 1974 were appealed to an appeals court. However, this would be a misleading comparison since, as Jerry Goldman has pointed out in "Federal District Courts and the Appellate Crisis," there are many more appealable decisions than there are trials, and furthermore the figures do not represent the tracing of individual cases to determine if they were indeed appealed. What we can suggest, however, is that the maximum appeals rate for tort cases in fiscal 1974 was likely to have been considerably less than that for other types of civil cases.

[43] Such procedural differences as exist are perhaps irrelevant. The difference in the size of the claims is not. Large claims are apparently more resistant to settlement than small claims. Thus for the federal courts, about 15 percent of the cases filed are settled by a court judgment, while in the New York City courts in 1957 where the median recovery was only $795 and the average $2,058, only 3.2 percent required a court judgment (see the study cited in note 44). Nevertheless, if one keeps this difference in mind, an analysis of state tort claims settlement is illuminating for understanding the dynamics of civil suit gatekeeping within the federal courts.

cases was trial completed and a verdict given. To quote the authors of this study, "Less than 2 percent of the claims made each year in New York City are directly controlled by court adjudication. . . . [T]hese adjudications account for only 3 percent of the money that changes hands. The other 98 percent of the claims are disposed of, and the money moved, by a bargaining process in which victims, defendants, lawyers, and insurance companies' representatives are the chief participants."[44]

In considering why this radical attrition in claims occurred as a court verdict was approached, it is important to note that 84 percent of those making claims (about 162,000) did achieve some recovery. This high rate of recovery emphasizes the extent to which "out-of-court" case disposal is a negotiated process leading to results at least minimally satisfying to both parties. The crucial role played by lawyers must also be noted. Practically all defendants, being insured, are represented by their insurance company's counsel. This is not true for accident victims. With claims where the victim retained a lawyer, the recovery rate was 90 percent. With claims where the victim did not, the recovery rate was only 65 percent. In cases where the fact/law situations were similar, the size of recovery was about twice as high for victims with lawyers as for those without.[45] Since the authors could not find any other factor that might distinguish lawyer from non-lawyer cases, they concluded that the very presence of a plaintiff's lawyer is important both for the size and chances of recovery.

A lawyer undoubtedly can make a stronger legal claim than can the

[44] Marc A. Franklin, Robert H. Chanin, and Irving Mark, "Accidents, Money and the Law: A Study of the Economics of Personal Injury Litigation," Columbia Law Review, 61 (1961), 1–39, reprinted in Rita James Simon (ed.), The Sociology of Law: Interdisciplinary Readings (San Francisco: Chandler, 1968), pp. 367–391. Quotation from pp. 373–374.

[45] Insurance companies obviously prefer to deal directly with victims and avoid having to negotiate with lawyers. Insurance company adjustors as a consequence take the initiative in trying to settle before the claimant sees an attorney. See H. Laurence Ross, Settled out of Court: The Social Process of Insurance Claims (Chicago: Aldine, 1970). Ross also noted (pp. 193–198) that settlements were considerably larger when an attorney represented the victim. Even for victims with lawyers, one study found that those who took an active interest in their case and shared decision making concerning the litigation with their lawyer wound up much better than those who were passive and had little participation in their own case. See Douglas E. Rosenthal, Lawyer and Client: Who's in Charge? (New York: Russell Sage Foundation, 1974).

typical layman. Furthermore, since the lawyer is paid only if recovery is made and the amount of payment varies directly with the size of recovery (contingent fee payment), the victim's lawyer has a direct interest in settling for as large an amount as possible. This makes it less likely that the victim can be bluffed into receiving no payment or an unfairly low one when he has a strong case. On the other hand, since lawyers are only paid if they win, some extremely weak claims are weeded out when victims go to a lawyer and are advised to drop the potential suit. The study's authors also suggested that a further reason why victims with lawyers do so much better than those without is that insurance companies sometimes will settle a relatively weak claim for a low amount when a lawyer is present to sustain "good will" for future cases.[46] Whatever the reasons involved, lawyers emerge as significant participants in civil suit gatekeeping by the out-of-court settlement of claims.

. Under federal rules of civil procedure, pretrial discovery procedures and the pretrial conference are vehicles for gatekeeping. Discovery procedures were instituted in 1938 to enable both sides to a civil suit to "discover" the facts and legal arguments the other side intends to use in the trial, thus eliminating surprises and cutting trial time. The implicit purpose of these rules is to encourage settlements before trial, thus saving all concerned much time and expense. In practice, there have been mixed results, and the rules have been used by some lawyers for dilatory purposes or for harassment or other strategic considerations.[47] Nevertheless, there is some evidence that for a majority of parties to a civil dispute, discovery of the opponent's

---

[46] The no-fault concept has attracted considerable attention as a means of relieving the courts of a substantial portion of automobile accident cases. Efforts to enact federal no-fault legislation finally resulted in the passage of such a bill by the Senate on May 1, 1974, but the 93rd Congress ended without the House having acted. Interestingly, some bar groups have opposed no-fault legislation, and it is probably more than coincidental that no-fault reduces the pool of potential clients. See *Congressional Quarterly*, July 20, 1974, p. 1886. The no-fault concept was extensively developed in a highly influential book written by two law professors, Robert E. Keeton and Jeffrey O'Connell. See their *Basic Protection for the Traffic Victim: A Blueprint for Reforming Automobile Insurance* (Boston: Little, Brown, 1965). For a discussion of the Keeton-O'Connell plan and other alternative proposals see Willis Park Rokes, *No-Fault Insurance* (Santa Monica, Calif.: Insuror's Press, 1971).

[47] See William A. Glaser, *Pretrial Discovery and the Adversary System* (New York: Russell Sage Foundation, 1968), pp. 3–37, 91 (especially note 4), 117–161.

evidence and argument is followed by a settlement before the case comes to trial.[48]

Rule 16 of the Federal Rules of Civil Procedure for the U.S. District Courts authorizes the judge, at his discretion, to "direct the attorneys for the parties to appear . . . for a conference to consider . . . matters as may aid in the disposition of the action." The judge thus has the opportunity to encourage a settlement and even to take an active part by, for example, stating what he thinks the case is worth (i.e., what he believes would be a reasonable settlement). Although district judges vary in the manner and extent to which they utilize pretrial conferences, there is evidence that suggests that they are used widely. In fiscal 1960, for example, more than 15,000 such conferences were convened. About two out of five conferences produced a resolution of the cases.[49]

The fact that so few cases are resolved by a verdict after trial should not be taken to mean that trials are relatively unimportant for systemic operations. The "threat" of a trial verdict underlies out-of-court negotiations. The prediction by both plaintiff's and defendant's lawyers as to what a verdict might be is the benchmark toward which an out-of-court settlement is aimed. There are certain aspects of trial, however, that may make an out-of-court settlement a better resolution than a trial verdict. For the defendant, in particular, trials cost money. Even for a large insurance company with its own legal staff, going to trial consumes expensive legal time and energy. Even if an out-of-court settlement is slightly higher than a possible verdict, the costs saved may make it a bargain. Going to trial has its costs for the plaintiff also. Getting a trial judgment takes time. In the federal system as a whole, in recent years the median time from when a note of issue is filed (signifying that the parties are ready) until trial has been 12 months. In a big metropolitan district such as the Southern

---

[48] *Ibid.*, pp. 91–101. However, in the Glaser study, pretrial settlement was even more likely when neither party utilized the discovery procedures! Furthermore, Glaser also found (pp. 102–103) that use of discovery procedures was associated with increased trial time. His data (p. 106) further suggested that discovery "might be associated with *more* surprise." Clearly, pretrial discovery is not the gatekeeping mechanism its proponents once suggested.

[49] Richard J. Richardson and Kenneth N. Vines, *The Politics of Federal Courts* (Boston: Little, Brown, 1970), p. 86. Also see their discussion on pp. 85–88. In general, see Maurice Rosenberg, *The Pretrial Conference and Effective Justice* (New York: Columbia University Press, 1964).

District of New York, the median time in fiscal 1973 was 28 months.[50] Particularly with a not-too-wealthy accident victim, for whom a speedy financial recovery may be more important than a possible big one, "delay in court" can be a crucial factor in bringing about an out-of-court settlement.

Although judges and lawyers frequently state that certain cases are "worth" so much at trial, this does not mean that any particular jury will arrive at that amount. Rather such statements are probabilistic in nature; that is, on the average such a case will yield such an award. The statistical nature of these predictions is well illustrated in an experiment by the Jury Project undertaken at the University of Chicago Law School.[51] An actual case was selected that was settled out-of-court for $42,000 just before verdict was to be rendered. The trial of this case was then reenacted before ten experimental "juries." The average verdict from the ten "juries" was, in fact, $41,000. This suggests that the lawyers in the real case were fairly accurate in assessing its worth in reaching settlement. The $41,000 average, however, was the result of verdicts that ranged all the way from $17,500 to $60,000. Only two verdicts were in accord with the average—one for $42,000 and one for $40,000.

In sum, the out-of-court resolution of a civil case may be less costly, certainly more speedy, and perhaps (but not necessarily) more "just" than its resolution by a verdict after trial.

Disposing of Criminal Cases Without Trial   Criminal case gatekeeping occurs at the trial court level of the federal judicial system both in the 91 district courts without local jurisdiction and those with such jurisdiction (including the U.S. District Court for the District of Columbia before fiscal 1972). The criminal case demands processed by both types of courts, however, differ.

Districts with local jurisdiction typically process criminal cases that violate the local criminal code (rather than a violation of a federal statute applicable nationwide) and include homicide, robbery, assault, burglary, or sex crimes. In fiscal 1973, about one-fourth of the criminal cases in the three districts with local jurisdiction concerned these

---

[50] In the federal district of New Mexico, the median was only three months. *Report, U.S. Courts, 1973*, Table C-10, pp. A-38-39.

[51] Harry Kalven, Jr., "The Jury, the Law and the Personal Injury Damage Award," *Ohio State Law Journal*, 19 (1958), 158–178.

crimes. In contrast, these offenses accounted for only 7 percent of the criminal cases commenced in the 91 district courts, which in turn have as their typical offenses auto theft, forgery and counterfeiting, larceny, and violations of the narcotics and immigration laws. Criminal cases processed in the three district courts and in the District of Columbia District Court before fiscal 1972 were more similar to those found in the state judicial systems than those found in the typical federal district court. However, both types of federal district courts process cases under the Federal Rules of Criminal Procedure, and there is reason to believe that their gatekeeping processes are similar.

The first step in the processing of a criminal case is typically arrest[52] (although some cases have as their first step—and are thus fed into the court system by—indictment as the result of a grand jury investigation). As soon after arrest as practicable, the accused must be presented before a judge or federal magistrate at which time he is formally advised of his rights to remain silent and to have a lawyer[53] and is considered for release on bail or on his own recognizance. The accused is also informed of his right to a preliminary examination by the court official. If from the evidence it appears to that official that there is probable cause to believe that an offense has been committed and that the defendant committed it, the case is then submitted by the U.S. Attorney's office to the grand jury. If an indictment is obtained, the case is formally commenced. Misdemeanors and cases where the accused waives a grand jury may also be commenced by a U.S. Attorney's filing of an Information. Whichever route is used, the accused is now a defendant and the case is commenced.

The next stage is arraignment. The defendant is taken before the trial judge where he is read the indictment or information, a lawyer

---

[52] Prior to arrest, substantial gatekeeping may also occur by the police or other public and private law enforcement officials. See James Q. Wilson, *The Varieties of Police Behavior* (Cambridge, Mass.: Harvard University Press, 1968), for a systematic study of different patterns of gatekeeping behavior by local police. Also see John A. Gardiner, *Traffic and the Police: Variations in Law-Enforcement Policy* (Cambridge, Mass.: Harvard University Press, 1969), especially pp. 150–165. In general, see the discussion and the citations within James Eisenstein, *Politics and the Legal Process* (New York: Harper & Row, 1973), pp. 84–97, 216–233 and Egon Bittner, "Florence Nightingale in Pursuit of Willie Sutton: A Theory of the Police," in Herbert Jacob (ed.), *The Potential for Reform of Criminal Justice* (Beverly Hills: Sage, 1974), pp. 17–44.

[53] Since Miranda v. Arizona, 384 U.S. 436 (1966), both federal and state law enforcement officials are also required to inform the accused of these rights upon the commencement of questioning.

is appointed if this has not already occurred, and the defendant enters his plea of guilty (including its substantial equivalent, *nolo contendere*) or not guilty.[54] If a guilty plea is entered, the next and final stage is sentencing by the judge. If the defendant pleads not guilty, preparation for trial begins. Any time before or during trial his plea may be changed to guilty and his sentence imposed. If acquitted, the process ends with his release.

Throughout the process substantial gatekeeping aimed at the avoidance of trial occurs. It takes two forms: (1) a decision not to proceed with the case; and (2) plea bargaining. The decision not to proceed is made by any of three systemic authorities: the U.S. Attorney's office (which is supervised by the Department of Justice), the initial committing judge or federal magistrate, or the grand jury. Of the three, most decisions not to proceed are made by the U.S. Attorney's office. The decision may take the form of either the dismissal of all charges or, with cases in the District of Columbia District Court, which only tries felonies and now only those in which a federal crime is concerned (which also are violations of the District of Columbia Criminal Code), a reduction of charges to a misdemeanor or the dropping of federal charges and referral to the District of Columbia Court of General Sessions. Plea bargaining entails negotiations between defense attorney and prosecutor. The objective is to reach an agreement whereby the accused will enter a guilty plea in return for a reduced charge or a favorable sentence recommendation. Although there may be cases where the prosecutor may feel that the seriousness or notoriety of the crime requires that "the book be thrown" at the defendant, there is evidence that suggests that plea bargaining occurs with some frequency in both the federal and state judicial systems.[55]

[54] Under the provisions of the Speedy Trial Act that became law in 1975, the time period from arraignment to trial is to be gradually reduced beginning with a 180 day maximum effective July 1, 1976 and culminating with a 60 day maximum starting July 1, 1979.

[55] A landmark study of plea bargaining is by Abraham S. Blumberg, "The Practice of Law as a Confidence Game: Organizational Cooptation of a Profession," *Law and Society Review*, 1 (1967), 15–39. Also see Albert W. Alschuler, "The Prosecutor's Role in Plea Bargaining," *University of Chicago Law Review*, 36 (1968), 50–112; Linda Ann Carstarphen, "Sentence Bargaining at the Local Level: Perceptions and Attitudes of Judges, Prosecutors, and Defense Attorneys," Ph.D. dissertation, University of Georgia, 1970; Jonathan D. Casper, *American Criminal Justice: The Defendant's Perspective* (Englewood Cliffs, N.J.: Prentice-Hall, 1972), pp. 77–99; Eisenstein, *Politics and the Legal Process*, pp. 110–119; George F. Cole, "The Decision to Prosecute," *Law and Society Review*, 4 (1970), 331–343, and *Politics and*

Figure 4.1 presents an analysis of felony case flow in the U.S. District Court for the District of Columbia for 1965.[56] Several characteristics of this case flow suggest criminal case gatekeeping. First, it should be noted that four out of five felony cases entering the system did not result in a felony conviction. Most of those cases that left the system did so because of decisions made by the prosecution, committing judge, or grand jury. Although most of these (over 60 percent) were referrals to the District of Columbia Court of General Sessions for processing as misdemeanors, the important point is that arrest for a felony is typically not the first step to a felony conviction. In this process the earlier the stage, the higher the exit rate. Sixty-six percent

the Administration of Justice (Beverly Hills, Calif.: Sage, 1973), pp. 195–208; Lynn M. Mather, "Some Determinants of the Method of Case Disposition: Decision-Making by Public Defenders in Los Angeles," Law and Society Review, 8 (1973), 187–216; Herbert Jacob, Urban Justice: Law and Order in American Cities (Englewood Cliffs, N.J.: Prentice-Hall, 1973), pp. 96–118; David W. Neubauer, Criminal Justice in Middle America (Morristown, N.J.: General Learning Press, 1974), especially pp. 194–223; Milton Heumann, "Plea Bargaining Systems and Plea Bargaining Styles: Alternate Patterns of Case Resolution in Criminal Courts," paper delivered at the 1974 Annual Meeting of the American Political Science Association. Plea bargaining was used by Special Prosecutor Leon Jaworski in the Watergate prosecutions. See "Watergate Plea Bargains are Defended by Jaworski: Replying to Criticism, He Terms Practice Fair, Legal, and Necessary," New York Times, June 19, 1974, pp. 1, 34.

[56] Figure 4.1 has been constructed from data contained in Joseph A. Navarro and Jean G. Taylor, "Data Analyses and Simulation of Court System in the District of Columbia for the Processing of Felony Defendants," in Task Force Report: Science and Technology (The President's Commission on Law Enforcement and Administration of Justice) (Washington, D.C.: Government Printing Office, 1967), pp. 199–215. This was a study of felony cases in the U.S. District Court for the District of Columbia for calendar year 1965. Unfortunately only two figures are presented with any high degree of certainty: 6,300 arrests and 1,600 cases commenced. All other figures are computed from percentages contained in the study. Moreover, in comparing the data found in this study with data, admittedly less precise, from Harry I. Subin, Criminal Justice in a Metropolitan Court: The Processing of Serious Criminal Cases in the District of Columbia Court of General Sessions (Washington, D.C.: Department of Justice, 1966), serious discrepancies are found. In that study the number of felony cases begun in the U.S. District Court in 1965 is put at 1,200. Furthermore, in checking the number of cases commenced in the U.S. Courts, Federal Offenders, 1967 (a publication that gives data by the fiscal rather than the calendar year), it appears that no more than about 1,100 cases were commenced. In sum, the figures presented in this analysis are somewhat in controversy. Therefore, they should be treated only as approximations. However, the Navarro and Taylor data are likely to be dependable since their study was based on the actual inspection of documents relating to each case.

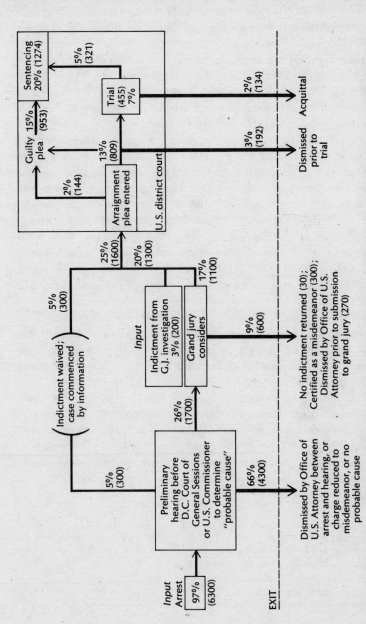

Figure 4.1 Felony case flow in the U.S. District Court for the District of Columbia, calendar year 1965. (Numbers prior to arraignment stage and all percentages rounded.) Source: Navarro and Taylor.

made their exit at the very start prior to or at the preliminary hearing. A further 9 percent left prior to or at the grand jury stage.

Commencement of the case by indictment or information marked a major watershed. Once that occurred, the chances for conviction were quite high. Of the approximately 1,600 cases commenced, only 12 percent left by dismissal. Acquittal accounted for another 8 percent. The remaining 80 percent ended with convictions.[57]

In the District of Columbia there are formalized negotiations by way of hearings in the U.S. Attorney's office prior to going to the Grand Jury.[58] In these hearings the Assistant U.S. Attorney in charge of the case, the arresting officer, defense counsel, and even the witnesses for both sides spend from twenty minutes to an hour discussing the case. In one study of such hearings, involving 64 felony complaints, the results were as follows: in 9 cases (14 percent) all charges were dropped; in 16 cases (25 percent) the original charge was maintained; in 39 cases (61 percent) the charge was reduced to a misdemeanor with the promise of a guilty plea.[59] Serious crimes were the most resistant to such bargaining. These, it might be noted, led to the highest number of sustained pleas of not guilty and thus the most trials.

Given the emphasis on plea bargaining before indictment, it is not surprising to find that the percentage of guilty pleas at arraignment, the next stage in the process, is low. Of the 1,600 cases arraigned in 1965, over 90 percent of the defendants entered a plea of not guilty. Between arraignment and trial, however, pleading guilty was again common. Almost 58 percent of those originally pleading not guilty changed their pleas. Either the defendant decided to "throw himself on the mercy of the court" or a last minute bargain was negotiated (e.g., some of the charges are dropped to assure a reduced sentence). When these guilty pleas were added to those made at arraignment, it was found that 75 percent of those convicted by the District of Columbia District Court never went to trial.

[57] Note that the conviction rate in the District declined by 1970, but then turned around so that by 1973 it was about at the 1965 level. See Table 4.8 and the discussion in the text. Note, however, that in fiscal 1974 there was an unusually large proportion of dismissals (over 26 percent) which in turn affected the conviction rate.

[58] Subin, *Criminal Justice*, pp. 42–48.

[59] *Ibid.*, p. 44.

As in civil cases we find doubtful (but not obviously weak) cases and cases involving the highest stakes most resistant (but certainly not immune) to gatekeeping. However, just as with most civil cases, the participants in most criminal cases want to avoid trial.[60] For the prosecution trial is expensive in terms of organization time, energy, and money. Moreover, prosecutors do not like to stain their conviction records, therefore, except in the strongest cases, a negotiated guilty plea is preferable to the risk of an acquittal at trial. Defense counsel, too, is motivated to negotiate in order to get his client off as lightly as possible. As a Department of Justice study notes, "Many defense attorneys consider the plea bargain a vital part of their service to the defendant."[61] Defense counsel is encouraged to do this by his knowledge that trial may be long and fruitless. Moreover, since many such lawyers are court-appointed and thus are not generously compensated by the court, or have private clients from whom chances of payment are questionable, it makes more financial sense to settle the case without going through a long and costly trial.

An obviously guilty defendant is discouraged from going to trial not only by the advice of his lawyer, but also by considerations of time and outcome. If he is not able to provide bail, the time spent in jail prior to a trial judgment is normally not deducted from any subsequent prison term. In the 90 districts in the states in fiscal 1973 the median time from filing a case to sentencing after a guilty plea was 3 months while the median time where conviction was the result of a jury trial was 5.8 months.[62] Even more important in a defendant's calculation in deciding whether or not to plead guilty are the differences in sentences of those pleading guilty compared to those convicted by trial. An analysis of sentences received by defendants convicted in 89 district courts[63] in fiscal 1971 shows that those sentenced

---

[60] Note that the highest New York state court, the New York Court of Appeals, endorsed and even encouraged plea bargaining in a series of three cases decided in October, 1974. Chief Judge Charles D. Breitel writing for an unanimous court observed: "In budget-starved urban criminal courts, the negotiated plea literally staves off collapse of the law enforcement system, not just as to the courts but also as to local detention facilities." As quoted in The New York Times, October 13, 1974, p. 70.

[61] Subin, Criminal Justice, p. 43.

[62] Report, U.S. Courts, 1973, Table D-6, pp. A-54, 55.

[63] The District of Columbia, Guam, the Canal Zone, and the Virgin Islands were excluded from analysis. The middle district of Louisiana had not yet been created.

after trial received more severe treatment than those sentenced after pleading guilty. This is also true when one holds prior criminal record constant.[64] Sentences after jury trial convictions were often two to three times more severe than sentences after guilty pleas for comparable crimes and defendants. There seems little doubt, therefore, that a trial—where the prosecution may "throw the book" at the defendant and the judge may discipline him with a harsh sentence for "wasting" the court's time—can be a risky business for the obviously guilty.

There is some evidence that suggests that the criminal case gatekeeping process has been in a state of flux. Generally in the federal courts through fiscal 1973 the conviction rate declined as did the proportion of guilty pleas. The decline in the conviction rate, however, was not due to an increase in acquittals. In fact, conviction after trial increased. The decline in the conviction rate was almost solely due to an increase in dismissals between arraignment and trial. This is shown in Table 4.8, which contains data from the 89 (90 in 1973) districts without local jurisdiction. The findings for the District of Columbia District Court are also presented in Table 4.8. One should note two distinguishing characteristics of the District of Columbia District Court. First, until mid-1971 the court had local jurisdiction over felonies committed in violation of the District of Columbia Criminal Code. Second, with no senators and party organizations involved in the judicial selection process the Nixon Administration, as others before it, could appoint precisely the sorts of judges they would have liked to appoint throughout the country had they a free hand. This meant that by 1973 the Nixon appointees as well as the Nixon-appointed U.S. Attorney's office could pursue a get-tough law-and-order policy. In any event, Table 4.8 suggests that for the District of Columbia District Court, in the 1970s there was a reversal of the trend of the 1960s so that by 1973 criminal defendant dispositions were closer to the national norm than for the other years cited in the table. Where the acquittals of the District of Columbia District Court had been about twice as high if not more than in the rest of the country, by 1973 they about matched the other districts. In 1967 the

[64] *Federal Offenders, 1971* (Washington, D.C.: Administrative Office of the U.S. Courts, 1973), pp. 14–17. This has been found at the state level as well. See, "Wide Disparities Mark Sentences Here," *New York Times,* September 27, 1972, pp. 1, 57.

Table 4.8   Trends in criminal case disposal in 89 district courts and the U.S. District Court for the District of Columbia by fiscal year

	1964	1967	1970	1973*
Types of disposition in 89 districts:				
All defendants disposed of after arraignment	33,381	31,535	36,356	46,724
Total convicted	87.4%	83.5%	77.5%	74.9%
(By guilty plea)	(78.7)	(73.3)	(66.3)	(62.1)
(By trial)	(8.7)	(10.2)	(11.2)	(12.8)
Total not convicted	12.6%	16.5%	22.5%	25.1%
(Dismissed)	(8.8)	(13.3)	(18.2)	(20.9)
(Acquitted)	(3.8)	(3.2)	(4.3)	(4.2)
Types of disposition in D.C. District Court:				
All defendants disposed of after arraignment	1,442	1,011	2,311	2,925
Total convicted	77.3%	72.2%	72.7%	77.9%
(By guilty plea)	(56.5)	(43.9)	(54.6)	(63.0)
(By trial)	(20.8)	(28.3)	(18.1)	(14.9)
Total not convicted	22.7%	27.8%	27.3%	22.1%
(Dismissed)	(16.2)	(14.7)	(18.9)	(17.5)
(Acquitted)	(6.5)	(13.1)	(8.4)	(4.6)

Source: Administrative Office of the U.S. Courts, *Federal Offenders,* 1967, 1971: *Annual Report, Administrative Office,* 1973.
*Disposition in 90 districts.

proportion of guilty pleas was markedly lower than in the other districts. In 1973 the proportion of guilty pleas had increased by close to 50 percent and matched that for the other districts. In fiscal 1967 the percentage of cases tried had increased to 41 percent, but by fiscal 1973 had come down to about 19 percent (just above the level of the other districts).

In contemplating these trends it is difficult not to associate the fall in convictions in the 90 districts to the Warren Court's policies concerning criminal procedure. The intent of these policies was to discourage aggressive police questioning and thus confessions and guilty pleas. The Nixon Court, however, has turned around the thrust of the Warren Court's policy making in the criminal-procedures area and has openly approved plea bargaining. In *North Carolina* v. *Alford*[65] the

[65] 400 U.S. 25 (1970).

Court suggested that plea bargaining is constitutional as long as the guilty plea is voluntary and implied that the Court would broadly construe voluntariness. In *Santobello* v. *New York*[66] the Court appeared to recognize the necessity of plea bargaining to prevent demand overload, although the Court ruled that the prosecution must keep its end of the bargain.

Supreme Court Gatekeeping The Judiciary Act of 1925 included among its provisions one that authorized the Supreme Court to issue the writ of certiorari at its discretion in place of the writ of error that until then practically guaranteed Supreme Court review as a matter of right. This provision was instituted so that the Court could protect itself from being overwhelmed by a rising tide of litigation and instead focus its energies on those cases its members deemed of special importance.[67]

[66] 404 U.S. 257 (1971). Chief Justice Burger speaking for the Court observed: "The disposition of criminal charges by agreement between the prosecutor and the accused, sometimes loosely called 'plea bargaining,' is an essential component of the administration of justice. Properly administered, it is to be encouraged. If every criminal charge were subjected to a full-scale trial, the States and the Federal Government would need to multiply by many times the number of judges and court facilities. Disposition of charges after plea discussions is not only an essential part of the process but a highly desirable part for many reasons. It leads to prompt and largely final disposition of most criminal cases; it avoids much of the corrosive impact of enforced idleness during pre-trial confinement for those who are denied release pending trial; it protects the public from those accused persons who are prone to continue criminal conduct even while on pre-trial release; and by shortening the time between charge and disposition, it enhances whatever may be the rehabilitative prospects of the guilty when they are ultimately imprisoned" 404 U.S. 257 (1971) at 260–261. The Supreme Court in its Amendments to the Federal Rules of Criminal Procedure sent to Congress in 1974 included Rule 11(e), which specifies the plea bargaining procedure to be used in federal courts. Within Rule 11(e)(1) there is the stipulation that the judge is not to participate in any such plea bargaining discussions.

[67] While accomplishing this purpose, the rationale for the Judiciary Act also, in the words of one study, "made dissent more acceptable and expected" since the major controversial cases on which the Court would be likely to focus its attention "are not necessarily and ineluctably subject to one 'correct' solution." The authors of the study, Stephen C. Halpern and Kenneth N. Vines, documented the sharp rise in dissent rates and behavior after the 1925 Act and concluded that the Act "may have been a necessary condition to maintain, promote and legitimate that development." See their "Dissent, The Judges' Bill and the Role of the U.S. Supreme Court," paper delivered at the 1974 Annual Meeting of the American Political Science Association.

Petitions for certiorari come in two forms: petitions *in forma pauperis,* which since 1947 have been placed on the Court's Miscellaneous Docket; and other petitions, placed on the Appellate Docket. Usually a petition *in forma pauperis* consists of a single typewritten or handwritten document drafted without professional aid. It often contains much that is irrelevant and leaves out essential information. The single copies go to the office of the Chief Justice whose clerks prepare memoranda analyzing the petitions; these go to the various justices. Only when a prisoner's life is at stake or the issue seems of distinct interest or importance is the petition itself circulated.

Petitions that go on the Appellate Docket are much more standardized. They are printed documents from ten to thirty pages in length setting forth the basis for Supreme Court jurisdiction, the questions asked to be reviewed, the facts pertinent to them, and the reasons why the Supreme Court should review these questions. Also appended are the judgments and opinions of the lower courts and (if involved) administrative agencies as well as a copy of the record. Respondents may enter a brief as to why certiorari should be denied, and petitioners may file a supplementary brief in reply. Each justice receives a copy of these documents, and the law clerks prepare memoranda summarizing the issues raised in the petitions.[68]

Each Miscellaneous and Appellate Docket petition is placed on the conference agenda and discussed if at least one justice so desires. Handling of petitions is expedited by use of a "special list" (an innovation of Chief Justice Hughes). Under this arrangement,[69] the chief justice reviews each petition; those that he considers to be obviously

---

[68] Since the 1972 term the four Nixon appointees—Chief Justice Burger and Justices Blackmun, Powell, and Rehnquist—along with Justice White dispensed with the practice of the preparation of memoranda by each justice's law clerks, and instead one or more law clerks prepare summaries for distribution to all the justices. However, Justices Douglas, Brennan, Marshall, and Stewart decided to continue to have their own clerks individually prepare summaries for themselves. This suggests that each of these justices are interested in certain kinds of issues and that their individual clerks will be sensitive to this when they review documents related to cases for certiorari or appeal.

[69] See the discussion by David J. Danelski, "The Influence of the Chief Justice in the Decisional Process of the Supreme Court," in Thomas P. Jahnige and Sheldon Goldman (eds.), *The Federal Judicial System: Readings in Process and Behavior* (New York: Holt, Rinehart and Winston, 1968), p. 150. Also see S. Sidney Ulmer, William Hintze, and Louise Kirklosky, "The Decision to Grant or Deny Certiorari: Further Consideration of Cue Theory," *Law and Society Review,* 6 (1972), 643, n. 6.

without merit he places on a list that is then circulated to all members of the Court prior to the judicial conference. If no member objects, the petition is rejected without discussion (i.e., "deadlisted"). Objection takes the petition off the list and it is discussed. If a minimum of four justices so vote, the petition is granted and the case is accepted for consideration on its merits. Otherwise it is rejected.

Despite the low acceptance rate for petitions (in the 1972 term, about one percent of Miscellaneous Docket petitions and about 8 percent Appellate Docket petitions were accepted[70]), the large numbers involved have meant that in the past such petitions typically accounted for about 75 percent of all cases that went to oral argument (although more recently that proportion has been reduced[71]). Thus a matter of keen interest to both practicing attorneys and to students of the Court has been determining what criteria the Court uses in accepting and rejecting cases.

Rule 19 of the Supreme Court's Rules ostensibly provides the gate-keeping criteria for the granting of the writ of certiorari. For example, Rule 19 specifies that certiorari will be granted if a lower court's ruling conflicts with a ruling of the Court, if a conflict in circuits exists, or if an "important" question is involved on which the Court has not ruled. Joseph Tanenhaus led a research team[72] that examined the opinions of cases for which certiorari had been granted and which were decided in the 1956–1958 terms and found that only about two out of three of them contained a reason for granting certiorari. In over half of these cases the reason given was the "importance of the issue," which of course is not a very illuminating reason. Tanenhaus concluded that Rule 19 reasons do not adequately explain the Court's certiorari gatekeeping. Rather, he hypothesized, the justices have had to develop some method for assessing the numerous petitions and for separating the frivolous ones from those that deserve careful study. This method, he suggested, is the search for readily identifiable *cues.* The presence of one or more of these cues would be a signal

---

[70] *Harvard Law Review,* 87 (1973), p. 310.

[71] See *Harvard Law Review,* 88 (1974), p. 277; and Mark W. Cannon, "Administrative Change and the Supreme Court," *Judicature,* 57 (1974), p. 338, n. 29.

[72] Joseph Tanenhaus, Marvin Schick, Matthew Muraskin, and Daniel Rosen, "The Supreme Court's Certiorari Jurisdiction: Cue Theory," in Glendon Schubert (ed.), *Judicial Decision-Making* (New York: Free Press, 1963), pp. 111–132.

to the judge that the petition warrants careful study. The absence of cues would mean that the petition can be safely discarded without further expenditure of judicial time. Careful study of a petition with cues would then occur to determine if certiorari should nevertheless be denied because of defects concerning jurisdiction, inadequacies in the record, lack of ripeness, or tactical inadvisability. Only those not weeded out by this process would be granted certiorari and either summarily affirmed, reversed, or scheduled for oral argument with the preparation of full opinion anticipated. Tanenhaus's concept of cue, therefore, is obviously a gatekeeping concept.

Tanenhaus and associates conducted an empirical test of cue theory.[73] They tested for the presence of four cues and hypothesized that, if any one of the four cues was present alone, then the likelihood of certiorari being granted would be greater than when no cues were present. They found that three of the four hypothesized cues met this test. The most potent cue was whether the federal government was a party to the case and urged review. Next was whether the case contained a civil liberties issue. Finally, dissension (whether among the judges of the court immediately below or between two or more courts and agencies) was a cue. A case with all three cues would have a 4 out of 5 chance of having certiorari granted. A case with none of these three cues would only have a 7 out of 100 chance of having the certiorari petition granted.[74] Although other cues might be formulated and tested, the findings of the Tanenhaus study provide strong evidence that the Supreme Court's control of demand input by certiorari gatekeeping during the time period studied was far from policy neutral. The justices most assuredly were responding to policy-oriented cues.[75]

S. Sidney Ulmer and colleagues also tested cue theory,[76] but unlike

[73] Ibid.

[74] Ibid., p. 129.

[75] Ulmer has found a relationship between voting to grant certiorari and voting on the merits of the cases. S. Sidney Ulmer, "The Decision to Grant Certiorari as an Indicator to Decision 'On the Merits,' " Polity, 4 (1972), 429–447; and his "Supreme Court Justices as Strict and Not-So-Strict Constructionists: Some Implications," Law and Society Review, 8 (1973), 13–32.

[76] Ulmer, Hintze, and Kirklosky, "The Decision to Grant or Deny Certiorari." Still another test of cue theory was conducted by Niel Thomas Zimmerman who examined the actual documents filed with the Court by the litigants in a random sam-

Tanenhaus who examined certiorari petitions that initially came to the Court, Ulmer studied those petitions that were not deadlisted and thus had been discussed at the weekly conferences. The only cue that emerged from the statistical analysis of these conference-discussed cases was whether the federal government was a party to the case and wanted the Court to review the case. This led Ulmer to suggest that a two-stage process may be at work. Initial screening may very well rely on a variety of cues such as those uncovered by Tanenhaus. But once these cases survive initial screening, and presumably many civil liberties cases were in this category, the most potent cue is the federal government's wishes concerning Supreme Court review.

Over the years more and more cases have come to the Court, and this has been of special concern to Chief Justice Warren Burger who has feared that demand input overload will soon overwhelm the Court. Unlike the lower federal courts whose demand overload, where it exists, is a result of the fact that these courts must decide the cases brought to them (assuming they have met such requirements as jurisdiction, standing, and the like), the Supreme Court's overload problem, such as it may be, lies in deciding what to decide. In 1972 Chief Justice Burger appointed a study group to examine this problem and to make recommendations.

Under the auspices of the Federal Judicial Center the study group, under the chairmanship of Harvard Law Professor Paul Freund and composed of leading legal scholars, came up with a proposal for a new court that would make decisions as to what cases the Supreme Court should consider and what cases should be denied review.[77] By taking from the Court the burden of having to select its cases for review, the justices presumably would be able to do a more thorough job on the cases they decide on the merits (the study commission was diplomatic in making this point). The new court would be *the national court of appeals* and would not only screen cases for the

---

ple of all cases (not just certiorari petitions) brought over a ten-year period (1957 through 1966). Zimmerman found that the most important cue was the position of the government. See his "The Decision to Decide: A Statistical Analysis of the Preliminary Decision-Making Process of the United States Supreme Court," Ph.D. dissertation, University of California (Riverside), 1970.

[77] *Report of the Study Group on the Case Load of the Supreme Court.* Excerpts from the report are reprinted in Walter F. Murphy and C. Herman Pritchett (eds.), *Courts, Judges and Politics,* 2nd ed. (New York: Random House, 1974), pp. 83–87. The entire report can be found in 57 Federal Rules Decisions 573–628 (1972).

Court, but would also decide certain cases in which different circuit courts made conflicting rulings on points of law.

Membership on the court would be limited to regularly serving appeals courts judges who have had a minimum of five years of appellate bench service. Appointments would be automatic from lists of judges by seniority and would alternate between the most senior and the most junior judges with the minimum of five years experience and would rotate by circuit. Seven judges would serve at any one time and appointments would be for three-year terms with the terms staggered to give continuity on the bench. A case denied review would be at the end of the legal line, although under the proposal the Supreme Court could, if it wished, take the initiative and call up the case on its own (how the justices would know very much about the case is not clear from the study group report).

Response from former and sitting members of the Supreme Court was negative. Former Justice Arthur Goldberg questioned the constitutionality of taking from the Court the responsibility for exercising its discretion in deciding which cases to hear.[78] Former Chief Justice Earl Warren opposed the proposed court as a political device that would hamper the Court from enforcing basic constitutional rights.[79] On the Court itself, Justices Stewart,[80] Brennan,[81] and Douglas[82] came out in opposition to the new court recommendation. Justice Douglas repeatedly made the point that the Court was not overworked and could handle the decisions to decide.[83]

Lower court judges too have found fault with the proposal, but at least one judicial critic, Judge Henry Friendly of the Second Circuit, also recognized that an overload problem will have to be faced if the trend of increased numbers of cases coming to the Court for review

[78] New York Times, January 1, 1973, sec. 4, p. 6.

[79] New York Times, May 2, 1973, p. 50.

[80] New York Times, January 9, 1973, sec. 4, p. 6.

[81] William J. Brennan, Jr., "National Court of Appeals: Another Dissent," University of Chicago Law Review, 40 (1973), 473–485.

[82] New York Times, January 9, 1973, sec. 4, p. 6.

[83] See, for example, New York Times, October 25, 1974, p. 14. For a systematic empirical analysis of the problem and a critique of the proposal, see Gerhard Casper and Richard A. Posner, "A Study of the Supreme Court's Caseload," Journal of Legal Studies, 3 (1974), 339–375. But see, Russell R. Wheeler, "The Supreme Court's Workload and the Demands on the Federal Appellate Courts," paper presented at the Annual Meeting of the Midwest Political Science Association, 1975.

continues.[84] Friendly's solution, also favored by some other judges, lies in contracting federal jurisdiction.[85]

The American Bar Association leadership, unenthusiastic about the national court of appeals proposal, appointed its own committee to study the problem, and that group came up with an alternative proposal for a national division of the U.S. courts of appeal.[86] Under the ABA proposal the Supreme Court would still make screening decisions on its own in federal criminal appeals and in certain civil cases. But appeals from the state courts, tax matters, and administrative agency cases would be screened by the national division which would also have authority to decide cases. Any case decided by the national division would be subject to Supreme Court review during a ninety-day period. If the Court did not act during that period, the decision would become final. The ABA proposal, however, did not receive as much attention as the Freund group's proposal, and by 1975 it appeared that neither had achieved anywhere near the backing necessary for legislative enactment. In mid-1975 the federal Commission on Revision of the Federal Court Appellate System recommended its own version of a national court of appeals.[87] As of this writing, it is doubtful that the Commission's proposal will be any more favorably received than the previous ones. Thus it is likely that the Supreme Court will continue to retain its full gatekeeping powers.

SUPPORT

Systems analysis suggests that in order to persist, a political system must maintain a minimum level of support among those who are

[84] *New York Times*, November 14, 1972, p. 35.

[85] Henry J. Friendly, *Federal Jurisdiction: A General View* (New York: Columbia University Press, 1973), and his "Averting the Flood by Lessening the Flow," in *Cornell Law Review*, 59 (1974), 634–657. Also see Shirley M. Hufstedler, "Comity and the Constitution: The Changing Role of the Federal Judiciary," *New York University Law Review*, 47 (1972), 841–870.

[86] *New York Times*, January 27, 1974, sec. 4, p. 9.

[87] See, Commission on Revision of the Federal Court Appellate System, *Structure and Internal Procedures: Recommendations for Change*, Preliminary Report, (Washington, D.C.: 1975), pp. 8–53. Chief Justice Burger and Justices White, Blackmun, Powell, and Rehnquist were reported as being favorably disposed toward the Commission's proposal while Justices Stewart, Marshall, Brennan, and Douglas were reported as being opposed to it. *New York Times*, June 21, 1975, p. 20.

politically relevant to it. This concept of support is distinct from the concept of feedback, although both are intimately related. (Each input to the system is instigated by systemic outputs; one way of inferring support attitudes is by looking at feedback activity.) Support, however, deals only with *attitudes* that may be related to systemic output, but may also be held as a result of early socialization or psychological predispositions toward governmental authority in general. Feedback, on the other hand, concerns only *behavioral responses* to output whose existence is transmitted back to the system. This includes *public expression* of support attitudes as well as a wide variety of actions (e.g., private and official noncompliance, court-curbing legislation, new litigation).

The concept of support insofar as it attempts to aid in explaining judicial behavior raises some problems. In American political and legal theory, federal judges are supposed to be insulated not only from the other branches of government and "politics" in general, but also from such considerations as whether their decisions are popular or not.[88] Judges who respond to the views of politicians, interest groups, or the public are considered by the organized bar to be acting "unprofessionally."[89] This makes it hard to know to what extent support is in fact an input variable processed by the judicial authorities.

Particularly unclear are both the effect and legitimacy of public opinion on judicial behavior. Some legal theorists have held that public opinion, insofar as it reflects contemporary community needs and values, should be considered in determining the general shape of judicial policy making but not in specific cases concerning unpopular litigants. Similarly, advocates of judicial restraint have emphasized the need for some minimal attention to public opinion. Alexander Bickel, for example, who was one of the leading modern proponents of judicial restraint, argued that, although the courts should not enforce public opinion, the Supreme Court in particular should avoid

[88] The classic statement concerning the insulation of the judicial branch is contained in *The Federalist,* No. 78. See Jacob E. Cooke (ed.), *The Federalist* (New York: World, 1961), pp. 521–530.

[89] On the other hand, the organized bar and members of the legal profession frequently express *their* views. This is seen by at least one legal commentator as an important check on judicial decision making. For example, the late Dean of Harvard Law School, Roscoe Pound, once observed that "Every [judicial] decision is subject to criticism by a learned profession, to whose opinion the judge, as a member of the profession, is keenly sensitive." See Pound's "Justice According to Law, III," *Columbia Law Review,* 14 (1914), 108.

cases and decisions that seriously violate community attitudes and values.[90] This, as Glendon Schubert noted, is a "strategy for survival."[91] It is, in other words, a working-out of a theory of support. Yet, many behavioralists have held that at the Supreme Court level, professions of judicial restraint are simply rhetoric. Harold Spaeth, for example, has presented evidence suggesting that judges who profess that certain decisions are based on considerations of judicial restraint are in fact using this as a rationale for arriving at decisions in accord with their more basic political attitudes and values.[92]

Nevertheless, the idea dies hard that at least at some crucial turning points in judicial history, the Supreme Court, as Mr. Dooley commented long ago, "follows the election returns." To put it in the more scholarly language of David Easton, "Where . . . support threatens to fall below [some] minimal level . . ., the system must provide mechanisms to revive the lagging support or its days will be numbered."[93] One major way, notes Easton, by which such lagging support may be "revived," is through changing systemic policy output. Whether the public is a relevant source of support for the federal judicial system and, if so, whether it produces the type of response that both the fictional Mr. Dooley and the scholarly Mr. Easton suggest, are questions worth considering.[94]

The analytical dimensions of support

Support may be highly different for different aspects or organizational units of the system.[95] Some aspects and units of the federal judicial

[90] Alexander Bickel, *The Least Dangerous Branch* (Indianapolis: Bobbs-Merrill, 1962).

[91] Glendon Schubert, *Constitutional Politics* (New York: Holt, Rinehart and Winston, 1960), p. 213.

[92] Harold J. Spaeth, "Judicial Power as a Variable Motivating Supreme Court Behavior," *Midwest Journal of Political Science*, 6 (1962), 54–82. But compare Joel B. Grossman, "Role-Playing and the Analysis of Judicial Behavior: The Case of Mr. Justice Frankfurter," *Journal of Public Law*, 11 (1962), 285–309.

[93] Easton, *A Framework for Political Analysis*, p. 124.

[94] For a general survey and assessment of the literature on public opinion and law, see Austin D. Sarat, "Law and Public Opinion: A Review and Critique," manuscript. Also see William J. Daniels, "The Supreme Court and Its Publics," *Albany Law Review*, 37 (1973), 632–661.

[95] Note that in this discussion of support, there is no consideration of intrasystemic support. This form of withinput is of interest as it is manifested by affirmance and

system have appeared to have experienced substantial increases and decreases in support over time. With others, basic agreement as to their legitimacy appears so widespread that support has remained consistently high and unchanging. Since the Civil War, for example, there has been little disagreement as to the definition of the political community over which the authority of the federal judicial system extends. Similarly, such basic regime rules as the supremacy of federal law, judicial review, and the isolation of the courts from direct popular control have not been the subject of any serious support problems in recent times. On the other hand, particular judges, courts, and the judicial interpretation of some regime rules (e.g., various parts of the Federal Rules of Criminal Procedure, the extent of federal jurisdiction, and the scope of the judiciary's authority vis-à-vis Congress, the President, and the states) have from time to time been the objects of large negative inputs of support.

Another consideration to be taken into account is where support comes from: the legal profession or segments thereof; national, state, or local party leaders, elected politicians, and other public officials; or the general public. It would seem that different sources of support have different consequences for the system.

The kind of support involved is still another consideration. The distinction should be made between diffuse and specific support. *Diffuse support* concerns the general good will, loyalty, and sense of legitimacy directed toward a political system regardless of any specific rewards people may feel they have received. *Specific support* refers to the positive or negative feelings people have in direct response to their perceptions of specific policy outputs. These two kinds of support are both analytically and empirically separable. A person, for example, may express general approval of the Supreme Court as the legitimate forum for constitutional adjudication, while at the same time expressing strong disapproval of many of its constitutional decisions.

---

reversal rates of judges and courts by the next court level as well as additional actions and remarks of judges and other authorities in the system. The empirical dimensions of such withinput have not been subjected to much scholarly scrutiny. An important exception is Richardson and Vines, *Politics of Federal Courts*, Chaps. 6 and 7. Also see Robert A. Carp, "The Scope and Function of Intra-Circuit Judicial Communication: A Case Study of the Eighth Circuit," *Law and Society Review*, 6 (1972), 405–426.

The focus here will be on the available evidence relating to both specific and diffuse support of the general public for the Supreme Court, particularly during the 1960s.

The Empirical Dimensions of the Supreme Court's Support   Beginning in the 1940s and on through the 1960s, the Supreme Court was the object of increasing disenchantment by those members of the public who responded to the queries of the pollsters.[96] The trend was apparently not uniform, however. It least affected diffuse support among those members of the public least aware of Court activities (the Court's marginal public); it most affected specific support among persons most aware (the Court's attentive public). By 1966, net specific support was strongly negative and increasingly so in some major policy areas such as criminal procedures; net diffuse support was positive but decreasing.[97] Although the Court still had a substantial number of strong positive supporters within its attentive public, much of the reason for its comparatively high diffuse support was the large positive support from its marginal public. This is seen in Table 4.9, which is based on a study by Walter Murphy and Joseph Tanenhaus of support data collected nationally in 1966.[98]

[96] See the 1949 and 1956 Gallup polls, the 1964 Michigan Survey Research Center, and 1964 Berkeley Survey Research Center surveys cited in Kenneth M. Dolbeare and Phillip E. Hammond, "The Political Party Basis of Attitudes toward the Supreme Court," *Public Opinion Quarterly*, 32 (1968), 23–24.

[97] According to the Gallup polls, positive diffuse support continued its downward plunge, reaching a low point in July, 1969. The Gallup surveys asked respondents to rate the Court as either "Excellent," "Good," "Fair," or "Poor." The proportion of "Excellent" and "Good" ratings dropped from 60 percent in the 1949 poll to 45 percent in 1967, 36 percent in 1968, and finally 33 percent in the 1969 poll. Conversely, the relatively unfavorable ratings of "Fair" and "Poor" rose from 14 percent in 1949 to 46 percent in 1967, 53 percent in 1968 to 54 percent in the 1969 survey. (The balance consisted of those unable or unwilling to rate the Court.)

[98] Walter F. Murphy and Joseph Tanenhaus, "Public Opinion and the United States Supreme Court: A Preliminary Mapping of Some Prerequisites for Court Legitimation of Regime Changes," *Law and Society Review*, 2 (1968), 357–384. Murphy and Tanenhaus, along with Daniel L. Kastner, reanalyzed the 1966 survey and tested a number of alternative hypotheses to explain differences in diffuse support. See Walter F. Murphy, Joseph Tanenhaus, and Daniel L. Kastner, *Public Evaluations of Constitutional Courts: Alternative Explanations*, Sage Professional Papers in Comparative Politics, Vol. 4, series no. 01-045 (Beverly Hills, Calif.: Sage, 1973). Although the reanalysis used a smaller number of respondents than utilized in the earlier Murphy and Tanenhaus articles based on the same 1966 survey, and the methodology employed in the reanalysis was more rigorous, the general findings

Table 4.9 Distribution of specific and diffuse support among Supreme Court's attentive and marginal publics, 1966

| Type of support | Attentive public[a] | | Marginal public[b] |
	Specific support	Diffuse support	Diffuse support
Strong positive[c]	5.4%	26.8%	27.5%
Moderate positive	15.2	14.9	37.0
Pro/con[d]	10.8	16.7	14.8
Moderate negative	41.5	14.7	16.7
Strong negative[c]	27.0	19.9	4.0
Unclassified		7.4	
Total	99.9%	100.4%	100.0%
	N = 596		N = 357

Source: Percentages are derived from data presented in Walter F. Murphy and Joseph Tanenhaus, "Public Opinion and the United States Supreme Court: A Preliminary Mapping of Some Prerequisites for Court Legitimation of Regime Changes," *Law and Society Review,* 2 (1968), 370 (Table 5), 377 (Table 9).
[a] Attentive public defined as the 46.2 percent of all respondents in the Murphy-Tanenhaus survey who offered specific likes and dislikes about the Supreme Court.
[b] Marginal public defined as the 27.6 percent of all respondents in the Murphy-Tanenhaus survey who offered diffuse opinions about the Supreme Court, but could not articulate any specific likes or dislikes.
[c] Very strong and strong categories in the Murphy-Tanenhaus study combined for purposes of this table.
[d] Positive and negative comments were about evenly balanced.

The Court in some (but not all) surveys taken in 1966 can also be seen as doing relatively poorly in its input of support as compared to the other major national political institutions of Congress and the presidency. The results from three surveys are shown in Table 4.10. The Murphy-Tanenhaus survey asked respondents to compare the Court and Congress. The Dolbeare study was based on a survey taken only in Wisconsin. Both showed the Court doing comparatively badly in terms of support. However, the national Harris survey, also reported in Table 4.10, asked respondents about their level of confidence in American institutions, and the Supreme Court in 1966, unlike Congress or the presidency, was the recipient of a (bare)

of the earlier studies that are used in the discussion here remain unrefuted. The reanalysis by Murphy-Tanenhaus-Kastner supports the basic proposition illustrated by Table 4.9. See Murphy, Tanenhaus, and Kastner, *Public Evaluations,* pp. 41, 51–52.

Table 4.10 Relative support for the Supreme Court as compared with other branches of government (confidence in actions taken by institutions of the national government)

	Supreme Court	Congress	Presidency
Trust Congress/Trust Court? (1966)[a]	37%	51%	—
Confidence that right action taken by (1966)[b]	28	50	35%
Great deal of confidence[c]			
1966	51	42	41
1972	28	21	27
1973	33	30	19

[a] *Source:* Walter F. Murphy, Joseph Tanenhaus, and Daniel L. Kastner, *Public Evaluations of Constitutional Courts* (Beverly Hills, Calif.: Sage, 1973), p. 11, national sample survey. Proportions are of those answering the question of in which institution, Congress or the Court, did respondent place greater trust. Twelve percent gave on-the-fence responses.

[b] *Source:* Kenneth M. Dolbeare, "The Public Views the Supreme Court," in Herbert Jacob (ed.), *Law, Politics, and the Federal Courts* (Boston: Little, Brown, 1967), p. 197. 1966 Wisconsin Survey.

[c] *Source:* Louis Harris and Associates, Inc., national sample survey as reported in Subcommittee on Intergovernmental Relations of the Senate Committee on Government Operations, *Confidence and Concern: Citizens View American Government* (Washington, D.C.: Government Printing Office, 1973), p. 33.

majority's positive diffuse support.[99] The reasons frequently mentioned by those who responded negatively in 1966 concerning the Court (and who had some knowledge of the Court's work) were its decisions concerning race, school prayers, and criminal procedures. (The reapportionment cases seemed to have elicited little awareness or negative support.)[100] In other words, the liberal-activist Warren Court was viewed unfavorably by many of its critics in the public as too liberal and too activist. The criminal procedures area was particularly a source of increasing negative support of the Supreme Court and American court systems (federal and state) in general during the 1960s. This is suggested by Table 4.11, which was constructed from a series of Gallup poll responses to the question, "Do you think the

[99] By 1972, as suggested by Table 4.10, positive diffuse support had plummeted across the three institutions. By 1973, however, Congress and the Court made some very modest gains in regaining public confidence, while the Watergate-mired Nixon Presidency plunged still lower in the public's esteem.

[100] Murphy, Tanenhaus, and Kastner, *Public Evaluations of Constitutional Courts*, p. 46.

Table 4.11 Public attitudes toward treatment of criminals by the courts, 1965–1969

	Too harshly	Not harshly enough	About right	No opinion	Total
			Courts treat criminals:		
April 1965	2%	48%	34%	16%	100%
August 1965	2	60	26	12	100
February 1968	2	63	19	16	100
February 1969	2	75	13	10	100

Source: Gallup Opinion Reports, no. 4 (September 1965); no. 33 (March 1968); no. 45 (March 1969).

courts in this area deal too harshly or not harshly enough with criminals?"[101]

It is appropriate to examine more closely the "public" of the public-opinion polls. In the Murphy-Tanenhaus study mentioned earlier, the authors found that 53.8 percent of the entire survey could not state anything they liked or disliked about the Court, and 34.7 percent would not even venture a guess at "what the main job of the Court is."[102] Similarly, in a national poll made in 1945, 40 percent did not know how many justices were on the Court. In another poll taken in 1949, 14 percent were unable to even name the highest court in the land. In 1973, the Harris poll revealed that 20 percent of the national survey thought that the Supreme Court is a branch of Congress.[103] Analysis of these and other poll results indicates that the "public" of public-opinion polling can be stratified into a hierarchy of groups on the basis of awareness, concern, and information.

At the bottom level are those members of society who neither

[101] Follow-up surveys in February, 1971, and December, 1972, revealed that three out of four respondents continued to feel that the courts did not treat criminals harshly enough. The 1971 survey was conducted by the Gallup organization for and reported in *Newsweek*, March 8, 1971, p. 39. The 1972 Gallup survey was reported in the *New York Times*, January 16, 1973, p. 15.

[102] "Public Opinion and the United States Supreme Court," pp. 360, 365.

[103] Both the 1945 and 1949 polls are cited in Kenneth M. Dolbeare, "The Public Views the Supreme Court," in Herbert Jacob (ed.), *Law, Politics, and the Federal Courts* (Boston: Little, Brown, 1967), pp. 194–212. The Harris poll is cited in *Confidence and Concern: Citizens View American Government* (Washington, D.C.: Government Printing Office, 1973), p. 250. Note that even 12 percent of the college-educated thought that the Court was a branch of Congress.

know nor care anything about Court behavior. Depending upon the survey question asked, this group's size varies between about 10 and 30 percent of the adult population as suggested by the various studies cited in Table 4.12. This segment of the public is generally unaware and apathetic about politics in general. They possess little or no general political knowledge. They tend not to vote.[104] Although the upper levels of this group sometimes respond to questions on "forced choice" public opinion polls, in general they are *politically irrelevant* as a source of either negative or positive support for the Court.

In setting the size of the Court's *politically relevant* public at from 70 to 90 percent of the adult population, there is serious danger of overstating the real percentage of those who hold meaningful opinions. Murphy and Tanenhaus note, "Forced choice questions of the

Table 4.12 Determining the size of the Supreme Court's politically irrelevant public

	Percent
"No Opinion" about any Supreme Court decision or aspect of Supreme Court behavior (Seattle, 1965)[a]	21
"Don't Know" when asked to rate Supreme Court's performance (Wisconsin, 1966)[b]	19
"Unclassified"—i.e., "no response" or "no opinion" in testing for diffuse support (national poll, 1966)[c]	29
Cannot answer question about what Supreme Court is supposed to do (Missouri, 1968)[d]	26
"No opinion" when asked to rate Supreme Court's performance (AIPO national surveys)[e]	
1963	16
1967	9
1968	11
1969	13
1973	12

[a] *Source:* John H. Kessel, "Public Perceptions of the Supreme Court," *Midwest Journal of Political Science,* 10 (1966), 174.

[b] *Source:* Kenneth M. Dolbeare, "The Public Views the Supreme Court," in Herbert Jacob (ed.), *Law, Politics, and the Federal Courts* (Boston: Little, Brown, 1967), p. 203.

[c] *Source:* Walter F. Murphy and Joseph Tanenhaus, "Public Opinion and the United States Supreme Court: A Preliminary Mapping of Some Prerequisites for Court Legitimation of Regime Changes," *Law and Society Review,* 2 (1968), p. 374.

[d] *Source:* Gregory Casey, "The Supreme Court and Myth: An Empirical Investigation," *Law and Society Review,* 8 (1974), 397.

[e] *Source:* AIPO polls 1963, 1967, 1968, 1969, 1973.

[104] Murphy and Tanenhaus, "Public Opinion," p. 368, note that 42 percent of these "unknowledgeables" did not vote in the 1964 Presidential election.

variety so typical in commercially conducted public opinion polls strenuously overestimate the Court's visibility because they solicit responses from people who may possess no meaningful information."[105] Kenneth Dolbeare illustrated this point in his 1966 Wisconsin study by asking respondents to indicate whether the Court had recently made a decision in different policy areas including some in which the Court had not, for example, Medicare, urban renewal, and the John Birch Society. He found that 52 percent claimed that the Court had made a decision about Medicare, 26 percent about urban renewal, and 23 percent about the John Birch Society.[106] This suggests that many respondents to poll questions venture opinions that are based on no or false information. Perhaps even more revealing as to the extent of the Court's relevant public was a Survey Research Center poll conducted in 1964 that began with a question that asked whether the respondent had paid any attention to what the Supreme Court had done in recent years; 58.7 percent indicated they had not.[107] These and other data suggest that the Court's politically relevant public can be divided into two groups.

The attitudes of the members of the first group are meaningful inputs of support to the Court. Its members demonstrate knowledge about the Court, hold strong opinions either pro or con, are highly likely to have recently read or heard about the Court and its activities,[108] and are easily able to articulate specific likes and dislikes. This segment of the population is the Court's *attentive* public. It constitutes roughly about 40 percent of the adult population. Evidence for this estimate is presented in Table 4.13. Murphy, Tanenhaus, and Kastner have suggested that attitudes toward public policy best accounted for the variation in support levels of the knowledgeables in the 1966 survey, but they also acknowledged that party allegiance was related to support with Democrats giving more positive diffuse support than Republicans.[109]

105 *Ibid.*, p. 360.

106 Dolbeare, "Public Views," pp. 199–201.

107 Murphy and Tanenhaus, "Public Opinion," pp. 360–361.

108 John H. Kessel, "Public Perceptions of the Supreme Court," *Midwest Journal of Political Science*, 10 (1966), p. 189, Table 12.

109 Murphy, Tanenhaus, and Kastner, *Public Evaluations of Constitutional Courts*, pp. 32–33. See Dolbeare and Hammond, "The Political Party Basis of Attitudes toward the Supreme Court," pp. 23–24. The argument, however, can be made that the partisans of the party in control of the White House will observe their

Table 4.13 Determining the size of the Supreme Court's attentive public

	Percent
Strong Court critic or supporter (Seattle, 1965)[a]	40.9
Intensity of attitude about the Supreme Court— "very strong" (Seattle, 1965)[b]	37.5
SRC polls—expression of specific likes and dislikes[c]	
1964	41.3
1966	46.2
"High knowledge" about the Supreme Court (Wisconsin, 1966)[d]	37.4
Awareness/Familiarity concerning Supreme Court decisions (Missouri, 1968)[e]	48.6

[a] *Source:* John H. Kessel, "Public Perceptions." "Strong critics" were those with scores of at least −2 and "strong supporters" with scores of at least +2 on the open-end questions scale presented in Kessel's Table 2.

[b] *Source:* Kessel, "Public Perceptions," derived from data presented in Table 12, p. 189.

[c] *Source:* Murphy and Tanenhaus, "Public Opinion," p. 360.

[d] *Source:* Dolbeare, "Public Views," p. 200. "High knowledge" defined as four or more correct identifications out of eight concerning policy areas in which the Court made a decision in recent years.

[e] *Source:* Gregory Casey, "The Supreme Court and Myth: An Empirical Investigation," *Law and Society Review,* 8 (1974), p. 415 n. 20. Those considered aware or familiar with Court decisions are those with scores of "2" and "3."

Opinions of the remainder of the politically relevant public are much less meaningful. The persons holding them are characterized by a low knowledge of the Court and a propensity to express diffuse support attitudes or respond to forced-choice questions without

---

President making appointments to the Court and will consider the Court part of their "government." Thus, when Republicans control the White House, Republicans should give more positive diffuse support than Democrats. The opposite should be true when Democrats control the White House. During the Republican Eisenhower Administration, a 1956 Gallup survey asking people to rate the Court found that, nationally, Republicans gave greater positive diffuse support than did Democrats (although when the South was excluded there was little difference in support levels). In the 1973 Gallup court-rating poll, with another Republican administration in power, Republicans gave greater positive diffuse support than did Democrats. The greatest gains in positive support from the previous survey, taken at the end of the last term of the Warren Court, were in the South. See *Current Opinion,* 1 (1973), 91. More specialized segments of the attentive public, however, may base support levels not on the basis of attitudes toward the party in power generalized to the Court but rather more on the basis of policy positions. For example, a survey in 1970 of congressional candidates revealed marked differences between Democrats and Republicans in terms of their positive support for the Court in the criminal procedures areas. Democrats gave considerably more positive support than did Republicans. *Congressional Quarterly,* October 16, 1970, pp. 2564–2565.

having enough information to spontaneously be able to articulate specific support opinions. They are perhaps better characterized as on the threshold of political relevancy and can be considered the Court's *marginal* public.

Members of each public, whether friend or foe of the Court, tend to be more like one another than like their attitudinal partners in other publics. This is not only true in terms of knowledge, access to recent information, and propensity to hold strong opinions, but also in such demographic and political variables as education, income, partisanship, political involvement, and general political knowledge. Being in the Court's *attentive*, as compared to its *marginal*, public is positively correlated with greater formal education, income, and general political knowledge. Republicans tend to be better represented than Democrats, Democrats better represented than Independents.[110] Of even greater interest is that by the late 1960s being in the Court's attentive public was also positively associated with political involvement, alienation from government, and a high sense of political efficacy. It seems hard to overemphasize the importance of these latter tendencies. To quote Murphy and Tanenhaus, "Individuals who tend to be aware of the Court . . . [and] vote often, . . . are [also] apt to distrust government and feel that it is generally unresponsive to their desires."[111] Dolbeare states, "People [with high knowledge about the Court] are the [same] ones with a high sense of political efficacy, for they are also the ones who say that they would act in some way to change a Court decision of which they disapprove."[112] When one couples these latter tendencies with the relatively low positive specific and diffuse support levels within this same segment of the public, it is clear that the Court in the late 1960s was approaching a crisis in its input of support. Some of the evidence has already been presented in Table 4.9. Evidence from two other studies is provided in Table 4.14. It is rather ironic that much of the Court's net positive support was attributed to members of the public who

---

[110] Note that party identification was found to be unrelated to knowledge of Court decisions in the 1968 sample survey of Missouri reported in Gregory Casey, "The Supreme Court and Myth: An Empirical Investigation," *Law and Society Review*, 8 (1974), 385–419 at 405–406.

[111] Murphy and Tanenhaus, "Public Opinion," p. 366.

[112] Dolbeare, "Public Views," p. 201.

Table 4.14 Diffuse support for the Supreme Court by knowledge of the Court

Respondents' rating of the Court	Wisconsin Survey, 1966[a] Knowledge of the Court		
	High	Medium	Low
Very good/good	54%	65%	64%
Fair	28	29	33
Poor	18	7	4
Total	100%	101%	101%
N =	92	196	221

Type of support	Seattle Survey, 1965[b] Read or heard about the Court in last year?	
	Yes	No
Court Supporter	51.7%	49.0%
Neutral	14.9	41.6
Critic	33.3	9.4
Total	99.9%	100.0%
N =	222	96

[a] *Source:* Dolbeare, "Public Views," p. 204.
[b] *Source:* Kessel, "Public Perceptions," p. 189, Table 12.

were least aware of its activities. To know the Court was not necessarily to love it.[113]

The positive support from the Court's marginal public does not assure the viability of the system. The demographic and political involvement attributes of the Court's marginal public indicate relatively low social and political power. When compared to the attentive public, they tend generally to have less formal education, less income, less political knowledge, less sense of political efficacy, and less of a propensity to vote and be politically active. These attributes hardly indicate an inclination to fight in the political arena for the Court's integrity. Perhaps the most important contribution of positive support from the marginal public, however, is in how it affects the behavior of

[113] Cf. Murphy, Tanenhaus, and Kastner, *Public Evaluations of Constitutional Courts,* pp. 41–43. The public opinion findings raise serious questions about traditional assumptions concerning the "role" of the Court as a legitimizer of the actions of government. See the extensive discussion on this matter by David Adamany, "Legitimacy, Realigning Elections, and the Supreme Court," *Wisconsin Law Review* (1973), 790–846.

political leaders. In an age when elected politicians are reportedly sensitive to public opinion polls, this relatively large positive diffuse support may discourage most politicians from initiating a drastic frontal attack on the Court (e.g., an impeachment proceeding against the Chief Justice; fundamental contraction of the Court's jurisdiction).

It is of interest to speculate whether and how the attitudes of the marginal public would be affected by a concerted propaganda campaign by those unfriendly to the Court in the Congress, the White House, and the state capitals. On the one hand, because members of the marginal public are so resistant to receiving new information about the Court, one might speculate that such a campaign would only slightly affect the positive support level. On the other hand, if the message were able to penetrate the formidable perceptual barriers, it might well result—given the low intensity with which positive support attitudes are held and the paucity of information upon which they are based—in the formation of new negative attitudes. It is likely that a crucial variable is the extent to which the controversial Court policies are perceived by the opinion-holders to affect them and the extent to which the policies require opinion holders to change their behavior patterns.[114]

Perhaps a better indication of the relative weakness of support attitudes of the Court's marginal public is gained by a more detailed consideration of the drop in positive support for the judicial handling of criminal defendants. This is an area where public awareness has increased sharply since 1964. It is also an area where anti-Court propaganda has been intense. To indicate how this criticism has differently affected the members of the Court's attentive and marginal publics, the rate of decline in positive support for the courts among respondents with a grade-school education (who tend to be among the Court's marginal public) and among those with a college education (who tend to be among its attentive public) is considered.[115] To indicate what is presumed to be differences in how the policies affect

[114] See the discussion in Dolbeare, "Public Views," p. 211.

[115] Murphy and Tanenhaus, "Public Opinion," pp. 367–368, note "the strength of the association between education and awareness [is strong] ($r = .44$), . . . Thirty-nine point six percent of the totally unaware group completed less than nine years of schooling and only 6.7 percent had any college work at all. For those aware of both the Court's activity and responsibilities, the comparable figures are almost reversed, 12.4 percent and 40.4 percent."

members of the public, the attitudes of those living in cities of more than 500,000 are compared with those living in rural areas under 2,500. (Inhabitants of major cities are most sensitized to crime as these cities have the highest crime rates.[116]) Since most studies seem to indicate that, at the most, local law enforcement officials have only been mildly hurt by Court decisions in their ability to make arrests and obtain convictions,[117] the statistics in Table 4.15 seem to indicate that anti-Court propaganda can significantly change support attitudes particularly (but not exclusively) within the Court's marginal public. The effect is greatest in communities where respondents presumably feel most threatened by the decisions. By 1969, then, it appears that a majority of the marginal public had joined ranks with a majority of the attentive public to deny the Court positive support particularly in the criminal procedures area. The July, 1969, Gallup survey found the smallest proportion (33 percent) of respondents giving the Court a favorable rating since such court-rating surveys were first conducted.[118]

The setting was ripe for a major assault on the Court, and in one sense the Nixon Administration actually mounted such an assault by successfully forcing Justice Fortas off the Court. Anti-Court sentiment was thereafter politically exploited through use of the law-and-order issue and the avowed nomination of conservatives to fill Court vacancies. When the dust finally settled, four appointments later,

[116] *Uniform Crime Report for the United States* (Washington, D.C.: Federal Bureau of Investigation, 1968), pp. 96–97, Table 6. Victimization surveys conducted by the Census Bureau for the Law Enforcement Assistance Administration in thirteen cities found that residents experienced at least two or three times more crime than was reported by the police. The results of the study were reported in some detail in *The New York Times*, April 15, 1974, pp. 1, 51. A Gallup survey reported in 1973 that 60 percent of the residents of the center cities said there was *more* crime in their areas than in the previous year. Half of the residents of the suburbs and 45 percent of the residents in the rural areas thought that crime had increased over the year (*New York Times*, January 16, 1973, p. 15). Perhaps most to the point, a national Gallup crime victimization survey taken in December, 1972, revealed that one out of three residents of central cities had been the victim of a major crime (robbed, mugged, suffered property damage) during the previous twelve months. The figure was about one out of five for residents of suburbs and about one out of eight for residents of rural communities. See *Current Opinion*, 1 (1973), 24.

[117] An early study that established this point was "Interrogations in New Haven: The Impact of *Miranda*," *Yale Law Journal*, 76 (1967), 1521–1648.

[118] *Current Opinion*, 1 (1973), 91.

Table 4.15 Decreasing support for courts in handling of criminals (by respondent's education and size of respondent's community, 1965–1969)

Type of respondent/ response	August 1965	Survey February 1968	February 1969
College education			
Courts treat criminals:			
Too harshly	1%	3%	3%
Not harshly enough	62	58	67
About right	28	20	18
No opinion	9	19	12
Total	100%	100%	100%
Grade school education			
Courts treat criminals:			
Too harshly	2%	3%	2%
Not harshly enough	56	63	78
About right	26	21	12
No opinion	16	13	8
Total	100%	100%	100%
Large urban community[a]			
Courts treat criminals:			
Too harshly	2%	2%	2%
Not harshly enough	63	68	78
About right	22	12	9
No opinion	13	18	11
Total	100%	100%	100%
Rural community[b]			
Courts treat criminals:			
Too harshly	1%	1%	2%
Not harshly enough	59	58	70
About right	30	24	19
No opinion	10	17	9
Total	100%	100%	100%

Source: AIPO Reports, no. 4 (September 1965); no. 3 (March 1968); and no. 45 (March 1969).

[a] "Large urban," defined in 1965 survey as cities with a population of 500,000 and over. In 1968 and 1969 surveys, "large urban" defined as cities with a population of one million and over.

[b] "Rural" defined as under 2,500 population.

President Nixon had his Nixon Court. With the Court's major shift to the right, particularly in the criminal-procedures area, and the absence of the Court as a major partisan issue in the 1970s, it is reasonable to expect an increase in positive support. In terms of specific support, with the Court's attentive public one could expect that many favorable supporters have become opponents of Court policies and former foes have become more favorable in their attitudes. Diffuse support also can be expected to be affected but less dramatically since the phenomenon of negative specific–positive diffuse support still presumably occurs.[119] The July, 1973, Gallup survey in fact showed an increase (4 percent) in favorable ratings of the Court from the previous 1969 survey and a decrease (8 percent) from the 1969 survey of the proportion giving the Court the poorest rating. A Survey Research Center study conducted during October and November, 1973, reported the results of a national sample survey in which people were asked how good a job each of fifteen major institutions was doing for the country. The Supreme Court was found to be the governmental institution given the highest rating and was seen as having the highest integrity.[120]

The Court's longevity as a bastion of a particular political philosophy is not secure during periods of low specific support. However, attempts to change the Court through either blatantly or deviously untraditional means will probably not only fail, but may even be counterproductive for the attacker. A widespread lack of popular positive support for a particular set of justices should not be taken as indicative of a lack of positive support for the Court as an independent institution. It is just this error that President Franklin Roosevelt seems to have made in pushing his 1937 court-packing plan.

[119] See Murphy, Tanenhaus, and Kastner, *Public Evaluations of Constitutional Courts,* p. 46, Table 11. Note there is the suggestion in data presented by Dolbeare, "Public Views," p. 209, that believers in the judicial myth (i.e., that judging is a mechanical business and that Supreme Court judges "decide cases strictly on the basis of what the Constitution says") have a greater tendency than nonbelievers to give the Court positive diffuse support. Presumably as long as there are believers in the myth, the Court is assured of some positive diffuse support. The Casey study, "The Supreme Court and Myth," suggests that members of the attentive public are the ones likely to be the myth-holders, thus the Court has perhaps more leeway in terms of diffuse support than its friendly critics have feared.

[120] *Institute for Social Research Newsletter,* 1 (1974), 8.

Roosevelt took the considerable evidence of widespread popular and congressional dissatisfaction with the "nine old men" of the Supreme Court as indicative of low support for the Court as an institution. His court-reform program was (and was almost immediately perceived as) not just an attack on the anti-New Deal justices, but also an attack on the Court's independence and decision-making procedures. The consequences for Roosevelt's own support were significant. Not only did he not get his plan passed, but, by pushing it, he provided a rallying point for his previously disorganized opposition.

President Roosevelt was not the only political authority to respond to the 1937 Court's low input of positive support. At least two crucial members of that Court, Hughes and Roberts, also seemed sensitive to its support problems. While FDR was attacking the Court as unresponsive to the nation's needs, they joined with the Court's liberal bloc of Stone, Brandeis, and Cardozo to renounce the Court's laissez-faire economic policies in favor of more progovernment policies.

The 1937 switch as an illustration of judicial responsiveness to a negative input of support raises a considerable number of questions as to the linkage between support input and judicial policy making. To say the least, the degree of negative support the Court received during the early New Deal, especially in 1936, was dramatic. It was transmitted to the Court not only from Congress and the White House, but also through the mass media, law reviews, and the statements and writings of a number of scholars at universities and their law schools. This input of negative support was reinforced by a number of strongly negative feedback actions taken by the President, Congress, state legislatures, and the electorate. FDR's court-reform plan itself was such a feedback action. So also was the overwhelming reelection of FDR and his congressional colleagues in 1936 after a campaign in which the New Deal was the major issue. In the same vein were the actions of Congress and state legislatures, which passed new economic regulatory and social welfare legislation after their first attempts had been rejected as unconstitutional.

The 1937 episode represents what in systems terms one ought to expect to be the normal responsiveness of authorities to falling positive support. However, it appears that such responsiveness is at best episodic. Such falling support does not produce the automatic alterations in policy output in the federal judicial system to the extent that occurs with other social and political systems. This raises the fundamental question of what are the determinants of the judicial conversion process by which inputs are processed to produce policy outputs, which is the subject of the following chapter.

FIVE
CONVERSION

THE study of judicial conversion is the study of decision making whereby input is processed by judges into output. How and why judges decide the way they do has for many decades held a certain fascination for lawyers, political scientists, and even judges themselves. We first examine the more traditional concepts and briefly describe the development of the field of judicial behavior which has used more advanced tools for the systematic study of conversion. The subsequent sections discuss various behavioral approaches and the facets of the conversion process that are explored by utilizing them.

FROM TRADITIONALISM TO BEHAVIORALISM

The oldest and most discredited explanation of conversion has been derisively called "mechanical jurisprudence." This was, for over a century, the official and widely accepted explanation of judicial and, notably, Supreme Court behavior. In the words of President Calvin Coolidge, "Men do not make laws. They do but discover them."[1] Judges in an exact, logical, and absolutely detached manner merely "find" the law that already exists and apply it mechanically to the case in hand. Or to use another metaphor, the judge is a legal slot machine. You put in the case and out comes *the law*, law that is only

[1] As quoted by Jerome Frank in *Law and the Modern Mind* (Garden City, N.Y.: Anchor, 1963), p. 35, n. 1.

discovered and known by the oracle–slot-machine judge. Justice Owen Roberts restated this view of judicial conversion in an often quoted passage in the important case of *United States* v. *Butler*[2] which declared the Agricultural Adjustment Act of 1933 unconstitutional. Roberts observed that "This Court neither approves nor condemns any legislative policy. Its delicate and difficult office is to ascertain and declare whether the legislation is in accordance with, or in contravention of, the provisions of the Constitution." How does the Court make this determination? Roberts suggested that what the Court does is "to lay the article of the Constitution which is invoked beside the statute which is challenged and to decide whether the latter squares with the former."

At odds with the notions of mechanical jurisprudence were the outspoken lawyers and judges associated with the so-called legal realism movement. Paternity is often attributed to Oliver Wendell Holmes who for a time before the turn of the century stood in the forefront of the assault on mechanical jurisprudence. Soon he was joined by others who developed the thesis that judging is a human process and judges have their own notions of public policy that are often transformed into their decisions. These scholars emphasized the wide range of discretion at the disposal of judges. They emphasized the opportunities for exercising choice in the interpretation or application of facts, statutes, the Constitution, rules of procedure and precedent. The high point of legal realism was in the 1930s. The major legal realists undertook to study judges, courts, and justice to "see it as it works."[3]

The legal realists of the 1930s, for the most part lawyers, constituted a small minority of the legal profession. Their common bond was a rejection of traditional jurisprudence and an ardent desire to grasp the reality of the judicial process. Most were what have been called "rule skeptics."[4] They were skeptical of the legal rules and legal norms ostensibly used by judges. Instead they were concerned with what was actually being decided, and the values being promoted by the judges. Another type of legal realist was the "fact skeptic," a

[2] 297 U.S. 1 (1936) at 62–63.

[3] The phrase was coined by Karl Llewellyn. See his *The Common Law Tradition: Deciding Appeals* (Boston: Little, Brown, 1960), pp. 508–510.

[4] See the discussion in Wilfred E. Rumble, *American Legal Realism* (Ithaca, N.Y.: Cornell University Press, 1968), Chap. 2.

position developed by Jerome Frank.[5] At the heart of this approach was a skepticism about the ability of trial courts to discover "facts." According to Frank each judge has his own set of idiosyncrasies that cannot help but affect his performance as a judge. The process of conducting a trial and the facts that emerge are in large part attributable to the judge: his likes and dislikes; what he had for breakfast; his relations with his wife and family; his anxieties, hopes, and aspirations; religious, social, economic, and political beliefs. For Frank each judge was unique, and the variables associated with each judge's decision making were viewed as so complex that without knowledge gained from a psychoanalysis of the judge it would be impossible to predict judicial behavior.[6]

Frank implicitly rejected empirical research on decision making. Some rule skeptics did attempt such research, but with few exceptions their work remained crude, as the realists were not concerned with developing rigorous methodology and theory to guide their research. Legal realism made little impact on the law schools, and business has gone on, at least until recently, more or less as usual.[7] Today the stock in trade at many law schools is the case analysis approach with its underlying assumption that case law develops rationally so that one may trace the logical connection between one case and the next. The focus is on legal logic and not the judges themselves. The basic implication is that *stare decisis* is the rule, not the exception, and as such guides judicial conversion. Much legal scholarship is thus in the more traditional vein: that is, a concern with case law in specific areas of the law, in particular, how the law developed or should develop; professional criticism of court policies concerning the standards, precedents, or reasoning of courts; or criticism of the unarticulated changes in policy. This scholarship, of course, is a source of feedback and is undoubtedly useful in pointing the way to policy change or even change of the regime rules.

About the same time that legal realism was in its heyday, the political science profession was undergoing an analogous upheaval that was destined to change the discipline radically.[8] Political science tra-

---

[5] See the discussion in Rumble, *American Legal Realism,* Chap. 3.

[6] Frank, *Law and the Modern Mind,* pp. 398–399.

[7] Cf. Rumble, *American Legal Realism,* pp. 238–239.

[8] See Albert Somit and Joseph Tanenhaus, *The Development of American Political Science* (Boston: Allyn & Bacon, 1967), Chaps. 9–14.

ditionalism, the exclusive emphasis on formal rules and institutions, was challenged by political science "realists" who insisted that the first order of the discipline is to focus on how politics and our political institutions really work. How are decisions in fact really made? Who gets what, when, and how? This quest for realism among political scientists was accompanied by the development and increasing use of quantitative and statistical techniques as well as a commitment to the scientific method.[9]

Political scientists who specialized in the field of constitutional or public law had largely followed the lead of the legal academics, and the thrust of their work was on legalistic analyses of cases. An increasing number of scholars, however, no doubt influenced by the trends in the other areas of the discipline, began to produce judicial biographies, political histories of the Supreme Court, case studies of particular decisions, descriptive studies of the social characteristics and selection processes of judges and other participants in the judicial process, and descriptive analyses of the activities of interest groups in their attempts to influence decision making.[10]

The breakthrough that began the development of the behavioral approach to judicial conversion was achieved by Professor C. Herman Pritchett who began where the legal realists left off.[11] His attention

[9] At the heart of the scientific method is a concern with assertions that can be proven true or false by empirically verifiable procedures. In order for an assertion or hypothesis to be testable, it is necessary to establish operational definitions of the phenomenon about which an hypothesis or hypotheses have been formulated. Typically, five steps or procedures are involved in the scientific method: (1) identifying a particular research question; (2) specifying one or more hypotheses; (3) gathering data that test the hypothesis; (4) analyzing the findings in terms of the hypothesis; and (5) assessing the findings in the context of other knowledge. See the discussion of these five steps by S. Sidney Ulmer in "Scientific Method and the Judicial Process," American Behavioral Scientist, 7 (December 1963), 21–22, 35–38.

[10] These areas of concern, along with an interest in the processing of cases at all court levels and the impact of court decisions, represent much of the research in the judicial area undertaken by political scientists in recent years. See David J. Danelski, "Public Law: The Field," International Encyclopedia of the Social Sciences, 13 (1968), 175–183; Glendon Schubert, "Judicial Process and Behavior, 1963–1971," in James A. Robinson (ed.), Political Science Annual, Vol. III (Indianapolis: Bobbs-Merrill, 1972), pp. 73–280.

[11] C. Herman Pritchett, "Divisions of Opinion among Justices of the U.S. Supreme Court, 1939–1941," American Political Science Review, 35 (1941), 890–898; and his two books, The Roosevelt Court: A Study in Judicial Politics and Values 1937–1947 (New York: Macmillan, 1948), and Civil Liberties and the Vinson Court (Chicago: University of Chicago Press, 1954).

was on the Supreme Court, and his concern was with the voting alignments and policy preferences of the judges. His theory of conversion was that all courts, but especially the Supreme Court, are political agencies and that judges are political actors whose attitudes toward the substantive issues are often decisive in shaping their votes and opinions. Pritchett focused on nonunanimously decided Supreme Court cases because they offered the most compelling evidence that the judges "are operating on different assumptions, that their inarticulate major premises are dissimilar, that their value systems are differently constructed and weighted, that their political, economic, and social views contrast in important respects."[12]

In the late 1950s Glendon Schubert, Joseph Tanenhaus, Sidney Ulmer, and others began to build on Pritchett's work and also to develop new methodologies for the study of judicial behavior. They were innovators in their use of cumulative scaling of judicial decisions and the use of the phi coefficient, factor analysis, and other statistical techniques to analyze judicial behavior. By the late 1960s, attention had turned to other American courts aside from the Supreme Court, further development of theories of judicial behavior (some by way of causal models), and the use of techniques developed to study the Supreme Court to study the courts of other countries.[13] These trends have continued well into the 1970s.

ATTITUDES AND DECISION MAKING

The attitudinal approach to conversion is the approach perhaps most identified with the field of judicial behavior. From the pioneering work of Pritchett to the work of the current generation of behavioral scholars, discovery and analysis of patterns of behavior that could be shown to represent judicial attitudes has been of primary research interest.[14] Voting behavior of individual judges is studied in order to discern regularities of behavior that might exist. The central hunch is that attitudes and values guide voting behavior and that the votes in

[12] Pritchett, *Roosevelt Court*, p. xii.

[13] See, for example, Glendon Schubert, "Behavioral Jurisprudence," *Law and Society Review*, 2 (1968), 407–428; and C. Herman Pritchett, "Public Law and Judicial Behavior," *Journal of Politics*, 30 (1968), 480–509. Also see Glendon Schubert and David J. Danelski (eds.), *Comparative Judicial Behavior* (New York: Oxford University Press, 1969); and Schubert, "Judicial Process and Behavior, 1963–1971."

[14] *Ibid.*

specific cases—what the authorities actually do—are more important in revealing their attitudes and values than are the rationalizations they provide in their written opinions telling us why they voted as they did.

This focus on *voting* behavior as providing the clue to judges' attitudes and values does not necessarily mean that written opinions are considered irrelevant for these concerns. They can and have been used as data for behavioral analysis,[15] and the computer content analysis method in particular has shown some promise of discerning underlying attitudinal dimensions.[16]

Among the principal methodologies used individually or in concert in judicial attitudinal research are bloc analysis and Guttman scaling. Many studies have used other statistical tools as well. Some of the major studies using these various methods will be briefly discussed particularly in terms of research concerning federal judges. It should be acknowledged, however, that blocs, scale patterns, or issue voting cannot be used to conclusively *prove* (in the scientific sense of the term) the attitudinal hypothesis as there is no measure of judges' attitudes and values independent of their votes. Thus we cannot say that attitudes *cause* votes when we have defined those attitudes in terms of the same votes. Nevertheless, it is clear that if the attitudinal hypothesis were invalid, neither repeated findings of bloc voting, scale patterns, nor consistent issue-oriented voting would be found. One, therefore, can have a firm basis for evaluating the attitudinal hypothesis taking into account two decades of research results from numerous studies.

Bloc analysis

C. Herman Pritchett was the first to study systematically judicial bloc voting. In his analyses of the Supreme Court, he theorized that atti-

---

[15] See, for example, Glendon Schubert, "Jackson's Judicial Philosophy: An Exploration in Value Analysis," *American Political Science Review*, 59 (1965), 940–963 and his "The Dimensions of Decisional Response: Opinion and Voting Behavior of the Australian High Court," in Joel B. Grossman and Joseph Tanenhaus (eds.), *Frontiers of Judicial Research* (New York: Wiley, 1969), pp. 163–195.

[16] See Werner F. Grunbaum, "Analytical and Simulation Models for Explaining Judicial Decision-Making," in Grossman and Tanenhaus (eds.), *Frontiers of Judicial Research*, pp. 307–334 and his "A Quantitative Analysis of the 'Presidential Ballot' Case," *Journal of Politics*, 34 (1972), 223–243. Also see Alan M. Sager, "From Brief to Decision: A Computer Simulation of the 1963 Supreme Court Term," paper presented at the 1969 Annual Meeting of the American Political Science Association.

tudes are the key to judicial conversion, that nonunanimously decided cases can best reveal attitudinal differences, and that judges with similar attitudes and values will tend to agree with each other in these cases and thus vote together forming "blocs." Pritchett analyzed the voting data in various ways, including the construction of matrices[17] of agreement scores (i.e., the percentage of nonunanimous cases in which every two-judge combination voted alike). He found two principal voting blocs, one consisting of judges who usually voted for "liberal" decisional results, and the other consisting of judges who typically opted for the more "conservative" solutions.[18]

Glendon Schubert in the late 1950s suggested refinements to Pritchett's method and introduced several indices, including the index of interagreement (i.e., the average agreement score of the justices in the hypothesized bloc).[19] In later years other methods of undertaking bloc analysis were devised and utilized.[20]

One scholar, S. Sidney Ulmer, undertook an extensive bloc analysis of the Supreme Court.[21] He began by assuming that the existence of a voting bloc at one point in time does not necessarily demonstrate that common attitudes and values account for the bloc voting phenomenon. It is possible, Ulmer suggested, for a voting bloc to represent a coalition of judges with a diversity of views who find it mu-

[17] A matrix is a rectangular array of entries by rows and columns.

[18] See the Pritchett works cited in note 11.

[19] Glendon Schubert, Quantitative Analysis of Judicial Behavior (New York: Free Press, 1959), Chap. 3.

[20] See S. Sidney Ulmer, "The Analysis of Behavior Patterns in the United States Supreme Court," Journal of Politics, 22 (1960), 629–653; Glendon Schubert, The Judicial Mind (Evanston, Ill.: Northwestern University Press, 1965); David J. Danelski, "Values as Variables in Judicial Decision-Making: Notes toward a Theory," Vanderbilt Law Review, 19 (1966), 721–740; John D. Sprague, Voting Patterns of the United States Supreme Court (Indianapolis: Bobbs-Merrill, 1968); Glendon Schubert, "Dimensions of Decisional Response." See the discussion by Walter Murphy and Joseph Tanenhaus, The Study of Public Law (New York: Random House, 1972), pp. 159–176, 190–194. Also see, H. Frank Way, "The Nixon Court: Two Models of Criminal Justice," paper presented at the Annual Meeting, A.P.S.A., 1974.

[21] S. Sidney Ulmer, "Toward a Theory of Sub-Group Formation in the United States Supreme Court," Journal of Politics, 27 (1965), 133–152. But cf. S. Sidney Ulmer, "Subset Behavior in the Supreme Court," in Sven Groennings, E. W. Kelley, and Michael Leiserson (eds.), The Study of Coalitional Behavior (New York: Holt, Rinehart and Winston, 1970), pp. 396–409; and David N. Atkinson and Dale A. Neuman, "Toward a Cost Theory of Judicial Alignments: The Case of the Truman Bloc," Midwest Journal of Political Science, 13 (1969), 271–283.

tually advantageous to vote together in the short run because, for example, they wish to dominate the Court by being on the winning side. A subgroup or bloc can be interpreted as representing common attitudes and values only if the voting bloc persists and thus has stability over time. The results of Ulmer's study of voting in non-unanimous cases decided by the Supreme Court from the 1946 term through the 1961 term are presented in Table 5.1 (along with similar analyses for some more recent terms). Ulmer found not only that

Table 5.1 Subgroups in the U.S. Supreme Court, 1946–1974 terms

	1946 (3)	
BL, MU, DO, RU	RE, BU	FR, JA, VI
	1947 (3)	
BL, MU, DO, RU	RE, BU, VI	FR, JA
	1948 (4)	
BL, DO MU, RU	RE, BU, VI	FR, JA
	1949 (3)	
BL, DO	RE, BU, VI, CL, MI	FR, JA
	1950 (4)	
BL, DO	RE, VI, CL BU, MI	FR, JA
	1951 (2)	
BL, DO, FR, JA	RE, BU, VI, CL, MI	
	1952 (4)	
BL, DO	RE, BU, MI VI, CL	FR, JA
	1953 (4)	
BL, DO	RE, BU WA, CL	FR, JA, MI
	1954–1955 (3)	
BL, DO, WA, CL	RE, BU, MI	FR, HA
	1956 (3)	
BL, DO, WA, BR	RE, CL	FR, HA, BU
	1957 (3)	
BL, DO, WA, BR	WH, BU, CL	FR, HA
	1958–1961 (2)	
BL, DO, WA, BR	WH, CL, ST, FR, HA	
	1962 (3)	
BL, DO, WA, BR, GO	WI, ST	CL, HA
	1968 (2)	
BL*, DO, WA, BR, MA, FO	WI, ST, HA	
	1969 (3)	
DO, BR, MA	WI, HA	ST, BG, BL*
	1970 (2)	
DO, BR, MA		ST, BG, BL*, HA, WI, BM
	1971 (2)	
DO, BR, MA, ST		BG, WI, BM, PO, RN
	1972 (2)	
DO, BR, MA		BG, WI, BM, PO, RN, ST

	1973 (3)	
DO, BR, MA	ST, PO, WI	BM, BG, RN
	1974 (2)	
DO, BR, MA		BM, BG, RN, ST, PO, WI

Legend:

BG	Burger	FR	Frankfurter	RE	Reed
BL	Black	GO	Goldberg	RN	Rehnquist
BM	Blackmun	HA	Harlan	RU	Rutledge
BR	Brennan	JA	Jackson	ST	Stewart
BU	Burton	MA	Marshall	WA	Warren
CL	Clark	MI	Minton	WH	Whittaker
DO	Douglas	MU	Murphy	WI	White
FO	Fortas	PO	Powell	VI	Vinson

Source: The 1946–1961 subgroups from S. Sidney Ulmer, "Toward a Theory of Sub-Group Formation in the United States Supreme Court," *Journal of Politics,* 27 (1965), p. 146, Table 1. Note that the positions of subgroups in the table should *not* be taken to mean that they were either "left," "right," or "center," in terms of their attitudes and values. The 1962 and 1968–1974 subgroups were derived from voting behavior on civil liberties cases only.

*Black's placement in this subgroup is an artifact of the method (the McQuitty technique) that requires that each justice be placed with the justice with whom he has the greatest correlation. Justice Black, however, exhibited such idiosyncratic behavior that in no meaningful sense can he be said to have "belonged" with a subgroup. For more on Justice Black see note 22 in the text.

voting blocs occurred during each term of the Court, but that there was a large extent of stability in the alignments over time. Although the nonunanimous cases studied covered a wide variety of issues, Ulmer found that the voting blocs actually voted together for the most part in a large proportion of nonunanimous decisions. Ulmer concluded that common attitudes and values underlie the formation of voting blocs. As Table 5.1 suggests, the blocs of more recent years continue to demonstrate enduring stability of membership, although there has been some fluctuation when new members have joined the Court.[22]

[22] One obvious exception was the bloc and voting behavior of Justice Hugo Black. Justice Black's voting behavior during the last half-dozen terms in which he sat was markedly different than his previous civil libertarian voting record. The annual surveys published by the American Jewish Congress demonstrated this. Prior to the 1963 term, Black was second only to Justice Douglas in his support of civil liberties as measured by the simple percentage of votes each term favoring civil liberties. In the 1963 and 1964 terms, Black moved to third place. In the 1965 and 1966 terms, he occupied fifth place. By the end of the 1967 term, Black was recorded in seventh place, and after the 1968 term, he earned placement in ninth place (i.e.,

It is beyond serious question today that the judges of the Supreme Court have their own conceptions of public policy and that their attitudes and values affect the thrust of their decision making. Bloc analysis of the Supreme Court has been instrumental not only in specifically demonstrating differences of views on the Court but in suggesting their magnitude. The four conservative Nixon appointees assure that there will be substantial cleavages manifested by voting blocs on the Supreme Court for years to come.

Bloc analysis of the courts of appeals has also repeatedly uncovered evidence of voting blocs on these courts,[23] lending further credence to the attitudinal approach to *judicial* and not just Supreme Court conversion.

One further word about bloc analysis is in order. The existence of voting blocs *suggests* that judicial attitudes are instrumental for judi-

---

the Justice *least* sympathetic to claims of civil liberties during the 1968 term). (As cited by Wallace Mendelson, "Hugo Black and Judicial Discretion," *Political Science Quarterly*, 85 (1970), 38–39.) Interestingly, in his last two terms (which coincided with the first two terms of the Nixon Court), Black was the most liberal of the *non*-liberal wing of the Court.

Black's shift from liberal to idiosyncratic conservative and his shift in bloc alignment as noted in Table 5.1 has met with conflicting explanations. Black's defenders found consistency in his behavior. See, for example, Mendelson, "Hugo Black"; A. E. D. Howard, "Mr. Justice Black: The Negro Protest Movement and the Rule of Law," *Virginia Law Review*, 53 (1967), 1030–1090; John M. Harlan, "Mr. Justice Black—Remarks of a Colleague," *Harvard Law Review*, 81 (1967), 1–3; Howard Ball, *The Vision and the Dream of Justice Hugo L. Black* (University: University of Alabama Press, 1974). Black defended himself in *A Constitutional Faith* (New York: Knopf, 1968). Also see S. Sidney Ulmer, "The Longitudinal Behavior of Hugo Lafayette Black: Parabolic Support for Civil Liberties, 1937–1971," *Florida State Law Review*, 1 (1973), 131–158. But cf. Glendon Schubert, *The Constitutional Polity* (Boston: Boston University Press, 1970), pp. 118–129. Note that Ulmer has argued in general that "no judge exhibits absolutely constant behavior patterns from one year to the next . . . [and] that over a long-enough period, marginal changes can lead cumulatively to major change in judge or behavior." See S. Sidney Ulmer, "Dimensionality and Change in Judicial Behavior," in James F. Herndon and Joseph L. Bernd (eds.), *Mathematical Applications in Political Science, VII* (Charlottesville: University Press of Virginia, 1974), p. 66.

[23] See the two studies by Sheldon Goldman, "Conflict and Consensus in the United States Courts of Appeals," *Wisconsin Law Review* (1968), 461–482 and "Conflict on the U.S. Courts of Appeals 1965–1971: A Quantitative Analysis," *University of Cincinnati Law Review*, 42 (1973), 635–658. Also see Burton M. Atkins, "Decision-Making Rules and Judicial Strategy on the United States Courts of Appeals," *Western Political Quarterly*, 25 (1972), 626–642 and Charles M. Lamb, "Warren Burger and the Insanity Defense: Judicial Philosophy and Voting Behavior on a U.S. Court of Appeals," *American University Law Review*, 24 (1974), 91–128.

cial conversion. The existence of voting blocs, however, does *not* imply that judges consider themselves members of a bloc, or that they caucus to discuss strategy, or that the bloc assumes a life of its own with bloc loyalties independent of attitudes affecting voting behavior. The assumption is simply that judges who have similar attitudes and values independently examine the issues before them and then vote alike. As one critic of bloc analysis concedes, bloc analysis "may still be a useful tool in describing the commonality of views shared by Justices."[24] However, the technique has a major drawback in that it can only provide a crude measure of attitudes and values. No account is taken of the variation in the case stimuli and thus the variations of the voting responses. The methodology of Guttman scaling, on the other hand, is attuned to this problem and has been used by students of judicial behavior for precisely this purpose.

Guttman scaling

Guttman scaling, sometimes referred to as cumulative scaling or scalogram analysis, was first developed by Louis Guttman in the early 1940s to determine whether a series of attitude questions on interview schedules measured the same underlying attitude.[25] Guttman suggested that if the questions in fact tap the same underlying attitudinal dimension, then the questions and responses can be arranged so that there is an attitudinal continuum indicating varying degrees of intensity of the underlying dimension. This pattern of responses is a *scale* and as such contains certain properties. We are able to determine where each question (i.e., stimulus) falls on the attitudinal continuum. We can also determine the break-off point of each respondent, that is, at what point the stimulus will produce a negative response in terms of the underlying attitudinal dimension. The scale is cumulative in that it represents a continuum and each item is ordinally related (i.e., contains more, less, or the same) to the items above and below it on the scale. Perhaps the most interesting property of a scale is that once you know a respondent's scale score, you can exactly predict his response to the items in the scale or, if he did not

[24] Joel B. Grossman, "Dissenting Blocs on the Warren Court: A Study in Judicial Role Behavior," *Journal of Politics*, 30 (1968), 1089.

[25] See the discussion and materials cited in Schubert, *Quantitative Analysis*, Chap. 5. In general see Gary M. Maranell (ed.), *Scaling: A Sourcebook for Behavioral Scientists* (Chicago: Aldine, 1974).

respond to certain items, what his responses ought to have been were he attitudinally consistent.

The conventional example of a scale is one in which the questions relate to the respondent's height, and the underlying dimension is thus height. For example, the following questions will normally produce a perfect scale:

1. Are you five feet tall or more?
2. Are you five feet, eight inches, tall or more?
3. Are you six feet tall or more?

These responses fall on a continuum. If we know the respondent's scale score (derived from his scale position which is fixed by the last consistent positive response) we can accurately predict his responses to the questions as well as fill in nonresponses.

Typically with attitude measurement the empirically obtained pattern of response differs from the perfect scale pattern because of a variety of reasons. For example, the respondent misunderstood or misinterpreted the question or he had great difficulty deciding how to respond. It is useful then to be able to measure the extent to which the empirically obtained scale corresponds to the perfect scale and indeed to formulate a criterion to determine when a pattern of responses can be said to represent a scale. Guttman proposed the coefficient of reproducibility (CR) for these tasks.[26] A CR of 0.90 (90 percent reproducibility) or more was suggested as indicating that the response pattern was a scale characterized by "unidimensionality," that is, a common attitudinal dimension.

Glendon Schubert took the lead in developing Guttman scaling for the analysis of Supreme Court voting behavior.[27] What Schubert did was to consider the cases as representing questions and the votes (not the opinions) of the justices to be the responses. Unanimously decided cases are eliminated from the scales, and in practice decisions with only one dissenting vote are eliminated from the computa-

[26] The coefficient of reproducibility is 1 minus the number of inconsistent responses (in terms of a perfect scale) divided by the number of items scored. CR measures the extent that one is able to correctly reproduce the responses from the respondents' scale positions or scale scores. See the discussion in Schubert, *Quantitative Analysis*, pp. 271–272.

[27] See Schubert, *Quantitative Analysis*, pp. 269–270, for references to other early work in adapting Guttman scaling for judicial research.

tions of CR to decrease the likelihood that CR will be spuriously high. In addition to CR other measures of scalability have been devised such as the coefficient of scalability (S) which takes into account all inconsistent responses and the maximum number of opportunities for inconsistent votes.[28]

Before a scalogram is constructed, it is necessary to hypothesize the existence of an attitude underlying the cases. The hypothesized attitude should be plausible; that is, it should make some sense to begin with and should not be trivial (in order to reduce the possibility of constructing a spurious scale).

Through the use of cumulative scaling of voting responses, Schubert, Ulmer, Danelski, Spaeth, and other students of judicial behavior have presented ample evidence *suggesting* that the justices have varying attitudes toward the substantive issues before them.[29] It has been fairly well established that, at least since 1946, two major underlying attitudinal dimensions have characterized most Supreme Court voting behavior in nonunanimously decided cases. They have been represented by two scales; the C (for civil liberties) and the E (for economic liberalism). The C scale, according to Schubert, contains all cases in which the primary issues involved a conflict between individual rights and liberties and governmental authorities.[30] The E scale, Schubert has suggested, contains cases whose underlying characteristic is that they involve "an underdog economic relationship . . . conflicts of interest between the economically affluent and the economically underprivileged."[31] The C and E scales for the 1973 term

[28] See the discussion in Schubert, *Judicial Mind*, pp. 79–81.

[29] Glendon Schubert, in particular, has developed an attitudinal or (as he calls it) a *psychometric model* of judicial conversion and has constructed an elaborate and sophisticated methodology with which to test it. See *Judicial Mind* and also his *The Judicial Mind Revisited: Psychometric Analysis of Supreme Court Ideology* (New York: Oxford University Press, 1974). Simply stated, the psychometric model considers cases to be stimuli and judicial votes to be responses that represent attitudes toward the substantive issues. What is important is the nature of the stimulus and the point where it falls along the value continuum as well as the individual judge's attitude and its point on the value continuum. For an extensive consideration of Schubert's extensive contributions see Fred Kort, "The Works of Glendon Schubert: The History of a Subdiscipline," *The Political Science Reviewer*, 4 (1974), 193–227.

[30] See the discussion in Schubert, *Judicial Mind*, pp. 99–127. The different types of civil liberties cases are discussed in *ibid.*, Chap. 6.

[31] *Ibid.*, pp. 127–128; also see pp. 127–146. Types of economic liberalism cases are discussed in *ibid.*, Chap. 6.

Table 5.2   1973 term, C scale

Cases	D	Br	M	S	W	P	Bl	Bu	R	Totals
94/1160	x									1–8
94/1263	x									1–8
94/1296	x									1–8
94/2080	x									1–8
94/2179	x									1–8
94/2274	x									1–8
94/2357	x									1–8
94/2253	x	x								2–7
94/2997	x	x								2–7
94/19	x	x	x							3–6
94/396	x	x	x							3–6
94/467	x	x	x							3–6
94/488	x	x	x							3–6
94/613	x	x	x							3–6
94/700	x	x	x							3–6
94/977	x	x	x							3–6
94/988	x	x	x							3–6
94/1179	x	x	x							3–6
94/1274	x	x	x							3–6
94/1494	x	x	x							3–6
94/1536	—	x	x							2–7
94/1780	x	x	x							3–6
94/1868	x	x	x							3–6
94/2116	—	x	x							2–7
94/2437	x	x	x							3–6
94/2485	x	x	x							3–6
94/2655	x	x	x							3–6
94/2963	x	x	x							3–6
94/3039	x	x	x							3–6
94/1734	—	x	x		x					3–6
94/2532	x	—	x			x				3–6
94/1323	x	x	x		x					4–5
94/1347	x	x	x			x				4–5
94/2800	x	x	x		x					4–5
94/2811	x	x	x		x					4–5
94/2416	x	x	x		x					4–5
94/3112	x	x	x		x					4–5
94/1234	x	x	x	x						4–5
94/1849	x	x	x	x						4–5
94/2464	x	x	x	x						4–5
94/2547	x	x	*	x						3–5
94/2887	x	x	x	x						4–5
94/2714	—	x	x	x	x					4–5
94/645	x	x	x	x					x	5–4
94/2191	x	x	x	x		*	x			5–3
94/2727	x	x	x	x	x	x				6–3
94/17	x	x	x	x	x					5–4

Table 5.2 1973 term, C scale, continued

Cases	D	Br	M	S	W	P	Bl	Bu	R	Totals
94/1820	x	x	x	x	x					5-4
94/2687	x	x	x	—	x	x				5-4
94/326	x	x	x	x	x	x				6-3
94/970	x	x	x	x	x	x				6-3
94/1228	x	x	x	x	x	x				6-3
94/1242	x	x	x	x	x	x				6-3
94/664	x	x	x	x	—	x	x			6-3
94/791	x	x	x	x	x	x	x			7-2
94/2290	x	x	x	x	x	—	x	x		7-2
94/303	x	x	x	x	x	x	—	x		7-2
94/740	x	x	x	x	x	x	—	x		7-2
94/1105	x	x	x	x	—	x	x	x		7-2
94/1076	x	x	x	x	x	x	x	x		8-1
94/2098	x	x	x	x	x	x	x	x		8-1
94/2496	x	x	x	x	x	x	x	x		8-1
94/2697	x	x	x	x	x	x	x	x		8-1
94/2842	x	x	x	x	—	x	x	—	x	7-2
Totals	60-4	56-8	54-9	26-38	19-45	19-44	13-51	8-56	2-62 / 257-317	257-317 / 574
Scale positions	64	57	55	27	18	16	11	9	1	
Scale scores	1.000	0.781	0.719	-0.156	-0.438	-0.500	-0.656	-0.719	-0.969	

$$CR = 1 - \frac{26}{475} = 0.945 \qquad\qquad S = 1 - \frac{26}{108} = 0.759$$

Legend:

D	Douglas	M	Marshall	Br	Brennan
S	Stewart	P	Powell	Bl	Blackmun
R	Rehnquist	Bu	Burger	W	White

* nonparticipation
x consistent vote in support of civil liberties claim
<u>x</u> inconsistent vote in support of civil liberties claim
   (blank) represents consistent negative vote
— inconsistent negative vote

Case citations from *Supreme Court Reporter* advance sheets. The numbers preceding the slash bar refer to the volume number; the numbers following the slash bar refer to the page citations.

Table 5.3 1973 term, E scale

Cases	D	Br	M	W	S	Bl	Bu	P	R	Totals
94/334	x									1-8
94/629	x									1-8
94/2157	x									1-8
94/2236	x									1-8
94/495	—	x		x̲	x̲					3-6
94/959	x	x	x							3-6
94/2140	x	x	x							3-6
94/1146	—	x	x			*		*		2-5
94/1151	—	x	x			*		*		2-5
94/427	x	x	x	x						4-5
94/2856	*	x	x	x						3-5
94/1186	x	x	x	x						4-5
94/2449	x	x	x	x						4-5
94/2578	x	x	x	x						4-5
94/1757	—	x	x	x	x					4-5
94/1895	x	x	x	—	x					4-5
94/2737	x	x	x	—	x			x̲		5-4
94/806	x	x	x	x	—	x				5-4
94/1099	x	x	x	x	—	x	x			6-3
94/2770	x	x	x	x	x	x	x			7-2
94/2223	x	x	x	x	*	x	—	x		6-2
94/2504	x	x	x	x	x	x	x	x		8-1

	D	Br	M	W	S	Bl	Bu	P	R	Totals
Totals	17-4	18-4	17-5	12-10	5-16	6-14	3-19	3-17	0-22 / 81-111	81-111 192
Scale positions	22	18	17	13	8	5	4	2	0	
Scale scores	1.000	0.636	0.545	0.182	-0.273	-0.546	-0.636	-0.818	-1.000	

$$CR = 1 - \frac{12}{147} = 0.918 \qquad S = 1 - \frac{12}{40} = 0.700$$

are presented in Tables 5.2 and 5.3. They demonstrate the polarization that has developed on the Nixon Court.

Harold Spaeth and associates have also undertaken extensive scaling of Supreme Court decisions. Particularly noteworthy about this work is the detailed development of attitude and value theory[32] and

[32] See Harold J. Spaeth and Douglas R. Parker, "Effects of Attitude toward Situation upon Attitude toward Object," *Journal of Psychology*, 73 (1969), 173–182; Harold J. Spaeth and David J. Peterson, "The Analysis and Interpretation of Dimensionality:

Spaeth's ongoing newspaper and radio predictions of upcoming Court decisions and votes (his high rate of correct predictions has itself won media attention[33]). Spaeth's method involves the use of refined category scales that differentiate between and among subject matter (attitude toward the situation) and the litigants or interests involved (attitude toward the object). The refined category scales provide the basis for determining attitudes, while values are defined as sets of interrelated attitudes. Spaeth and associates have identified three major values for the Warren and Nixon Courts: Freedom (including rights of criminal defendants and First Amendment freedoms scales), Equality (encompassing political, economic, and racial discrimination scales), and New Dealism (covering economic activity and government regulation scales). Spaeth has made his predictions after subjectively determining what attitudes are involved in upcoming cases and the strength of the claims being made. Spaeth then compares the past behavior of the judges on the particular refined category scale and makes his predictions accordingly.[34] Spaeth has been able to correctly predict over nine out of ten decisions. Over a decade earlier Schubert, who originated a similar method, correctly predicted reapportionment cases that were then coming to the Court.[35] By successfully predicting Supreme Court voting behavior using past behavior as measured through the use of cumulative scal-

---

The Case of Civil Liberties Decision-Making," *Midwest Journal of Political Science,* 15 (1971), 415–441; Harold J. Spaeth, David B. Meltz, Gregory J. Rathjen, and Michael V. Haselswerdt, "Is Justice Blind: An Empirical Investigation of a Normative Ideal," *Law and Society Review,* 7 (1972), 119–137; and Harold J. Spaeth and David W. Rohde, *Supreme Court Decision Making* (San Francisco: Freeman, in press). Spaeth and colleagues draw heavily on the attitude and value theory developed by Milton Rokeach. See Rokeach's *Beliefs, Attitudes and Values* (San Francisco: Jossey-Bass, 1968) and his "The Nature of Attitudes," *International Encyclopedia of the Social Sciences,* 1 (1968), 449–457. In general, see Jarol B. Manheim, *The Politics within: A Primer in Political Attitudes and Behavior* (Englewood Cliffs, N.J.: Prentice-Hall, 1975). For an application of scaling and attitude and value theory to the pre-1945 Supreme Court see Donald Leavitt, "Changing Issues, Ideological and Political Influences on the U.S. Supreme Court, 1893–1945," paper presented at the 1974 Annual Meeting of the American Political Science Association.

[33] See, for example, "Computer Helps Predict Court Rulings," *New York Times,* August 15, 1971, sec. 1. p. 75; "Court Handicappers: Computer Predictions of Supreme Court Decisions," *Newsweek,* 84 (August 12, 1974), 53.

[34] Spaeth and Rohde, *Supreme Court Decision Making,* Chap. 7.

[35] Glendon Schubert, "Prediction from a Psychometric Model," in Glendon Schubert (ed.), *Judicial Behavior: A Reader in Theory and Research* (Skokie, Ill.: Rand McNally, 1964), pp. 548–587.

ing, we have still more evidence of the plausibility of the attitudinal hypothesis (although such prediction techniques make some observers uncomfortable because of the subjective aspects of identifying the strength of the case stimuli).

It should be clear, however, that only collegial courts with a constant membership are potentially suitable for scalogram analysis. The three-judge appeals court panel with shifting membership, the specially constituted ad hoc three-judge district court panel, and the single-judge district court are therefore not amenable to such analysis. Although most appeals courts occasionally decide cases *en banc* (i.e., the entire membership of the particular appeals court decides the case), such cases for most circuits are usually too infrequent to allow for meaningful cumulative scaling particularly on the E dimension. C scales, however, have been constructed for some circuits (by combining several years' worth of *en banc* cases[36]).

Guttman scaling has been the subject of some criticism,[37] in part over the criteria used to establish a valid scale and the manipulations used to achieve the least number of inconsistencies. There has also been serious question of the assumption of unidimensionality, the argument being that cases often concern many issues and that to focus on one dimension distorts the complexity and neglects the richness of "law." These charges have been answered by Glendon Schubert and Sidney Ulmer[38] (the precise rebuttal need not concern us here). What is of great importance is that all but the most adamant antibehavioralists concede that cumulative scaling is useful *at least* as the beginning of analysis. It is also apparent that the continued successful cumulative scaling of Supreme Court decisions underscores the plausibility of the attitudinal interpretation of judicial conversion.

[36] See Goldman, "Conflict on the U.S. Courts of Appeals 1965–1971," pp. 652–656. Also see Charles M. Lamb, "Warren Burger and the Insanity Defense: Judicial Philosophy and Voting Behavior on a U.S. Court of Appeals," *American University Law Review*, 24 (1974), p. 118.

[37] See, for example, Joseph Tanenhaus, "The Cumulative Scaling of Judicial Decisions," *Harvard Law Review*, 79 (1966), 1583–1594; Sprague, *Voting Patterns*, pp. 9–11, 73–77, 157–160; Edward J. H. Weissman, "Mathematical and Statistical Models of Judicial Behavior," paper presented at the 1969 Annual Meeting of the American Political Science Association, pp. 3–7.

[38] Glendon Schubert, "Ideologies and Attitudes, Academic and Judicial," *Journal of Politics*, 29 (1967), 3–41; S. Sidney Ulmer, "The Dimensionality of Judicial Voting Behavior," *Midwest Journal of Political Science*, 13 (1969), 471–483.

Other methods

The attitudinal assumption has also been tested by other methods such as simple correlational analysis of scores given to the votes of judges. This method has been used particularly for the analysis of voting behavior of lower federal court judges. One study using these methods examined the voting behavior of appeals court judges and found that there were significant positive correlations in the voting behavior of judges on various issues.[39] There was a marked tendency for a judge who tended to support the claims of the criminally prose-cuted to support the individual presenting a civil liberties claim against the actions of government, the labor union or employee in controversies with management, the underdog claim in private eco-nomic cases, and claims by the physically injured. The interpretation of these results was that a liberalism-conservatism voting syndrome exists on the appeals courts just as it does on the Supreme Court.[40] A study by Burton Atkins of voting behavior on the District of Co-lumbia circuit involved the scaling of *en banc* criminal procedures decisions and the determination of pro-defendant (liberal) and anti-defendant (conservative) judges on that broadly defined set of is-sues.[41] Atkins found that panels dominated by judges identified by the scale as liberal produced a considerably larger proportion of liberal decisions than those panels dominated by previously identi-fied conservatives. For the deep South Fifth Circuit on the racial

[39] Sheldon Goldman, "Voting Behavior on the United States Courts of Appeals, 1961–1964," *American Political Science Review*, 60 (1966), pp. 378–379 and Sheldon Goldman, "Voting Behavior on the United States Courts of Appeals Revisited," *American Political Science Review*, 69 (1975), pp. 491–506.

[40] Note that the study of ideological voting patterns has also made use of factor analysis, a mathematical technique, enabling one to extract the underlying dimen-sions in a correlation matrix. The method is a data-reduction method in that it cuts through the multitude of surface relationships to uncover the essential com-monalities. Factor analysis of a matrix of phi coefficients is an integral part of the methodology used by Schubert (see *Judicial Mind* and *Judicial Mind Revisited*). Schubert discusses another data-reduction technique, smallest space analysis, in his "Dimensions of Decisional Response," pp. 181–185. See the discussion of factor analysis in Murphy and Tanenhaus, *Study of Public Law*, pp. 208–212.

[41] Burton M. Atkins, "Decision-Making Rules and Judicial Strategy on the United States Courts of Appeals," *Western Political Quarterly*, 25 (1972), 626–642. Also see Burton M. Atkins, "Judicial Behavior and Tendencies toward Conformity in a Three Member Small Group: A Case Study of Dissent Behavior on the United States Court of Appeals," *Social Science Quarterly*, 54 (1973), 41–53.

segregation issue, Atkins and Zavoina found convincing statistical evidence suggesting that the attitudes of the judges during the tense period of the early 1960s were likely to have been taken into account by the Chief Judge of the circuit in making panel assignments in race cases.[42] Other work as well concerning the appeals courts has lent support for the attitudinal explanation of judicial voting behavior.[43]

BACKGROUNDS AND DECISION MAKING

Closely associated with the attitudinal approach to judicial conversion is the backgrounds approach. The focus of this approach is on the various socioeconomic, political, and professional backgrounds (or attributes) of judges as they may be associated with judicial behavior. The type of questions asked in background/behavior analysis are: Does it make a difference in terms of how a judge will decide cases if he is, for example, Catholic rather than Protestant? older rather than younger? a Democrat rather than a Republican? from a lower social class rather than a higher social class? has an Ivy League law school education rather than a public law school education? from a small law firm rather than a large Wall Street–type firm? The assumption has been that, just like anybody else, a judge is a product of his experiences and that a knowledge of certain backgrounds may be the key to understanding that judge's decisional behavior. The problem, of course, is to differentiate between those backgrounds that may be directly relevant for judicial behavior and those that are not. Earlier, in Chapter 3, some backgrounds of federal judges were discussed. The implication was that these were likely to be related to their decision making. This implication deserves closer scrutiny.

Essentially, background studies suggest that certain backgrounds are conducive to the formation of certain attitudes that in turn may affect the decisional behavior of the judge; that is, these backgrounds provide the foundation or the setting for the development of attitudes and values. However, each judge's attitudes and values have

[42] Burton M. Atkins and William Zavoina, "Judicial Leadership on the Court of Appeals: A Probability Analysis of Panel Assignments in Race Relations Cases on the Fifth Circuit," *American Journal of Political Science*, 18 (1974), 701–711.

[43] See the citations contained in Goldman, "Voting Behavior, 1961–1964," p. 375, n. 6; Goldman, "Conflict on the U.S. Courts of Appeals 1965–1971," p. 636, n. 3; and Goldman, "Voting Behavior Revisited," p. 491, n. 2.

been tempered by a host of experiential, institutional, and interpersonal variables once on the bench. Political party affiliation is one background variable that has been thought to be a summary variable of relevant backgrounds and attitudes. But party affiliation, as well as other attributes, has not been considered identical to attitudes or values. Nevertheless, those undertaking background/behavior analysis assume that some relationships between discrete backgrounds and judicial behavior can be found, and the testing of this has been at both the group and individual levels.

Aggregate background/behavior analysis of the Supreme Court is particularly difficult because only a small number of justices sit at any one time and generalizations from such a small group may not be too reliable. Some analysts have considered the entire past and present membership of the Supreme Court for purposes of analysis, but such attempts raise methodological problems (such as the comparability of attributes from different social and economic periods), and the results have not been conclusive.[44] Lower federal courts with large numbers of judges seem to be better suited for such analysis.

One extensive study of appeals court judges and the cases they decided during fiscal 1965 through fiscal 1971 included tests of the relationships of certain background variables to decision making.[45] The findings were that, *in the aggregate*, most of the demographic variables for the most part could not be directly related to voting behavior. Party affiliation, however, proved to have a moderately strong association with voting behavior on issues involving economic liberalism and, to a lesser extent, political liberalism. The age variable seemed to be associated to some extent with political liberalism issues and to a lesser extent with economic issues. Religion had a relatively minor association with primarily economic issues. Thus, judges who were Democrats, younger judges, and Catholics tended to be more "liberal" than those who were Republicans, older judges, and

[44] See John R. Schmidhauser, *"Stare Decisis*, Dissent, and the Backgrounds of the Justices of the Supreme Court of the United States," *University of Toronto Law Journal*, 14 (1962), 194–212. Cf. S. Sidney Ulmer, "Dissent Behavior and the Social Background of Supreme Court Justices," *Journal of Politics*, 32 (1970), 580–598 and Ulmer's study "Social Background as an Indicator to the Votes of Supreme Court Justices in Criminal Cases: 1947–1956 Terms," *American Journal of Political Science*, 17 (1973), 622–630.

[45] Goldman, "Voting Behavior Revisited."

Protestants. However, background variables were much weaker than attitudinal variables in their association with judicial behavior. The study did not downplay background variables, but rather concluded that their primary importance lies in the part they play in shaping the hierarchy of values, the philosophy, outlook, and attitudes of *individual* judges.

Three studies of federal district court judges also tested the nexus of backgrounds to behavior. Kenneth Vines conducted a study concerned with southern district court judges and their decisional behavior in cases involving Negro civil rights. He found somewhat of a tendency for southern judges with cosmopolitan backgrounds (e.g., they were born outside the state in which they served as district judges, they went to a law school in a state other than the one in which they sat as judges, they had ties and contacts outside the district) rendered more pro–civil rights decisions than those without such backgrounds.[46] Kenneth Dolbeare studied the voting behavior of a sample of federal district judges situated in urban areas but did not discover any relationship between backgrounds (including party affiliation) and decisional behavior.[47] Thomas Walker's study of federal district judges found little association between party and civil liberties voting behavior.[48]

When the unit of analysis is the individual and not the group, the relationship of backgrounds to behavior becomes more impressive. The mainstay of such analysis is judicial biography. One assessment of fifteen major judicial biographies (all but two of them concerned Supreme Court justices) found that, with only one exception, every

[46] Kenneth N. Vines, "Federal District Judges and Race Relations Cases in the South," *Journal of Politics*, 26 (1964), 338–357.

[47] Kenneth M. Dolbeare, "The Federal District Courts and Urban Public Policy: An Exploratory Study (1960–1967)," in Grossman and Tanenhaus (eds.), *Frontiers of Judicial Research*, pp. 373–405.

[48] Thomas G. Walker, "A Note Concerning Partisan Influences on Trial-Judge Decision Making," *Law and Society Review*, 6 (1972), 645–649. It is possible that the methods used by Dolbeare and Walker were responsible for their finding no relationship between backgrounds and decisional results. Because there were insufficient numbers of cases for each judge to enable the researchers to quantify individually the behavioral tendencies of each judge, it was necessary to treat the judges and cases as fungible. Studies that *have* found some relationship between backgrounds (such as party) and voting behavior have generally been based on aggregating the decision scores of individual judges (i.e., judges were not considered to be fungible).

biographer sought to demonstrate the relationship of the particular judge's backgrounds to his subsequent judicial behavior.[49] In a study of the appointment of Pierce Butler to the Supreme Court, David Danelski utilized cumulative scaling to demonstrate the relationship of Butler's experience as a railroad lawyer (in the context of his previous experiences) to his subsequent voting behavior in support of railroads and utilities in rate and valuation cases.[50] Danelski also suggested that Butler's Roman Catholicism accounted for his dissenting behavior in at least two cases (one in which the Court upheld the constitutionality of Virginia's law authorizing compulsory sterilization of the feeble-minded and the other in which the Court ruled that a former resident alien, an unmarried woman who was living with a married man, was entitled to readmission to the United States).[51] In a study of Justice Harold Burton, Danelski convincingly linked Burton's American Legion background to his policy orientation as a justice.[52]

It would appear, then, that the investigation of the relevance of backgrounds to behavior is essentially an examination of those life experiences (and attributes that presumably characterize those experiences) that mold certain attitudes, shape the value hierarchies, and affect the way the individual perceives and interprets reality. Life experiences and attributes are numerous, and the combinations of different backgrounds are obviously countless. Even the same discrete attribute—such as religion, race, type of law school attended, or type of law practice engaged in—masks a multitude of varying individual experiences. It should therefore be no surprise that, although aggregate analysis has shown relatively minor statistical relationships,[53] analysis of individual judges strongly suggests a rela-

[49] J. Woodford Howard, Jr., "Judicial Biography and the Behavioral Persuasion," American Political Science Review, 65 (1971), p. 712.

[50] David J. Danelski, A Supreme Court Justice Is Appointed (New York: Random House, 1964), pp. 186–189.

[51] Ibid., pp. 189–190.

[52] David J. Danelski, "Legislative and Judicial Decision-Making: The Case of Harold H. Burton," in S. Sidney Ulmer (ed.), Political Decision-Making (New York: Van Nostrand Reinhold, 1970), pp. 121–146.

[53] But see Ulmer, "Social Background as an Indicator," and Stuart S. Nagel, "Multiple Correlation of Judicial Backgrounds and Decisions," Florida State University Law Review, 2 (1974), 258–280.

tionship of an individual's backgrounds to his subsequent decision making. The point of course is not that judges are necessarily prisoners of their past, but that at least part of their judicial behavior is probably accounted for by their attitudes and philosophical outlook as it has been shaped by their life experiences.

SMALL GROUP ANALYSIS

A judge comes to the bench with numerous attitudes and a hierarchy of values formed during a lifetime of experiences and perhaps even an inchoate judicial philosophy. If appointed to a collegial court he discovers that decision making is a group endeavor and not simply an individual act made in isolation. It is this small group nature of collegial court decision making that provides another perspective on judicial conversion. This perspective, sometimes with explicit reference to social psychological concepts, suggests a focus on various types of group interaction in the process of rendering decisions and suggests that the group condition itself affects the kinds of decisions made.[54] The principal data are mined from the private papers of deceased judges.[55]

Walter Murphy, a leading small group analyst of the Supreme Court, suggests that much of the interaction among the justices (and presumably judges on other collegial courts) may be governed by strategic considerations of individual justices. In his major study entitled *Elements of Judicial Strategy*, Murphy considered various interpersonal activities in which a policy-oriented justice could engage and which would directly or indirectly enhance his influence with his colleagues and thus promote acceptance of his strongly held policy views.[56] Such activities include persuasion, bargaining, friendship, and social amenities. A brief discussion of each follows. Small group leadership analysis that explicitly utilizes social psychological concepts

[54] See in general S. Sidney Ulmer, *Courts as Small and Not So Small Groups* (Morristown, N.J.: General Learning Press, 1971).

[55] Cf. Eloise Snyder, "The Supreme Court as a Small Group," *Social Forces*, 36 (1958), 232–238. Snyder's study relied on voting data; her work, however, is perhaps closest in approach to the attitudinal studies. Thomas Walker's work also relied in large part on voting data. See the reference in note 109.

[56] See Walter F. Murphy, *Elements of Judicial Strategy* (Chicago: University of Chicago Press, 1964), especially Chaps. 3, 7, and 8.

will also be examined along with some additional considerations of the small group approach.

Persuasion

One course of action open to a judge on a collegial court is to attempt to persuade his colleagues through logical argument of the correctness of his view of the particular case before them. With the Supreme Court, the weekly judicial conferences offer the primary forum for such activity. Subsequent face-to-face meetings and the circulation of memoranda and drafts of majority, concurring, and dissenting opinions are other vehicles for maintaining a dialogue among justices as well as permitting policy-oriented justices to press their views.

Were all the justices to hold their policy views on the same matter before them with the same intensity of commitment, negotiation rather than persuasion would characterize all interpersonal relationships. But the available evidence suggests[57] that (1) the attitudes of all justices on all matters are not held with the same intensity; (2) some issues before the Court are sufficiently novel or present a multiplicity of conflicting values so that at least some justices are open to persuasion; and (3) in complex cases some justices may have initial difficulty in identifying issues, and they may be swayed by a policy-oriented justice's arguments concerning the depiction of the problem.

Several examples of the use of persuasion by a justice with strongly held policy views under these varying circumstances can be found in the papers of Supreme Court justices. For example, in 1947 the Vinson Court considered the issue of indirect state aid to parochial schools by way of subsidizing the transportation costs of parochial school students (the case *Everson* v. *Board of Education*[58] concerned a New Jersey statute permitting such subsidies).[59] This forced the Court to consider the prohibition against the establishment of religion found in the First Amendment and its application to the states through the Fourteenth Amendment. When the transportation subsidy was first discussed in conference, Justice Rutledge vigorously ar-

[57] See, for example, the biographies cited in Howard, "Judicial Biography," and the various empirical analyses cited in this chapter.

[58] 330 U.S. 1 (1947).

[59] The discussion in the text is drawn from J. Woodford Howard, Jr., "On the Fluidity of Judicial Choice," *American Political Science Review*, 62 (1968), 54.

ticulated his policy view that there must be an absolute separation between church and state and that the line must be drawn with the subsidy in question. Rutledge argued, "First it has been books, now buses, next churches and teachers. Every religious institution in the country will be reaching into the hopper for help if you sustain this. We ought to stop this thing at the threshold of the public school."[60] Justice Frankfurter was the only other justice who voted in the preliminary voting against the subsidy, and his policy views too were strongly held and expressed. Rutledge's and Frankfurter's use of logical argument won over only Justices Jackson and Burton, one vote short of a majority. Frankfurter made an unsuccessful effort to gain the support of Justice Murphy. In one note to Murphy, Frankfurter spiced his intellectual arguments with an emotional appeal by writing "You have a chance to do for your country and your Church such as never come to you before—and may never again."[61] Justice Black, writing for the majority, agreed with the minority's insistence on absolute separation of church and state but held that the subsidy to the parents of parochial school students did not violate that standard. For Justice Black, the New Jersey statute was essentially a secular public welfare measure that the Court had no business invalidating. Justice Black's persuasive powers kept the votes of Chief Justice Vinson and Justices Douglas, Reed, and Murphy. Justice Murphy, a devout Catholic[62] and undoubtedly the most cross-pressured of all the justices in this case, told confidants that he had *prayed* over the church-state issue[63] before allowing himself to be persuaded by Black's opinion.

Another example of persuasion at work in the small group milieu of the Supreme Court can be seen with the case of *Martin* v. *Struthers*[64] decided in 1943.[65] The case concerned the constitutionality of an anti–doorbell-ringing ordinance of the city of Struthers, Ohio, that sought to protect the daytime repose of night-shift industrial workers. Proselytizing Jehovah's Witnesses had violated the

[60] *Ibid.* Note that the source for Rutledge's remarks was the conference notes of Justice Murphy.

[61] J. Woodford Howard, Jr., *Mr. Justice Murphy* (Princeton, N.J.: Princeton University Press, 1968), p. 450.

[62] *Ibid.*, p. 444.

[63] *Ibid.*, p. 450.

[64] 319 U.S. 141 (1942).

[65] The discussion is drawn from Howard, *Mr. Justice Murphy*, pp. 291–294.

ordinance, setting in motion the litigation that came before the Court. Chief Justice Stone argued in conference that the ordinance violated the "preferred freedoms" of the First Amendment, and Justices Murphy, Douglas, and Rutledge agreed. A majority led by Justice Black disagreed, and Black being the senior justice with the majority exercised his opinion-assignment prerogative and assigned the task to himself. Black saw the Struthers ordinance as protecting the privacy of the home and believed that the right to privacy in the home was a legitimate subject of concern for a municipality. After Justice Black circulated a second revision of his majority opinion and after he read the sharply worded dissent by Justice Murphy in which Murphy was joined by Douglas and Rutledge, Black changed his mind. The Chief Justice generously permitted Black to write the opinion for the new majority, and in it Black made clear that First Amendment considerations had priority over privacy in this case, but that both values are not necessarily mutually exclusive. Struthers was invited to write a more carefully drafted ordinance protecting both rights.

Still another example of persuasion is suggested by the decision making in the case of *Terminiello* v. *Chicago*.[66] Terminiello was convicted of inciting a breach of the peace by delivering a virulently racist speech at an indoor rally while an angry crowd protested outside the hall. Justice Douglas first perceived that speech as the functional equivalent of throwing a burning stick into a warehouse of dynamite. He initially voted with Vinson, Frankfurter, Jackson, and Burton to sustain the conviction. However, after considering the views of Murphy, Rutledge, and Black, Douglas reevaluated the case and perceived it as clearly a case in which freedom of speech was abridged. Joined by Justice Reed, a new majority was formed, and Justice Black assigned Douglas to write for the majority. Douglas's opinion contained a stirring defense of free speech and did not betray his initial "misperception" of the matter.[67]

Bargaining

Another principal form of intracourt activity is bargaining and negotiating over votes and opinions. A judge with strongly held views can be expected to do this, and the small group literature contains many

[66] 337 U.S. 1 (1949).

[67] Howard, *Mr. Justice Murphy*, p. 484.

examples attesting to this phenomenon. It is now believed that Justice Brandeis engaged in either tacit or explicit bargaining during the Taft Court (the 1920s), often circulating a dissenting opinion and then withdrawing it once he was able to make changes in the majority opinion.[68] Brandeis himself admitted that the "great difficulty of all group action, of course, is when and what concession to make."[69] When there is a close division on a case, any one justice's bargaining power may be enhanced. For example, in an 1889 case, Justice Gray put the squeeze on Justice Miller who had written the majority opinion in a case where the vote was 5–3. Gray in a note sent to Justice Miller said:

After a careful reading of your opinion in *Shotwell* v. *Moore*, I am very sorry to be compelled to say that the first part of it (especially in the passage which I have marked in the margin) is so contrary to my convictions, that I fear, unless it can be a good deal tempered, I shall have to deliver a separate opinion on the lines of the enclosed memorandum.

I am particularly troubled about this, because, if my scruples are not removed, and Justices Field, Bradley and Lamar adhere to their dissent, your opinion will represent only four judges, half of those who took part in the case.[70]

Justice Miller made the necessary revision.

Justice Stone frequently negotiated with his colleagues both as an associate justice and as Chief Justice. For example, one note to Justice Frankfurter contained the following: "If you wish to write, placing the case on the ground which I think tenable and desirable, I shall cheerfully join you. If not, I will add a few observations for myself."[71]

Another documented example of intracourt bargaining occurred during the deliberations over the 1941 Meadowmoor Dairies case.[72] Only the year before, Justice Murphy speaking for the Court in the Thornhill[73] and Carlson[74] cases had stated that picketing was a con-

---

[68] Alexander Bickel (ed.), *The Unpublished Opinions of Mr. Justice Brandeis* (Cambridge, Mass.: Harvard University Press, 1957); and Murphy, *Judicial Strategy*, p. 201.

[69] Quoted in Bickel, *Unpublished Opinions*, p. 18, as cited by Murphy, *Judicial Strategy*, p. 57.

[70] As quoted by Murphy, *Judicial Strategy*, pp. 57–58.

[71] *Ibid.*, p. 59.

[72] Milkwagon Drivers Union v. Meadowmoor Dairies, 312 U.S. 287 (1941).

[73] Thornhill v. Alabama, 310 U.S. 88 (1940).

[74] Carlson v. California, 310 U.S. 106 (1940).

stitutionally protected exercise of freedom of speech. The Meadowmoor case involved a state court injunction prohibiting picketing in a labor dispute that had a context of bloodshed and violence. The Court was split on this issue. Justice Frankfurter circulated a draft of the majority opinion and Justices Black and Reed prepared separate dissents. Justice Murphy first considered writing an opinion expressing his own views, but then took the advice of his law clerk who in a memo urged Murphy:

[T]ake advantage of your eminently strategic position. All three will try to woo you. Wouldn't it be better to work out your own views? Then pick the opinion that comes the closest. Then start work (à la Stone) on that. The name of Murphy in this case means much. It adds great weight to the opinion bearing it since you wrote Thornhill. I'd act accordingly.[75]

Murphy found that Frankfurter's opinion came closest to his views, and he transmitted them to him. Frankfurter revised his opinion accordingly and sent the revision to Murphy along with a memorandum stating in part: "You know how eager I have been—and am—to have *our* Milk opinion reflect your specially qualified expert views. . . . So here is my effort to translate the various suggestions into terms that would fit into, and truly strengthen, *our* opinion. *Of course* I am open for any further suggestion."[76] In the published decision, Frankfurter emphasized the extreme violence that underlay the labor dispute and justified the injunction. Frankfurter specifically noted, "We do not qualify the Thornhill and Carlson decisions. We reaffirm them." Murphy's Thornhill opinion was quoted to demonstrate that it was not inconsistent with the Meadowmoor decision.

There is a suggestion in the literature that the nature of the negotiations may vary from Court to Court. It appears that the justices of the Taft Court were more likely to bargain over votes than opinions than were the justices of the Stone or Vinson Courts.[77] One reason was that unlike the later Courts, the custom on the Taft Court was not to dissent unless absolutely necessary.[78] The type of leadership provided by the Chief Justice, the various personalities and value orien-

[75] As quoted in Murphy, *Judicial Strategy*, p. 58.

[76] *Ibid.*, p. 59. Italics added.

[77] *Ibid.*, p. 198.

[78] David J. Danelski, "The Influence of the Chief Justice in the Decisional Process of the Supreme Court," in Thomas P. Jahnige and Sheldon Goldman (eds.), *The Federal Judicial System* (New York: Holt, Rinehart and Winston, 1968), pp. 158–160.

tations of the justices, the type of issues coming to the Court, the level and nature of specific and diffuse support for the Court may also be relevant for the kind and extent of negotiations that take place.

There is some evidence that a negotiations process similar to that on the Supreme Court occurs on the various courts of appeals.[79] One appeals judge, the late Simon Sobeloff of the Fourth Circuit, told one of the authors:

It is very difficult to get unanimity on the court but the judges on the circuit try to reach consensus. It is a bargaining, give-and-take process as each judge is a different being with different views. Often a judge would rather bargain with his peers and achieve a decision, although not as broad-sweeping as he would want but nevertheless in the right direction, than write a ringing dissent while having no influence on the outcome of the case.[80]

An appeals judge from another circuit remarked, "We don't like to dissent. It's a last resort. To avoid it, the judges engage in further conferences, additional research, and exchange of memos."[81] The nature and kind of bargaining, however, may vary with the circuit, the issues, and the personalities and value orientations of the judges (just as, of course, with the Supreme Court).

Friendship and social amenities

Those using the small group approach are also interested in the friendship and social amenity patterns among the judges insofar as they may be related to the exercise of influence. For example, it appears that Justice Stone's transformation from a conservative to what Chief Justice Taft considered a "radical" was in part due to his close friendship with Holmes and Brandeis. As an intimate friend of Stone suggested, it was "respect and liking for Holmes and Brandeis that turned him from his earlier attitudes."[82] A close friendship can reinforce attitudes as well, as is suggested, for example, by Justice Murphy's close friendship with Justice Rutledge.[83] Justice Arthur Goldberg's revelation that he and Chief Justice Warren had daily

[79] See Goldman, "Conflict and Consensus," pp. 479–480; Marvin Schick, *Learned Hand's Court* (Baltimore: Johns Hopkins Press, 1970).

[80] Goldman, "Conflict and Consensus," p. 479.

[81] *Ibid.*

[82] Alpheus T. Mason, *Harlan Fiske Stone: Pillar of the Law* (New York: Viking, 1956), p. 254, as cited in Murphy, *Judicial Strategy*, p. 53.

[83] Howard, *Mr. Justice Murphy*, pp. 425–426.

conferences with each other raises an interesting question about the friendship patterns on the Warren Court.[84]

When a newly appointed justice first takes his seat on the Court, he may be the subject of wooing from several of his judicial colleagues.[85] Once on the bench, a new justice in particular, but undoubtedly others as well, will appreciate praise for his written opinions. Examples of praise adorn the papers of most justices. For example: "I congratulate you most sincerely and heartily on having written an opinion which . . . will be a landmark in the history of the Court,"[86] or "If Justice Brandeis could read it [the opinion] he would be proud of his successor."[87] However, unlike persuasion and bargaining, the relationship of friendship and social amenity patterns to decision making is uncertain.[88]

Leadership

Social psychologists have conducted numerous investigations of the nature of small group decision making.[89] From this research two types of leadership have been defined: task leadership and social leadership.[90] David Danelski utilized these concepts in his study of

[84] Television interview with former Justice Arthur Goldberg on NET Journal: Documentary on Earl Warren, July 7, 1969.

[85] See, for example, Murphy, *Judicial Strategy*, pp. 49–50.

[86] *Ibid.*, p. 51.

[87] *Ibid.*, p. 52.

[88] James Sterling Young, *The Washington Community 1800–1828* (New York: Harcourt Brace Jovanovich, 1969), pp. 76–77, notes that until 1845 the justices of the Supreme Court roomed and took meals at a common table in the same lodging house on Capitol Hill. Quoting Justice Story, " 'The Judges here live with perfect harmony . . . in the most frank and unaffected intimacy. We are all united as one.' " Young himself observes that "The unanimity of their [the Supreme Court's] case decisions provides little food for political analysis beyond the observation that their single-mindedness on policy questions conformed to the fraternal character of their life style." John Schmidhauser has argued that this constant social interaction helped Chief Justice John Marshall to dominate the Court. See Schmidhauser's *The Supreme Court: Its Politics, Personalities, and Procedures* (New York: Holt, Rinehart and Winston, 1960), pp. 111–114.

[89] See, for example, the studies cited in Thomas W. Madron, *Small Group Methods* (Evanston, Ill.: Northwestern University Press, 1969). Also see Graham S. Gibbard, John J. Hartman, and Richard D. Mann (eds.), *Analysis of Groups: Contributions to Theory, Research and Practice* (San Francisco: Jossey-Bass, 1974).

[90] See the citations in Danelski, "Influence of the Chief Justice," pp. 151–152, nn. 22–25.

the influence of the Chief Justice in the small group situation of the Supreme Court, in particular at the weekly Court conferences.[91] Danelski suggested that the task leader of the conference is that member who is concerned with getting the job done and who consequently "makes more suggestions, gives more opinions, orients the discussion more frequently, and successfully defends his ideas more often than the others."[92] He is held in high esteem by his colleagues. The social leader of the conference is concerned with maintaining friendly relations within the group. He is the diplomat who strives to lessen tension and to promote consensus. He "attends to the emotional needs of his associates by affirming their value as individuals and Court members"[93] and consequently is well liked.

Danelski suggested that the Chief Justice by virtue of the fact that he presides over the conference has the best opportunity to be either or both task and social leader. Relying on the private papers of several justices, Danelski studied leadership patterns on the Taft, Hughes, and Stone Courts. He found that during the Taft Court, Taft was the social leader of the conference in coalition with Van Devanter who was task leader. This positive sharing of leadership led to a productive and congenial Court despite ideological differences on the bench. Justice Brandeis attested to this with his observation, "Things go happily in the conference room. The judges go home less tired emotionally and less weary physically than in [former Chief Justice] White's day."[94]

Chief Justice Hughes was apparently both task and social leader, and conference productivity reached a new high.[95] However, the situation under Chief Justice Stone was substantially different. Stone was a poor task leader and was challenged by Justice Black. Stone was unprepared to assume social leadership, and cleavages on the Court became more pronounced and more personal. Conferences were long, frequently continuing into the evening and requiring additional days. It took the Court twice the amount of conference time to decide the same number of cases decided by the Hughes Court.[96]

[91] *Ibid.*

[92] *Ibid.*, p. 151.

[93] *Ibid.*, p. 152.

[94] As quoted in *ibid.*, p. 153.

[95] *Ibid.*, p. 154.

[96] *Ibid.*, p. 156.

The Chief Justice, whoever he is, has the opportunity at almost every stage of the decisional process to exercise some influence. At the first stage of the process, that of deciding which cases will be heard by the Court, the Chief Justice has an advantage by virtue of the special list procedure. During the conference discussion of *certiorari* petitions as well as cases to be decided, the Chief Justice presents his views first, and his ability to structure discussion can be a source of influence. When he votes with the majority, the Chief Justice assigns the writing of the Opinion of the Court either to himself or another with the majority. This assignment power of the Chief Justice is one of great importance because the particular justice chosen to speak for the Court[97] (1) may approach the case differently than would another majority justice in terms of the grounds on which the opinion is based or its narrowness or breadth (thus possibly furthering the Chief Justice's own policy preferences), (2) may make the decision more or less acceptable to the public, (3) may enable the Chief Justice to retain the narrow majority, and (4) may win over dissenters to the majority:[98] There are other considerations in the use of the assignment power. A Chief Justice may wish to distribute the workload equally, or he may wish to take advantage of the expertise of a particular justice,[99] or he may have a special regard for the ability

[97] Discussion of the assignment power is drawn from Danelski, "Influence of the Chief Justice," pp. 156–158.

[98] Examples can be found in David J. Danelski, "The Assignment of the Court's Opinion by the Chief Justice," paper presented at the Annual Meeting of the Midwest Conference of Political Scientists, 1960; also see Danelski, "Legislative and Judicial Decision-Making," p. 139.

[99] Justice Brennan observed of Chief Justice Warren: "He bent over backwards in assigning opinions to assure that each Justice, including himself, wrote approximately the same number of Court opinions and received a fair share of the more desirable ones." William J. Brennan, Jr., "Chief Justice Warren," *Harvard Law Review*, 88 (1974), 2. But see the contrary empirical evidence in S. Sidney Ulmer, "The Use of Power in the Supreme Court: The Opinion Assignments of Earl Warren, 1953–1960," *Journal of Public Law*, 19 (1970), 49–67; William P. McLauchlan, "Research Note: Ideology and Conflict in Supreme Court Opinion Assignment, 1946–1962," *Western Political Quarterly*, 25 (1972), 16–27; and David W. Rohde, "Policy Goals, Strategic Choice, and Majority Opinion Assignments in the U.S. Supreme Court," *Midwest Journal of Political Science*, 16 (1972), 652–682. On the other hand some empirical support for Brennan's assertion can be inferred from the findings of Gregory James Rathjen, "Policy Goals, Strategic Choice, and Majority Opinion Assignments in the U.S. Supreme Court: A Replication," *American Journal of Political Science*, 18 (1974), 713–724. These studies are not contradictory but rather suggest

of an associate. However, as Danelski points up, "every assignment presents the Chief Justice with an opportunity for influence."[100] The final stage is when the opinions have been circulated and are being debated, modified, or rewritten. The Chief Justice as the administrative head of the Court is at the nucleus of activity. Ordinarily the Chief Justice will know the status of each case and the position of each justice. He can potentially use this knowledge for his own policy goals by, for example, delaying the announcement of a case in order to work for unanimity, trying to persuade a wavering justice, or taking the lead in accommodating differences. In sum, the office of Chief Justice provides him "with an opportunity for influence, but it does not guarantee it."[101]

One of the outstanding examples of leadership on the Supreme Court was Chief Justice Earl Warren's skillful, patient, persuasive, and diplomatic marshalling the Court to an unanimous vote and opinion in *Brown* v. *Board of Education*.[102] Today one might think that the justices ought to have had no hesitation in striking down apartheid as violating the Constitution, but there is evidence that reveals otherwise. Three of the justices were Southerners and one of the non-Southerners had given indications that he was racially prejudiced.[103] The legislative history of the Fourteenth Amendment was ambiguous as to the intent of the framers concerning racially segregated public schools. As soon as he came to the Court in October, 1953, Chief Justice Warren was faced with the school segregation cases and he

---

that Warren in civil liberties but *not* in economic cases (according to the Rathjen study) assigned majority opinions to himself or to the justice closest to his views on the particular civil liberties issue raised in order to have the Court make policy closest to his own policy preferences. Opinion assignment in the economic cases may have been used in part to equalize the workload. Note also that there is some evidence of expertise being a consideration in opinion assignments on the courts of appeals. See Burton M. Atkins, "Opinion Assignments on the United States Courts of Appeals: The Question of Issue Specialization," *Western Political Quarterly*, 27 (1974), 409–428.

[100] Danelski, "Influence of the Chief Justice," p. 158.

[101] *Ibid.*, p. 160.

[102] See S. Sidney Ulmer, "Earl Warren and the *Brown* Decision," *Journal of Politics*, 33 (1971), 689–702.

[103] See S. Sidney Ulmer, "Bricolage and Assorted Thoughts on Working in the Papers of Supreme Court Justices," *Journal of Politics*, 35 (1973), pp. 306–308; and Jack Anderson and Carl Kalvelage, *American Government . . . Like It Is* (Morristown, N.J.: General Learning Press, 1972), p. 69.

realized that there was division on the Court on the issue.[104] At an early conference on the school cases, Warren gave his view that racial segregation was based on a premise of Negro inferiority and that such a premise was inconsistent with the Thirteenth, Fourteenth, and Fifteenth Amendments to the Constitution. But Warren also persuaded his colleagues not to take a formal vote, but instead to discuss the issues during subsequent conferences. As Warren himself later observed: "We did not polarize ourselves at the beginning."[105] Usually at the end of other business at the weekly conferences, Warren would turn the group's attention to the Brown and companion cases. Warren was also active outside the conference room, and there is evidence that suggests he personally sought to persuade doubting justices.[106] The justices finally voted, and Warren assigned himself the job of writing the Opinion of the Court. In the spring of 1954, Warren personally circulated drafts of the opinion and sought to accommodate various suggestions of his colleagues as well as to work on the waverers.[107] On May 17, 1954, the Supreme Court announced its historic *unanimous* decision, and it is clear that unanimity was the result of the task and social leadership exercised by the Chief Justice.

Other aspects of small group analysis

Experimental research by social scientists with small groups in a laboratory setting has resulted in studies that suggest that group decision making is a markedly different enterprise than individual decision making and that groups make different kinds of decisions than individuals do acting alone. We have already seen how this appears to be true in terms of the federal judicial system when we previously considered interaction patterns particularly on the Supreme Court and when we discussed leadership. There are other small group concepts, most of which have not been put to use by students

[104] Ulmer, "Earl Warren and the *Brown* Decision," pp. 690–692. Chief Justice Warren also indicated this in an interview on public television, broadcast and produced by WGBH (Boston), on December 11, 1972.

[105] Warren television interview, (WGBH) Boston, December 11, 1972.

[106] Ulmer, "Earl Warren and the *Brown* Decision," p. 699. Anderson and Kalvelage report that Warren took the draft of his *Brown* opinion to Justice Robert Jackson who was in a hospital and by Jackson's bedside Warren explained it to him (*American Government*, p. 69).

[107] Ulmer, "Earl Warren and the *Brown* Decision," pp. 698–699.

of courts primarily because of the difficulties involved in so doing. Nevertheless such small group concepts as group accuracy (groups have been found to make fewer errors than individuals), reference group (a group with which an individual identifies), communication net (who communicates with whom in the small group), conformity and deviance (to group norms and decisions) and the "risky shift" (the greater willingness to take risks as one shifts from the individual to the group) may have potential for aiding our understanding of collegial court processes.[108] One student of courts, Thomas Walker, tested the risky-shift concept by comparing the behavior of federal district judges in civil liberties cases when they sat alone and when they served as members of three-judge district courts.[109] He found that the same judges tended to support the civil liberties claim more when they served on three-judge courts than when sitting alone (i.e., they behaved differently in a group context, thus leaving open the possibility that they took greater risks). In a survey of the judges, Walker found that about four out of five respondents claimed they had no preference in terms of a single judge or collegial court when it came time to make an unpopular decision. But of those with a preference, over three out of four claimed they preferred the three-judge court as opposed to the one-judge court as the vehicle for making controversial decisions.[110]

Evaluation of the approach

Ideally, the investigation of collegial courts utilizing the tools and approach of small group analysis should be conducted by first-hand observation of the judicial conference at work. Of course, this is impossible. Thus, the major reliance must be on the reports of justices or persons who were the recipients of revelations by the justices as to the interpersonal relationships and conference proceedings on the Court. Such reports and revelations are available from several sources: the private papers of deceased judges; private interviews with judges; and the public writings, speeches, or interviews of judges and their close associates or relatives.

[108] See the discussion in Ulmer, *Courts as Small and Not So Small Groups.*

[109] Thomas G. Walker, "Judges in Concert: The Influence of the Group on Judicial Decision-Making," Ph.D. dissertation, University of Kentucky, 1970.

[110] *Ibid.*, pp. 99–104. Walker found that Southern judges preferred the collegial court more than judges from the other regions (pp. 103–104).

Several Supreme Court justices and Chief Justices have kept voluminous files of their correspondence, exchange of memoranda with their colleagues, drafts of opinions with the comments of colleagues, diaries or notes taken of the conference proceedings, and other pertinent papers related to their work. Such collections of private papers of justices have been indispensable to the judicial biographer. They are of equal value to the small group analyst. Small group analysts following the lead of David Danelski have mined the unusually extensive private papers of Chief Justices Taft and Stone as well as of other justices. Students of the appeals courts are beginning to investigate the wealth of private papers of appeals court judges that can shed light on the small group behavior on those courts.[111] Perhaps the most valuable papers are those of justices who have died before having had the opportunity to edit their papers.

However, the use of private papers has several distinct drawbacks. First, not all judges keep extensive accounts of court deliberations. Second, most justices stipulate that their papers are not to become available for public inspection until their colleagues who served with them are no longer on the bench. This, of course, means that there is a considerable lag between the time the justice sat and the time that the papers become available for examination by scholars. Third, the conference notes taken by one justice may not necessarily be complete and objective reportage. His strongly held policy views and the nature of his interpersonal relationships with his colleagues may affect a justice's papers so as to distort events and mislead the scholar. Similarly, after a justice has the opportunity to edit his papers in order to dispose of confidential or potentially embarrassing materials, the papers may be of little value to the small group analyst.

Personal interviews with Supreme Court justices are extremely difficult, if not impossible, for scholars to arrange. Access has been somewhat easier to lower federal court judges, but judges are careful not to reveal specifics about the intracourt relationships and maneuverings—precisely the sort of information so vital for small group analysis. Memoirs, public interviews, the writings and speeches of justices and their close associates and relatives may occasionally contain pertinent data suitable for analysis.

One of the difficulties with most data sources for small group anal-

---

111 See, for example, Schick, *Learned Hand's Court.*

ysis is that the analyst has little control over the extensiveness of the data to be collected. Small group processes, however, have been inferred from quantitative analysis of voting behavior of the sources and nature of conflict and consensus and the extent to which the Chief Justice has exercised leadership to further his policy goals by use of his opinion-assigning powers.[112] Reliance on justices' papers has with few exceptions resulted in less precise analyses than studies dependent upon other behavioral approaches to conversion. Yet the value of the small group studies and of the approach itself is considerable. The small group studies, for example, have fleshed out the workings of the Supreme Court, suggesting a more sophisticated and complex decision-making context than might be surmised from the more quantitative attitudinal analyses. What is more, these studies are compatible with the attitudinal approach and in a general sense provide additional evidence supporting the attitudinal thesis. If the justices display fluidity and not rigidity in their responses to the cases before them, if they have difficulty perceiving or digesting the facts of a case within their attitudinal frame of reference, if their votes can be swayed by persuasion, negotiation, interpersonal relationships, the leadership of the Chief Justice, or appeals to their sense of institutional loyalty, it is because the justices are human beings and not judicial slot machines. The small group studies have sensitized students of courts to these considerations.

FACT PATTERN ANALYSIS

The fact pattern approach to judicial conversion seems to bear somewhat of a resemblance to the more traditional approach still used by most of the legal profession. Both suggest that judicial decisions turn on the facts presented in the case, and both seemingly underplay individual attitudes in favor of a focus on institutional decision making. However, unlike traditional legal analysis, fact pattern analysis does not contain the assumption that courts examine the law and apply it to the legally relevant facts of the case. Fact pattern analysis is

[112] See, for example, the studies cited in footnote 99. Also see the numerous studies by S. Sidney Ulmer that have utilized the diary and papers of Justice Harold Burton such as "The Decision to Grant Certiorari as an Indicator to Decision 'On the Merits,'" *Polity*, 4 (1972), 429–447. Also see Glendon Schubert, "Policy without Law: An Extension of the Certiorari Game," *Stanford Law Review*, 14 (1962), 284–327.

not only concerned with legally relevant facts (i.e., those facts that clearly fall within the purview of the statute invoked in the case), but also with legally irrelevant facts (such as the race of the defendant in criminal cases). Furthermore, fact pattern analysis, unlike traditional analysis, hypothesizes but does not assume that courts are consistent in the type of facts used as a basis of decision. Finally, unlike traditional analysis, fact pattern analysis enables the researcher to determine what combinations of facts are more important than others for reaching a result for one or the other party involved in the litigation. Fact pattern methods (provided the court has been found to be consistent) can potentially yield precise weightings or combinations of facts that permit the researcher to predict the decisional results of future cases.

Essentially, then, fact pattern analysis is concerned with uncovering, by systematic examination of a set of decisions, the patterns of facts that are related to decisional results. In the words of Fred Kort, a leading fact pattern analyst, the objective is "to obtain a precise and exhaustive distinction between combinations of facts that lead to decisions in favor of one party and combinations of facts that lead to decisions in favor of the opposing party."[113] The approach originated in the 1930s with the late legal realist Herman Oliphant[114] and has been developed by Kort, Reed Lawlor,[115] Stuart Nagel,[116] and S. Sidney Ulmer.[117]

[113] Fred Kort, "Simultaneous Equations and Boolean Algebra in the Analysis of Judicial Decisions," in Jahnige and Goldman (eds.), Federal Judicial System, p. 167.

[114] Herman Oliphant, "Facts, Opinions, and Value Judgments," Texas Law Review, 10 (1932), 127–139. See the discussion of Oliphant's work in Rumble, Legal Realism, pp. 159–161.

[115] See Reed C. Lawlor, "Personal Stare Decisis," Southern California Law Review, 41 (1967), 73–118, and his other works cited therein.

[116] See Stuart S. Nagel, The Legal Process from a Behavioral Perspective (Homewood, Ill.: Dorsey, 1969), Chaps. 10–13.

[117] See the following articles by S. Sidney Ulmer: "Supreme Court Behavior in Racial Exclusion Cases: 1935–1960," American Political Science Review, 56 (1962), 325–330; "Mathematical Models for Predicting Judicial Behavior," in Joseph Bernd (ed.), Mathematical Applications in Political Science—III (Charlottesville: University of Virginia Press, 1967), pp. 67–95; "The Discriminant Function and a Theoretical Context for Its Use in Estimating the Votes of Judges," in Joel Grossman and Joseph Tanenhaus (eds.), Frontiers of Judicial Research (New York: Wiley, 1969), pp. 335–369.

The study of fact patterns requires content analysis to ascertain the facts in a predetermined set of decisions. Fred Kort has demonstrated two different methods for studying fact patterns.[118] One method, utilizing algebraic solutions to simultaneous equations, allows one to calculate the weight of each fact. Equations are written expressing the facts present in the cases and the number of judges voting for or against the plaintiff or defendant. Because there may be many facts whose weights are unknown and relatively few cases, factor analysis is used to reduce the number of facts to factors. Once the weights of different facts or factors are determined, it is possible to predict the decision of future cases given their facts. Both the factor analysis and the solving of simultaneous equations are done by computer.

The second method Kort has demonstrated utilizes Boolean algebra. Unlike the method of simultaneous equations, the objective is not to calculate weights for each fact or factor, but rather to derive a compound statement that will precisely indicate what combination of facts is necessary in order for the court to render a pro or con decision. Because there may be thousands of combinations of facts (if not more), it is necessary to rely on computers to derive the compound statement. Other fact pattern analysts, although using different statistical techniques, have essentially been concerned with either deriving the weights of facts in order to ascertain their relative importance or have been concerned with the combinations of facts that produce pro or con decisions.

Theoretical basis for fact pattern analysis

Reed Lawlor and S. Sidney Ulmer in particular have used fact pattern analysis to study individual judicial behavior, and both articulated theories of conversion. Lawlor theorized that each judge follows personal stare decisis; that is, he is logically consistent in his behavior from case to case as to the weights he assigns to different facts.[119]

Ulmer's theory of conversion is more elaborate. Ulmer has argued that although human behavior is a function of the interdependence and interaction of three basic dimensions—the psychological, the organic, and the environmental—it is useful to abstract the last dimension for purposes of empirical analysis.[120] Ulmer assumed that a

[118] Kort, "Simultaneous Equations and Boolean Algebra."
[119] Lawlor, "Personal Stare Decisis."

judge's decision is "a behavioral response to some perceived aspect of environment."[121] More specifically Ulmer contended that judges respond to signs or signals contained within or associated with the cases before them. These signs designate or represent something (e.g., an occurrence or state of affairs), and they are interpreted by the judge in accordance with his values and his calculus of the costs involved in choosing decisional alternatives. Ulmer's focus was on the individual judge, and he used the statistical technique of discriminant analysis to establish the weights and direction (either pro or con) of the signs.

Although Ulmer's fact pattern approach, and to some extent Lawlor's, is consistent with the attitudinal approach, the principal empirical research concerns an analysis of the statistical relationship between facts or signs and the decisions of judges. This raises the question of whether the facts cited by judges and their perceptions of what these facts represent are substantially subjective or whether they accord with objective reality. Ulmer considered this and argued that "the judge is not free to dream signs or to ignore those that all others see. Thus the fact that the judge identifies a particular sign does not mean that the signs exist only in his subjective."[122] Where many identify signs and agree as to what they represent (such as a beating with a rubber hose signifying coercion), their beliefs may be considered to represent objective reality.[123]

In his study of Justice Frankfurter, Ulmer relied on lower court records to identify the presence or absence of the hypothesized relevant signs. Lawlor, too, concerned himself with the question of subjectivity and objectivity and furthermore conducted an empirical analysis in which he compared the fact content of briefs with the fact content of judicial opinions.[124] He found that the court asserted that certain facts were present or absent in contradiction to the assertions in the briefs in only a minute portion of the cases.[125]

[120] Ulmer, "Discriminant Function," p. 339.

[121] *Ibid.*, p. 342.

[122] *Ibid.*, p. 358, n. 45.

[123] *Ibid.*

[124] Reed C. Lawlor and H. T. Fehn, "A Study of Appellate Briefs," Report no. 4, in Reed C. Lawlor, *Judicial Opinions: Analysis and Prediction* (Reports to the National Science Foundation, 1968), mimeographed.

[125] *Ibid.*, p. 22.

Race as a fact

One fact that has been considered by fact pattern analysts is the race of the litigants, in particular whether black Americans are involved. This fact is ordinarily not legally relevant in criminal cases. Yet fact pattern studies of the Supreme Court by Kort, Nagel, and Ulmer have found that the fact that a criminal defendant was black was related to a decision *favorable* to him. This is not to suggest that all black defendants receive favorable judgments, but rather that race is one of many facts that lead toward favorable decisions. Kort, in his study of involuntary confession cases, found that the fact that the defendant was black was associated along with 21 other variables with a prodefendant decision.[126] Nagel also examined involuntary confession cases and found that the fact that the defendant was a black American in a Southern jurisdiction was relevant to a decision in favor of the defense.[127] Ulmer, in his study of Justice Frankfurter, found that the fact (or sign) that the complaining party was black (or a lower court judge or attorney defined the case as one of Negro rights) was related to Frankfurter's decisions. In the 1959–1960 terms, Frankfurter responded favorably (thirteen of fifteen cases) with the appearance of the "Negro sign."[128] On the other hand, there is evidence that suggests that many Southern and other lower court judges have responded negatively to black litigants because of their race,[129] particularly in criminal sentencing.

Sentencing behavior and fact patterns

Sentencing behavior of trial court judges has come under increasing scrutiny in the 1970s. There is evidence that suggests that trial judges are often arbitrary and inconsistent from the standpoint of

[126] Fred Kort, "Content Analysis of Judicial Opinions and Rules of Law," in Glendon Schubert (ed.), *Judicial Decision-Making* (New York: Free Press, 1963), p. 137.

[127] Stuart S. Nagel, "Using Simple Calculations to Predict Judicial Decisions," *American Behavioral Scientist*, 4 (1960), 24.

[128] Ulmer, "Discriminant Function," p. 365. Also see Ulmer's study of Earl Warren, "Support for Negro Claimants in the Warren Court: The Case of the Chief Justice," *Jurimetrics Journal*, 11 (1971), 179–188.

[129] See, for example, Kenneth N. Vines, "The Role of Circuit Courts of Appeal in the Federal Judicial Process: A Case Study," *Midwest Journal of Political Science*, 7 (1963), 305–319; Jack W. Peltason, *Fifty-Eight Lonely Men: Southern Federal Judges and School Desegregation* (New York: Harcourt Brace Jovanovich, 1961); Comment, "Judicial Performance in the Fifth Circuit," *Yale Law Journal*, 73 (1963), 90–133; Charles V. Hamilton, *The Bench and the Ballot: Southern Federal Judges and Black*

legal criteria in their sentencing patterns and that there are wide disparities among judges in their sentencing of similar defendants convicted under the same statutes. Legally irrelevant considerations seem to frequently influence sentencing. Blacks have been found to be sentenced to longer prison terms than whites convicted of the same offense. For example, the Federal Bureau of Prisons records reveal that in fiscal 1970 the average sentence for whites convicted of income tax evasion was 12.8 months, but was 28.6 months for non-whites. For drug offenses the average sentence for whites was 61.1 months, but for nonwhites it was 81.1 months.[130]

Socioeconomic considerations—that is, whether the crime and criminal were white collar or blue collar—have also been related to sentencing patterns. In fiscal 1972, for example, 36.5 percent of those convicted of the white-collar crime of income tax fraud were sentenced to prison for an average sentence of 10.4 months, while 69 percent of those convicted of the blue-collar crime of auto theft were sentenced to prison for an average sentence of 35.3 months.[131]

There appears to be a relationship between still other legally irrelevant facts and criminal sentencing. Whether the defendant en-

---

Voters (New York: Oxford University Press, 1973). Also see, Haywood Burns, "Can a Black Man Get a Fair Trial in This Country?" New York Times Magazine, July 12, 1970, pp. 5 ff; Marvin E. Wolfgang and Marc Riedel, "Race, Judicial Discretion, and the Death Penalty," The Annals of the American Academy of Political and Social Science, 407 (1973), 119–133; Isaac D. Balbus, The Dialectics of Legal Repression: Black Rebels Before the American Criminal Courts (New York: Basic Books, 1973); Walter G. Markham, "Chromatic Justice: Color as an Element of the Offense," paper presented at the Annual Meeting of the A.P.S.A., 1974. But note that a reanalysis of the major empirical studies of sentencing behavior and the race of the defendant found the statistical evidence for racial discrimination in sentencing by judges to be weak. See John Hagan, "Extra-Legal Attributes and Criminal Sentencing: An Assessment of a Sociological Viewpoint," Law and Society Review, 8 (1974), 357–383.

130 This was reported in the New York Times, September 27, 1972, pp. 1 ff. But note that these analyses did not take into consideration prior convictions; thus, John Hagan's reservations of other studies as reported in "Extra-Legal Attributes" may be applicable here. Note that Herbert Jacob and James Eisenstein also found that race did not emerge as statistically important in sentencing. See their paper "Sentences and other Sanctions Imposed on Felony Defendants in Baltimore, Chicago, and Detroit," presented at the Annual Meeting of the A.P.S.A., 1974.

131 Federal Offenders in United States District Courts, 1971 (Washington, D.C.: Administrative Office of the U.S. Courts, 1973), pp. 149, 157. Also see Marvin E. Frankel, Criminal Sentences: Law without Order (New York: Hill and Wang, 1973), pp. 23–24.

tered a plea of guilty (and plea bargained) or whether he was convicted after a jury trial is apparently an important consideration as shown by the much more severe sentences for those who go to trial and are convicted. With some offense categories such as marijuana and other narcotics laws violations, sentences in fiscal 1971 were from two to three times longer than for defendants who entered a plea of guilty and presumably had plea bargained.[132] Defendants with no lawyer (or their own privately retained counsel) come off better at sentencing time than those with assigned counsel.[133] Other legally irrelevant facts that seem to be related to some judges' sentencing patterns have been discussed by Federal District Judge Marvin Frankel in his study of criminal sentences appropriately subtitled "Law without Order."[134] Another study by a psychoanalyst who is also a law school professor was based on interviews with judges and demonstrated that even the "best" judges continually use legally irrelevant criteria in their sentencing, often without realizing it.[135]

One of the most rigorous studies of sentencing disparity in the federal courts was conducted by a subcommittee of the Second Circuit Committee on Sentencing Practices in conjunction with the Federal Judicial Center.[136] The 1974 study involved all 43 active district court judges and 7 senior judges who participated in a sentencing simulation experiment. The judges were given the same set of presentence reports and asked to render sentences. For the first time in

---

[132] *Federal Offenders, 1971*, pp. 14–15.

[133] *Ibid.*, pp. 8–9. Also see Stuart S. Nagel, "Effects of Alternative Types of Counsel on Criminal Procedure Treatment," *Indiana Law Journal*, 48 (1973), 404–426.

[134] Frankel, *Criminal Sentences*. Also see Stuart Nagel and Lenore J. Weitzman, "Double Standard of American Justice," *Society*, 9 (1972), 18–25, 62–63, and their study "Women as Litigants," *Hastings Law Journal*, 23 (1971), 171–198, for evidence of sexual discrimination in the judicial process. But cf. Hagen, "Extra-Legal Attributes."

[135] Willard Gaylin, *Partial Justice: A Study of Bias in Sentencing* (New York: Knopf, 1974). Also see Keith D. Harries and Russell P. Lura, "The Geography of Justice: Sentence Variations in U.S. Judicial Districts," *Judicature*, 57 (1974), 392–401.

[136] Anthony Partridge and William B. Eldridge, *The Second Circuit Sentencing Study: A Report to the Judges of the Second Circuit* (Washington, D.C.: Federal Judicial Center, 1974). Another rigorous study that examines federal judge sentencing behavior in selective service cases is Beverly Blair Cook, "Sentencing Behavior of Federal Judges: Draft Cases—1972," *University of Cincinnati Law Review*, 42 (1973), 597–633.

sentencing studies it was possible to control the case stimuli by having different trial judges respond to the same "cases." Furthermore, most of the "cases" were based on real cases previously decided in the circuit.

The results were startling. Second Circuit district judges responding to the same presentence reports varied widely in their sentences. For example, in one case half the judges gave a sentence from one to three years of *probation*, while one-fourth of the judges gave prison sentences from six months to three years. In another case, the sentences varied from five years to eighteen years and a fine, with the median sentence being ten years.[137] The study also found that it made no difference in terms of disparity whether judges had a number of years of trial court experience or whether they were relative newcomers to the bench.[138]

In some respects the search for fact patterns that are associated with individual judges' sentencing behavior is similar to the study of attitudes. One can consider the response of a judge to a particular combination of facts as representing the judge's attitudes toward the litigant and situational characteristics of the cases. The fact pattern approach as applied to collegial courts, in the hands of some practitioners, has provided more of a focus on institutional responses. The approach, whether in the context of individual or institutional decision making, by examining all the legally relevant *and* legally irrelevant facts alerts us to the wide range of discretion available and used by judges. Perhaps, most importantly, it also aides us in documenting the use of that discretion by courts and individual judges.

JUDICIAL ROLE ANALYSIS

Of all the approaches discussed, judicial role analysis offers perhaps the most ambiguous and yet potentially the most comprehensive explanation of judicial conversion. It is ambiguous in that the concept of judicial role can and has been defined differently, and little systematic attention has been devoted to formulating and testing judicial role hypotheses. It is comprehensive in that in its broadest form, the judicial role concept can be used to order the just discussed conversion variables to provide a general model of conversion.

137 *The Second Circuit Sentencing Study,* pp. 6–7.
138 *Ibid.,* pp. 34–35.

The concept of role as used by social scientists is tied to the concept of position; that is, the researcher examines the role of those who occupy particular positions such as federal district court judge, federal appeals judge, or associate justice of the Supreme Court. The judicial role may be defined as the "set of normative expectations concerning the official behavior of an incumbent of a . . . [judicial] position."[139] Judicial role behavior may be defined as those activities of a judge that manifest his perceptions of what he ought to and can do (as well as the converse) as a judge.[140] Thus, his attitudes and values are filtered through a role screen and are manifested by role behavior. From the more traditional legal literature as well as from some behavioral analyses, there appear to be some elements of role for which there is wide consensus among judges, that is, common role behavior. These may be considered the *institutional role elements*. There also appear to be some elements of role that, on the basis of divergent patterns of judicial behavior, suggest the absence of common interpretations and perceptions. These may be considered *variable role elements*. Both will be discussed and followed by a consideration of the potential of role analysis to provide the basis for a comprehensive causal model of conversion.

Institutional role elements

Institutional role elements, as just defined, are those about which a wide consensus apparently exists in terms of normative expectations and about which a uniformity exists for the most part in actual behavior. They are likely to have been initially fostered during the ongoing legal socialization process that law students undergo and to which practicing lawyers are constantly exposed. New judges, too, are socialized in terms of the judicial role.[141] Institutional role ele-

[139] David J. Danelski, "Conflict and Its Resolution in the Supreme Court," *Journal of Conflict Resolution*, 11 (1967), 76.

[140] Joel B. Grossman, "Dissenting Blocs on the Warren Court: A Study in Judicial Role Behavior," *Journal of Politics*, 30 (1968), 1071. Also see Russell Wheeler, *Extrajudicial Behavior and the Role of the Supreme Court Justice* (Morristown, N.J.: General Learning Press, 1975).

[141] See Robert Carp and Russell Wheeler, "Sink or Swim: The Socialization of a Federal District Judge," *Journal of Public Law*, 21 (1972), 359; Beverly Blair Cook, "The Socialization of New Federal Judges: Impact on District Court Business," *Washington University Law Quarterly*, (1971), 253–279. In general, see, Charles H. Sheldon, *The American Judicial Process: Models and Approaches* (New York: Dodd, Mead, 1974), Chap. 3.

ments may be considered insofar as they concern or relate to public behavior of judges, procedural aspects of decision making, and substantive aspects of decision making.

Public Behavior   There is an image of a federal judge that is probably widely perceived by most Americans. He is a late middle-aged or elderly black-robed gentleman who is dignified and learned. This institutional image is in part fortified by an accepted judicial etiquette whereby judges are treated with deference by other authorities (particularly other court personnel). Judges also address each other on the bench and in their opinions with respect and courtesy, referring to each other, for example, as "brother."

It is also expected that judges will appear to be and will be in fact impartial when processing litigation. A judge who has or had any involvement with one or more of the litigants or any substantial stake in the resolution of the controversy is expected to excuse himself from the case. Judges on appellate courts are also expected to maintain secrecy about conference deliberations. Prior to judgment day, judges do not reveal their views of the case nor do they predict how the case will be decided. Even then, it is traditional for judges not to reveal the course of deliberations nor to elaborate upon the decision itself.[142] These institutional elements of the judicial role as well as others (some of which are specified in the American Bar Association's Canons of Judicial Ethics) are associated with the public image of the judiciary, an image that is no doubt distinct from the image of other political authorities such as legislators or Presidents.

Procedural Aspects of Decision Making   There are various institutional role elements related to procedural aspects of decision making. The special judicial position of federal district judge, the trial judge of the federal system, connotes particular activities in the conduct of trials, for example, the maintenance of decorum in the courtroom

---

[142] But see the revelations in Nina Totenberg, "Behind the Marble, Beneath the Robes," *New York Times Magazine*, March 16, 1975, 15, 58–67. Totenberg claims to have obtained interviews with justices, law clerks, and friends of the justices among others. The article contains juicy accounts of conference deliberations over cases involving school busing, abortion, and the Nixon tapes. That such information could be obtained brings into doubt notions of widespread consensus concerning conference secrecy. On the other hand, given the unflattering portrait of Chief Justice Burger unveiled in the article one could speculate that perhaps only one disgruntled justice and his entourage might have spilled the beans to Ms. Totenberg.

and scrupulous attention to correct trial procedures. The positions of appeals court judge and associate justice of the Supreme Court also suggest institutional role elements concerned with procedure. One study of appeals judges suggested that panel conferences on most circuits are conducted in a spirit of give-and-take or accommodation in an effort to reach decisional consensus and thus avoid public dissension. The extent of accommodation in practice, however, apparently depends upon the circuit, issue, ideological or attitudinal gaps that must be spanned, and personal relationships of the judges with one another.[143] Nevertheless, the role of appellate judge or associate justice contains the element of negotiation institutionalized through the conference and the practice of circulating drafts of opinions for comments and suggestions.[144]

The position of Chief Justice of the Supreme Court is also a specialized role as will be recalled from previous discussion of leadership and the small group approach. The Chief Justice chairs the conference, makes opinion assignments when he votes with the majority, first presents his views of the issues and how he is inclined to vote[145] (he is followed by his colleagues in order of seniority), and has special gatekeeping responsibilities (recall the special list procedure). He also has the opportunity to exercise task and social leadership in order to promote an efficient and harmonious Court.

Other institutional role elements include the norm that judges on a collegial bench will not change their votes just before the decisions are to be announced. A court would be in a constant turmoil if this were not common practice.

Substantive Aspects of Decision Making   Institutional role elements that concern or affect the substance of decisions include the norms of *stare decisis* and adherence to the obvious requirements and intent

---

[143] Goldman, "Conflict and Consensus," p. 479.

[144] See the comments of Howard, "Fluidity of Judicial Choice," p. 55.

[145] Chief Justice Earl Warren explained in a television interview what happens next: "[We] go on until everybody has spoken . . . [and] generally stated his views. . . . [If] everyone is agreed that the outcome should be one way there's no need of taking a [formal] vote. But if there is a division [of opinion] . . . we start with the junior member of the Court and vote upwards instead of going from the Chief Justice down to the junior member of the Court." Warren television interview (WGBH), Boston, December 11, 1972, transcript pp. 7–8.

of the law. The uses of dissent, at least on the Supreme Court, also appear to fit the pattern of institutional role elements.

Although the legal realists argued forcefully that *stare decisis* is a meaningless norm because precedents are plentiful and can always be found to support one's view, the rule of precedent is still maintained by the bar and bench as a decision-making norm. The crucial question, however, is whether *stare decisis* is merely pro forma or whether it does in fact shape the substance of decisions. The answer is that there is some evidence suggesting that to a limited extent *stare decisis* is related to substantive decision making. The majority of all decisions (with *per curiams* included) decided by the Supreme Court are decided unanimously, and many (particularly the *per curiam* decisions) are specifically decided on the authority of precedent. One scholar, Werner Grunbaum, who conducted a computer simulation of the 1962 and 1963 terms, concluded that "judicial attitudes alone are insufficient to explain judicial behavior" and that in unanimously decided cases "justices are influenced by the lawyers' model governing traditional *stare decisis*."[146] There is other evidence that concerns the appeals courts.

Typically at least four out of five cases are unanimously decided by the various appeals courts. One study involving interviews with a large sample of appeals judges found that most judges not only recognized the expectation that they follow Supreme Court precedent, but suggested that when the precedent involves policy set by the Supreme Court, stare decisis *is* largely responsible for encouraging decisional consensus on the appellate courts. This should not be taken to mean that all or most unanimous appellate panels achieve unanimity *because* of precedent alone, but the limited evidence suggests that *stare decisis* is probably responsible for at least a part of those decisions.[147]

[146] Werner F. Grunbaum, "Analytical and Simulation Models for Explaining Judicial Decision-Making," in Grossman and Tanenhaus (eds.), *Frontiers of Judicial Research*, p. 329.

[147] See the discussion in Sheldon Goldman, "Backgrounds, Attitudes and the Voting Behavior of Judges," *Journal of Politics*, 31 (1969), 214–222. Also see Francis M. Rich, Jr., "Role Perception and Precedent Orientation as Variables Influencing Appellate Judicial Decision-Making: An Analysis of the Fifth Circuit Court of Appeals," Ph.D. dissertation, University of Georgia, 1967. Also of interest in terms of the general research problem is the article by Bradley Canon and Dean Jaros: "External

Of course, *stare decisis* as an institutional role element raises some problems. It is difficult to conclusively prove that *stare decisis* operates for all judges on some minimal basis to influence the substance of policy making. A judge may claim he is following precedent, but it may also be that the precedent coincides with his attitudes and values. The empirical analyses of *stare decisis*, such as Glendon Schubert's analysis of Justice Clark[148] and his later work in *The Judicial Mind*, suggested that *stare decisis* is really a role variable, that justices differ in their perceptions and evaluations of *stare decisis* as a norm. Sophisticated qualitative analysts such as Martin Shapiro have argued that *stare decisis* is typically a facade for what really amounts to incremental changes in policy.[149] Further role behavior research will be necessary to demonstrate the extent to which *stare decisis* can be considered an institutional role element with import for substantive decision making.

When one examines the norm that judges should follow the obvious requirements and intent of the law, one turns to what has always been considered at the heart of the judicial function. To some scholars the mention of this as an institutional role element may seem superfluous, indeed, belaboring the obvious. Yet the emphasis of political analyses of judges' behavior is on their use of discretion, and one may lose sight of the fact that not every case offers judges a wide range, or perhaps even any range, of decisional alternatives.

One classic example of this is the famous 1833 Court opinion in the case of *Barron* v. *Baltimore*[150] in which Chief Justice John Marshall

---

Variables, Institutional Structure and Dissent on State Supreme Courts," *Polity*, 3 (1970), 175–200. For some suggestive evidence concerning state trial and appellate court judges, see Thomas D. Ungs and Larry R. Baas, "Judicial Role Perception: A Q-Technique Study of Ohio Judges," *Law and Society Review*, 6 (1972), 343–366. Also see, John T. Wold, "Political Orientation, Social Backgrounds, and Role Perceptions of State Supreme Court Judges," *Western Political Quarterly*, 27 (1974), 239–248. For an analysis based on mail questionnaire responses by middle-level appellate court judges in Austria and Switzerland, see Victor E. Flango, Lettie M. Wenner, and Manfred W. Wenner, "The Concept of Judicial Role: A Methodological Note," *American Journal of Political Science*, 19 (1975), 277–289.

[148] Glendon Schubert, "Civilian Control and Stare Decisis in the Warren Court," in Schubert (ed.), *Judicial Decision-Making*, pp. 55–77.

[149] Martin Shapiro, "Stability and Change in Judicial Decision-Making: Incrementalism or Stare Decisis?" *Law in Transition Quarterly*, 2 (1965), 134–157; and see, in general, Martin Shapiro, "Toward a Theory of Stare Decisis," *Journal of Legal Studies*, 1 (1972), 125–134.

[150] Barron v. Baltimore, 7 Peters 243 (1833).

was compelled to rule that the Bill of Rights provided limitations on Congress but not the individual states. One obscure example concerns another activist justice, some 110 years later, who wrote to a colleague explaining his vote in a case, "I am constrained to concur, though I wish, as I know you do, that there was some tenable way to reach the opposite result."[151] There are undoubtedly numerous other examples that could be mentioned. However, it should be noted that there have been no studies demonstrating more precisely the extent to which there are cases with no meaningful decisional alternatives because of the requirements of law. Presumably the Supreme Court, which determines for the most part which cases it hears, is *least* concerned with such cases. The district courts and the appeals courts, which do not have a similar discretionary power over their dockets, would be expected to be *most* concerned with such cases.

There is some evidence that suggests that before 1940 the accepted norm of the Supreme Court was not to dissent unless absolutely necessary, that is, unless a great principle and/or major constitutional issue was at stake.[152] This, of course, affected the strategy and tactics of negotiation related to the substance of the Court's opinion (as will be recalled from the discussion of small group behavior). Since 1940 this expectation appears to have been changed. Certainly the much greater frequency of dissents and special concurrences suggest as much. As for the operating norms on the appeals courts, not much is known except that the rate of dissent is markedly less than that of the Supreme Court and also that dissent rates vary by circuit.[153]

Role variables

A norm more difficult to define than those just discussed is that judges are expected to dispense "justice." Although "rendering justice" is a norm widely recognized by judges, their role behavior suggests vastly different perceptions and interpretations of justice. This indeed goes to the essentials of conversion—the backgrounds and conditioning experiences of the judges and the emergent attitudes and values that may culminate in a judicial philosophy that may lead one judge to view the equities of a case in an entirely different man-

---

151 As quoted in Howard, "Fluidity of Judicial Choice," p. 49.

152 Danelski, "Conflict and Its Resolution," pp. 78–79.

153 Goldman, "Conflict and Consensus," pp. 463–464; and Goldman, "Conflict 1965–1971," pp. 638–639.

ner from another judge. For example, one study reported the contrasting views of criminal justice of two judges on the District of Columbia circuit. One judge remarked, "Our main goal is to see that no man loses his life, liberty, or indeed, his property unless he is clearly guilty. . . . [However] if a man is guilty I will not look for procedural niceties. [What is important is that] justice should be done."[154] His colleague, on the other hand, stated:

The primary goal of the judge is to do justice. . . . Settled principles of law are used to guide a court to a just result. When it is clear that these principles or precedents will produce an injustice, then you must strain the principles to get a just result. . . . I feel our society is responsible for Negro crime and my position is that society must dot the i's and cross the t's when it brings a criminal case [with a black defendant] before me.[155]

Another role variable, one that has especially occupied the attention of students of the Supreme Court, concerns each justice's perception of what the higher courts ought to do and can do in determining public policy for the nation. The popular discussion usually centers around the catch-all terms of "activism" (i.e., the position that courts should not hesitate to foster policies beneficial to society) and "restraint" (i.e., the courts should defer to the popularly elected branches of government in *their* determination of suitable public policy). Obviously one can be activist on one issue and restrained on another. Justice Frankfurter was closely identified with the restraint philosophy, particularly when the issue involved state criminal procedures. He observed, for example, in a 5–4 decision in which his vote condemned a black criminal defendant to death:

I cannot rid myself of the conviction that were I to hold that Louisiana would transgress the Due Process Clause if the State were allowed, in the precise circumstances before us, to carry out the death sentence, I would be enforcing my private view rather than that consensus of society's opinion, which for purposes of due process, is the standard enjoined by the Constitution.[156]

Justice Frankfurter, however, was apparently less restrained in his embrace of more conservative economic positions in his later years

154 Goldman, "Conflict and Consensus," p. 478.

155 *Ibid.* There is some evidence that different urban political systems recruit judges with markedly different role concepts in terms of rendering justice. See Martin A. Levin, "Urban Politics and Judicial Behavior," *Journal of Legal Studies*, 1 (1972), 193.

156 Louisiana ex rel Francis v. Resweber, 329 U.S. 459 (1947), at 471. As quoted in Danelski, "Conflict and Its Resolution," p. 76.

on the bench.[157] In sum, it is apparent both from the more traditional analyses of decisional output and philosophical statements by judges as well as from empirical analyses[158] that judges differ as to the proper function of higher courts in a democracy. Although the terms "activism" and "restraint" may be an oversimplification of a complex reality, they do suggest the variable nature of this role element.

The varying personality characteristics of judges also can be thought of as affecting their role behavior. Jerome Frank[159] and Harold Lasswell,[160] among others, in their studies have suggested that the personality variable may lurk beneath the ostensible philosophical and attitudinal differences of judges.[161]

Role and a dynamic causal model of conversion

The role concept may be utilized in the construction of a causal model of judicial conversion. Such an endeavor represents a level of analysis different from that presented thus far in that a causal model seeks to account for all the relevant variables and to specify precisely how they are interrelated.[162] Building a causal model in the mathematical sense involves developing a system of equations the solution of which determines which variables are causes and which are effects

---

[157] Harold J. Spaeth, "Warren Court Attitudes toward Business: The 'B' Scale," in Schubert (ed.), *Judicial Decision-Making*, pp. 79–108.

[158] See in particular, Harold J. Spaeth, "Judicial Power as a Variable Motivating Supreme Court Behavior," *Midwest Journal of Political Science*, 6 (1962), 54–82. J. Woodford Howard, Jr., interviewed appeals court judges on the Second, Fifth, and District of Columbia Circuits and found some differences in the judges' role concept. Five judges saw their judicial work as innovating (akin to the activist position). Nine took the opposite position and asserted that their job was not to judicially legislate, but to confine themselves to the case at hand and avoid innovation whenever possible (similar to the restraint stand). Most (twenty) had what Howard considered the "realist" role concept; that is, they acknowledged more restraints than did the "innovators," but also more need and room for innovation than did the "interpreters" (or restraint-oriented judges). "Role Perceptions and Behavior in Three U.S. Courts of Appeals," paper presented at the Annual Meeting of the American Political Science Association, 1974.

[159] *Law and the Modern Mind*.

[160] Harold Lasswell, *Power and Personality* (New York: Norton, 1948), pp. 61–88.

[161] In general, see Fred I. Greenstein, *Personality and Politics: Problems of Evidence, Inference, and Conceptualization* (Chicago: Markham, 1969).

[162] See Abraham Kaplan, *The Conduct of Inquiry* (San Francisco: Chandler, 1964), pp. 327–369, for a discussion of what distinguishes causal explanations from predictive and functional ones.

Figure 5.1 Dynamic causal model of judicial conversion. *Legend:* B—backgrounds and attributes; P—political characteristics; S—professional socialization; R—role concept; G—group interaction; F—fact patterns; V—vote; ⤸ — feedback

(as well as specifying which variables serve as linking mechanisms).[163] Implicit in such analysis is the assumption that there are regularities of behavior and that the discovered uniformities suggest a dependence of effect on cause under specified conditions all other things being equal. There are various alternative methods of causal model building, the details of which are more appropriately discussed in more advanced technical writings.[164] Neither is it necessary to be concerned here with their mathematics, for what is about to be suggested is only at best a first step toward developing a testable causal model of judicial conversion.[165]

Figure 5.1 presents an arrow diagram of a dynamic causal model of judicial conversion in which the role concept is central. As can be observed, the model suggests that backgrounds are causally related to certain political characteristics (such as party affiliation, partisan activism, and political attitudes and values). These political characteristics, in turn, are causally related to the role concept espoused by

[163] See Hayward R. Alker, Jr., "Causal Inference and Political Analysis," in Joseph L. Bernd (ed.), *Mathematical Applications in Political Science, II* (Dallas: Southern Methodist University Press, 1966), pp. 7–43. In general, see Fred Kort, "A Special and a General Multivariate Theory of Judicial Decisions," paper presented at the Annual Meeting of the American Political Science Association, 1974.

[164] See the discussion and citations in *ibid.*

[165] Also see Edward J. Weissman, "Mathematical Theory and Dynamic Models," pp. 367–395, and Glendon Schubert, "Two Causal Models of Decision-Making by the High Court of Australia," pp. 335–366, in Schubert and Danelski (eds.), *Comparative Judicial Behavior*. But cf. Alan M. Sager, "From Brief to Decision: A Computer Simulation of the 1963 Supreme Court Term," paper presented at the Annual Meeting of the American Political Science Association, 1969.

the judge. Attitudes and values are at the heart of a judge's role concept, but they are assumed to be not as baldly political as they were before his ascending the bench. Rather, attitudes and values are manifested in terms of what the judge believes he can and ought to do and how he in fact acts as a judge. The kind and extent of professional socialization is also causally related to the judge's role concept as are various on-the-bench collegial experiences. The model, however, takes into consideration that the judge's role concept (i.e., his attitudes and values in the context of how he believes judges should decide cases) is subject to change over time due to feedback from previous decisional output. Presumably increased age and experience are also taken into account by this dynamic aspect of the model. The judge's role concept as well as the facts of the case and the group experience related to discussing the case (conferences, circulation of drafts of opinions and memoranda, etc.) cause the judge to vote as he does.

The challenge of such a model is to devise operational procedures by which to quantify and then measure the variables. It would be necessary to specify the types of cases and voting responses to be studied. It would also be necessary to devise indices by which to measure the variables. For example, B (backgrounds) might be a composite of weighted attributes;[166] P (political characteristics) could consist of a composite index of party affiliation and activism as well as political attitudes and values held before ascending the bench (perhaps determined through a content analysis of pre-judicial speeches or writings[167] or perhaps as ascertained through extensive interviewing of the judge and those who knew him before his judicial career began); S (professional socialization) could weight bar association activism, legal honors and writings, and types of legal experience; R (role concept) could perhaps be operationally determined through extensive use of scaling of previous voting behavior[168] and/or deter-

---

[166] Possibilities are suggested in the work of Rodney L. Mott, Spencer D. Albright, and Helen R. Semmerling, "Judicial Personnel," *Annals of the American Academy of Political and Social Science*, 67 (1933), 143–155.

[167] See Danelski's use of content analysis in his "Values as Variables" and "Legislative and Judicial Decision-Making: The Case of Harold H. Burton."

[168] The Schubert method as presented in the original and revisited *Judicial Mind*, and that used by Harold Spaeth and David Rohde, *Supreme Court Decision Making*, seem to be suggestive for classifying judges as to role concept.

mined by content analysis of previous opinions; G (group interaction) might possibly be discerned through a combined index measuring the amount of conference time spent on a case, the number of drafts circulated, the extent and nature of behind-the-scenes negotiations (presumably conference notes and diaries can provide such data), and the number of concurrences and dissents and how they are in accord or differ from previously discovered bloc patterns; and F (fact patterns) can be found through the use of any of the established techniques. V, of course, refers to the vote or votes that we hypothesize are caused by the preceding variables. It should also be stressed that the votes to be explained (the dependent variable) cannot also be used to determine any of the variables (the independent variables) that presumably cause those votes. Only past behavior would be used for those measures.

These, then, are the rudiments for developing a causal model of judicial conversion. It should be apparent, however, that serious difficulties await the model builders. Not only are there problems of operationalizing the variables and measuring them, there are also formidable technical problems as well.[169] For the present, however, it may be useful to consider such a model as presented in Figure 5.1 (which was suggested in part by the studies reported earlier in this chapter) as a working model of behavior. It also suggests a more complex empirical theory of judicial conversion than those presented earlier.

[169] See Weissman, "Mathematical Theory and Dynamic Models," pp. 389, 394, n. 18; Schubert, "Two Causal Models"; Alker, "Causal Inference," p. 13. Also see Dennis J. Palumbo, "Causal Inference and Indeterminancy in Political Behavior: Some Theoretical and Statistical Problems," paper presented at the Annual Meeting of the American Political Science Association, 1969. But see Kort, "A Special and a General Multivariate Theory."

SIX
OUTPUT

I N studying judicial output we are primarily concerned with the formal decisions by which demands fed into the federal judicial system are finally and authoritatively disposed. This concern also includes a focus on the rules and norms that underlie the disposition of particular demands. In discussing output within the framework of political systems analysis, Easton distinguishes three different subconcepts as relevant to the main concept of output. These are *authoritative* output (the binding decisions of the authorities), *associated* output (which includes the statements that interpret, clarify, or build on authoritative output, but also encompasses other activities related to the judge's official position), and *outcomes* (the immediate effects or consequences of authoritative and associated outputs). In this chapter these concepts are considered (but with special attention to authoritative output and to the U.S. Supreme Court).

Traditionally, in their analyses of federal judicial output, historians, political scientists, and legal scholars have tended to focus almost exclusively on the decisions (authoritative outputs) and opinions (associated outputs) of the Supreme Court, especially in the "important" cases. The most highly regarded scholars have supplemented their keen analyses of Court decisions and opinions with extensive historical and judicial biographical research. They have used the Court's output as the springboard for understanding the place of the federal courts in American democracy. The literature produced by the major traditionalist (in method) legal scholars is rich and, indeed, indispensable for serious students of the federal judicial system.

Despite the fact that Supreme Court decisions and opinions constitute the most analyzed and perhaps the most interesting single species of output of the federal judicial system, their study must be approached with some care and sophistication. Although Supreme Court decisions and opinions (and the policies they represent) often have broad effect on the behavior of persons and institutions both in and out of government, the Court is, after all, only one of over 100 courts in the federal system. The combined output of the lower federal courts greatly exceeds that of the Supreme Court. Furthermore, Supreme Court (as well as lower court) decisions and opinions are but one species of output among a whole set of political outputs that determine the shape of public policy and the nature of social behavior in America. Consistent judicial gatekeeping—that is, the application of such systemic rules as those dealing with jurisdiction and justiciability—has meant that over broad periods of time some areas of public policy and social life, potentially within the Supreme Court's jurisdiction, have been left almost exclusively under the control of the state courts or other political institutions such as Congress, the state legislatures, or local governments.

When the Supreme Court decides an issue "on the merits," its decision does not unambiguously determine the decisions of subsequent cases raising similar questions, particularly in the lower courts. Even when the Court has made specific authoritative rulings, compliance problems can occur under the rules of the system. When the Supreme Court acts as an appellate court, its decisions and opinions are technically intrasystemic in nature. The Supreme Court (after it rules on the merits) either affirms the lower court's ruling or sends the case back to the lower court for final disposition "not inconsistent" with the decision and opinion of the Court. Some lower courts have thus been able to turn a Supreme Court "winner" into a "loser" after all.[1] Therefore, to understand the outcome and impact

[1] For example, in a study of all cases remanded by the Court to state courts between 1941 and 1951, it was found that of the 175 cases involved there was further litigation in 46, and in just under half of these the party successful in the Supreme Court was unsuccessful in the state court following remand. See "Evasion of Supreme Court Mandates in Cases Remanded to State Courts since 1941," *Harvard Law Review*, 67 (1954), 1251–1259. Jerry K. Beatty's study of the last ten years of the Warren Court revealed that in about 27 percent of the cases remanded to the state courts, the winners at the Supreme Court level ultimately became losers. See his study, "State Court Evasion of United States Supreme Court Mandates during the Last Decade of the Warren Court," *Valparaiso University Law Review*, 6 (1972), 260–285.

of Supreme Court output, we must consider not only that output itself, but also the systemic rules and processes that influence or bear upon it.

THE RELATIONSHIP OF INPUT RULES TO OUTPUT

The federal judicial system's rules of jurisdiction and justiciability mean that certain areas of public policy never or almost never become the object of authoritative judicial output. Excluded are most questions of foreign policy, including decisions about diplomatic recognition, foreign aid, treaty making, whether to go to war, and military operations. Rather, judicial policy making has been almost solely concerned with domestic affairs. Even in this area, broad questions involving governmental spending for public works, natural resource and technological development, conservation, and the raising of revenue have rarely been subjected to judicial control. Only in those areas where constitutionally protected individual rights are threatened—for example, in cases concerning equal treatment, just compensation for expropriated property, and political freedom—have the courts played any autonomous policy-making role at all. Judicial interference is also rare in the internal organization, procedures, and activities of the legislative and executive branches of government. Although cases are litigated concerning the hiring and firing of certain specific classes of employees, the validity of election procedures and districting, and the treatment of private citizens by legislative committees and executive officials, the questions involved rarely change the essential structure, procedures, or policy-making proclivities of the legislative and executive branches of government. The important exceptions to this generalization (and these *are* extremely important exceptions) are judicial policies concerning racial discrimination by or within governmental agencies, legislative malapportionment, and, of course, the behavior of law enforcement officials, an area of executive action closely related to the judiciary's control over criminal law.

In assessing the extent to which systemic rules limit judicial output, one should recognize the fact that these rules are to a broad degree self-defined and self-enforced. They are, therefore, subject to change. On rare occasions they have been changed by Congress either by legislation (e.g., the removal of the federal judiciary's jurisdiction over certain classes of *habeas corpus* cases following the Civil War)[2] or in conjunction with the states through constitutional amendment (e.g., the Eleventh and Sixteenth Amendments). Historically, however, most changes in the rules determining systemic input have been engineered by the federal judicial system itself through Supreme Court decisions.

Sometimes the change in jurisdictional rules is explicit, as in *Fay* v. *Noia*[3] (expanding the availability of federal *habeas corpus* for state prisoners) and *Baker* v. *Carr*[4] (announcing that state legislative malapportionment was a justiciable federal question). Other times the triggering judicial decision is more substantive in nature, but because the social or governmental behavior involved is widespread, a specific decision or set of decisions has the effect of promoting or stifling large amounts of litigation. *Brown* v. *Board of Education*,[5] for example, was a substantive decision that, by overruling the "separate but equal" doctrine of *Plessy* v. *Ferguson*,[6] generated vast amounts of litigation attacking segregationist laws and official activities which had developed under the protective mantle of the Plessy decision. Conversely, the many post-1937 economic decisions in which the Supreme Court left standing most state and all federal laws concerning the power to regulate economic life as well as the frequent denial of certiorari in cases challenging the constitutionality of such legislation have served to stifle litigation raising similar questions in more recent years.

GATEKEEPING AND THE NATURE OF SUPREME COURT OUTPUT

Many cases and controversies that are disposed of by gatekeeping contain issues that might well be fit subjects for Supreme Court review and decision making. In Chapter 4 the mechanisms of gatekeeping and some of its empirical dimensions were discussed in the analysis of how the judicial system protects itself from demand input overload. If gatekeeping were carried on in a completely random

[2] See, Ex Parte McCardle, 6 Wall. 318 (1868); 7 Wall. 506 (1869).

[3] 372 U.S. 391 (1963).

[4] 369 U.S. 186 (1962).

[5] 347 U.S. 483 (1954).

[6] 186 U.S. 537 (1896).

manner, then these processes would be of no greater interest than as an economical way by which a vast number of cases are disposed of with minimal expenditure of judicial time, energy, or resources.

But this is not so. Gatekeeping processes, at least at the Supreme Court level, have important implications by determining at any particular time which issues will be the subject of Court output and which will not. This is clearly understood by the justices and was the basis for the opposition on the part of so many justices and former justices to proposals that would diminish or eliminate the Court's gatekeeping authority. It is of interest to examine, by way of a formal model, litigant and judicial gatekeeping to see how these processes affect the Court's policy output.

At the outset it is apparent that, despite the policy dimension to gatekeeping, individual gatekeeping decisions in themselves generally stimulate little public controversy or interest.[7] This is not hard to understand, for when the members of the Court gatekeep by dismissing an appeal or denying a petition for certiorari, only rarely is the decision accompanied by any display of intracourt dissension. Such decisions ordinarily do not make good copy for the communications media. Perhaps more important is the fact that there is generally no one point upon which criticism of gatekeeping decisions can focus since only the result is announced and not the reasons behind the decisions. With denials of certiorari the decisions even formally lack any assessment of the merits of the claims pressed. At the most, a denial of certiorari may represent an approval of lower court decision making; at the least, it is a nondecision, that is, a decision not to do anything. Because they involve the Court neither in new policy departures nor in the overt responsibility for existing policy, such nondecisions are generally perceived as not being politically salient. Nondecisions, however, when consistently made, are a form of policy making. Until the 1920s, for example, the consistently made nondecision that First Amendment liberties would not be enforced by the federal courts on the states was a policy with profound political im-

[7] One notable exception to this general rule was the case of James Earl Ray, the man accused of murdering Martin Luther King. By confessing to the crime, Ray avoided a trial and also the death penalty. This example of plea bargaining aroused widespread criticism. See New York Times, March 11, 1969, p. 16. Ray later maintained that he was pressured into the plea bargain by his lawyer and claimed he did not commit the murder. See New York Times, October 22, 1974, p. 25.

plications. Not until the 1925 case of *Gitlow* v. *New York*[8] did the Court finally reverse its position.

Most gatekeeping is a product of decision making by litigants and their lawyers. These include decisions to settle civil cases out of court, to plead guilty (with and without promises of a prosecutorial *quid pro quo*), plaintiff and prosecution decisions not to proceed to trial, and the decision of the losing party not to appeal the trial or intermediate appellate court decision. We therefore start our model of gatekeeping by a consideration of the factors involved in making such decisions.[9]

Litigant-lawyer gatekeeping doubtless involves some rough-and-ready form of cost-benefit analysis. Initially involved are calculations by the litigant of (1) the utility of a favorable judgment in terms of psychic satisfaction, prestige, money, freedom, and so forth; (2) the cost of going on with litigation in terms of time, money, psychic frustration, and so forth; and (3) the perceived probability of a favorable decision from a trial or appellate court. Representing the utility by U, the cost of litigation by C, and the perceived probability of a favorable judgment by p, we note that for any litigant, a, if[10]

$$U_a p_a \gg C_a$$

then the litigant will be inclined to press for a formal court judgment. If, on the other hand,[11]

$$U_a p_a \ll C_a$$

the litigant will be inclined to avoid further litigation by a gatekeeping solution. These solutions are of two types: (1) complete renuncia-

---

[8] 268 U.S. 652 (1925).

[9] It should be emphasized at this point that the model presented is a formal model. As such it is based on considerations of how the various actors involved in litigation should behave if they wish to maximize their interests with a minimal risk of extreme loss. As a formal description of how rational participants in litigation should act, it is valid even if no real-life persons act in the way described (though if this were the case, we would want to know why). However, there is suggestive evidence, some of it previously discussed in Chapter 4, that leads us to believe that many litigants behave in accordance with the formal model.

[10] This inequality may be read: "For litigant *a* the utility of a favorable judgment multiplied by its probability is *much greater* than the cost of litigation."

[11] This inequality may be read: "For litigant *a* the utility of a favorable judgment multiplied by its probability is *much less* than the cost of litigation."

tion of all reward (*nonnegotiated gatekeeping*)—for example, no recovery in a civil suit or full payment of requested damages, a non-bargained guilty plea or the decision not to prosecute, complete acceptance of a trial or circuit court's (unfavorable) judgment—and (2) a negotiated settlement or bargained guilty plea (*negotiated gatekeeping*). If the first option is exercised, then a gatekeeping solution is resorted to regardless of litigant b's calculations.[12] If the second option is sought, then b's calculations become important. If b's calculations indicate that

$$U_b p_b \ll C_b$$

then negotiated gatekeeping is sought. What then must be determined is the worth, W, of the case for both a and b: for example, the size of the damages, the acceptable criminal charge with its projected penalties, and so on. If[13]

$$W_a = W_b$$

then a negotiated settlement or plea bargain occurs. If, however,[14]

$$W_a \neq W_b \text{ or } U_b p_b \gg C_b$$

[12] This is not quite true since if it is *known* that b is willing to negotiate, negotiated gatekeeping may still occur. However, if it is known that b will not negotiate or his calculations are unknown or disguised (b is bluffing), nonnegotiated gatekeeping will occur by a.

[13] $W_a = W_b$ is not meant to represent an exact equality. This is because the Ws do not represent exact figures but rather zones of acceptability. If we represent the situation by two overlapping circles, $W_a = W_b$ is the intersection between the two circles. The case is negotiated in the area of intersection with the exact settlement or bargain being determined by the negotiating skill of the respective parties and their lawyers. $W_a \neq W_b$ represents the condition when W_a and W_b do not intersect. Thus there is no possible negotiated result.

[14] Both the utility of winning the case, U, and its worth, W, must be separately considered because these are not the same things. The latter includes only such settlement-related factors as the amount of damages or length and nature of a criminal sentence. The former also includes such other factors as psychic satisfaction of winning, prestige, and the desire to establish a formal policy ruling. For example, in a tax case a business firm may not be very much concerned with the amount of money it would have to pay as a settlement. It may, however, be very much concerned with obtaining a formal ruling on a point of tax law, particularly if there is a good probability that the ruling will be in the firm's favor.

then a formal systemic resolution in terms of an authoritative court judgment will still be sought.

Litigant-lawyer gatekeeping is encouraged by a number of aspects of the judicial process. The costs of litigation, C, for both a and b are often high as compared to their utilities, U. This is particularly true for civil litigation and appellate review. The legal skill and familiarity with judicial and jury behavior of both litigants' lawyers mean that the perceived probabilities of a favorable court judgment for one side or the other tend to be the same; that is, there is a tendency for

$$p_a = 1 - p_b$$

Usually these probabilities approach zero for one side and unity for the other; that is, there is often little doubt by both lawyers as to what the *general* court judgment will be. At the same time, the *specific* decision is typically less predictable. There is always the chance that an "unexpected" assessment of damages or sentence will occur in terms of leniency or severity for the "losing" party. The specific result of a negotiated settlement, on the other hand, is much more predictable.

Stated conversely, this means that cases that go to trial and are pressed for appellate review for an authoritative output are those where either U_a or U_b or both are high (e.g., cases involving high stakes in monetary value, criminal penalties, prestige, or issues of public policy) and cases where p_a and p_b approach 0.5 (cases whose decisional results are ambiguous). Most favored, of course, are cases that combine both features.

Whether a case leads to the highest authoritative output of a Supreme Court ruling accompanied by a written opinion is dependent upon how the Court's members respond to the demand for such treatment by a petitioner for certiorari or appellant. Here we are interested in the exercise of judicial rather than litigant-lawyer gatekeeping. At this stage questions of utility and decisional predictability once again play an important role. Utility considerations are suggested by the Court's giving special scrutiny and a higher acceptance rate to petitions where a prisoner's life is at stake as well as cases where the federal government favors review. But of greatest import are the justices' calculations of their own utilities in having the Court render an authoritative judgment on the specific questions of public policy presented. The process of filtering out cases where judicial utilities are low, either because the case is considered "frivolous" or its treatment would involve the Court in unwanted political controversy, is highly formalized in the exercise of granting certiorari petitions through the mechanisms of the chief justice's special list and the "rule of four."

It should not be thought that Supreme Court gatekeeping only allows acceptance of cases involving important social interests or policy questions, while rejecting cases lacking these characteristics. Cases that are avoided because of the tactical consideration that a judicial decision would place the Court in the center of a storm of controversy are rejected not because the issues or interests are unimportant, but rather because they are considered too important. Even many frivolous cases that are rejected may contain important issues affecting widespread and powerful interests. It is not their lack of important issues that make these cases frivolous, rather it is because the points of law challenged are considered so well settled as to be beyond question, at least for the time being. This is the current status of cases questioning the constitutionality of state and federal authority to regulate the economy. Importance or utility, therefore, as a criterion for judicial selection of cases for Supreme Court review, refers to the subjective evaluation by each member of the Court. In other words, to pass Supreme Court gatekeeping, a case must present issues upon which at least four members of the Court feel it is time for the Court to act. As already suggested, the cue of the federal government's favoring review and the question of a litigant's life or death are two objective criteria creating this subjective importance. A further, and perhaps as important, variable giving a case subjective importance is whether the issue raised falls into an area of stable judicial policy or not; that is, *is* the decisional result of the case in doubt?

Decisional ambiguity as an important criterion is indicated by the findings of Tanenhaus and his colleagues that both lower court dissension and conflict in circuits are relevant for the granting of certiorari.[15] Its importance is further suggested by the fact that the re-

[15] Joseph Tanenhaus, Marvin Schick, Matthew Muraskin, and Daniel Rosen, "The Supreme Court's Certiorari Jurisdiction: Cue Theory," in Glendon Schubert (ed.), *Judicial Decision-Making* (New York: Free Press, 1963), pp. 111–132.

versal rate for cases accepted on certiorari, at least in the past, has run about 50 percent.[16]

When it affects a whole area of the law, decisional ambiguity doubtless springs from deeply felt societal tensions. It may be created by changing patterns in social life (e.g., economic and technological development) that render old rules and norms inapplicable to the newly created modern conditions. For example, American industrialization generated severe economic and social dislocations that gave rise to numerous demands on the larger political system as well as the federal and state judicial systems. As a result, during most of the latter nineteenth and early twentieth centuries, there was widespread instability in the law governing economic life, especially involving employer-employee and manufacturer-consumer relationships. The Supreme Court as well as Congress and the state legislatures spent considerable time and energy on redefining the law of business regulation. This example suggests a simple causal model for explaining the surge and decline in cases that are considered important and thus deserving of Supreme Court time and policy-making creativity.

Old patterns of stable social life are broken by (economic and technological) developments leading to new patterns of social interaction. Such increasing social conflict generates increasing demands on legislative and judicial systems for new rules and norms. Legislative and/or lower level judicial authorities may respond by creating such new rules and norms, and the Supreme Court may then legitimize them by reinterpreting or changing the previously established legal norms. This cycle continues until a new pattern of stable social relationships is established.

A similar process occurs when previously thwarted demands are made amenable to authoritative treatment by decisions made solely by the judicial authorities. Such a situation has characterized the Court's confrontation with the issues of racial segregation, sexual equality, and legislative malapportionment. In fact, it has often been stated by admirers of the judiciary that one contribution that the courts, and especially the Supreme Court, uniquely make for conflict resolution in American society is to offer oppressed groups a forum

[16] Glendon Schubert, *Quantitative Analysis of Judicial Behavior* (New York: Free Press, 1959), pp. 43, 62.

for treating demands that otherwise are untreatable because of the control exercised by entrenched majorities, whether they be in a national or local electorate, a legislative body, or a local governmental area such as a school district. Here a favorable judicial decision encourages litigation calling for new judicial decisions and often legislation creating new rules and norms. In the broader sense, conflict is thereby enhanced rather than resolved as new issues demand the attention of political authorities. Thus legal instability continues to make such issues subjectively important for members of the Court.

This demand-flow/gatekeeping model of what cases and issues ultimately become formal output following Supreme Court review illuminates some empirical characteristics of Court policy making. First, it has often been noted that the Court concentrates its energies on certain questions of public policies during certain specific historical periods, for example, economic issues from after the Civil War until the mid-1930s, civil rights and civil liberties since then. These policy proclivities of the Court are often explained in terms of judicial attitudes, backgrounds, or political sensitivities. However, as just suggested, an understanding of Court output also requires consideration of the nature of the demands made on the system as well as the nature of gatekeeping at any one point or period in time.

It has also been suggested by some observers of the American judiciary that trial courts typically enforce norms, while the Supreme Court makes policy.[17] The norm-enforcement role of trial courts is suggested by such facts as: only rarely do specific cases at trial generate much public or professional attention or controversy; few trial judgments, particularly at the state judicial level, are accompanied by a written opinion which then stands as a precedent for lawyers and other courts; and, last, only somewhat less rarely is the basic decision of who will win (but not the size of the damages or the severity of the sentence) a matter of considerable doubt. In other words, individual cases within the trial courts are fairly routinized affairs affecting and of interest to only the specific parties involved. Cases that the Supreme Court reviews, especially those involving oral argument and a written opinion, tend to have just the opposite characteristics.

The norm-enforcement–policy-making dichotomy is at heart a qual-

---

[17] Cf. Herbert Jacob, *Justice in America*, 2nd ed. (Boston: Little, Brown, 1972), pp. 21–39.

itative distinction. An analysis of gatekeeping, however, suggests that the real distinction is more properly a quantitative one. Because the district courts, especially at the pretrial stage but also at trial, handle predominantly routine cases that are important only to the specific litigants involved, this dichotomy is doubtlessly reinforced. Although some trial judges do show a propensity for creative policy making when called upon to do so, both the hierarchical nature of the system and the general atmosphere created by handling mostly routine cases discourages this even when a novel situation begs such a response. Moreover, as Richardson and Vines have shown,[18] the pressing of questions calling for judicial creativity may not even occur until after the trial record has been searched, and thus such questions are not raised as the central issue of the case until the first appeal.

As cases move up the court system hierarchy, litigant/lawyer, and judicial gatekeeping filter out the routine cases and promote for extensive Supreme Court consideration cases that on the whole call for judicial creativity. The very expectation that the Court will concentrate on such cases as well as the knowledge that the Supreme Court is the court of last resort with constitutional equality, if not superiority, to the states, Congress, and the executive encourages its members to be creative policy makers. As Wells and Grossman have pointed out,[19] the case or controversy context of adjudication has meant that *both* the Supreme Court and the lower courts are involved in the problem-solving exercise of authoritatively resolving unique conflicts between specific individuals and institutions through the application of certain standards (provided by such legal sources as the Constitution, statutes, and the body of precedent that makes up the evolving legal tradition) to specific sets of facts.

ADJUDICATION AS POLICY MAKING

The concrete specific context of adjudication has important implications for the manner in which judicial policy making proceeds, the types of questions that can be handled successfully, and the ability of

[18] Richard J. Richardson and Kenneth N. Vines, "Review, Dissent, and the Appellate Process: A Political Interpretation," *Journal of Politics,* 29 (1967), 597–616.

[19] Richard S. Wells and Joel B. Grossman, "The Concept of Judicial Policy-Making," *Journal of Public Law,* 15 (1966), 286–307.

the federal judiciary and especially the Supreme Court to change social behavior through its power to define legal rules and norms. Like the authorities of bureaucratic systems in general, the authorities of a judicial system strive to bring decisional ambiguity under control in the areas over which it has competence. This makes adjudication more than just a process by which concrete conflicts are resolved in the here and now. It is also an enterprise by which judges try to eradicate decisional ambiguity through the authoritative announcement of what norms are currently being applied to cases. Each decision, therefore, may be seen as a declaration of current policy. Appellate court decisions in particular and the opinions associated with them stand as a communications output telling other judges, public officials, members of the bar, and private citizens what to expect from litigation. In effect, when any court authoritatively decides a case it says, "This is what this court will do when presented with this situation again." When that court is the highest court in the system, its decision in a case in effect states, "This is what all courts [in the system] will [should] do when presented with this situation again."

Without this future orientation to judicial outputs, court judgments would be like the arbitrary granting of favors by a capricious sovereign. Such a situation would have serious implications for the legitimacy of the judiciary. Moreover, it would probably result in an intolerably high level of demands for trial and appellate review as litigants pressed their cases until all remedies were exhausted in the search for a favorable decision. When one combines this antigate-keeping effect of unpredictability with the cultural concepts that posit that judicial decision making is only legitimate when it represents the consistent application of known law, then it should be obvious that the pressures toward predictability in judicial decision making are great. This drive toward consistency is, of course, at the heart of the legal concept of *stare decisis*.

Before the days when legal philosophers recognized that courts ought to be responsive to changing social needs and conditions as well as to be consistent, *stare decisis* was emphasized as *the legal norm*. The law that courts enforced was seen as stable and knowable through the analysis of constitutional provisions, statutes, and past precedents. Each judicial output was seen as an application of that knowable law. Since, however, trial judges could err in making decisions, appellate courts, particularly the one court of last resort (the

Supreme Court), were a structural necessity to see that lower court consistency and correctness were maintained. Supreme Court decisions and opinions, therefore, were conceptualized as the vehicles by which the lower court judges—and all other interested persons, for that matter—were informed as to what the law was.

As our demand-flow/gatekeeping discussion of appellate review suggests, the situation is not as simple. Stability in the law is constantly broken by new legislation and judicial interpretations aimed at making legal norms more responsive to contemporary social needs, demands, and ideas. Thus, as the courts, especially the Supreme Court, focus on legal areas at which such demands for change are aimed, that law enters into a state of becoming rather than being.

Judicial gatekeeping and the case-by-case aspect of adjudication allow the Court to engineer legal change incrementally. For example, in attacking racial segregation in the public schools, the landmark case that announced the major policy that such practices are forbidden by the "equal protection clause" of the Fourteenth Amendment (*Brown* v. *Board of Education*) was preceded by a series of less dramatic and less far-reaching cases that had slowly chipped away at the separate-but-equal doctrine in law and graduate schools.[20] Even the Brown case itself was announced in a way that allowed for further incremental change. The separate-but-equal doctrine upon which segregation laws had rested was not declared unconstitutional per se —a ruling that would have meant that all legally maintained segregation in every aspect of social life from residential housing to miscegenation laws would immediately have been struck down—rather it was declared unconstitutional in *public education* because social science research indicated that such segregation had a deleterious effect on Negro children. This attempt at social theorizing made the decision less comprehensive in scope than would have the ruling of per se unconstitutionality. The incremental effect of the Court's reasoning should be plain. It meant that for other segregation laws to be struck down the Supreme Court had to take up these laws one at a time (e.g., public parks, public transportation, public libraries, and so on) and consider whether they too would be declared unconstitutional.

[20] Missouri ex. rel. Gaines v. Canada, 305 U.S. 337 (1938); Sweatt v. Painter, 339 U.S. 629 (1950); McLaurin v. Oklahoma State Regents, 339 U.S. 637 (1950), among others. Also see Albert P. Blaustein and Clarence C. Ferguson, Jr., *Desegregation and the Law*, 2nd ed. (New York: Vintage, 1962), pp. 95–113.

The Court's method of disposing of the Brown case, the "all deliberate speed" formula, also contained an obvious incremental aspect. Here, however, the incrementalism was concerned more with the pace of implementation at the district court level than with the shape or scope of the basic policy. Yet even this created a certain step-by-step growth in judicial policy making. First, state laws that met the letter of the Brown ruling but evaded its spirit (e.g., closing of all public schools and state financing of private "whites only" schools) were struck down. Then the more substantive plans (e.g., freedom of choice) that allowed marginal but did not provide for total desegregation were attacked. Eventually even delaying tactics based on the "all deliberate speed" formula itself were declared invalid. Finally, the lower courts began to move on various forms of *de facto* (i.e., what occurs in practice although not legally required, as opposed to legally imposed or *de jure*) segregation. Ultimately, the Supreme Court made it clear in *Keyes* v. *School District Number 1, Denver, Colorado*,[21] that *de facto* school segregation as a result of actions deliberately taken by the local school authorities, which had the effect of maintaining the separation of the races, was indistinguishable from *de jure* segregation and was thus in violation of the equal protection clause of the Fourteenth Amendment. The Denver case was to northern school segregation what *Brown* v. *Board of Education* was to Southern school segregation.[22]

The incremental approach in the articulation of legal norms dealing with civil rights meant that it took the Court almost two decades to erect the necessary legal structure for the elimination of *de jure* segregation, and almost another two decades to eliminate *de facto* segregation. Even now, many of the behavioral remains of the old patterns of segregation still exist in both North and South. Their final eradication depends in part on continued litigation in the lower courts and determined administrative action. This has led some to

[21] 413 U.S. 921 (1973).

[22] The Nixon Court, however, subsequently in a sharply divided decision concerning the Detroit metropolitan area ruled that desegregation plans can only be imposed on the local governmental unit in which it has been proven that official actions by the school authorities promoted racial segregation. Thus, even when the problem is shown to be an areawide one fostered by state action or inaction in terms of discriminatory real-estate practices or nonenforcement of antidiscrimination statutes, school desegregation remedies are limited strictly to the geographical locality in which it is proved that the actions of *school authorities* have maintained segregation of the races. Milliken v. Bradley, 94 S. Ct. 3112 (1974).

charge that the "all deliberative speed" formula was itself responsible for the long delay. However, it should be kept in mind that the pressures for incrementalism in striking down *de jure* (and even *de facto*) segregation were strong. Broad areas of social life and deeply held cultural mores have had to be changed. To prevent the Brown decision from becoming a gigantic "self-inflicted wound" that would have severely undermined the Court's support and been unenforceable as well, time had to be given to allow for Congress, the executive branch, and the nation at large to adjust. Indeed, it should be noted that incrementalism can be found in practically all subject areas where the Court has fashioned new policies, be they the civil rights of black Americans or the civil rights of women.

In pointing to Supreme Court incrementalism, a word of caution is in order. Although from time to time members of the Court as well as various legal scholars have called attention to the merits of such an approach, it should not be implied that a step-by-step growth in judicial policy is necessarily due to the fact that certain policy goals are set and then a crablike movement toward those goals is undertaken in order to "break the news gently." Although there is statistical evidence that suggests that such a tactic may be consciously carried out by certain members of the Court,[23] when one looks at the Court as a whole, much less conscious psychological mechanisms seem to be involved.

The Supreme Court's dual appellate jurisdiction over federal and state courts also leads to a certain type of incrementalism, that is, initially fashioning policies that only apply to its federal jurisdiction and then extending them through constitutional interpretation to the states. This process is quite obvious in the Court's policy making in the area of criminal procedure. The reasons the Supreme Court initially had been more creative in handling cases dealing with federal rather than state criminal procedure included the lack of any inhibitions arising from considerations of federalism, the direct supervisory role formally given the Supreme Court over the lower federal courts, its participation in rule making for the federal system as a whole, and the fact that in federal cases the Court is typically involved in statutory interpretation rather than constitutional adjudication. Members of the Court have had fewer qualms about the legitimacy, informational base, or ability to do irreparable harm in

[23] See Schubert, *Quantitative Analysis,* pp. 214–254.

modifying federal rules than they have had with state rules. Not only are the Court's statutory interpretations amenable to remedial congressional action through legislation, but also the number of persons affected is much smaller, given the difference between federal and state criminal jurisdiction. Thus we see, particularly in the areas of search and seizure, and post arrest and appellate procedures, that policy thrusts through federal rule making and case decisions preceded similar thrusts into state criminal procedures.

Policy making by adjudication implies a number of limits on the scope and impact of judicial policies. Some of these have already been suggested in the discussion of the system's regime rules concerning jurisdiction and justiciability, gatekeeping, and incremental decision making. Other limitations are inherent in the adversary method of processing cases, the nature of legal remedies, and the format (i.e., court rulings and opinions) by which policies are announced. It is to these latter limitations that we now turn.

The adversary method means that for a case to arise there must exist social conflicts between identifiable persons and/or institutions.[24] The impact of judicial policy thrusts is furthered when the injured parties readily attack evasion of those policies either because they are well organized (e.g., the NAACP and civil rights) or because of the strong personal interests involved (e.g., when the rights of criminal defendants are involved). The adversary method also limits judicial output in that it limits information input. American trial judges are not expected to independently gather evidence and search for the truth. Judge John J. Sirica's handling of the Watergate-related trials raised some eyebrows because of his insistence at getting at the truth as much as at the sensational aspects of the revelations.[25] Trial

[24] When social consensus exists, judicial control is very difficult to establish and maintain. This seems evident, for example, in the fate of the school prayer decisions where noncompliance has been substantial. Cf. Richard M. Johnson, *The Dynamics of Compliance* (Evanston, Ill.: Northwestern University Press, 1967); William K. Muir, *Prayer in the Public Schools* (Chicago: University of Chicago Press, 1967); and Kenneth M. Dolbeare and Phillip E. Hammond, *The School Prayer Decisions: From Court Policy to Local Practice* (Chicago: University of Chicago Press, 1971).

[25] See, for example, Robert M. Smith, "T-r-u-t-h or T-r-i-a-l?," *New York Times*, November 4, 1974, p. 37. Note that the Court of Appeals praised Sirica when it upheld the conviction of G. Gordon Liddy. The appeals court wrote: "Judge Sirica's palpable search for truth in such a trial [involving the integrity of the nation's political system] was not only permissible, it was in the highest tradition of his office as a Federal judge. And although his execution of this objective presented problems, as must be acknowledged, they were not the kind that deprived de-

courts ordinarily process only information provided them by opposing counsel as that information survives cross-examination and standards of evidence. Although appellate courts may receive, in addition to the trial record and standard appellate briefs, additional informational input from factual Brandeis-type and *amicus curiae* briefs (and from each new crop of law clerks as well), even these courts are limited to an extent by the adversary method.

Judicial policy making (and constitutional policy making, in particular) is also limited by the nature of legal remedies. The Court essentially says either yes or no to governmental activity. Because where the line falls between the permissible and the forbidden is difficult to pinpoint and the affected instances of behavior are numerous, the promotion of a judicial policy may take numerous cases extending over many years. The Court normally does not articulate its policies in the form of codes of what is permissible and what is forbidden;[26] thus, even after years of adjudication, there still may be substantial confusion as to just what is judicial policy. For example, this confusion was long apparent in the law dealing with obscenity.[27] In short, judicial remedies are relatively unsuccessful for controlling policy in an area that requires a comprehensive plan of positive action. In such areas often the most appropriate judicial response is to return these problem areas to Congress or the executive whose regime rules do allow for comprehensive plans of positive action.[28] This is in effect what the Court did after 1936 with regard to the regulation of economic life.

---

fendants of a fair trial." As quoted in *The New York Times*, "Appellate Court Praises Sirica As It Upholds Liddy Conviction," November 9, 1974, p. 16.

[26] In recent years one decision that seems to be an exception to this general statement has been Miranda v. Arizona, 384 U.S. 436 (1966), the opinion of which includes detailed instructions to police as to how they should behave when they wish to question a criminal suspect. Another might be Roe v. Wade, 410 U.S. 113 (1973) in which the Court sought to specify what sort of legislation regulating abortion would pass constitutional muster and what would not.

[27] When the Nixon Court sought to change but also clarify matters in the key 1973 obscenity decisions, the Court's efforts only resulted in continued confusion. See Miller v. California, 413 U.S. 15 (1973); Paris Adult Theatre v. Slaton, 413 U.S. 49 (1973); United States v. 12 200-Ft. Reels of Super 8mm Film, 413 U.S. 123 (1973); and United States v. Orito, 413 U.S. 139 (1973).

[28] The Nixon Court would have liked to have been able to turn obscenity back to the state legislatures and Congress, but obscenity may be such a unique policy area that it is impossible for the courts to remove themselves from deciding the constitutional questions that invariably arise without an absolutist policy of total

The impact of judicial policy making where it implies new patterns of social behavior is strongly limited by the format in which policies are announced. The bare outlines of each case disposed of by the Supreme Court—that is, the facts, the legal questions considered, and who won—provide important cues as to contemporary judicial policy for the area of the law under consideration. Yet because each case is always to some extent unique and the factual and legal questions may be many and complex, a case decision (absent an opinion) may leave many questions in doubt. In "important" cases, therefore, associated output by way of the Court's opinion can be seen as a device to clarify and interpret the underlying considerations behind the case's disposal.

But there are opinions and opinions. Some serve to clarify, others confuse. In *Brown* v. *Board of Education,* for example, the fact that the Court was able to produce an unanimous opinion helped to establish Court policy in what was bound to be a controversial and complex subject. In *Reynolds* v. *Sims,*[29] the "one man–one vote" policy announced in the Court's opinion served as a fairly definitive guide for subsequent district court action. However, the Court is often unwilling or unable to agree on only one policy option. Sometimes this occurs because members of the Court in fact *want* to leave open more than one option. Other times a consensus is lacking among the Court majority as to what policy considerations lie behind a specific decision; that is, a Court majority may agree on authoritative but not associated output.

Youngstown Sheet and Tube v. *Sawyer*[30] is a prime example of such a case. Although the Court ruled that the federal government's seizure of the nation's steel mills was forbidden when based on presidential authority alone, the opinions that represented the views of the justices in the majority had little to offer as policy guides for future presidents and courts. The case was decided 6 to 3 against the government. Justice Black wrote the opinion for the Court. Each of his colleagues on the winning side also wrote a concurring opinion, and each disagreed to some extent with the Black opinion

---

permissibility. Thus in 1974 the Court had to clarify its 1973 position in the case over the alleged obscenity of the film *Carnal Knowledge.* See Jenkins v. Georgia, 94 S. Ct. 2750 (1974).

[29] 377 U.S. 533 (1964).

[30] 343 U.S. 579 (1952).

as well as with each other's concurrences. The same phenomenon was demonstrated with the Pentagon Papers case in 1971[31] and with the 1972 decision striking down capital punishment.[32]

Although these cases are perhaps extreme examples, most opinions representing the majority's view suffer from their ambiguities. This is perhaps unavoidable, as the Court's opinion reflects the negotiations and bargaining that were necessary to attract a majority. Such compromises mean that areas of intramajority contention and conflict will be papered over by ambiguous phrases. Moreover, often the thrust of this opinion is made less understandable by concurrences and dissents that misstate or exaggerate the majority's intent.

Needless to say, opinion ambiguity and intra-Court dissension can seriously affect the impact of the case on social behavior. They can be seized upon by the Court's critics for challenging the rationality and legitimacy of the Court's ruling.[33] They can provide the opportunities for subsequent private, official, and judicial evasion and noncompliance.

In summary, as our analysis of judicial output indicates, the nation is not ruled by "nine old men" of the Supreme Court. This is true even for those areas of the law in which there are frequent judicial policy pronouncements. Instead, we have a much more complex situation. There are important and broad areas of national policy where there is no judicial policy. In those areas where federal judicial policy does exist, although the Supreme Court often plays a primary

[31] New York Times Company v. United States, 403 U.S. 713 (1971).

[32] Furman v. Georgia, 408 U.S. 238 (1972).

[33] Some justices appear to be alerting the opposition with their dissents. For example, Justice Black in one dissent noted, "I regret very much that this Court by its hasty, summary reversal, is providing its critics with such choice ammunition for their attacks." Recznik v. City of Lorain, 393 U.S. 171 at 174 (1968). Another apparent example of this is a dissent by Justice Stewart in which he observed, "It seems to me that those of us who dissented in Miranda v. Arizona . . . remain free not only to express our continuing disagreement with that decision, but also to oppose any broadening of its impact." Orozco v. Texas, 394 U.S. 324 at 331 (1969). Justice Marshall in Milliken v. Bradley declared: "The Court today takes a giant step backwards. . . . I cannot subscribe to this emasculation of our constitutional guarantee of equal protection of the laws and must respectfully dissent. . . . Today's holding, I fear, is more a reflection of a perceived public mood that we have gone far enough in enforcing the Constitution's guarantee of equal justice than it is the product of neutral principles of law." 94 S. Ct. 3112 at 3145, 3146, 3161 (1974).

role in setting this policy, it does so in conjunction with the lower federal and state judiciaries. Often intervention by the Court is sporadic and aimed more at legitimizing governmental policy or preserving the status quo rather than creating new legal norms. However, when judicial policy making is aimed at the definition of new norms of behavior, the results of the new policy may be in doubt. There are numerous instances where Court policies have been totally or partially nullified. This has occurred quite legitimately, for example, when Congress has passed new legislation overturning a Court ruling on statutory interpretation or in the few instances when a constitutional ruling of the Court has been repudiated by a constitutional amendment. Of course, there are less legitimate ways of avoiding compliance that run the gamut from benign neglect to outright defiance. There are other occasions when Court policy defining new legal norms may be followed by official action and social behavior that complies both with the letter and spirit of that policy. In such instances it may truly be said that the Court exercises a "final say" in national policy making.

OUTPUT TRENDS: SOME GENERAL CONSIDERATIONS

Although detailed discussion of the substantive policies promoted by the Supreme Court and the lower federal courts is beyond the scope of this book, a few very general comments in addition to the preceding references to substantive output are in order.

In terms of constitutional policy making, the basic trend since 1937 has been apparent.[34] The Court in 1937 and beyond rejected the legal doctrines so carefully built in the preceding half-century

---

[34] See Glendon Schubert, *The Constitutional Polity* (Boston: Boston University Press, 1970), Chap. 1; Alpheus T. Mason, *The Supreme Court from Taft to Warren* (New York: Norton, 1964), Chaps. 3–6; Robert G. McCloskey, *The American Supreme Court* (Chicago: University of Chicago Press, 1960), pp. 136–231; Archibald Cox, *The Warren Court: Constitutional Decision as an Instrument of Reform* (Cambridge, Mass: Harvard University Press, 1968); Alexander M. Bickel, *The Supreme Court and the Idea of Progress* (New York: Harper & Row, 1969); James F. Simon, *In His Own Image: The Supreme Court in Richard Nixon's America* (New York: McKay, 1973). Also see Tinsley E. Yarbrough, "The Nixon Court and the First Amendment," paper delivered at the 1974 Annual Meeting of the American Political Science Association; Leonard W. Levy, *Against the Law: The Nixon Court and Criminal Justice* (New York: Harper & Row, 1974).

that stated that economic regulatory legislation could be constitutionally challenged because the judges thought that the law was inherently a deprivation of liberty or property without due process of law. Rejected too were allied doctrines in the commerce and taxation areas, all of which allowed the Court to preempt economic policy making for the nation. The Court, of course, had used its laissez-faire economic policies in favor of powerful corporate and financial interests, and in turn the Court had received potent political support. After the so-called Constitutional Revolution of 1937, the Court has almost always conceded to government the right to control economic policy. However, the Court has not removed itself from economic policy making. Rather, the Court has been very heavily involved in statutory interpretation of the glut of economic regulatory legislation that thickens the statute books. Thus, less dramatically than through constitutional adjudication, the Court has nevertheless influenced economic policy.[35] However, the most prominent thrust of Court policy making since 1937 has been in the realm of civil liberties, and it is here that Court output has had a profound effect on American life.

Why civil liberties came to dominate the constitutional output of the Court in the last several decades can perhaps be answered. First, it must be recognized that the Roosevelt pro–New Deal appointees to the Court were sympathetic to these issues. Second, the members of the Court, as most perceptive Americans, undoubtedly became more self-conscious of basic freedoms in an age that saw the rise of brutal fascist and communist totalitarianisms. Third, it should be kept in mind that the Court as an institution has historically been activist on behalf of one or another set of values. Historically, the Court has played an active role in American life. Had it not embraced and promoted some constitutional values, the Court would have been surrendering a vital portion of its institutional power. Finally, individuals and groups emerged willing to press civil liberties claims. Three broad areas of civil liberties in which the libertarian activism of the post-1937 Court (especially during the last half of Chief Justice Warren's tenure) was pronounced concerned First Amendment freedoms, constitutional rights of criminal de-

[35] See Martin Shapiro, *Law and Politics in the Supreme Court* (New York: Free Press, 1964); and also his book, *The Supreme Court and Administrative Agencies* (New York: Free Press, 1968).

fendants, and the equal protection of the law (i.e., racial and electoral discrimination).[36]

As suggested earlier (and as considered in the following chapter), the federal judicial system has entered a new constitutional era fashioned by the Nixon Court. Unlike the 1937 constitutional revolution the Court has not made, at least through the 1974 term, wholesale reversals of liberal Warren Court doctrines, nor has it repudiated constitutional doctrines that permit the exercise of power in any subject matter area. Rather the Nixon Court has sought to limit and reinterpret those policies particularly in (but not confined to) the realm of criminal procedures.[37] The strategy seems to be that of incrementalism so that policies disliked by the Nixon Court majority, for example, the Miranda policy, will eventually be so eroded that by the time the Court comes around to formally announcing their demise, for all intents and purposes those policies will long have been reversed.

Yet it should be emphasized that not only has the Court *not* given up the broad constitutional doctrines that permit substantive policy making, but the Nixon Court has revived the substantive due process doctrine and has used it as the constitutional basis in certain areas of civil liberties, for example, the abortion decision of *Roe* v. *Wade*. This decision, a decidedly "liberal" one, also suggests that new areas of civil liberties, such as the rights of women, are being developed by the Nixon Court. Thus, while many important Warren Court policies have in effect been turned around, there are other and even new areas in which the Court is demonstrating a creative will of its own (thereby being true to the institutional traditions of the Court). Thus the Nixon appointments to the Supreme Court and the staffing of the lower judiciary with Nixon (and Ford) appointees has had an effect on substantive output.[38]

36 See, for example, Lucius J. Barker and Twiley W. Barker, Jr. (eds.), *Civil Liberties and the Constitution*, 2nd ed. (Englewood Cliffs, N.J.: Prentice-Hall, 1975).

37 See, in general, Simon, *In His Own Image*; Yarbrough, "The Nixon Court and the First Amendment"; and Levy, *Against the Law*. Also see, H. Frank Way, "The Nixon Court: Two Models of Criminal Justice," paper presented at the Annual Meeting, A.P.S.A., 1974.

38 See Sheldon Goldman, "Voting Behavior on the U.S. Courts of Appeals Revisited," *American Political Science Review*, 69 (1975), p. 497, n. 24; and Jon Gottschall, "The Nixon Appointments to the United States Courts of Appeals: The Impact of the Law and Order Issue on the Rights of the Accused," Ph.D. dissertation, University of Massachusetts, 1975.

ASSOCIATED OUTPUT

In some respects the distinction between authoritative and associated judicial output is difficult to discern. After all, in accord with the definitions proposed at the beginning of this chapter, a judicial policy can consist of both a binding decision by the authorities (authoritative output) and the opinion elaborating upon the principle used to decide the case (associated output). The previous considerations in fact did blur any distinction between the two forms of output, and it is plausible to argue that for purposes of analysis of judicial policies as they are articulated in decisions and opinions such a distinction is unnecessary.[39] However, there are other forms of judicial output that intuitively are not of the same character as binding judicial decisions and policies. In judicial opinions, for example, *obiter dicta* (judicial asides) may anticipate new policy directions or may imply certain consequences of the policy that were not actually decided upon by the Court. Incrementalism in policy making, as suggested earlier, is largely fostered by such dicta.

Furthermore, there are other on-the-bench aspects of judicial behavior that can be considered a form of output, for example, the attitudes and demeanor of trial judges toward the attorneys and litigants appearing before them. One of the serious charges brought against Judge G. Harrold Carswell during the Senate controversy over his Supreme Court nomination in 1970 was that, as a trial judge, he was openly hostile to civil rights lawyers appearing before him.[40] His behavior can be considered to have represented a policy output for which he ultimately was held accountable. Participating in a case in which one has some (however minor) tangible interest can also be thought of as a form of output. Judge Clement Haynsworth's nomination to the Supreme Court in 1969 suffered badly because of such charges brought against him.[41]

Off-the-bench activities of judges can also be conceptualized as forms of output when they concern the judge by virtue of his official

[39] This is the position taken by Joel B. Grossman in his "A Model for Judicial Policy Analysis: The Supreme Court and the Sit-In Cases," in Joel B. Grossman and Joseph Tanenhaus (eds.), *Frontiers of Judicial Research* (New York: Wiley, 1969), p. 420.

[40] *New York Times*, February 3, 1970, p. 15.

[41] See *Congressional Quarterly*, September 26, 1969, pp. 1766–1767; November 14, 1969, pp. 2244–2245; November 21, 1969, pp. 2310–2311.

capacity. The financial dealings of Justice Fortas and what they purportedly represented made him a vulnerable member of the Court and ostensibly began the chain of events that led to his resignation.[42] The speeches and writings of judges are also output-type activities, particularly when they concern matters of controversy. When he was on the Court of Appeals for the District of Columbia, Judge Burger delivered an address that presented his legal philosophy concerning criminal procedures.[43] Apparently this talk caught the attention of Richard Nixon and eventually led to Burger's elevation to the chief justiceship of the Supreme Court.[44] The writings of Justice Douglas, particularly his book *Points of Rebellion*,[45] led to a serious congressional campaign for his impeachment. In announcing his intent to press for Douglas's impeachment, then–Republican House Minority Leader Gerald Ford stated that Judges Carswell and Haynsworth "have been denied seats on the bench for statements that are much less reprehensible than those made, in my opinion, by Justice Douglas."[46]

Associated output, then, encompasses those activities of the judicial authorities that are not direct orders and rulings in specific cases. As such, associated output covers a wide variety of on- and off-the-bench behavior that has the imprimatur of the judge in his official position. That output, too, can be thought of as resulting from processing input and feedback. Just as with authoritative output, it can be expected to change under certain circumstances. No doubt the Fortas-Haynsworth-Douglas controversies have affected many forms of associated output.[47]

[42] See the discussion in Chapter 1.

[43] Julius Duscha, "Chief Justice Burger Asks: 'If It Doesn't Make Good Sense, How Can It Make Good Law?' " *New York Times Magazine*, October 5, 1969, p. 30.

[44] *Ibid.*

[45] William O. Douglas, *Points of Rebellion* (New York: Random House, 1970).

[46] *New York Times*, April 14, 1970, p. 27.

[47] Note that in August, 1972, the American Bar Association approved a revised and stricter set of Canons of Judicial Ethics. The Judicial Conference of the United States in April, 1973, went even further in the first code of ethics for federal judges that body had ever adopted. Among the provisions of the new code were requirements of periodic disclosure of compensation, gifts, and of other outside income and that judges should refrain from business dealings or participate in any case in which they have a financial interest in the matter that might raise questions of

Until the last decade or two, analysis of judicial decision making normally ceased after considering the results of particular rulings in terms of the behavior and fortunes of those directly affected. Such results or *outcomes* of judicial output include, for example, the exchange of money in the payment of damages, the imprisonment of those convicted of crimes, the release of those not convicted, and the dropping of legal actions against those accused of violating statutes declared invalid.

The reason that analysis of output ended with a consideration of outcomes was because it was generally assumed that specific decisions, particularly by the Supreme Court, had the effect of settling the issues raised at least for the time being. As the recent history of civil rights and school prayer decisions has shown, however, what is legally a settled question may, in terms of behavioral compliance, not be a settled question at all. Sometimes, but certainly not always, private citizens and public officials evade, resist, and even openly defy the Court's policy. Thus it is necessary to study not only what the courts decide, but also the rate of compliance or *impact* to gain a full understanding of the judicial system's contribution to the governing of society.

Sometimes, too, but not always, once a case is decided its outcome gives rise to forces in society that have the effect of creating new systemic inputs or *feedback*. Included are new litigation, new information about how current Court policy channels social behavior, and even the institution of new regime rules concerning substantive and/or procedural law. Attention is given to these processes in the following chapter.

---

their impartiality. See *Congressional Quarterly*, April 14, 1973, p. 820. Congress in late 1974 passed the Judicial Disqualification Act that incorporated the ABA and Judicial Conference codes. Under the legislation that affects Supreme Court justices, lower federal court judges, magistrates, and bankruptcy referees, these officials are *required by law* to disqualify themselves in any proceeding in which their impartiality is plausibly open to question, including cases in which the official has even a small financial stake that could be affected by the court's decision. For other circumstances requiring disqualification see *Congressional Quarterly*, November 30, 1974, p. 3226. In general, see the discussion of off-the-bench activities of justices in Russell R. Wheeler, *Extrajudicial Behavior and the Role of the Supreme Court Justice* (Morristown, N.J.: General Learning Press, 1975).

SEVEN
IMPACT AND FEEDBACK

THE concepts of impact and feedback, although analytically distinguishable, are empirically closely related to each other. Information on the rate of compliance, the mechanisms used to affect that rate, and the broad social, economic, and political consequences of the implementation and attempts to implement policy output are important feedback data and activities. Various feedback responses in turn may vitally affect impact. Thus these analytically separate concepts are treated here as an empirical whole. Impact and feedback phenomena take a variety of forms, such as verbal comment by the communications media, politicians, and interest group leaders; various actions of evasion, noncompliance, and protest by lower court judges, public officials, and the public-at-large; new litigation aimed at narrowing or broadening court policy; and various responses by the major national political institutions of Congress and the presidency in enforcement, legislation, and judicial selection. It will be recalled that impact and feedback phenomena were earlier considered in our analysis of judicial selection and the input of support. Here some other aspects of these two highly interrelated phenomena will be considered.[1]

[1] An extensive consideration of impact and feedback phenomena can be found in Stephen L. Wasby, *The Impact of the United States Supreme Court: Some Perspectives* (Homewood, Ill.: Dorsey, 1970). Cf. Wasby's distinction between "impact" and "compliance," pp. 28–32. Also see James P. Levine, "Methodological Concerns in Studying Judicial Efficacy," *Law and Society Review*, 4 (1970), 583–611; Malcolm Feeley, "Coercion and Compliance: A New Look at an Old Problem," *Law and*

There are, of course, several dramatic episodes in American history when politically unpopular court decisions triggered anticourt responses. These include, for example, the attempt by a Jeffersonian-dominated Congress to use impeachment as a weapon for cleansing Federalist judges from the federal courts; the overturning of *Chisholm* v. *Georgia*[2] and *Pollock* v. *Farmers' Loan*[3] by the Eleventh and Sixteenth Amendments; and FDR's attempt to change Supreme Court policy by changing its size (a tactic used by Republicans of the 1860s and by others earlier). Obviously such court-curbing activities were immensely important negative feedback to the Court. However, not all feedback is either as dramatic or as tinged with partisan and ideological controversy. Neither is all feedback as episodic as the preceding examples imply, nor is it always so bound up with basic questions of constitutional law, judicial powers and constitutional legitimacy. There are such clearly legitimate forms of congressional and presidential feedback as the passage of remedial legislation and the use of the appointment process to staff the courts with those in ideological agreement with current political authorities. Furthermore, the common law tradition allows extensive room for certain other kinds of feedback. Foremost among the latter are the use of litigation as a feedback device and the recognition by judges of professional comment and criticism in court decision making.

LITIGATION AS A VEHICLE FOR FEEDBACK

Litigation is one of the most important ways by which the Supreme Court receives feedback. In fact, the incremental nature of judicial policy making suggests that such feedback is not only expected, but it is even invited. When it ventures to change long-standing legal norms or practices, the Supreme Court's initial decision rarely so settles the law as to make subsequent appeals so frivolous as to only

---

Society Review, 4 (1970), 505–519. See the comments of S. Sidney Ulmer concerning the problems of defining impact in his "From 'Academic Stuff' to Judicial Behavior: A Continuing Search for Identity," *Polity*, 6 (1974), pp. 387–388. Also see Nathan Hakman, "The Impact of Judicial Opinions: Another Critical Analysis of Political Science Folklore," paper presented at the 1974 Annual Meeting of the American Political Science Association.

[2] 2 Dall. 419 (1793).

[3] 157 U.S. 429 (1895); 158 U.S. 601 (1895).

be fitting for lower court enforcement. Rather, the initial decisions may be so ambiguous as to invite further appeals, thus allowing for additional policy consideration, definition, and clarification.

Baker v. *Carr* illustrates this phenomenon well. That decision was a landmark in that it broke with precedent and made legislative apportionment a justiciable question, but it provided very little guidance as to what standard should be applied not only by the District Court for the Middle District of Tennessee to which the case was remanded, but also to other district courts which would obviously receive similar litigation. The Court's opinion stated, "The right asserted is within the reach of judicial protection under the [Equal Protection Clause of the] Fourteenth Amendment." It was also asserted that, "Judicial standards under the Equal Protection Clause are well developed and familiar."[4] But, of course, at this time the judicial standards provided by the Equal Protection Clause concerning legislative apportionment were anything but well developed and familiar. Thus this case, rather than stifling further appeals by "settling" the law, invited them by "unsettling" it. Such cases of course came, and two years later in *Reynolds* v. *Sims*[5] the Court again took up the issue and provided the one man–one vote standard. After that, other cases made their way to the Court asking for greater clarification of the one man–one vote standard, such as whether it applied to local governing boards and special purpose districts, as well as the extent of permissible deviation from perfect mathematical equality.

Other policy areas in which the Supreme Court has been involved can also illuminate the use of litigation as a vehicle for feedback. In the obscenity area, the Nixon Court sought to change the more liberal Warren Court standards in order to permit state and local authorities to crack down on "hard core" pornography. The 1973 cases, which announced the new more restrictive standards,[6] far from resolving the issues, exposed the Court to much new litigation as the problems of differentiating obscenity from constitutionally protected free speech remained as difficult as before. Indeed, in 1974 the

[4] Baker v. Carr, 369 U.S. 186 at 237, 226 (1962).

[5] 377 U.S. 533 (1964).

[6] Miller v. California, 413 U.S. 15 (1973); Paris Adult Theatre I v. Slaton, 413 U.S. 49 (1973).

Supreme Court had before it the case in which the Georgia Supreme Court had ruled that the widely acclaimed motion picture *Carnal Knowledge* was obscene.[7] In this policy area, new litigation continues to keep the Court apprised of the impact of its obscenity policy and the difficulties of implementation.

The same is true, to take another example, with the Court's policy concerning the admissibility of confessions. *Miranda* v. *Arizona*[8] was the culmination of a series of cases that brought feedback information to the Court as to the implementation of its previous "due process" policy concerning the questioning of suspects and the use of statements and confessions against the defendant in court. Finally in Miranda the Court spelled out the procedures that must be followed before statements and confessions extracted from the suspect can be used against him (the constitutional basis was the Fifth Amendment right against self-incrimination and the Sixth Amendment right to counsel as these rights have become part of the Fourteenth Amendment due process guarantees that the states must respect). But here, too, litigation continued transmitting (negative) feedback responses to the Court. Finally in *Harris* v. *New York*, after several years of intense negative feedback and with the emergence of the Nixon Court, a new majority shifted gears and modified the Miranda policy. Under *Harris*, statements and confessions obtained in violation of the Miranda standards can be introduced at the trial to impeach the credibility of the defendant's on-the-stand testimony (when it contradicts what was said during interrogation).[9] Confession cases continued to come to the Court well into the 1970s and the Miranda policy about a decade after its launching seemed not to have accomplished the purposes for which it was designed (i.e., the elimination of *any* form of coercion to produce statements or confessions from those arrested).[10]

Feedback via litigation occurs to some extent in every case that is

[7] Jenkins v. Georgia 94 S. Ct. 2750 (1974). Note that the Supreme Court reversed the Georgia Supreme Court and held *Carnal Knowledge* not to be obscene.

[8] 384 U.S. 436 (1966).

[9] Harris v. New York, 401 U.S. 222 (1971). Note that the Court imposed the Harris policy on a state judicial system that had attempted to reject it. See Oregon v. Haas, 95 S. Ct. 1215 (1975).

[10] See Michael Wald, Richard Ayres, David W. Hess, Mark Schantz, and Charles H. Whitebread, II, "Interrogations in New Haven: The Impact of *Miranda*," *Yale Law Journal*, 76 (1967), 1519–1648; Richard H. Seeburger and R. Stanton Wettick, Jr.,

appealed and even with many that never proceed beyond the trial stage. Interest groups use test cases quite deliberately to channel feedback to the courts. At times legislative and executive officials also use their powers in law making and law enforcement to generate feedback. One of the more dramatic (and controversial) examples of such feedback occurred after the National Industrial Recovery Act (NIRA) was declared unconstitutional in the Schechter case.[11] President Roosevelt then urged Congress to pass a new NIRA-like statute for regulating the bituminous coal industry. In the face of charges that the proposed law was unconstitutional, Roosevelt wrote a letter to the chairman of the House subcommittee in which the bill was pending. This letter said in part,

Manifestly, no one is in a position to give assurance that the proposed act will withstand constitutional tests. . . . But the situation is so urgent and the benefits of the legislation so evident that all doubts should be resolved in favor of the bill, leaving to the courts, in an orderly fashion, the ultimate question of constitutionality. A decision by the Supreme Court relative to this measure would be helpful as indicating, with increasing clarity, the constitutional limits within which this Government must operate.[12]

The bill became law. It was soon struck down as unconstitutional in *Carter* v. *Carter Coal Co.*[13] But within a year, quite similar legislation did withstand the test of constitutionality in *National Labor Relations*

"*Miranda* in Pittsburgh—A Statistical Study," *University of Pittsburgh Law Review*, 29 (1967), 1–26; Richard J. Medalie, Leonard Zeitz, and Paul Alexander, "Custodial Police Interrogation in Our Nation's Capital: The Attempt to Implement Miranda," *Michigan Law Review*, 66 (1968), 1347–1422; Neal A. Milner, "Comparative Analysis of Patterns of Compliance with Supreme Court Decisions: *Miranda* and the Police in Four Communities," *Law and Society Review*, 5 (1970), 119–134; Neal A. Milner, *The Court and Local Law Enforcement: The Political Impact of Miranda* (Beverly Hills, Calif.: Sage, 1971); Otis H. Stephens, Jr., *The Supreme Court and Confessions of Guilt* (Knoxville: University of Tennessee Press, 1973); James W. Witt, "Noncoercive Interrogation and the Administration of Criminal Justice: The Impact of Miranda on Police Effactuality," *Journal of Criminal Law*, 64 (1973), 320–332; David W. Neubauer, *Criminal Justice in Middle America* (Morristown, N.J.: General Learning Press, 1974), pp. 163–188; Cecile Ruth Stolbof, "The Impact of Mapp and Escobedo on Law Enforcement in New Jersey," Ph.D. dissertation, Rutgers University, 1972; Richard W. Long, "Miranda and the Police: the Impact of the Miranda Decision in Medium Size Missouri Cities," Ph.D. dissertation, University of Missouri (Columbia), 1973.

[11] 295 U.S. 495 (1935).

[12] *The Public Papers and Addresses of Franklin D. Roosevelt* (1938), Vol. 4, pp. 297–298.

[13] 298 U.S. 238 (1936).

Board v. Jones and Laughlin Steel Corporation,[14] and within five years after Carter was announced it was explicitly overturned in United States v. Darby.[15] This switch in judicial policy, of course, followed sustained and forceful negative feedback concerning the Court's conservative activism.

PROFESSIONAL COMMENT AND CRITICISM AS FEEDBACK

Students of the law have long recognized the legitimacy and potential ability of professional comment and criticism in influencing judicial outputs. The dual notion of the courtroom lawyer as advocate and officer of the court, the casebook approach in law schools where opinions and decisions are analyzed and criticized, the role given the organized bar in making changes in legal procedure, and the existence and the prominence of law reviews and professional journals all suggest that feedback from the legal profession is widely accepted and expected. Much of this feedback occurs within the context of litigation itself, for example, through briefs and oral argument. It also occurs within the context of opinion writing and in off-the-bench activities of fellow judges. In this section two aspects of professional feedback to the Supreme Court are considered: feedback from members of the lower courts and feedback from the law reviews.

Lower court feedback to the supreme court

Decisions of the Supreme Court articulate norms that lower courts are supposed to follow in deciding cases. With the lower federal courts, the supremacy of the Supreme Court theoretically extends to all matters within their jurisdiction, while with the state courts, it extends to all questions touching matters of federal law and ultimately even the determination of whether federal law is applicable. Although the complexities and courtesies created by the doctrine of federalism generally mean that the Supreme Court supervises the federal courts more closely than it does the state courts, state judges have long acknowledged that Supreme Court rulings indeed represent the highest judicial voice in the land. As Walter Murphy noted in his analysis of Southern state judicial attitudes toward the Supreme Court's school desegregation rulings, "When pressed, no state

[14] 301 U.S. 1 (1937).
[15] 312 U.S. 100 (1941).

supreme court has yet failed to concede that the School Segregation cases are the law of the land and binding on the lower [state] courts."[16]

The Court's supremacy, however, has not made lower court judges merely its silent servants. The most common form of feedback from lower court judges has been both on- and off-the-bench praise and criticism of the Court's decisions. A dramatic instance of off-the-bench criticism was the 1958 report by the Conference of State Chief Justices on federal-state relationships. In this report, adopted by a vote of 36–8, the Court was strongly criticized for "press[ing] the extension of federal power [over the states] and press[ing] it rapidly."[17] Significantly, however, the chief justices prefaced their report by noting that they have an "obligation . . . to uphold respect for the law" and that this obligation includes being bound even by those Supreme Court policy pronouncements that they believe to be wrong.

Closely related to off-the-bench verbal feedback is that rendered by lower court judges from the bench. For example, in 1969 the Court of Appeals for the Second Circuit sitting *en banc* reversed the dismissal by two district judges of state prisoners' applications for writs of *habeas corpus*.[18] The prisoners had asserted that their guilty pleas were not voluntary, but had been induced by illegally obtained confessions that their lawyers allegedly refused to attempt to challenge. The dissent suggested the dissenters' disagreement with the Warren Court's liberal policies in the confessions area. This prompted a concurring (with the majority) opinion by Judge Irving Kaufman that chided the dissenters with the observation that "Judges must be careful lest their personal predelictions lead them to ignore the constitutional requirements set forth by the Supreme Court, by indulging in sophistic games of distinction-making because they do not approve of the Court's constitutional determinations."[19]

[16] Walter F. Murphy, "Lower Court Checks on Supreme Court Power," *American Political Science Review*, 53 (1959), 1019–1020.

[17] Conference of State Chief Justices, *Report of the Committee on Federal-State Relationships as Affected by Judicial Decisions*, as reprinted in Robert Scigliano (ed.), *The Courts* (Boston: Little, Brown, 1962), p. 461.

[18] U.S. Ex Rel. Ross v. McMann, 409 F.2d 1016 (1969).

[19] *Ibid.* at 1026.

Mere verbal feedback may have little direct effect on case outcomes and the rate of compliance, but lower court judges do not always limit themselves to unhappy compliance when they disagree with Supreme Court policy. Such judges have at times provided encouragement for legislative attempts to circumvent a Court decision. For example, following the Court's ruling in *Mallory* v. *United States*[20] that a ten-hour delay between Mallory's arrest and arraignment represented an "unnecessary delay" under Rule 5(a) of the Federal Rules of Criminal Procedure, Federal District Judge Alexander Holtzoff [the trial judge on the Mallory case and a member of the advisory committee that had drafted Rule 5(a)] testified before a Senate subcommittee concerning the Mallory case. He told the senators that when the rule had been drafted, a proviso that confessions obtained during a period of "unnecessary delay" be forbidden had been considered and rejected because it was felt that this would punish the public more than delinquent police officials. He furthermore reminded the subcommittee that the Mallory case was an instance of statutory interpretation and therefore could be overturned by a simple act of Congress. Congress did in fact follow Holtzoff's suggestion some years later in the Omnibus Crime Act of 1968. To cite another example, U.S. Court of Appeals Judge Henry Friendly demonstrated his dismay with the Miranda policy when he publicly advocated severe restrictions by way of constitutional amendment on the use of the self-incrimination guarantee of the Fifth Amendment.[21] Lower court judges have also on occasion used less legitimate means to blunt a Supreme Court decision. The most illegitimate means is, of course, outright defiance of a Supreme Court ruling. However, open and publicized defiance is usually corrected by the processes of appellate review.

Outright refusal to comply is not the only on-the-bench option left to lower court judges who disagree with Court policies. Working in the interstices of the law and making use of the ambiguities inherent in Supreme Court opinion writing, lower court judges are often able to evade the spirit of current Court policies while observing the letter of its decisions. For example, of the approximately

[20] 354 U.S. 449 (1957). Note that in this case the Court's ruling reversed the conviction of Mallory, a confessed rapist.

[21] *New York Times,* "Court Scored by Top Judge Here: A Jurist Nixon May Name Urges Curbs on Liberal Trend," November 10, 1968, sec. 1, p. 73.

twenty cases decided between 1941 and 1951 where Supreme Court "winners" became state court losers on remand, in only one case was there outright defiance.[22] In all the others, the case outcome was changed by a lower court's interpretation of the Supreme Court's ruling. A similar finding of state court evasion was revealed in a study of the last decade of the Warren Court that determined that over one out of four winners at the Supreme Court level eventually became state court losers.[23]

Evasion, of course, does not only concern cases on remand. It is a phenomenon that affects much trial and intermediate appellate court decision making. The pervasiveness of evasion is difficult to ascertain and is, of course, more characteristic of some fields of the law, levels of the judiciary, and areas of the nation than others. In recent history perhaps the most systematic evasion occurred during the 1950s and 1960s when Southern state courts had responsibility for implementation of the Supreme Court's decisions dealing with the civil rights of black Americans. Some evasion by some state courts of the Supreme Court's criminal procedures decisions has also been documented.[24]

The most obvious effect of evasion is to retard the impact of Supreme Court decisions and to stifle broad extension of rulings into areas of social behavior related to those the Court has dealt with explicitly. This dual effect was quite obvious in Southern court

---

[22] Note, "Evasion of Supreme Court Mandates in Cases Remanded to State Courts since 1941," *Harvard Law Review*, 67 (1954), 1251–1259.

[23] Jerry K. Beatty, "State Court Evasion of United States Supreme Court Mandates during the Last Decade of the Warren Court," *Valparaiso University Law Review*, 6 (1972), 260–285. Also see Ronald Schneider, "State Court Evasion of United States Supreme Court Mandates: A Reconsideration of the Evidence," *Valparaiso University Law Review*, 7 (1973), 191–195 and Jerry Beatty's rejoinder which follows on pp. 197–200. Cf. Hakman, "The Impact of Judicial Opinions."

[24] See Bradley C. Canon, "Reactions of State Supreme Courts to a U.S. Supreme Court Civil Liberties Decision," *Law and Society Review*, 8 (1973), 109–134; Donald E. Wilkes, Jr., "New Federalism in Criminal Procedure: State Court Evasion of the Burger Court," *Kentucky Law Journal*, 62 (1973–1974), 421–451; Neil T. Romans, "The Role of State Supreme Courts in Judicial Policy Making: *Escobedo, Miranda,* and the Use of Judicial Impact Analysis," *Western Political Quarterly*, 27 (1974), 38–59. Also see Stephen L. Wasby, "Communication of the Supreme Court's Criminal Procedure Decisions: A Preliminary Mapping," *Villanova Law Review*, 18 (1973), 1086–1118, for a broader view of the place of state courts in the process of transmitting the Supreme Court's criminal procedures policies down to the local law enforcement authorities.

response to *Brown* v. *Board of Education*. Evasion itself may lead to direct litigative feedback to the Court as cases marked by lower court resistance are appealed. This gives the Court an opportunity to reiterate more clearly its initial policy. It also provides the chance for a second judicial look at the policy in light of its impact. With the school segregation cases, the result of reexamination was for the Court to call for even more forceful and far-reaching implementation as well as an extension of the decision to other areas of social life and governmental action. In some other areas of the law, the second look offered by a lower court's narrow interpretation of a Supreme Court ruling has led, at least temporarily, to the Court's accepting that interpretation and thus indicating the limits of its initial decision.[25]

Not all judicial feedback is aimed at retarding the thrust and impact of Supreme Court policy making. Lower court judges off the bench often publicly express support for newly articulated Court rulings and even urge their expansion. Positive feedback to evolving judicial policy also occurs within the context of lower court decision making. Some lower court judges on occasion have even decided cases on the basis that the Supreme Court was likely to rule that way. An example of such action can be found in a decision by Fourth Circuit Court of Appeals Judge John J. Parker concerning a West Virginia law compelling all children attending public school to salute the flag. This included children of the Jehovah's Witnesses sect for whom such action represents a violation of their religious beliefs. Parker held the law unconstitutional despite the fact that just two years earlier a similar Pennsylvania law had been upheld by the Court in the Gobitis case.[26] In rendering his decision, Parker noted that three of the Gobitis majority had subsequently confessed error and that two others had retired. Upon appeal to the Court, Parker's prediction held true, and Gobitis was formally overruled.[27]

However, second-guessing the Court is far from being an accepted tactic. A number of jurists have, in fact, disavowed it and in the words

[25] A noted example of this is Zorach v. Clauson, 343 U.S. 306 (1952), which limited the earlier decision in McCollum v. Board of Education, 333 U.S. 203 (1948). The issue was released time from the public schools for religious education.

[26] Minersville School District v. Gobitis, 310 U.S. 586 (1940).

[27] West Virginia State Board of Education v. Barnette, 319 U.S. 624 (1943).

of one, "We should leave it to the Supreme Court to overrule its own cases."[28] Furthermore, second-guessing is not necessarily a successful tactic. Some thirty years after Judge Parker's decision, another Fourth Circuit Judge (and another senatorial reject on ideological grounds for a Supreme Court seat), Clement Haynsworth, who was no doubt aware of the Court's consistent extension of the right to counsel during the previous decade, ruled that the right of indigents to free counsel applied to their taking their appeals beyond the first appeal to the highest state court and the U.S. Supreme Court. Judge Haynsworth, as it turned out, incorrectly anticipated the Nixon Court, which by a divided vote in *Ross* v. *Moffitt*[29] overruled him.

The court and the law reviews

Prior to the 1930s, there were very few citations of law reviews in Supreme Court opinions.[30] By the early 1930s citations became more numerous. Those who cited reviews during this period and those who did not fell into two groups corresponding to the Court's liberal and conservative wings. Those who most cited review articles were Brandeis, Stone, and Cardozo—all members of the Court's liberal, pro–New Deal bloc. McReynolds, Van Devanter, Butler, Sutherland, and Roberts—the five justices who were most anti–New Deal— practically never cited reviews. Since the early 1940s, however, when the number of opinions with citations to reviews reached about twenty per term, there have been no obvious ideological or background differences between those who cite law review articles and those who do not.

The citation of review articles is an important modern manifestation of how professional comment and research is fed into judicial policy making. To a surprisingly large degree (over 80 percent of the time), review citations in Supreme Court opinions are not taken from references within briefs, but rather reflect the justices' and their clerks' own research efforts.

Reviews are edited by the best students at each law school. Issues contain unsigned articles called "Notes" written by individual edi-

---

28 As quoted in Murphy, "Lower Court Checks," p. 1027.

29 Ross v. Moffitt, 94 S. Ct. 2437 (1974).

30 This section relies heavily on Chester A. Newland, "Legal Periodicals and the United States Supreme Court," *Midwest Journal of Political Science*, 3 (1959), 58–74.

tors as well as signed articles by legal scholars, judges, and legal administrators. In the last decade an increasing number of the signed articles have also been contributed by political scientists. Obviously not all reviews are of equal quality nor, of course, are members of the Court equally responsive to all reviews or all commentators. As a result a few reviews and authors are cited quite frequently, while most others are cited only rarely or never. In an analysis of citations to law reviews in Supreme Court opinions between 1924–1956, Chester A. Newland found that the *Harvard Law Review* was cited most frequently (399 times), followed by the *Yale Law Journal* (194), and the *Columbia Law Review* (176). Thereafter the number of citations to particular reviews fell off rapidly. As for the authors most frequently cited, Newland found that Felix Frankfurter (28) and Charles Warren (27) led the list.

One must be careful in assessing such quantitative data. Most citations stand only as minor references in an opinion. Articles from such often-cited sources as the *Harvard Law Review* may be inconsequential, while a single reference to a rarely cited journal may be important. Only a few times has an article apparently had a major influence on an opinion.

A famous instance of such an influential article concerned one by Charles Warren, which appeared in 1923 in the *Harvard Law Review*.[31] It was a critique of Justice Story's opinion in *Swift* v. *Tyson*[32] interpreting the Federal Judiciary Act of 1789. The Court's ruling in that case resulted in the establishment of a federal "common law" for diversity cases in the federal courts, while equivalent cases tried in state courts were subject to the "common law" of the respective states. Since the federal courts' diversity jurisdiction is nonexclusive (i.e., either a state or federal court can try the case), litigants were encouraged to shop around for the court system with the most favorable common law.

In analyzing the historical background to Swift, Warren wrote,

It now appears from an examination of the Senate files . . . that if Judge Story and the Court had had recourse to those Files in preparing the de-

---

[31] Charles Warren, "New Light on the History of the Federal Judiciary Act of 1789," *Harvard Law Review*, 37 (1923), 49–132, as cited by Newland, "Legal Periodicals and the United States Supreme Court," p. 66, n. 11.

[32] 16 Pet. 1 (1842).

cision . . . it is highly probable that the decision would have been different, and that the word "laws" in Section 34 would have been construed to include the common law of a state as well as the statute law. This conclusion will probably be reached by anyone who examines the original slip of paper on which the amendment containing Section 34 was written, and which is, with little doubt, in Ellsworth's handwriting.[33]

In a 1928 case, Holmes used the Warren article as a basis for his dissent writing, "An examination of the original document by a most competent hand has shown that Mr. Justice Story probably was wrong if anyone is interested to inquire what the framers of the instrument meant."[34] Thereafter criticism of Swift proliferated in the reviews. Finally, in *Erie R.R.* v. *Tompkins*,[35] Swift was overruled. In writing the opinion, Brandeis cited 22 different articles. In commenting on the Warren article, Brandeis wrote, "[I]t was the more recent research of a competent scholar, who examined the original document, which established that the construction given to it by the Court was erroneous." As Newland noted, "The decisive influence of Warren's article in Brandeis' interpretation of the Judiciary Act of 1789 could hardly be made more plain."[36]

Thus far only activities within the legal community have been surveyed.[37] Now we turn to a consideration of phenomena occurring outside the courts and the legal profession. The activities of the communications media, local officials, interest group spokesmen, private citizens, Congress, and the President will be discussed in terms of how they affect impact and contribute to feedback. Attention is first focused on the media because they stand as the communications linchpin that links judicial output to citizen and even official response. Typically, the only information that most Americans have about court decisions—and this includes many public officials as well as private citizens—is through the media. How the media

[33] Warren, "Federal Judiciary Act," p. 85, as cited by Newland, "Legal Periodicals," p. 67, n. 13.

[34] Black and White T. & T. Co. v. Brown and Yellow T. & T. Co., 276 U.S. 518 at 535 (1928), as cited by Newland, "Legal Periodicals," p. 67, n. 15.

[35] 304 U.S. 64 (1938).

[36] Newland, "Legal Periodicals," p. 66.

[37] For another and more extensive view of the professional critics including those representing the American Bar Association, see Clifford M. Lytle, *The Warren Court and Its Critics* (Tucson: University of Arizona Press, 1968), pp. 94–107.

report and cover court activities, in particular those of the Supreme Court, goes a long way in illuminating how and why private citizens and public officials respond to judicial output the way they do.

THE COURTS AND THE COMMUNICATIONS MEDIA

To understand the relationship of the communications media to the courts, it is necessary to understand how the media in general influence governmental policy and affect its implementation. Through newspapers, news magazines, radio, and television, the "newsworthy" events of the daily lives of the political authorities and the decisions they make or are in the process of making are reported and interpreted. Information about policy decisions is transmitted outward to those who are the objects of that policy, and information about the reception and impact of decisions is fed back to the policy makers. Through their operations, the communications media serve not only to transmit the activities of others but also as a source of feedback itself in that the media highlight and bring to consciousness various problem areas of social life and governmental activity, interpret them for both the public at large and governmental policy makers, and render value judgments. Obviously the media are neither so monolithic nor so universally believed that they can make and break policy and policy makers at will. However, the media are widely acknowledged to have a major influence on the public. Thus, the way news is handled, interpreted, and evaluated in editorials can help to stimulate positive or negative attitudes about governmental institutions and policies. This in turn may be an important variable in what policies are made and how they are received.

The influence of the media is generally well understood by those who aspire to and hold high positions of political power. It is also generally recognized that those who collect, report, and interpret the news are not totally unbiased as to either persons or policies. In fact most of those with some policy to promote make use of these biases (along with the media's need for news) to generate approval for some policies and to destroy it for others. News releases, press conferences, speeches, and even demonstrations and acts of civil disobedience are used for getting one's name and face (and, of course, views) onto the printed page and on the television screen. Through these devices even those with few friends in the press can get into the headlines, but those with even just a few friends can do much more. Favored reporters and columnists are fed "leaks" and given access to otherwise inaccessible materials. Through background sessions, off-the-record briefings, and other similar devices, high-ranking government officials are able to get potential policies aired to test public reactions without having to have their names associated with the proposed policy. In sum, through these and other ways, political authorities use an often-willing press to create public opinion supporting the making and implementation of governmental policies.

In this scramble for media attention and favor, the courts are at a distinct disadvantage. The judiciary's critics in Congress, in the executive branch, in local officialdom, and at the head of pressure groups can all use the devices just outlined in attacking the courts. At the same time, long-standing traditions and expectations related to the judicial role discourage judges from responding in like manner. Although some individual judges have made their views known through public speeches, interviews, and writings, it is largely the official and formal aspects of courtroom activity and its end products of case disposition and published opinions that constitute the sources for newsmen covering the courts. Some crucial aspects of case processing and policy making, such as what occurs in Supreme Court conferences and what policies are considered only to be subsequently rejected, are never disclosed at the time. "Trial balloons" and news "leaks" are forbidden. Many judges refuse to be interviewed privately by newsmen. Thus to a large degree, judicial authorities must rely upon the perceptions of reporters and commentators in the transmission of judicial policy to the American people.

A number of aspects of judicial decision making and of media reporting, however, serve to blur and distort the policy messages that judicial opinions and decisions are meant to convey. This is especially true of Supreme Court decision making, where the decisions are often the subject of sharp professional disagreement and where the interests rallying behind the opposing sides are highly organized and vocal.

Many judicial policy pronouncements and decisions enunciate or are based on threshold criteria. For example, in the Mallory case, the Court ruled that the ten-hour delay between arrest and arraignment exceeded the threshold implied by the term "unnecessary delay" in Section 5(a) of the Federal Rules of Criminal Procedure. Thus Mallory's conviction, resulting from a trial in which a confession made during this ten-hour period was admitted, was declared invalid and he was set free. It was irrelevant to the Court's ruling that Mallory was a chronic criminal and that a brutal rape was the crime to which he had confessed. Similar irrelevancies also marked the Escobedo and Miranda[38] cases, yet it was just these irrelevancies that made the cases newsworthy for the media. By emphasizing their outcomes rather than the rules of law being articulated, the media stressed the fact that the Court through its actions had freed chronic and violent criminals. "Good" civil libertarian decisions, in other words, often result in a bad press.

A second source of news distortion has been the lack of professional training by most of those who write about the Court. Only a handful of Court reporters have had some legal training, and even fewer (three were mentioned in a study published in 1968) have law degrees.[39] Although there is a high level of reporting found in the major newspapers serving the Washington community (such as *The New York Times, Washington Post, Washington Star, Wall Street Journal,* and *Christian Science Monitor*), news distortion grows rapidly as one retreats to the hinterland. Most non–Washington-oriented papers get their first and often only news on Court decisions from the wire services (AP and UPI), although many papers also subscribe to either *The New York Times* or *Washington Post–Los Angeles Times* press services, which also have regular Court reporters. Rarely in covering the Court is the text of an opinion itself sent out. With the wire services the pressure for speed, brevity, and dramatic news content result in the initial stories written by Court "regulars" being constantly cut and revised both by wire service rewrite men and local reporters and editors. Much accuracy is lost in this process as inexact journalistic language replaces the exact language of the Court, and background information and speculation of the initial reporter is taken as the content of the Court's opinion. "Denial of certiorari" becomes "dismissal of an appeal." A reporter's background inclusion of the language of the lower court's opinion may result in that language being attributed to the Supreme Court, when in fact the lower court's

[38] Escobedo v. Illinois, 378 U.S. 478 (1964); Miranda v. Arizona, 384 U.S. 436 (1966).

[39] David L. Grey, *The Supreme Court and the News Media* (Evanston, Ill.: Northwestern University Press, 1968), p. 134, n. 27.

decision was merely summarily affirmed in a memorandum order. The far-ranging language of a concurrence or even a dissent may form the basis of a story purporting to portray what actually was decided.

Adding to distortion in press coverage of what the Court did is that by the second day after the decision is rendered, stories focus on reaction to the Court's decision rather than the decision itself. This often means that newsmen without legal training who have not read the full text of the opinion ask similarly untrained and uninformed laymen, whose interests may be strongly affected by the decision, for their views of the Court's action. In the stories thus generated, extreme and highly contentious statements are generally played up to the detriment of those more restrained and ambiguous statements, since the former are more "newsworthy."

Often, in all fairness to the media, many of the extreme views found in such stories are indeed worth reporting, since they may coincide with the opinions of highly placed members of the legal community including even members of the Court itself. This is well illustrated in the media's coverage of reaction to the Court's ruling in *Engel* v. *Vitale*,[40] the New York School Prayer case.

In his majority opinion, Justice Black reasoned that since the prayer in question was drafted and recommended by the New York State Board of Regents (a governmental agency) for reading in the state's public schools, this represented a violation of the Establishment Clause of the First Amendment (as applied to the states through the Fourteenth Amendment) and was thus unconstitutional. Even before it was announced, the opinion was already marked by extreme controversy and misstatement. Justice Douglas, in a concurring opinion, suggested that the Court's interpretation of the Establishment Clause raised serious questions about the validity of numerous governmental activities in the religious realm. In a footnote he included such practices as the hiring of chaplains for Congress, the armed forces, and the service academies; the use of the Bible for administering oaths; governmental aid for busing of parochial school students; tax deductions for contributions to religious institutions; and even the

[40] 370 U.S. 421 (1962). The discussion of the press and the Engel decision that follows is based on Chester A. Newland, "Press Coverage of the United States Supreme Court," *Western Political Quarterly*, 17 (1964), 15–36; and Grey, *Supreme Court and the News Media.*

Treasury's use of the motto "In God We Trust." Justice Stewart, in dissent, suggested that the decision also extended to the Court's practice of having its marshal declare "God save the United States and this Honorable Court," the prayers said at the beginning of each daily session of the House and Senate, and the Presidential practice of calling on God's aid at his inauguration.

Douglas's concurrence and Stewart's dissent soon provided a focus for the Court's critics. Black's more narrowly based opinion, which only countered Douglas's and Stewart's questions in a short footnote, was soon forgotten. Added to this initial misstatement of the Court's ruling were the adverse reactions of prominent people. For example, the President of the American Bar Association stated that the ruling meant the elimination from coins of the motto "In God We Trust."[41] The Chief Justice of the Pennsylvania Supreme Court was reported as saying that the "First Amendment sometimes aids reds and criminals more than other citizens." Professor Mark De Wolfe Howe of the Harvard Law School was quoted as saying, "Justice Black's opinion is ridiculous." The Chief Justice of Indiana was reported as criticizing the ruling on the ground that the First Amendment applied only to Congress. Joined to this flurry of criticism from within the legal profession were the strong condemnations by many Roman Catholic and Protestant clergymen. All this criticism received extensive media attention. Although a few high governmental and religious leaders spoke in defense of the Court, generally their comments were only published in the locality where their views were offered. In fact, the only defense that received wide and prominent coverage was that made by President Kennedy in his June 27, 1962, press conference three days after the decision was announced.

The Engel decision clearly touched many sensitive nerves within the nation. Yet the misstatements and the emphasis on irresponsible criticism that characterized its treatment by the media have occurred on other occasions. Typically, the emphasis is on decisions more concerned with symbols than concrete matters affecting vast numbers of citizens. Major economic cases generally receive only the most cursory coverage by the media. On the same day Engel was announced, the Court disposed of forty other cases (15 by full opinion

[41] This example and those that follow are taken from Newland, "Press Coverage of the United States Supreme Court."

and 25 by memorandum orders). Many of these had important and wide-ranging policy dimensions, but the only other cases that received wide media attention were one dealing with homosexuals and another striking down a California narcotics law. Among the other cases announced that day was one that set forth a major new step in antitrust policy, but this case was given attention in only the New York and Washington papers. Although judgments in this area are always subjective, one may well question how many life styles and what vital social interests were substantially affected by Engel.

This brings us to a consideration of what role the media actually play as feedback channels to the courts. Certainly in the aftermath of a widely reported decision, editorial writers, columnists, and even reporters see themselves as sources of feedback to whom judicial authorities should listen. In making an assessment one should look at who receives the feedback, its content, and how it fits in with the policy views of those receiving it. One suspects that most lower court judges are subjected to different media feedback to Supreme Court decision making than are members of the Court itself. For the members of the high Court it is likely that only the prestige papers serving the Washington community—*The New York Times* and *Washington Post* in particular—are seen, read, and perceived of as references. District and circuit court judges, particularly those living outside the Northeast, might be more likely to read the papers serving their local regions. One might speculate that since the Washington and the Northeastern press in general tended to be more pro-Court than the press in other regions during the Warren Court years, the effect was to reinforce the Warren Court's liberal activism. At the same time a more critical press elsewhere in the country, read by the more locally oriented judges at the trial court level as well as by the local law enforcement establishments and the general public, promoted a more negative reception of the liberal Court's output.[42]

It should be remembered, however, that current regional divisions

[42] These views are given some added weight concerning an area of criminal law by the findings reported by Bradley Canon in "Reactions of State Supreme Courts to a U.S. Supreme Court Civil Liberties Decision," pp. 127–128. Canon found that Northeastern state supreme courts were more positive than Southern and Midwestern courts in their response to the Warren Court's Mapp policy prohibiting illegally obtained evidence from being introduced in state trials, Mapp v. Ohio, 367 U.S. 643 (1961). The Western state supreme courts, however, were found to be close to the Northeastern courts in terms of favorable response to Mapp.

are not nearly as great or divisive as in some earlier periods, largely because of improvements in transportation, communications, and economic development. In communications, television network news and the news magazines have served to transmit the type of Court-supporting views typical of the Eastern prestige press to all sections of the nation. But local and regional resistance to Supreme Court decisions does occur and is usually supported by regional media. This has been particularly characteristic of the responses to the Court's decisions on civil rights and school prayers. In contrast to the problems of compliance and strongly negative attitudes that these decisions produced among the public in various localities, one might note the generally favorable public opinion response (of those few members of the public with opinions) the Court had and the high rate of compliance that has occurred with regard to the reapportionment decisions. It is probably not unimportant that these decisions were greeted with praise by the big urban dailies throughout the country.

Returning to the example of the Engel case, it is of interest to note that the justices of the Supreme Court were not oblivious to the storm of criticism and confusion that greeted that decision. As one scholar who interviewed most of the justices noted,[43] the justices were sufficiently "shaken" by the 1962 feedback so that when the 1963 Schempp case concerning Bible reading and the Lord's Prayer was to be decided, steps were taken "to avoid a recurrence of the confusion." These steps included (1) assigning the task of writing the Court's opinion to Justice Clark rather than a more partisan libertarian activist; (2) "emphasis in the majority opinion on the importance of religion and on historical background for perspective"; (3) lengthy concurring opinions by Justices Brennan and Goldberg that sought to precisely clarify the dimensions of the Court's decision. (Note also that Justices Clark, Brennan, and Goldberg were affiliated with the Protestant, Roman Catholic, and Jewish faiths, respectively—perhaps a conscious attempt to appeal to their co-religionists.)

As far as the Supreme Court is concerned, it is likely that occasionally the feedback transmitted and generated by the media has some immediate effect on the substance of Court policies. For example, Justice Felix Frankfurter recorded in his diary that, in the fall

---

[43] Grey, *Supreme Court and the News Media*, p. 87. The quotations in this paragraph are from *ibid*.

term after the first Flag Salute case[44] had been decided (the vote was 8–1 against the First Amendment claims of the Jehovah's Witnesses), Justice Douglas remarked to him, "Hugo [Justice Black] would now not go with you in the Flag Salute case." Frankfurter wrote that he replied: "Why, has he reread the Constitution during the summer?" to which Douglas responded, "No, but he has read the papers."[45] When the feedback suggests positive support, it may have the effect of encouraging the justices to do what they were going to do anyway. When negative, the amount of misstatement and distortion inevitably involved may sensitize the justices to problems of communication and public relations.

Media comment is also quite important in an indirect way as it both reflects and shapes public and political opinion. By praise and criticism of specific outputs and general Court behavior, the media provide vital inputs of information and opinion for politicians, public officials, interest group leaders, and private citizens that help determine their responses to judicial policy making. In the deep South, for example, the constant drumfire of a critical press attacking the legitimacy of the Brown decision tended to isolate those political and judicial authorities who were predisposed to carry out the Court's policy during the 1950s and early 1960s. This rendered the formula of "all deliberate speed" into one of "all determined resistance." With other decisions, such as those concerned with reapportionment, a press generally supportive of the Court was instrumental in achieving fairly rapid compliance. In general, however, the press is neither so monolithic nor so one-sided as the preceding two examples imply. Even in the same newspaper, a Court decision may be praised on the editorial page and criticized by a columnist or in a political cartoon. The press thus shares in the process by which the judiciary and judicial decision making are removed from narrow confines and thrust forward as a subject fit for political controversy.

[44] Minersville School District v. Gobitis, 310 U.S. 586 (1940).

[45] As cited in S. Sidney Ulmer, "Bricolage and Assorted Thoughts on Working in the Papers of Supreme Court Justices," Journal of Politics, 35 (1973), p. 296, n. 26. Note that Justices Douglas and Murphy who also had voted with the majority in the Gobitis case too changed their minds. In 1943, with the additional votes of two new appointees, a new majority overturned Gobitis in West Virginia State Board of Education v. Barnette, 319 U.S. 624 (1943).

COMPLIANCE BY LOCAL OFFICIALS AND PRIVATE CITIZENS

Constitutional law casebooks as well as many studies of judicial policy making often imply that a knowledge of the law as it really is can be found merely by looking at the content of judicial (i.e., Supreme Court) opinions and decisions. The obvious implication of such a formulation is that what the law really is, is also a description of how members of the political community behave. Doubtless with some types of judicial policy this is true. For example, when the Court in 1895 ruled an early form of the income tax constitutionally invalid, such tax collections ceased. And, some 57 years later, when the Court declared presidential seizure of the steel mills illegal, management of the mills was immediately returned to their private owners. The outcomes of these decisions thus seem fairly obvious. One of the reasons that their enforcement was so rapid was that they involved well-organized, well-financed, and highly articulate groups who had a substantial self-interest in seeing that enforcement occurred. Moreover, compliance involved the action of only a limited number of highly visible public officials. Yet there are many areas of the law where neither of the above litigant characteristics is true. Sometimes, even though there are those in society with an interest in enforcement, those opposing enforcement hold a monopoly or near monopoly of money, legal skill, and other forms of political and social power. In such cases compliance may become a massive problem as the fate of the Brown decision well shows.

After *Brown* v. *Board of Education* was announced, there was no sudden disappearance of racially segregated school systems. In fact, a full decade after Brown, only about 3 percent of the black school children in the South were attending integrated schools.[46] (By 1972, however, the proportion was about 91 percent, a better integration record than the rest of the nation, but this was achieved after several years of heavy pressure from the federal government. Even so, this figure is misleading as over half the black students attended schools that had a large majority of black students.[47]) By 1972, a large major-

[46] As cited by G. Theodore Mitau, *Decade of Decision* (New York: Scribner's, 1967), p. 68.

[47] *New York Times*, May 12, 1974, p. 42. Also see Harrell R. Rodgers, Jr., and Charles S. Bullock, III, *Law and Social Change: Civil Rights Laws and Their Consequences* (New York: McGraw-Hill, 1972), p. 95.

ity of Southern school districts had formally eliminated dual school systems (de jure segregation). Nevertheless (nonlegally required) de facto segregation, particularly in the urban areas of the entire nation, has remained a serious problem. Indeed in 1974 at the time of the twentieth anniversary of the handing down of the Brown decision, the proportion of blacks nationwide in predominantly black schools was close to that found in 1954 when the Brown decision was announced.

If the intent of the Brown policy and subsequent decisions was not just to end legal segregation by race but to achieve a fully integrated society, that policy is far from successful. Yet a 1970 Gallup poll suggests that there may be cause for a glimmer of optimism. White Southern opinion on the subject of school racial integration apparently underwent a major reversal. In 1963 in response to the question "Would you, yourself, have any objection to sending your children to a school where a few of the children are Negroes?" 61 percent of the Southern white respondents objected to racial integration. By 1970, only 16 percent said they would object (the figure was 6 percent for non-Southern white parents).[48] Furthermore, the formidable opposition to enforcement by the local authorities appears to have lessened, at least in comparison with previous decades. Whether the South as well as the rest of the nation will move toward full racial integration within education is still, however, in grave doubt.[49]

If one surveys the whole spectrum of judicial policy, it is not difficult to find other areas where the originally objectionable patterns of behavior have long persisted in the face of a Court ruling. Earlier it was mentioned how evasion by lower court judges could yield such a result. It is also of interest to note the activities, backgrounds, and attitudes of local officials and private citizens as they relate to the pattern of compliance to Court policies that run counter to local mores.

To consider this question further, it is of interest to examine the findings of one study by Robert Birkby which was concerned with the

[48] New York Times, May 3, 1970, p. 53.

[49] See the discussion in Rodgers and Bullock, Law and Social Change, Chap. 4. Also see their paper "Compliance to Coercion: Southern School Districts and School Desegregation Guidelines," paper presented at the 1974 Annual Meeting of the American Political Science Association and their book Racial Equality in America: In Search of an Unfulfilled Goal (Pacific Palisades, California: Goodyear, 1975), Chap. 5.

responses by Tennessee school boards to the Court's 1963 Schempp and Curlett decisions forbidding devotional religious activities (Bible reading and the Lord's Prayer) in public schools.[50] Coupled with the earlier Court rulings, these decisions in effect made illegal the use of public school facilities and faculties for religious instruction or devotional purposes. The study of religion, however, including the Bible, was still permissible "when presented objectively as part of a secular program of education."[51] Although the national outpouring of negative public criticism was not as great as that which met the Engel decision, the Tennessee "Bible belt" did not take kindly to the Schempp and Curlett decisions.

In the national response to Schempp, some school districts that previously had engaged in the forbidden practices ceased having them altogether. In many others no change occurred at all and religious exercises went on as before. In yet a third category of districts, previous procedures were changed and "voluntary" religious exercises replaced "required" ones, a change that represented a surface attempt at compliance by misreading the Court's decisions.

In Tennessee prior to the Schempp decision, devotional Bible reading was required under state law. After Schempp, which invalidated such a law, the State Commissioner of Education was reported as saying that it was permissible to still have Bible readings, but that decision was left to local school officials. To analyze compliance Robert Birkby in late 1964 and early 1965 sent questionnaires to school superintendents and school board members in Tennessee's 152 school districts. Responses from 121 school districts were received. In 70 districts, no change in practices was reported as having occurred following Schempp; in 50, devotional exercises were made discretionary with the decision being left to the classroom teacher; and in 1, all devotional exercises were reported as having been stopped. Thus in Tennessee more than a year after the Court spoke, massive noncompliance and evasion were commonplace, and, moreover, school officials were willing to admit their noncompliance in a questionnaire. There was little doubt that the school officials knew they were

---

[50] The following discussion is drawn from Robert H. Birkby, "The Supreme Court and the Bible Belt: Tennessee Reaction to the 'Schempp' Decision," *Midwest Journal of Political Science*, 10 (1966), 304–319.

[51] School District of Abington Township v. Schempp, 374 U.S. 203 at 225 (1963).

violating the Court's Schempp policy because that decision had been well (and unfavorably) publicized.

In looking at noncompliance in Tennessee, the question was raised as to why in some districts changes were made in the direction of compliance and in others nothing at all happened. To better understand the dynamics of compliance, Birkby first looked for distinguishing social and economic differences between the 70 districts in which no change occurred and the 51 others where some minor surface change took place, and he found no differences in degree of urbanization, religious heterogeneity, whether or not there was articulate local opposition to devotional exercises, and in the socioeconomic backgrounds of school board members.

After obtaining these negative results, Birkby looked more closely at the reasons that school board officials themselves gave for why they changed or did not change procedures and he found that changes toward compliance generally occurred where board members and superintendents saw the Court as the legitimate arbiter of the school prayer issue. Although some thought the Court's policy "correct" and others disagreed, in general the more important consideration was that as public officials and citizens they believed they were obliged to adhere to "the law" as announced by the Court and to disregard local public demands for the now-forbidden practices. But, of course, the changes they instituted could not in any meaningful sense be considered compliance. Prayers were still recited only now they were "voluntary" and at the teacher's "discretion." In districts marked by no formal change whatsoever, officials generally felt that the Court in the school prayer and other areas had consistently misinterpreted the Constitution and that its decisions lacked legitimacy. Thus Birkby found that the only essential difference between school districts where officials took some surface steps to comply with the Court's ruling and those in which it was totally disregarded was attitudinal; that is, how the officials saw their roles as public officials and citizens when the Court ruled on a question of law.

Kenneth Dolbeare and Phillip Hammond also studied compliance to the school prayer decisions[52] and they relied not only on a ques-

[52] Kenneth M. Dolbeare and Phillip E. Hammond, "Local Elites, the Impact of Judicial Decisions, and the Process of Change," paper presented at the 1969 Annual Meeting of the American Political Science Association; Kenneth M. Dolbeare and Phillip E. Hammond, "Inertia in Midway: Supreme Court Decisions and Local Re-

tionnaire survey but also on intensive interviewing of local educational system officials, teachers, and community notables. Their focus was on one Midwestern state and they found that, with the exception of the major city in the state and three university towns, there was *no* compliance with the Court's decision in the rest of the state. This was true even for communities that reported in the questionnaire that they were complying! Dolbeare and Hammond examined four communities in the state, two that had indicated compliance and two that had reported continuing religious practices. In all four, prayer and Bible reading and other religious activities continued as if the Supreme Court had never spoken. The researchers came to the conclusion that officials at the state and local levels had no motivation to implement the Court's policy. None had strong feelings about the First Amendment violations their school systems were engaging in and they all felt that stirring up controversy over religion in the schools would cost them more politically than they would benefit and would jeopardize their own goals and priorities. Furthermore, local elites wanted to avoid conflict and they believed that the implementation of the prayer rulings would produce undesirable community cleavage. The Court's policies themselves were incorrectly understood by local school officials and this may have been one way of rationalizing inertia. Finally, there were no routine governmental channels that would force officials to face up to the Court rulings. There remained only the costly and time-consuming, as well as personally stressful, route for individuals to sue their local school board.

Interestingly, in two other studies on the impact of the prayer rulings, it was found that there *was* compliance essentially because of the actions of certain local school officials who assumed leadership roles in obtaining compliance.[53] This points up the crucial role of local officials for compliance to Court decisions, be they in the prayer, school desegregation,[54] or criminal procedures[55] areas. These and

---

sponses," *Journal of Legal Education*, 23 (1971), 106–122; Kenneth M. Dolbeare and Phillip E. Hammond, *The School Prayer Decisions* (Chicago: University of Chicago Press, 1971).

[53] Richard M. Johnson, *The Dynamics of Compliance* (Evanston, Ill.: Northwestern University Press, 1967); and William K. Muir, *Prayer in the Public Schools* (Chicago: University of Chicago Press, 1967).

[54] In particular see Bullock and Rodgers, "Compliance to Coercion: Southern School Districts and School Desegregation Guidelines."

[55] See, for example, Michael M. Ban, "Local Compliance with Mapp v. Ohio: The Power of the Supreme Court," Ph.D. dissertation, Harvard University, 1973; Bradley

other studies suggest that local officials and the citizenry alike engage in some rough cost-benefit calculations when it comes to compliance with Court decisions.[56] A challenging question is how can the Court make policy in which it is likely that the costs of evasion will outweigh the benefits, and indeed what can the Court do to maximize the costs of evasion.[57] The other side of the coin is to examine what sorts of decisions produce the most and the least compliance and under what circumstances information of noncompliance will be fed back to the Court and what then can the Court do about it. Dolbeare and Hammond have suggested that noncompliance increases as (1) the degree of change required by the Court policy increases; (2) the number of persons who must comply increases (as opposed to a few conspicuous public officials); and (3) enforcement depends upon the actions of local courts.[58]

Does law change attitudes? Are attitudes the necessary catalyst for behavioral compliance? These are questions that have only recently been the subject of systematic inquiry and the returns are far from in. One might speculate that on the basis of their extensive opinion-writing activity and their behavior as judges that most justices assume answers to these questions in the affirmative at least as far as the long run is concerned. Some of the studies that have been conducted thus far suggest that, even in the short run, attitude change may indeed

---

C. Canon, "Is the Exclusionary Rule in Failing Health? Some New Data and a Plea against a Precipitous Conclusion," *Kentucky Law Journal*, 62 (1973–1974), 681–730; Bradley C. Canon, "Taking Advantage of a Quasi-Experiment Situation: The Impact of *Mapp v. Ohio*," paper presented at the 1974 Annual Meeting of the American Political Science Association. Also see the citations presented earlier in note 10.

[56] See Don W. Brown and Robert V. Stover, "An Economic Approach to Compliance with Court Decisions," paper presented at the 1974 Annual Meeting of the American Political Science Association; Rodgers and Bullock, *Law and Social Change*; Bullock and Rodgers, "Compliance of Southern School Officials." Also see Frederick M. Wirt, *Politics of Southern Equality: Law and Social Change in a Mississippi County* (Chicago: Aldine, 1970) and Don W. Brown, "Cognitive Development and Willingness to Comply with Law," *American Journal of Political Science*, 18 (1974), 583–594.

[57] See the discussion in Brown and Stover, "An Economic Approach to Compliance," pp. 7–16.

[58] Dolbeare and Hammond, "Local Elites," p. 13. Brown and Stover, "An Economic Approach to Compliance," stressed the number of people who must comply and the coercive sanctions and noncoercive sanctions available.

come about to some extent, although the relationship of attitudes to compliance is of course complex.[59]

FEEDBACK FROM THE PRESIDENT AND CONGRESS

Since the spirited battles between FDR and the conservative anti–New Deal Court of the early- and mid-1930s, presidential criticism of the Supreme Court has been rare. President Truman did, of course, verbally lash back after the steel seizure decision, but the dust soon settled and he complied. President Eisenhower, although no staunch defender of the Court in its more liberal thrusts at protecting civil rights and liberties, still never openly attacked the Court while in office and in fact supported the Court's policy on school desegregation by federalizing the troops in Little Rock. Presidents Kennedy and Johnson were open supporters of the Warren Court in the face of rising congressional criticism and falling public approval. Even President Nixon in the first year of his Administration, although he had campaigned for a more conservative judiciary, did not openly and directly attack the Court. No constitutional amendments were called for. No blatantly anti-Court legislation was proposed. In the main, the Nixon Administration's strategy to reshape judicial policies into a more conservative mold involved the following: the nomination of more conservative judges to the federal bench (and forcing Justice Fortas, the most vulnerable liberal, off the Court); a disinclination to vigor-

[59] See Muir, *Prayer in the Public Schools*. Also see Neal Steven Steinert, "The Supreme Court as an Effector of Attitude Change in Mass Publics: A Quasi-Experimental Approach," Ph.D. dissertation, Emory University, 1973; Austin Sarat, "Compliance and the Law: An Attitude Perspective," Ph.D. dissertation, University of Wisconsin (Madison), 1973 and his "Support for the Legal System: An Analysis of Knowledge, Attitudes, and Behavior," *American Politics Quarterly*, 3 (1975), 3–24; Jarol B. Manheim, *The Politics Within: A Primer in Political Attitudes and Behavior* (Englewood Cliffs, N.J.: Prentice Hall, 1975, pp. 8, 23–24. Attitude change may be a gradual process taking decades. See the discussion in Canon, "Is the Exclusionary Rule in Failing Health?" pp. 727–729. For a more pessimistic view of the ability of law to change attitudes, see the study by Harrell R. Rodgers, Jr., and Roger Hanson, "The Rule of Law and Legal Efficacy: Private Values versus General Standards," *Western Political Quarterly*, 27 (1974), 387–394. The issue of compliance to the criminal law is tackled in a review article of punishment and deterrence studies by Charles R. Tittle and Charles H. Logan, "Sanctions and Deviance: Evidence and Remaining Questions," *Law and Society Review*, 7 (1973), 371–392.

ously prosecute cases aimed at insuring full implementation of certain Court policies and last, a failure to act on behalf of the goals underlying the Court's concern for minority rights which was demonstrated by opposing integration-oriented school busing, proposing amendments to the Voting Rights Act that would have had the probable effect of lessening its impact, failing to vigorously defend the legal services component of the poverty program, and supporting public aid to segregated private schools formed to evade the law.

In contrast to recent presidents, Congress in the 1950s and 1960s actively engaged in anti-Court activity and criticism. Perhaps the reason for the contrast is that the presidency, despite the size and extent of the White House staff and official family, is at heart ordinarily only one man elected through one national election. For much of the period from 1940 until 1968, victorious presidential candidates have had in their winning coalitions groups who have approved of or benefited by Court output. During this same period, most of the major groups who were strongly anti-Court—for example, segregationists, religious fundamentalists, economic reactionaries—found few friends within the White House. Furthermore, presidents during this period for the most part occupied much the same moderate-to-liberal end of the political spectrum as did many members of the Court. All these factors reinforced the normal expectation that the President supports the law of the land as ultimately determined by the Court.[60]

Congress, on the other hand, is an institution of 535 members. When any one of these members attacks the Court, this is viewed as an attack from Congress. Moreover, there are many aspects of Congress that encourage individual members to make such attacks. Members are elected from different constituencies, some of which are far removed both ideologically and geographically from the "liberal establishment centers" whose views are widely considered to have dominated the White House and the Supreme Court until the presidencies of Nixon and Ford. The minorities with whose liberties the Court was concerned—for example, Negroes, communists, atheists—are either far removed from or, even worse, perceived as a direct

[60] See, in general, Robert Scigliano, The Supreme Court and the Presidency (New York: Free Press, 1971).

threat by the citizens of such constituencies. Furthermore, accepted conceptions of the congressional role leave large room for unrestrained criticism and court-curbing activities when they express constituency and regional interests and cultures.

The most dramatic and visible conflicts between Congress and the Court have concerned cases involving constitutional interpretations.[61] Without the Court's overruling itself, many of these decisions can be fully reversed only by constitutional amendment. Managing any piece of controversial legislation through Congress is typically a long, difficult, complicated, and often unfruitful process. With a constitutional amendment these difficulties are multiplied by the requirement of a two-thirds vote and the fact that the issues typically become highly charged with symbolism. Although the initial contention of those who would overturn a particular decision may be that it was the Court that violated the Constitution, sponsoring an amendment makes the amenders themselves open to the charge that they are tinkering with the handiwork of the Founding Fathers.[62] Even if it clears Congress, the amendment must still win approval of three-fourths of the states. The sum result is that changing a Court decision by amendment is typically a highly unpromising route. Before 1971, the last time it had been done successfully was in 1913 with the passage of the Sixteenth Amendment overturning the Court's anti–income tax decision of some eighteen years earlier. In 1970 the Court ruled that congressional legislation enfranchising 18, 19, and 20 year olds was only constitutional as applied to federal (as opposed to state) elections.[63] This decision, had it stood alone, would have cre-

---

[61] In general see C. Herman Pritchett, *Congress versus the Supreme Court* (Minneapolis: University of Minnesota Press, 1961); Walter F. Murphy, *Congress and the Court* (Chicago: University of Chicago Press, 1962); Lytle, *Warren Court and Its Critics*, pp. 10–49; Lucius J. Barker and Twiley W. Barker, Jr., *Freedoms, Courts, Politics: Studies in Civil Liberties*, rev. ed. (Englewood Cliffs, N.J.: Prentice-Hall, 1972); Robert J. Steamer, *The Supreme Court in Crisis* (Amherst: University of Massachusetts Press, 1971). Also see John R. Schmidhauser and Larry L. Berg, *The Supreme Court and Congress: Conflict and Inter-Action, 1945–1968* (New York: Free Press, 1972).

[62] Note, for example, the fate of the so-called Becker Amendment, which was aimed at overturning the Court's rulings on prayers in the public schools. See William M. Beaney and Edward N. Beiser, "Prayer and Politics: The Impact of *Engel* and *Schempp* on the Political Process," *Journal of Public Law*, 13 (1964), 475–503.

[63] Oregon v. Mitchell, 400 U.S. 112 (1970).

ated chaos at the polls, thus there was widespread agreement that a constitutional amendment was needed, and the Twenty-Sixth Amendment giving 18 year olds and older the right to vote in *all* elections quickly won approval in Congress and in the state legislatures.

Head-on conflict between the Court and Congress over constitutional cases concerning federal power have been relatively rare, however. From 1789 through February, 1975, there were only 114 decisions striking down congressional legislation in whole or in part.[64] Court curbs on presidential powers have even been rarer. Since the late 1930s when a humbled Court overruled its attempts to limit narrowly the national government's power to regulate the economy, the Supreme Court has been quite restrained in setting limits on Congress and the President. In contrast to the conservative Courts of the late nineteenth and early twentieth centuries, which broadly questioned the federal government's power to govern, the modern Court in striking down federal legislation has dealt mostly either with laws that lacked procedural safeguards but could be repaired by remedial legislation, or with fairly marginal civil libertarian areas involving relatively few persons. Even the Youngstown case, a potentially stunning defeat to President Truman in his attempt to guard against the military and economic consequences of a stoppage in steel production during the Korean War, was not a denial of power to the federal government, but merely a denial of that power to the President without supporting congressional action. The famous Nixon Tapes case,[65] although it led to Nixon's downfall, was itself a very narrow ruling relating to the integrity of the criminal judicial process. The Court in its unanimous decision left open ample room for the presidency to

[64] See, Henry J. Abraham, *The Judicial Process,* Third Edition (New York: Oxford University Press, 1975), pp. 280–294; Congressional Quarterly, *The Supreme Court: Justice and the Law* (Washington, D.C.: Congressional Quarterly, 1973), pp. 113–118. Also see Edward S. Corwin, *The Constitution of the United States of America: Analysis and Interpretation* (Washington, D.C.: Government Printing Office, 1964), pp. 1387–1402. See, in general, Dean Alfange, Jr., "Congressional Power and Constitutional Limitation," *Journal of Public Law,* 18 (1969), 103–134; Jonathan D. Casper, "The Supreme Court and National Policy Making," *American Political Science Review,* 70 (1976), in press.

[65] United States v. Nixon, 94 S. Ct. 3090 (1974). For a journalistic account of the behind-the-scenes deliberations of the Court in this case (based on interview findings but whose veracity has not been independently confirmed by others), see Nina Totenberg, "Behind the Marble, Beneath the Robes," *New York Times Magazine,* March 16, 1975, pp. 58, 67.

maintain executive privilege in matters of legitimate national interests. The modern Court's permissive attitude toward federal power, therefore, may well explain much of the amicable relationship that has existed between the President and the Court.[66]

In contrast to the relative infrequency of Court decisions overturning acts of Congress and exercises of presidential power, cases overturning state and local laws either as unconstitutional or as a violation of federal statutory law or treaties are much more common. From 1789 through the end of the Court's 1974 term, there were over 900 cases in which this occurred.[67] The rate had accelerated during the years of the Warren Court as attention was focused on state cases. As compared to federal cases, these cases involved an inordinately high number whose principal issue was constitutional. For example, in the Warren Court's 1967 term, of the cases decided with full written opinion, approximately 80 percent of the cases concerning state laws and procedures involved a constitutional question, while only about 30 percent of the federal cases did so. With the subsequent Nixon Court, one finds, for example, in the 1973 term, that about 78 percent of the cases concerning state laws and procedures involved a constitutional question as compared to about one-fourth of the federal cases raising constitutional issues.[68]

A large number of state cases decided on constitutional grounds, like similar federal cases, can only be reversed by a constitutional amendment. In fact, during the 1960s the two most serious and near successful attempts at Court-reversing amendments concerned state law cases. These were the so-called Becker Amendment, which would have reversed the Schempp decision and thus allowed school prayers, and the Dirksen Amendment, which would have partially reversed the one man–one vote doctrine of *Reynolds* v. *Sims*. Both these proposed amendments died as victims of the complexities and procedural pitfalls of the legislative process in Congress. The Becker Amend-

---

[66] The Court in Train v. City of New York, 95 S. Ct. 839 (1975) ruled that funds appropriated by Congress could not be impounded by the executive branch. Although this was a blow at the Nixon Administration, it was administered after Mr. Nixon's departure and was a narrow ruling upholding Congress's constitutional legislative powers. In this respect it was similar to Youngstown Sheet and Tube Co. v. Sawyer (steel seizure case), 343 U.S. 579 (1952).

[67] Abraham, *The Judicial Process*, p. 280. Also see Casper, "The Supreme Court and National Policy Making."

[68] *Harvard Law Review*, 87 (1974), 278–280.

ment was killed by the determined opposition of the then–Chairman of the House Judiciary Committee, Representative Emanuel Celler, who refused to report the bill out of committee; the Dirksen Amendment was killed by a filibuster by Senate liberals. After the Court's 1973 decision preventing the states from prohibiting abortion during the first two trimesters of pregnancy,[69] constitutional amendments were introduced in Congress but they were aborted in committee.

In face of the great difficulties in reversing Court constitutional policy making by constitutional amendment, Court critics in Congress have turned to other means for modifying and changing this type of Court output. These include such heavy-handed techniques as threats of impeachment and attempts to remove Supreme Court and perhaps total federal jurisdiction from areas where Court policies are disliked. Impeachment, as a political weapon, has always been difficult to administer. However, it should be noted that it was an impeachmentlike process that senatorial critics of the Court's liberal activism used when thwarting President Johnson's promoting of Associate Justice Fortas to the Chief Justice's chair. Furthermore, once the Nixon Administration came to power, disclosure of allegations of Fortas's impropriety in financial arrangements was used to force his resignation (amidst the righteous indignation of primarily conservative congressional critics of the Court). However, the symbolism of judicial ethics and considerations of judicial policy proved to be a two-edged sword, which liberals used against conservatives to defeat President Nixon's first nominee for the seat vacated by Fortas, Southern conservative Judge Clement Haynsworth. After the defeat of Nixon's second nominee to the Fortas seat, Judge G. Harrold Carswell, also a Southern conservative (his alleged mediocrity as a jurist was an additional issue), the Republican conservatives in Congress allied with anti-Court Democrats to revive the campaign to impeach liberal Justice Douglas. Although then–House Judiciary Committee Chairman Emanuel Celler once again moved to protect the Court in general and Justice Douglas in particular, the depth of anti-Court hostility was prominent.[70] (Note that when Nixon nominated Harry Blackmun, a

[69] Roe v. Wade, 410 U.S. 113 (1973). See Marilyn Falik, "The Impact of the Supreme Court Decision on Abortion: Political and Legislative Resistance v. Court Reactions," paper presented at the 1974 Annual Meeting of the A.P.S.A.

[70] See *Congressional Quarterly*, April 17, 1970, p. 1045; *New York Times*, June 7, 1970, p. 38; Milton Viorst, "Bill Douglas Has Never Stopped Fighting the Bullies of Yakima," *New York Times Magazine*, June 14, 1970, p. 52.

Midwestern conservative with impeccable professional credentials to the Fortas seat, the Senate gave its unanimous consent, thus tacitly acknowledging the prevailing displeasure with civil libertarian Court policies and the legitimacy of the President's using his appointment powers to rectify the situation.)

Attempts at curbing Court policy making by removal of jurisdiction, a device that succeeded in the aftermath of the Civil War, have failed to get congressional approval in recent years, although there have been some near misses with this ploy in several areas.

In sum, most negative congressional feedback to the Court in recent decades toward its constitutional decision making has been merely verbal (although some legislation concerning criminal law and court-ordered busing for purposes of school desegregation are notable exceptions).[71] Statements have been made on the floor, hearings held to establish a forum for the Court's critics, legislation and constitutional amendments proposed and defeated. This typical unsuccess on the part of congressional Court critics rests on the fact that for most of the recent past friends of the Court have been nearly as numerous, though not necessarily as vocal, as its enemies. Thus the Court's friends have been able to keep most feedback by congressional critics directed into relatively harmless channels. In some areas, particularly civil rights during the 1960s, Congress passed vital legislation aimed at forwarding the implementation of Court-initiated policy.

To emphasize only what Congress has not done or cannot do in the face of unwanted constitutional policy making by the Court is somewhat misleading. As applied to the recent history of Court-congressional relationships, it tends to imply a will in Congress that is perhaps only marginally there. Congress, and particularly the Senate during the 1960s, contained a sufficient number of backers of the Warren Court's liberal activism to protect the Court from congressional retaliation.

The second reason that it is misleading to focus on the ineffectualness of congressional responses to constitutional policy making is that many cases decided by the Court do not rest on constitutional grounds. For example, of the 157 cases deemed important enough by the Court in its 1973 term to warrant disposal by full written opinions, in only 78 (49 percent) was the principal issue constitu-

[71] In general see Schmidhauser and Berg, *The Supreme Court and Congress.*

tional.[72] The remainder primarily concerned judicial interpretations of federal legislation, which, of course, can be overturned by regular congressional legislation. Even among decisions that are normally listed as constitutional, there are a number that also can be changed simply by congressional legislation. For example, such cases occur when the Court, in lieu of any clear congressional policy, is called upon to uphold federal interests under the commerce power in the face of state activities inhibiting the free flow of commerce. A famous instance of congressional reversal of such Supreme Court policy making concerned a bridge built under a Virginia charter over the Ohio River. The bridge was built in such a way as to obstruct river navigation. Pennsylvania, acting in the interest of its citizens whose rights were "abridged," asked the Court for and was granted an injunction instructing the company to alter the structure as to not obstruct river traffic.[73] Congress then passed a bill declaring the bridge "a lawful structure" and required boats operating on the Ohio to be so regulated as not to interfere with it. The Court subsequently ruled the act a constitutional use of Congress's power over commerce.[74]

Congressional reversal of Court legislative interpretations and constitutional policy making of the type just discussed has been found to occur with occasional frequency. In a survey of congressional activities from 1945 to 1957, it was found that Congress overruled Court decisions 21 times in this period.[75] Although the circumstances under which this occurred varied, in a large number of cases congressional reversals were marked by the common theme of returning the law to the "common understanding" that had existed prior to the Court's action. For example, in *United States* v. *South-Eastern Underwriters Ass'n*,[76] the Court reversed prior doctrine and held that insurance companies in fact operate in interstate commerce and thus are sub-

[72] *Harvard Law Review*, 87 (1974), 278–280.

[73] Pennsylvania v. Wheeling and Belmont Bridge Co., 13 How. 518 (1852).

[74] Pennsylvania v. Wheeling and Belmont Bridge Co., 18 How. 421 (1856).

[75] Note, "Congressional Reversal of Supreme Court Decisions: 1945–1957," *Harvard Law Review*, 71 (1958), 1324–1336. Also see Harry P. Stumpf, "The Political Efficacy of Judicial Symbolism," *Western Political Quarterly*, 19 (1966), pp. 299–300, Table 1. See Schmidhauser and Berg, *The Supreme Court and Congress*, pp. 142–144, 171–176; Justin J. Green, John R. Schmidhauser, and Larry L. Berg, "Variations in Congressional Responses to the Warren and Burger Courts," *Emory Law Journal*, 23 (1974), 725–743.

[76] 322 U.S. 533 (1944).

ject to federal antitrust law. Congress, taking into account the pattern of state insurance regulation that had grown up over the years, then reversed the decision. Certain specific restrictive practices were outlawed, and the states were to continue to regulate the industry. In return the industry was given back its federal antitrust immunity.

FEEDBACK AND COURT POLICY MAKING

The federal judicial system and the Supreme Court as its highest and most visible policy-making organ has always received some minimal level of feedback. Law journals and the mass media always have had some reaction to court behavior, even if that reaction is the journalistic equivalent of "good job, well done." Alternatively, judicial authorities inevitably from time to time make errors in their interpretation of congressional legislation. These often occur not because of any great policy disagreement with the legislative branch, but merely because Congress's latent and often unarticulated intent is incorrectly perceived. Sometimes such rulings are allowed to stand. Other times Congress, with its greater fact-finding devices, interest group sensitivity, and mechanisms for complex policy making, will pass remedial legislation. In these and other ways a minimal or background level of feedback is maintained.

Over the history of the nation since constitutional government was established, there have been times when the level of negative feedback to the Court has risen sharply above this background. Thus, presidents normally during their terms in office have considered it as part of the presidential role to back or at least neutrally enforce Court policies as the sole legitimate interpretation of the law. Presidents Jefferson, Jackson, Lincoln, Franklin Roosevelt, and to some extent, Nixon eschewed that role and attacked the shape of Court policy, seeking to change it while in office. Similarly in Congress there have been some periods marked by attempts to curb the Court and others when the relationship between the two branches was friendly.

Stuart Nagel in a study of Court-curbing legislation up through 1959[77] found that 1802–1804, 1823–1831, 1858–1869, 1893–1897, 1922–1924, 1935–1937, and 1955–1959 were periods in which there was a high frequency of Court-curbing attempts through legislation.

[77] Stuart S. Nagel, *The Legal Process from a Behavioral Perspective* (Homewood, Ill.: Dorsey, 1969), pp. 260–279.

Also analyzed was whether or not the Court retreated in its policy stands and the overall or "composite success" of the Court-curbing attempts. Nagel suggested that only the following periods achieved "composite success": 1802–1804, 1823–1831, 1858–1869, and 1935–1937 (although he notes that there was a partial judicial retreat in the 1955–1959 period).[78]

As can be readily surmised, these composite success periods fall within the administrations of presidents noted for their particularly hostile attitudes toward the Court. (Of course, the dates of the Nixon Administration are excluded by Nagel since his analysis ended with 1959). We can note that with the exception of the 1922–1924 period, each high-frequency Court-curbing period falls within a period in which electoral realignment (as identified by critical election theory) produced a new political era.

Briefly, critical election studies have dealt with patterns of voting behavior. These studies have indicated that voters are typically quite stable in their partisan allegiances and such ancillary behavior as turn-out and ticket splitting. However, as an empirical phenomenon it has been found that about once every generation-and-a-half this electoral stability breaks down in one or more tightly grouped "critical elections" in which prior partisan allegiances are permanently and massively changed along with ancillary voter behavior. Although there has been some dispute as to which elections in American history have met these criteria, notably with regard to the earlier history of the Republic, in general the elections of 1828, 1864, 1896, 1928–1936, and 1964–1968 have been identified as having critical election characteristics. (Elections prior to 1824 are normally unanalyzed because of a lack of sufficient popular voting data, although the election of 1800 is generally thought to have at least some critical election attributes.)

To understand the phenomenon further, consider the election of 1888. The voting pattern for that election was more or less the same as the voting patterns of every election back to 1876. This was a pattern in which the two parties were very close, ticket splitting was rare, turnout high, and party allegiances very strong. With 1896 and the

[78] Ibid., p. 262, Table 21-2. See the discussion of court-curbing during these periods in David Adamany, "Legitimacy, Realigning Elections, and the Supreme Court," Wisconsin Law Review (1973), pp. 825–841. Also see, Richard Funston, "The Supreme Court and Critical Elections," American Political Science Review, 69 (1975), in press. But cf. Casper, "The Supreme Court and National Policy Making."

election of McKinley, voting behavior altered significantly. Partisan-ship became much more regionally based, turnout fell, major shifts toward a party (landslides) became more common. This pattern stayed more or less undisturbed until the election of 1928. In that election and subsequently the elections of 1932 and 1936 the New Deal Democratic coalition came into being.

Using this theory along with a consideration of public policy out-puts and presidential styles, it has been argued elsewhere that Ameri-can political history can therefore be split into five major periods:[79] the Federalist-Jeffersonian (1789–1828), the Jacksonian (1828–1860), the First Republican (1860–1896), the Second Republican (1896–1932), and the New Deal Era (1932–1968). (As students of American history will recognize, these periods more or less coincide with those suggested by traditional political historians.) These periods can be briefly summarized, although at the risk of oversimplification.

The Federalist-Jeffersonian period, although split into two parts (Federalist dominated from 1789 to 1800, Jeffersonian dominated from 1800 to 1828), still had the overall unity of the federal govern-ment under the control of a fairly select elite of merchants and planters concerning itself with the problems of Constitution build-ing, union, and creating economic and political stability in the face of intrigues and tensions both foreign and domestic. The Jacksonian period saw the disappearance of the old Federalist and Jeffersonian Republican parties and their replacement by the mass-based Demo-crats and Whigs. The common man, at least symbolically, took con-trol of government through widespread political participation in the party system and administration. The balance of political power shifted westward, and major party political competition existed everywhere. The major public policy concerns were state-based governmental encouragement of economic development as indus-trial takeoff proceeded regionally in the North and the drive toward a compromise solution on slavery.

Lincoln's election signaled a start of a new period, although the period's stable electoral alignments did not take shape until 1864,

---

[79] Thomas P. Jahnige, "Critical Elections and Social Change: Towards a Dynamic Explanation of National Party Competition in the United States," *Polity*, 3 (1971), 465–500. Also see Walter Dean Burnham, *Critical Elections and the Mainsprings of American Politics* (New York: Norton, 1970). Cf. Funston, "The Supreme Court and Critical Elections."

after four years of Lincoln's leadership. By 1860, however, the Whigs had disintegrated and the Democratic Party split in two; the Republicans had blossomed forth full grown and victorious. The dominant themes of this period were, of course, the Civil War, the protection of the freed slaves, the reconstruction of the South, and, most important, the protection and promotion of industry and capitalism.

The significant result of the election of 1896 was to propel the Republican Party into a position of overwhelming dominance. The party system created was one in which one-party states, both Democratic and Republican, were quite common. Dramatic shifts in public policy and symbolism are somewhat harder to find than with previous realignments. This is perhaps due to the continuing dominance of the Republican Party and that party's continuing support of big business. Also this was the first party-system realignment that did not witness the disappearance of one or both of the system's major party components. It should be noted, however, that this period was marked by the almost complete halt to all attempts to protect Negroes, the first serious attempts at economic regulation, and the first major entrance of the United States into imperialism and great-power politics.

With the realignments of 1928–1932, the dominant party once again shifted, and although partisan cleavages were still strongly regional, these began to break down. Economic cleavages became more important in determining one's vote, particularly outside the South. The public policy concerns were the welfare-warfare state and certainly by the Truman Administration a growing concern with civil rights (which dominated national politics through the Administration of Lyndon Johnson). It appears that the politics that began with FDR came to an end with the elections of Richard Nixon in 1968 and 1972. Had the Watergate-related scandals not fatally undermined the Nixon Administration, Nixon might well have been able to solidify for the Republican Party the moderate-right coalition including a sizable portion of blue-collar workers and lower-middle-class white "ethnic" groups that twice put him in the White House. (Had the aftermath of Watergate and the severe economic recession of the mid-1970s not occurred, President Ford might have been able to put that coalition together again.) The party system is now in a state of flux.

What, one well might ask, does all this have to do with feedback to the Supreme Court. The answer is perhaps deceptively simple.

Negative feedback to the Court has historically shown its greatest increases when old party system periods have come to an end and new ones are in the process of beginning. These are times when critical electoral realignments change the nature of politics and the groups in power. Because of the inevitable lag between when elected authorities of the "new politics" (i.e., electoral realignments) are put into office and sitting judges recruited under the old regime are replaced, the judiciary typically becomes suddenly out-of-tune with the times. Although retirement, death, and the selection process eventually correct the situation, this takes time.[80] In the interim, criticism, evasion, and Court-curbing attempts by President and Congress increase. This is suggested by the coincidence of Court-curbing periods found by Nagel and the presidential periods just discussed.[81]

Where does this leave us? In the first place it appears that the observation of popular commentators that the country in 1968 shifted to the right is supported by data that have special relevance for the judicial system. For example, the combined presidential vote in 1968 of Court-opponents Nixon and Wallace was 57 percent of the popular vote; by 1970 a substantial portion of those surveyed considered themselves "conservative" rather than "liberal," a result that has been repeated well into the 1970s;[82] by almost 2 to 1, those surveyed in 1970 advocated the appointment of conservatives rather than liberals to the Supreme Court, and similar results, too, have been found in later years although with a somewhat smaller margin favoring conservatives;[83] and negative feedback to the Warren Court's liberal policies, particularly in the realm of criminal procedures, reached a peak in the late 1960s and conservative attitudes

[80] For a discussion of the time lag between the rise of a new political era and an agreement in judicial policy making, see Robert A. Dahl, *Pluralist Democracy in the United States: Conflict and Consent* (Skokie, Ill.: Rand McNally, 1967), pp. 154–170. Cf. Casper, "The Supreme Court and National Policy Making," and Funston, "The Supreme Court and Critical Elections."

[81] Also see Adamany, "Legitimacy, Realigning Elections, and the Supreme Court," pp. 841–846. Cf. Funston, "The Supreme Court and Critical Elections."

[82] *New York Times*, April 19, 1970, p. 58. A 1974 Gallup Poll reported 38 percent of the national sample consider themselves "conservative," 26 percent consider themselves "liberal," and 36 percent were undecided. *Current Opinion*, 2 (June 1974), 61.

[83] See *Current Opinion*, 1 (September 1973), 91.

on matters of criminal law and procedures persisted into the 1970s.[84] Even those looking to youth as a source of hope for a liberal future had their faith tested with the results of the Survey Research Center study of the 1968 election, which showed that, outside the South, Wallace had his greatest support (by age group) in the under-30 set.[85] Nixon's overwhelming landslide reelection in 1972 further emphasized the shift in party attachments and the electoral shift to the right.

What this all suggests is that the federal judicial system of the Warren Court era, characterized by civil libertarian output, could have been expected to be transformed in accord with the new political era, and indeed, as we have seen earlier, the Court, particularly in the criminal procedures areas but in other areas as well, was so transformed. This was a source of obvious bitterness for the liberal Warren Court holdovers who on numerous occasions lamented that the new composition of the Court was the principal reason for the change in policy.[86]

Responding to feedback during the Nixon Court era has not necessarily meant a change only from liberal policies to conservative ones. At the federal district court level, it has been demonstrated by Beverly Cook that the sentencing behavior of judges of selective service law violators during the Vietnam War changed as public opinion (as measured by opinion surveys) concerning the war and the draft changed.[87] As public opinion over the years became more

[84] See the surveys cited in Chapter 4.

[85] Philip E. Converse, Warren E. Miller, Jerrold G. Rusk, and Arthur C. Wolfe, "Continuity and Change in American Politics: Parties and Issues in the 1968 Election," *American Political Science Review*, 63 (1969), p. 1103.

[86] That the Nixon Court was indeed adjusting its output in certain policy areas in response to negative feedback was explicitly recognized by Justice Marshall in his dissent in the Detroit school busing case when he observed: "Today's holding, I fear, is more a reflection of a perceived public mood that we have gone far enough in enforcing the Constitution's guarantee of equal justice than it is the product of neutral principles of law." Milliken v. Bradley 92 S. Ct. 3112 (1974) at 3161. In another instance Justice Stewart in a dissent charged the majority with "A basic change in law upon a ground no firmer than a change in our membership. . . ." Mitchell v. W. T. Grant Company 94 S. Ct. 1895 (1974) at 1914.

[87] See Beverly Blair Cook, "Decision-Making by Federal Trial Judges: Reference Groups and Local Culture," paper presented at the 1973 Annual Meeting of the American Political Science Association. Also see Beverly Blair Cook, "Public Opinion and Federal Judicial Policy," manuscript.

antagonistic to the war and the draft, judges became more lenient in their sentencing, so that by 1972 there was a turnaround in sentencing patterns in that a majority of violators were given probation. Thus it should be emphasized that the courts continually can be found responding to negative feedback.[88] During the transformation of an old to a new party system, however, the judiciary of the old regime is likely to be incapable of adequately responding to the intensified negative feedback and the new demands of the new coalition.

Because of the Watergate scandals and the economic crisis of the mid-1970s, the new electoral coalition that had seemed so promising for the Republicans came apart. As of this writing there is uncertainty as to whether the economic crisis in particular will stimulate a rebuilding of the old New Deal Democratic coalition and if so how stable it will be. In short, an unstable economic and political era can be expected to affect the judicial system. In a world of uncertainties, perhaps the only certainty that we can expect is change.

[88] See G. Gregory Fahlund, "Feedback in the Judicial Process: The Warren Court and Criminal Procedure," Ph.D. dissertation, University of Massachusetts, 1971; and his "Retroactivity and the Warren Court: The Strategy of a Revolution," *Journal of Politics*, 35 (1973), 570–593.

EIGHT
EASTONIAN SYSTEMS ANALYSIS
AND LEGAL RESEARCH

EASTONIAN systems analysis has been used in the preceding chapters to help understand and organize the major scholarly materials in the literature on judicial process and behavior. It is now appropriate to reflect on some of the gaps in our knowledge as well as some promising research areas and to focus on the questions about which one becomes cognizant through the use of systems analysis.[1]

SUGGESTED QUESTIONS FOR FURTHER STUDY

The input concept of *demands* alerts us to several lines of potential research that could help supplement the fragmentary knowledge we now have. These include determining who, in terms of backgrounds and status characteristics, institutes litigation and the kinds of demands made, the frequency of repetition of demands, the extent to which they mirror the wishes of the public and its constituent groups and the extent to which they reflect cleavages within the society,

---

[1] Note that the research questions suggested in this section need not be confined to the federal judicial system. Studies of the various state judicial systems and cross-national studies of judicial systems cannot help but broaden our understanding of judicial systems in general. Glendon Schubert has provided an extensive bibliography in his "Judicial Process and Behavior, 1963–1971," in James A. Robinson (ed.), *Political Science Annual, III* (Indianapolis: Bobbs-Merrill, 1972), pp. 73–280. Also see Glendon Schubert and David J. Danelski (eds.), *Comparative Judicial Behavior* (New York: Oxford University Press, 1969); Theodore L. Becker, *Comparative Judicial Politics* (Skokie, Ill.: Rand McNally, 1970); Henry Robert Glick and Kenneth N. Vines, *State Court Systems* (Englewood Cliffs, N.J.: Prentice-Hall, 1973); and Herbert Jacob, *Urban Justice* (Englewood Cliffs, N.J.: Prentice-Hall, 1973).

the relationship between refusal of the courts to consider certain demands and public support for the courts, and whether some individuals or groups are better able to make demands than others, and how this is related to stress on the judicial system.[2]

Research attention is also directed at *demand input overload* as a source of stress on the system, which can be caused by either (1) a preponderance of demands that take an excessive amount of time to process, or (2) by exceeding the volume of demands that the system is efficiently able to accommodate. Specification of which type of demand overload exists is the starting point for analysis of "delay in court" or "court congestion" phenomena. Such questions as what types of demands consume an "excessive" amount of time to process and why are relevant.[3] For example, a pertinent question to ask is whether and to what extent Supreme Court decisions in various legal areas such as criminal procedures have been related to demand overload. One question here is whether such decisions have, in fact, greatly increased the amount of time that both trial and appellate courts spend on such cases.

The concept of demand input overload because of excessive volume suggests consideration of what types of demands are responsible for excess volume. The underlying causes behind these demands deserve study. So does whether something can be done to decrease their volume such as decriminalization of "victimless" crimes or the adoption of the no-fault concept in areas of civil law

---

[2] Some of these research questions were considered in a major study of wage garnishment and consumer bankruptcy in four Wisconsin cities. See Herbert Jacob, *Debtors in Court* (Skokie, Ill.: Rand McNally, 1969). Questions of who uses the courts and why are attracting the attention of political scientists. See, for example, Craig Wanner, "The Public Ordering of Private Relations: Initiating Civil Cases in Urban Trial Courts," *Law and Society Review*, 8 (1974), 421–440; Joel B. Grossman and Austin Sarat, "Litigation in the Federal Courts: A Comparative Perspective," *Law and Society Review*, 9 (1975), in press; Joel B. Grossman and Austin Sarat, "Courts and Conflict Resolution: Problems in the Mobilization of Adjudication," *American Political Science Review*, 69 (1975), 321–346.

[3] See, for example, Daniel J. Meador, *Appellate Courts: Staff and Process in the Crisis of Volume* (St. Paul: West, 1974); Paul D. Carrington, "Crowded Dockets and the Courts of Appeals: The Threat to the Function of Review and the National Law," *Harvard Law Review*, 82 (1969), 542–617; Gerhard Casper and Richard A. Posner, "A Study of the Supreme Court's Caseload," *Journal of Legal Studies*, 3 (1974), 339–375; Henry J. Friendly, "Averting the Flood by Lessening the Flow," in *Cornell Law Review*, 59 (1974), 634–657; and Wesley G. Skogan, "Traffic and the Courts," in Herbert Jacob (ed.), *The Potential for Reform of Criminal Justice* (Beverly Hills, Calif.: Sage, 1974), pp. 131–172.

such as tort and family law, or whether systemic capacities should be enlarged by adding more judges and courts. The last consideration also suggests research into whether there might be diseconomies of scale involved in system enlargement. Furthermore, one might also investigate whether the "delay in court" phenomenon itself is not a systemic mechanism for frustrating the presentation of certain classes of "frivolous" demands.[4]

An obvious subject of inquiry suggested by Eastonian systems analysis is the relationship between changes in such regime rules as jurisdiction and justiciability and demand input overload. What would be the effect on the federal judicial system (as well as the larger political system) if certain subject areas were added to or withdrawn from its courts' jurisdiction?

Certain regime rules, such as discovery rules, negotiated guilty pleas in criminal cases, and pretrial conferences facilitate a reduction in demands that require further processing. Yet additional research would be helpful for our understanding of their ability to reduce stress. How are these processes perceived and evaluated by the participants—litigants, lawyers, and judges?[5] What modifications or

[4] The area of judicial administration has begun to attract the attention of political scientists. See Peter Graham Fish, *The Politics of Federal Judicial Administration* (Princeton, N.J.: Princeton University Press, 1973); Howard R. Whitcomb and Russell Wheeler, "The Literature of Court Administration," *Arizona State Law Journal* (1974), pp. 689–722; and Russell Wheeler and Howard R. Whitcomb, *Perspectives on Judicial Administration: Readings in Court Management and the Administration of Justice* (Englewood Cliffs, N.J.: Prentice-Hall, 1976). Also see Lucinda Long, "Innovation in Urban Criminal Misdemeanor Courts," in Jacob (ed.), *The Potential for Reform*, pp. 173–206.

[5] See William A. Glaser, *Pretrial Discovery and the Adversary System* (New York: Russell Sage Foundation, 1968); Abraham S. Blumberg, *Criminal Justice* (Chicago: Quadrangle, 1970); Jonathan D. Casper, *American Criminal Justice: The Defendant's Perspective* (Englewood Cliffs, N.J.: Prentice-Hall, 1972); and George F. Cole, *Politics and the Administration of Justice* (Beverly Hills, Calif.: Sage, 1973). Journalists also have a continuing interest in some of these questions. See, for example, Selwyn Raab, "Plea-Bargains Settling 8 of 10 Homicide Cases: Reduced Charges Found to Bring Probation or 10 Years at Most," *New York Times*, January 27, 1975, p. 1. The need is great for continuing empirical research concerning what actually happens when certain reforms are implemented. One such reform, the omnibus hearing, which is supposed to do for criminal case processing what discovery procedures are supposed to do for civil case processing, was implemented in the Federal District Court located in San Diego, California. Raymond T. Nimmer studied the "reform" there and found that it *increased* the amount of case processing time. See Nimmer, "Judicial Reform: Informal Processes and Competing Effects," in Jacob (ed.), *The Potential for Reform*, pp. 207–234.

additions to these formal and informal rules would encourage demand input reduction? What are the effects of nontrial settlements on the ability of the larger political system to cope with stress?

The demand-regulating mechanism of gatekeeping also suggests several research questions. With regard to lawyers as gatekeepers, such questions include asking the extent to which requests to handle litigation are denied and whether such refusal is a function of the proposed litigation, the status of the litigants, or the type and status of lawyers involved. Government attorneys also gatekeep by their decisions to prosecute or initiate litigation. How they exercise their discretion is of great interest. One might also look at the activities of interest groups in accepting and rejecting requests to sponsor litigation.[6] A related domain of research interest is determining the extent to which lawyers and interest groups change or modify the content of proposed litigation in order to enhance the prospects of their client's winning. Involved in such an investigation would be determining how these strategies are arrived at,[7] their success, and the significance of these modifications in demands for the disturbances within the environment that originally led to the demands. Similarly, one might look at how judges perform their gatekeeping tasks. This would involve investigating the effectiveness of procedures and techniques (such as those concerning the pretrial conference) as gatekeeping mechanisms, the sorts of demands likely to fall victim to judicial gatekeeping techniques, and the extent (and why) demands are transformed as they move from one court level to the next.[8]

[6] Suggestive research related to this can be found in two articles by Nathan Hakman, "Lobbying the Supreme Court—An Appraisal of 'Political Science Folklore,'" *Fordham Law Review*, 35 (1966), 15–50; and "The Supreme Court's Political Environment: The Processing of Noncommercial Litigation," in Joel B. Grossman and Joseph Tanenhaus (eds.), *Frontiers of Judicial Research* (New York: Wiley, 1969), pp. 199–253.

[7] See, for example, Jonathan D. Casper, *Lawyers before the Warren Court* (Urbana: University of Illinois Press, 1972); and Stuart A. Scheingold, *The Politics of Rights: Lawyers, Public Policy, and Political Change* (New Haven, Conn.: Yale University Press, 1974).

[8] See Richard J. Richardson and Kenneth N. Vines, "Review, Dissent, and the Appellate Process: A Political Interpretation," *Journal of Politics*, 29 (1967), 597–616. Carl Baar has argued that demand overload has transformed the very nature of judicial institutions so that courts and judges are becoming less judicial and more bureaucratic in their behavior. See his "Will Urban Trial Courts Survive the War on Crime?" in Jacob (ed.), *The Potential for Reform*, pp. 331–352.

The Supreme Court, in particular, is a court where the judges show broad discretion through the grant or denial of certiorari in selecting which demands are to be seriously treated. Although several studies of the exercise of this discretion have been undertaken, there is more work to be done in this area. Analogous research might also be conducted for lower courts in terms of the relationship of certain variables (such as the government's position in the case) and the extensiveness of formal (as opposed to cursory) court consideration.

Although Easton's analysis of support has stimulated landmark empirical research explicitly using the concepts of specific and diffuse support,[9] there remain a number of other questions that no doubt deserve extensive exploration. These include such questions as the identification of the members of a political system crucial for judicial system support,[10] the differences in both types of support for contemporary judicial authorities as distinct from the regime rules, and the relationship of judicial activities to the input of support for the larger political system. Regarding this last point, one might examine, for example, the relationship of the civil libertarian activism of the Warren Court to stress on the American political system. The concept of support also raises such questions as to how diffuse and specific support are generated, maintained, and lost.[11] How is a belief in court legitimacy inculcated in members of the political community, and to what extent is this done by the family, schools, groups, and the mass media?[12] To what extent does the legitimacy

[9] Walter F. Murphy and Joseph Tanenhaus, "Public Opinion and the United States Supreme Court," in Grossman and Tanenhaus (eds.), *Frontiers of Judicial Research*, pp. 273–303; and Walter F. Murphy, Joseph Tanenhaus, and Daniel L. Kastner, *Public Evaluations of Constitutional Courts: Alternative Explanations*, Sage Professional Papers in Comparative Politics, Vol. 4, series no. 01-045 (Beverly Hills, Calif.: Sage, 1973).

[10] Particularly suggestive is the study by Gregory Casey, "The Supreme Court and Myth: An Empirical Investigation," *Law and Society Review*, 8 (1974), 385–419. Also see Micheal W. Giles, "Lawyers and the Supreme Court: A Comparative Look at Some Attitudinal Linkages," *Journal of Politics*, 35 (1973), 480–486.

[11] Some suggestive research on some of these points was conducted by Richard L. Engstrom and Micheal W. Giles. See their "Expectations and Images: A Note on Diffuse Support for Legal Institutions," *Law and Society Review*, 6 (1972), 631–636. Also see, Austin Sarat, "Support for the Legal System," *American Politics Quarterly*, 3 (1975), 3–24.

[12] There is serious question as to whether the courts are deemed to have legitimacy beyond that of an equal branch of government. See the discussion by David Adamany, in his "Legitimacy, Realigning Elections, and the Supreme Court," *Wisconsin Law Review*, (1973), 790–846.

of the judicial branch rely upon an adherence by the judges to the common notions of judicial role behavior? What has been the import, if any, of the teaching and research of several generations of politically and behaviorally oriented public law college teachers on diffuse support? Perhaps even of more importance is investigating the import of the legal realism movement on the role conceptions of the judicial authorities and how this relates to the input of support for the system.

The concept of withinput suggests research into reversal rates of one court level by the next, the responses of lower court judges to changes in policy by the higher court and to its specific directives, the extent of lower court compliance with such directives or policy, as well as dicta and off-the-bench commentary of lower court judges regarding higher court pronouncements.[13] Also suggested is research on the operations of judicial councils and conferences as they process as well as reflect withinput.[14]

Despite Easton's disclaimer, systems analysis is suggestive for research on judicial conversion. The systems framework gives some of the findings of current research on judicial behavior a significance that otherwise might go unnoticed. It also suggests lines of research concerning the relationship of input to conversion. For example, how do judges perceive the stimuli of demands, support, and withinputs, and how do these perceptions affect their behavior both within the decision-making milieu of the one-judge trial court and of the small groups on collegial courts?[15]

The conversion-output linkage also raises some questions. These include considerations of the ways in which regime rules structure decision-making institutions and processes and the effect this has on systemic output. The extent and nature of the import of certain

[13] See Richard J. Richardson and Kenneth N. Vines, *The Politics of Federal Courts* (Boston: Little, Brown, 1970), pp. 129–138 for analyses of reversals of district courts by appeals courts.

[14] See Peter G. Fish, "The Circuit Councils: Rusty Hinges of Federal Judicial Administration," *University of Chicago Law Review*, 37 (1970), 203–241. But note the new proposals to create a new council of judges with major disciplinary powers over lower court judges. *New York Times*, March 9, 1975, sec. 4, p. 5.

[15] In general see, S. Sidney Ulmer, *Courts as Small and Not So Small Groups* (Morristown, N.J.: General Learning Press, 1971); and Thomas G. Walker, "Judges in Concert: The Influence of the Group on Judicial Decision-Making," Ph.D. dissertation, University of Kentucky, 1970.

regime rules on actor behavior is, of course, a subject for empirical inquiry.[16] This is part of the general research question of the relationships between the ways in which judges perceive various aspects of their role and judicial output. Also of concern is the relationship of judge to jury and how they mutually influence each other and thus influence output.[17]

Research questions of interest regarding output include investigating the differences (if any) in the conversion process when the outputs involve intrasystem concerns (e.g., rules of civil procedure) and when they do not, and the difference in judicial responses to intrasystem output that produces negative feedback and other output that receives similar feedback. The distinction between authoritative and associated output raises a number of questions for a judicial system among which are the relationship between authoritative and associated outputs, the types of feedback generated by associated outputs and how they differ (if at all) from feedback to authoritative outputs, whether judges respond differently to feedback from associated outputs than they do to feedback from authoritative outputs, the distinction (if any) between authoritative and associated outputs in their effect on systemic stress, and the circumstances under which output failure is most likely to occur and what types of output are most susceptible to failure.[18]

The relationship of output to input suggests research into the correlation between demand satisfaction and the inputs of both specific and diffuse support[19] as well as the generation of new demands.

[16] See, for example, Burton M. Atkins, "Some Theoretical Effects of the Decision Making Rules on the United States Courts of Appeals," *Jurimetrics Journal*, 11 (1970), 13–23; and Burton M. Atkins, "Decision-Making Rules and Judicial Strategy on the United States Courts of Appeals," *Western Political Quarterly*, 25 (1972), 626–642.

[17] See in general Howard S. Erlanger, "Jury Research in America: Its Past and Future," *Law and Society Review*, 4 (1970), 345–370.

[18] See Don W. Brown and Robert V. Stover, "An Economic Approach to Compliance with Court Decisions," paper presented at the 1974 Annual Meeting of the American Political Science Association. In general see Stephen L. Wasby, *The Impact of the United States Supreme Court* (Homewood, Ill.: Dorsey, 1970), especially Chap. 8.

[19] See David J. Danelski, "The People and the Court in Japan," in Grossman and Tanenhaus (eds.), *Frontiers of Judicial Research*, pp. 45–72.

The concept of systemic feedback also raises several other questions crucial for judicial systems analysis. These include determining the nature of the impact of and feedback responses to various kinds of court outputs; what differences in response patterns are found from various institutions, groups, and individuals, both within and outside the judicial system; what are the correlates of compliance and noncompliance to authoritative and associated outputs; and what is the communications process by which court policies are transmitted to those expected to comply?[20]

When the process of information feedback is considered, one confronts questions concerning the channels for this feedback. For example, what newspapers, magazines, and professional journals do judges read? What social activities and off-the-bench professional associations provide information feedback channels? What are the variables associated with how judges perceive and evaluate feedback? And how accurate are their perceptions? Inherent in systems analysis is the crucial assumption that the authorities are responsive to feedback and that this is manifested by the new outputs. Analysis of a judicial system requires quantitative and qualitative analyses of court outputs to test this. In particular, one might ask whether the responsiveness to feedback and the willingness to modify outputs is an institutional or an individual characteristic. We might ask whether it is episodic in character (a switch in time that saves nine) or a more consistent characteristic of judicial behavior.[21] If the crucial link for systems analysis between feedback and new output is found not to operate in the conventional sense for judicial systems, the fundamental question remains: what enables a judicial system to maintain stress below the critical point and thus persist? This would suggest examination of the ability of other political subsystems to adjust their own output (particularly concerning judicial selection and the regime rules under which the judicial system operates) in response to negative feedback from judicial output.

[20] See, for example, Richard M. Johnson, The Dynamics of Compliance (Evanston: Northwestern University Press, 1967), Chaps. 3–6; and Stephen L. Wasby, "Communication of the Supreme Court's Criminal Procedure Decisions: A Preliminary Mapping," Villanova Law Review, 18 (1973), 1086–1118.

[21] See G. Gregory Fahlund, "Feedback in the Judicial Process," Ph.D. dissertation, University of Massachusetts, 1971; and Beverly Blair Cook, "Decision-Making by Federal Trial Judges: Reference Groups and Local Culture," paper presented at the 1973 Annual Meeting of the American Political Science Association.

LIMITS OF SYSTEMS ANALYSIS

There are obvious difficulties with Eastonian political systems analysis. Perhaps most obvious is its essential ambivalence: Is it sets of hypotheses awaiting empirical testing, or is it really a theory grounded on empirical findings? The answer is simply that it is both. Political systems analysis was suggested by numerous empirical studies and thus can be considered descriptive of political reality. Its concepts then serve as organizing concepts. Yet, these concepts within the context of the analytical framework built with them suggest a wide variety of hypotheses concerning interactions within the system and various systemic mechanisms and processes. However, these hypotheses have been generally, rather than narrowly, formulated.

To be sure this has left some scholars dissatisfied with systems analysis. As one critic has warned, "Any putative theoretical effort which cannot achieve, to an appreciable extent, the requisite semantic and syntactic precision can remain substantially insulated against empirical test and is consequently devoid, in large part, of explanatory significance."[22] It would appear that the desired semantic precision is lacking with such concepts as "input," "demand," "support," "withinput," "gatekeeping," "output," "feedback," and so forth. However, Eastonian analysis does not preclude the formulation of operational criteria and their concrete application to specific sets of empirical data. Indeed, in this and previous chapters some possible criteria have been suggested. Nevertheless, this is no substitute for the major empirical undertaking that will ultimately develop the criteria and test the utility of the concepts. Political systems analysis in its present form, it must be acknowledged, has its limits.

Another major limitation to the use of political systems analysis is that description is emphasized to the apparent exclusion of prescription. The stress is on what *is,* and there is a danger that the systems analyst can implicitly use his analysis to defend or maintain the status quo. Thus, under the guise of empirical theory, systems analysis can potentially, if inadvertently, assume a politically conservative posture. Yet systems analysis is not necessarily incompatible

[22] A. James Gregor, "Political Science and the Uses of Functional Analysis," *American Political Science Review,* 62 (1968), 462. For another more recent critique see J. S. Sorzano, "David Easton and the Invisible Hand," *American Political Science Review,* 69 (1975), 91–106.

with normative consideration of systemic processes and output. Systems analysts simply try to distinguish between norms (what should be) and facts (what is). Perhaps the best way for the systems analyst to avoid the problem is to explicitly articulate policy preferences and the norms (whatever they may be) against which the system is evaluated. Proposals for reform would then be not simply in the realm of making the system more efficient (which, of course, implicitly reflects a conservative value), but rather shaping the system so that it can better accomplish those ends and produce those outputs that the analyst thinks it should. The observant student will be quick to realize that for the most part we have not taken our own advice. Rarely in the previous chapters have we explicitly stated our own norms against which we measured the operations and output of the federal judicial system. Our excuse, perhaps lame, is that our essential purpose was description and that prescription would have fundamentally altered the nature of this enterprise. Which brings us back to the original point of this paragraph!

How, then, can one assess, on balance, the current and prospective utility of the judicial systems approach? Perhaps the key to such an assessment lies with the criteria suggested by Karl Deutsch for the evaluation of a mode of analysis (or model), that is, the degree to which the model carries out four distinctive functions: the organizing, the heuristic, the predictive, and the mensurative.[23]

The *organizing* function concerns the ability of the model to order and relate disjointed data (and the analyses based on them) into an integrated and meaningful whole. If it is serving this function well, the model should indicate and illuminate heretofore unperceived interconnections and similarities. To a large degree, the evaluation of whether this function is being served or not rests upon the aesthetic experience of the observer. If what was originally murky and disjointed becomes meaningful, clear, and intuitively more simple, then the model is fulfilling the organizing function. Parenthetically, it might be noted that an explanation may be extremely satisfying without making any sort of quantitative predictions. The theory of evolution, for example, seems to be such an explanation.

The *heuristic* function concerns the ability of the model to raise new questions, suggest new relationships, or lead to previously un-

[23] Karl Deutsch, *The Nerves of Government* (New York: Free Press, 1963), pp. 8–10.

observed or unanalyzed data through new lines of empirical research. For example, the theory of evolution directed its adherents both to look for various "missing links" as well as allowing them to structure previously mysterious and unexplained fossils into a satisfying explanation.

The *predictive* function involves the production of verifiable predictions. As Deutsch noted, there is broad range in the explicitness of the predictions that may be made:

At one extreme we find simple yes-or-no predictions; at higher degrees of specificity we get qualitative predictions of similarity or matching, where the result is predicted to be of this kind or of that kind, or of this particular delicate shade; and at the other extreme we find completely quantitative predictions that may give us elaborate time series that may answer the questions of "When?" and "How Much?"[24]

When it implies the latter modes of prediction, a model then serves the *mensurative* function. The measurement in which it deals may vary "all the way from simple rank orderings to full-fledged ratio scales."[25]

Although Deutsch noted that they are "distinct," the organizing, heuristic, predictive, and mensurative functions are not unrelated to one another. Rather, they stand in a loose hierarchical arrangement. Thus a model must first present some satisfying organization and explanation for known data before it can make predictions, even if these predictions are only heuristic in nature. As one moves up the hierarchy, the successful fulfillment of each function becomes increasingly difficult. This characteristic of the functional criteria implies that in testing the adequacy of the model against them one gets a relative measure for evaluating the model's power and utility. One should note that the model need not satisfy the more difficult criteria—in particular, prediction and measurement—in order to be judged valuable.

In assessing whether judicial systems analysis has organizational utility, one's judgment must be relative. This necessitates our brief examination of three other frameworks whose scope is sufficiently general as to be competitors to the judicial systems approach. These are (1) the approach offered by traditional jurisprudence; (2) the

24 *Ibid.*, p. 9.
25 *Ibid.*

"bureaucratic" approach;[26] and (3) the "political" or "conventional" approach, which likens court behavior to the behavior of other political institutions, such as Congress or political parties.[27]

It hardly seems necessary to elaborate the reasons why the traditional approach is unacceptable. Although it may well serve as an important delineation of the norms to which judicial system authorities strive to adhere, the model does not adequately explain existing empirical data. A major contribution of legal realism, the sociology of law, and judicial behavior has been to show how great the deviation is between the real behavior of courtroom actors and that posited by the traditional model. Moreover, as an explanation, the traditional model simply cannot explain such crucial events as the "switch" in judicial policy during the Supreme Court's 1936 term[28] or the Nixon Court's marked change of direction particularly in the criminal procedures area. The killing blow, as Chapter 5 suggested, has been the quantitative work that shows better prediction of judicial behavior than does the traditional model.[29] Thus, although it has important implications for system behavior as a normative injunction, the traditional model cannot be considered an explanatory model. It suggests an extensiveness of activity that does not exist; it leaves untreated and unexplored too much activity; it makes predictions that simply are not borne out in the empirical world.

The bureaucratic model, whose most concise and clear formulation is still that by Max Weber, although more comprehensive in

[26] The original and still one of the best articulations of this approach is to be found in Max Weber, *The Theory of Social and Economic Organization* (New York: Free Press, 1964), pp. 329–341. Modern students of court behavior who have used various components of this model include Abraham Blumberg, *Criminal Justice*; Frank J. Sorauf, "Zorach v. Clauson: The Impact of a Supreme Court Decision," *American Political Science Review*, 53 (1959), 777–791; Martin Shapiro, *The Supreme Court and Administrative Agencies* (New York: Free Press, 1968).

[27] The classic of this genre is Jack W. Peltason, *Federal Courts in the Political Process* (New York: Random House, 1955).

[28] Cf. Felix Frankfurter, "Mr. Justice Roberts," *University of Pennsylvania Law Review*, 104 (1955), 313–316.

[29] Also see S. Sidney Ulmer, "Mathematical Models for Predicting Judicial Behavior," in Joseph L. Bernd and Archer Jones (eds.), *Mathematical Applications in Political Science, III* (Charlottesville: University of Virginia Press, 1967), pp. 67–95; and Fred Kort, "A Special and a General Multivariate Theory of Judicial Decisions," paper presented at the Annual Meeting of the American Political Science Association, 1974.

scope than the traditional model, has the disability of leaving un-treated and/or unexplained (particularly appellate) court behavior in which creative policy making rather than more simple conflict resolution through rule application predominates. Like the tradi-tional model, it also leaves unanalyzed activity external to the system that affects its output—activity that, in systems terms, is subsumed under the categories of "support" and "feedback." Thus the bureau-cratic model is at best incomplete in scope. It is still, however, highly suggestive. In its post-Weberian form,[30] it has much to offer both conceptually and as a guide to research. Its functional content makes it easily absorbed into a systems approach.

The "political" or "conventional" model is to some extent the mirror image of the bureaucratic model. Its strength lies in its treat-ment of those areas of behavior where the bureaucratic model is weakest. Conversely, it is weakest in those areas where the bureau-cratic model is strongest. Of all the models discussed, it shows the least formalization. To call the courts—like Congress and the presi-dency—"political" institutions does not take us very far. When a more precise operational content is given the term "political," it seems either too general or too specific. Thus, for example, if by "political" one means Easton's definition of politics as the authorita-tive allocation of values, then courts are obviously political. But one is then left with the problem of differentiating judicial processes and the processes characteristic of Congress and the presidency. If, on the other hand, one reads into the term "politics" the drive for power, partisan self-interest, and constituent sensitivity normally imputed to more popularly recruited political leaders, much judicial behavior seems unexplained and unexplainable. Thus, the political model suffers from a lack of semantic precision and the almost complete absence of formalization. Finally, there is an obvious neglect in the model toward a phenomenon whose discussion perme-ates both the traditional and bureaucratic models, that is, the ability of normative considerations as independent variables to affect judicial role playing.

[30] Weber emphasized formal considerations, rules and norms and authority pat-terns, almost exclusively. Later students of bureaucracy, among them Peter Blau and Robert K. Merton, built on Weber's work, particularly in their emphasis on in-formal organization and the dysfunctional aspects of formal rules and authority relationships.

When one turns to the systems model one finds at least partial elimination of some of the disabilities affecting the other models. Of all the models discussed, systems analysis can integrate and order the broadest range of what intuitively seems to be the significant data. This very comprehensiveness of the approach is one of its most striking merits. It can order and integrate phenomena treated by both the bureaucratic and political models. It can "make sense" out of the normative considerations involved in traditional jurisprudence. At the very minimum then, judicial systems analysis has greater organizational power than does its competitors. It appears to have the ability to produce greater clarity and to satisfyingly integrate the many, otherwise disjointed, materials found in legal and judicial studies.

The heuristic value of the judicial systems framework—its ability to suggest new lines of judicial system research and its potential for reinterpreting data already collected in previous studies—is, we believe, a striking merit of the approach.

Our assessment is radically and discouragingly different when we turn to the ability of systems analysis to serve the more formally demanding functions of prediction and measurement. The predictive statements found in systems analysis as distinct from its descriptive statements characteristically maintain that systemic processes tend toward certain states: for example, a system strives to prevent "demand overload," maintain a positive input of support, preserve systemic integrity, and so on. These statements, however, and the processes suggested by them are presented in metaphorical rather than linguistically or mathematically precise language. Simply put, the various concepts of systems analysis as presently given in the Eastonian literature are not defined or linked to one another by a calculus (language) having terminological invariance. It is as if one created a physics that stated that mass/energy, angular and linear momentum, electrical charge, and so on were conserved without having a calculus or set of operational definitions for measuring, identifying, or linking the empirical phenomena signaled by the terms mass, energy, momentum, charge, or conserve. Without such a set of operational procedures for identifying phenomena and an invariant calculus linking them, it is difficult to test the correspondence between the putative theory and the empirical world. In short, systems analysis does not, in its present state, make hard, quantitatively testable predictions.

Judicial systems analysis offers researchers a comprehensive set of categories for organizing and relating data, an impressive number of important heuristic insights, and the ability to handle microcosmic studies displaying predictability. However promising this may be, systems analysis has yet to yield a theory of judicial system behavior. For it to do so will require the development of operational definitions for precise identification and measurement of systemic parameters and a formalized calculus for relating these parameters to one another. That such precision is possible is suggested in particular by the mathematically sophisticated judicial conversion literature. Nevertheless, systems analysis, in spite of some severe shortcomings, provides a major analytical tool for students of public law and judicial behavior. It has been increasingly used[31] and has and should continue to provide solid analytical payoffs.

[31] Schubert correctly predicted in 1968 that "tomorrow systems analysis will be the conventional mode of discourse in the field." See his "Behavioral Jurisprudence," *Law and Society Review*, 2 (1968), p. 426.

INDEX

Goldman, Jerry, 87n, 105n, 107n, 115n, 116n, 117n
Goldman, Sheldon, 49n, 57n, 60n, 68n, 69n, 70, 72n, 73n, 77n, 164n, 172n, 173n, 174n, 175n, 184n, 202n, 203n, 205n, 206n, 233n
Gorai, Patricia, 78n
Gottschall, Jon, 233n
Goulden, Joseph C., 49n, 76n, 99n
Government Legal Services Corporation. See Legal services program
Graham, Fred P., 12n
Grant, Ulysses S., 62
Gray, Horace, 182
Green, Justin J., 271n
Greenstein, Fred I., 207n
Gregor, A. James, 287n
Grey, David L., 252n, 253n, 256n
Grossman, Joel B., 2n, 15n, 18n, 49n, 52n, 55n, 62n, 63n, 66n, 89n, 138n, 160n, 165n, 176n, 193n, 200n, 203n, 222, 223n, 234n, 280n, 282n, 285n
Grunbaum, Werner, 160n, 203
Guam, courts of, 23, 26
Guilty pleas, 128–130. See also Plea bargaining
Guttman, Louis, 165–166

H

Habeas corpus, 21, 100n, 102, 108n, 116n, 214, 243
Hagan, John, 197n, 198n
Haines, Charles G., 78n
Hakman, Nathan, 89n, 238n, 245n, 282n
Halpern, Stephen C., 130n
Hamilton, Alexander, 43n
Hamilton, Charles V., 196n
Hammond, Phillip E., 140n, 145n, 227n, 261–263
Hanson, Roger, 264n
Harlan, John M., 15, 56n, 162–163, 164n
Harries, Keith D., 198n
Harris, P. M. G., 67n
Harris, Richard, 66n
Harris v. New York, 240
Haselswerdt, Michael V., 171n
Haynsworth, Clement, 14, 15n, 55n, 63–64, 66, 77, 234–235, 247, 269
Henderson, A. M., 42n
Herndon, James, 1n, 164n
Hess, David W., 240n
Heumann, Milton, 37n, 124n
Hintze, William, 131n, 133n
Hobbs, Douglas S., 8n

Holmes, Oliver Wendell, 62, 64, 156, 184, 249
Holtzoff, Alexander, 244
Hoover, Herbert, 65
Howard, A. E. D., 164n
Howard, J. Woodford, Jr., 106n, 177n, 179n, 180n, 181n, 184n, 202n, 205n, 207n
Hufstedler, Shirley M., 136n
Hughes, Charles Evans, 8–11, 131, 153, 186

I

Illinois v. Allen, 39n
Impact. See Compliance; Feedback
Impeachment, 238, 269
In forma pauperis, 32, 109, 131
Indictment, 122, 126
Information, 122, 126
Information feedback, 7, 286. See also Feedback
Injunction, 26, 39
Input, 3–7, 10–11, 14–15, 75, 79, 95–154, 221, 279–285. See also Withinput
Institutes, court personnel, 97
Interest groups, 4, 89, 115, 137, 227, 241
Interstate Commerce Commission, 22, 26, 43, 100n

J

Jackson, Andrew, 34, 62, 67, 272
Jackson, Donald D., 49n, 55n, 56n, 60
Jackson, Robert H., 162–163, 180–181, 189n
Jacob, Herbert, 91n, 122n, 124n, 143n, 197n, 221n, 279n, 280n, 281n, 282n
Jahnige, Thomas P., 2n, 10n, 16n, 131n, 183n, 274n
Jaros, Dean, 203n
Jaworski, Leon, 124n
Jefferson, Thomas, 34, 238, 272, 274
Jencks, Christopher, 69n
Jenkins v. Georgia, 229n, 240n
Johnson, Earl, Jr., 86n
Johnson, Lyndon B., 12, 50, 54, 64, 65n, 66n, 69–71, 84, 102n, 264, 269, 275
Johnson, Richard M., 227n, 262n, 286n
Johnson v. Louisiana, 39n
Johnson v. Mississippi, 20n
Jones, Archer, 290n
Joslyn, Nancy, 90n
Judges, federal, 243–247. See also Courts of Appeals; District Courts; Supreme Court

Output, 3, 6–8, 10–11, 14–15, 75, 211–236, 284–285

P

Palumbo, Dennis J., 210n
Parenti, Michael, 65n
Paris Adult Theatre v. *Slaton*, 228n, 239n
Parker, Douglas R., 170n
Parker, John J., 15n, 65, 246–247
Parole, 26, 97–98
Parole board, 48n
Parsons, Talcott, 34n, 42n
Partridge, Anthony, 198n
Peltason, Jack W., 196n, 290n
Pennsylvania v. *Wheeling and Belmont Bridge Co.*, 271n
Pentagon papers case. *See New York Times Co.* v. *United States*
Per curiam decisions, 33, 110
Percy, Charles, 51n
Personality variable, 207
Peterson, David J., 170n
Plea bargaining, 26, 36–37, 90, 100n, 123, 126, 127–130, 198, 215n, 216–218
Plessy v. *Ferguson*, 214
Points of Rebellion, 235
Police, 21, 47n
Political liberalism, 175
Political party affiliation, as component of causal model, 208–209
   and judicial decision making, 174–176
   and judicial selection, 57–59
   and policy considerations, 59–61, 75
   and support, 145, 146n, 147n
Political questions, 112–113
Pollock v. *Farmers' Loan and Trust Co.*, 113, 238
Poor, rights of, 84–85
Posner, Richard A., 135n, 280n
Pound, Roscoe, 137n
Powell, Lewis, 15, 56n, 63–64, 131n, 136n, 162–163, 168–170
Precedent, 156. *See also* Stare decisis
President, the, 48, 50, 52, 57, 62, 74, 77, 80, 141, 229, 237, 249, 264–265, 267–268
Pretrial conference, 119–120
Prisoner petitions, 102, 107–109, 116n
Prisoners, rights of, 21, 102n
Pritchett, C. Herman, 87n, 134n, 158–161, 266n
Probation, Division of, 24–25, 48n, 97–98
Proffer v. *United States*, 114
Psychometric model, 167n

Public defenders, federal, 86, 89
Public interest lawyers, 102n
Public opinion, 137–154, 250, 277–278
Puerto Rico, courts of, 18, 23, 26

R

Race, and judicial selection, 65, 71
Rathjen, Gregory James, 9n, 171n, 187n
Reapportionment, 26, 100n, 113, 239. *See also Baker* v. *Carr*
Recznik v. *City of Lorain*, 230n
Redmont, Robert, 36n
Reed, Stanley F., 162–163, 180–181, 183
Regime rules, 3–5, 17, 96, 111–115, 139, 226–227, 281–282, 284
Rehnquist, William, 15, 56n, 63, 72, 131n, 136n, 162–163, 168–170
Religion, and judicial selection, 64, 69–71
Reproducibility, coefficient of, 166
Republican Party, 77, 238, 274–275
Restraint, judicial, 42, 113, 206–207
Reyes v. *United States*, 114
Reynolds v. *Sims*, 229, 239, 268
Rich, Francis M., Jr., 203n
Richardson, Richard J., 26n, 29n, 68n, 113–114, 120n, 139n, 222, 282n, 284n
Riedel, Marc, 197n
Risky shift, small group concept of, 190
Roberts, Owen, 8–11, 153, 156, 247, 290n
Robinson, James A., 158n, 279n
Rodgers, Harrell R., Jr., 258n, 259n, 262n, 263n, 264n
Roe v. *Wade*, 228n, 233, 269n
Rohde, David W., 9n, 171n, 187n, 209n
Rokeach, Milton, 171n
Rokes, Willis Park, 119n
Role, judicial, 33–42, 38–40, 83–84, 199–210, 251, 291
Role, of jury, 37–39. *See also* Juries
Role, of lawyers, 35–41. *See also* Lawyers; Plea bargaining
Romans, Neil T., 245n
Roosevelt, Franklin D., 9–10, 62, 67, 72, 74, 152–153, 232, 238, 241, 272, 275
Roosevelt, Theodore, 62
Rosen, Daniel, 132n, 219n
Rosenberg, Maurice, 120n
Rosenthal, Douglas E., 118n
Ross, H. Laurence, 118n
Ross v. *Moffitt*, 115n, 247
Rule of four, 31, 109, 219
Rule skeptics, 156

Supreme Court (*Continued*)
  behavior of judges
    and backgrounds, 175–177
    bloc analysis of, 160–165
    cumulative scaling of, 166–172
    and fact pattern analysis, 195–196
    role, 200–207
    as a small group, 178–189
  demand input overload, 134–136
  demands on, 108–110
  docket
    appellate, 109–110
    miscellaneous, 109
    original, 109
  feedback to, from
    communications media, 250–257
    compliance rates, 258–264
    congress, 265–272
    law reviews, 247–250
    litigation, 238–242
    lower courts, 242–247
    presidents, 264–265
  feedback and policy making, 272–278
  gatekeeping, 130–136, 214–222
  jurisdiction, 20, 28, 30–33, 109, 213–214
  law clerks to justices, 87
  opinion assignment, 9, 187–188, 202
  opinion of the court, 42, 187
  and plea bargaining, 129–130
  policy making, 222–233. *See also* Chief Justice
  selection of judges, 48
    consequences of process, 74–78
    geographic considerations, 63–64
    ideology, 62–63
    religious-ethnic considerations, 64–65
    and the Senate, 65–66
  support for, 137–154
Sutherland, George, 8–9, 247
Sweatt v. *Painter*, 224n
Swift v. *Tyson*, 19n, 248–249
System, definition of, 2

T

Taft, William H., 184, 186, 191
Taft Court, 182–183
Tanenhaus, Joseph, 2n, 89n, 132–134, 140–147, 148n, 149n, 152n, 157n, 159, 160n, 161n, 172n, 173n, 176n, 193n, 203n, 219n, 234n, 282n, 283n, 285n
Taney, Roger B., 62, 64
Tax Court, 23, 25, 106
Taylor, Jean G., 124n

Terminiello v. *Chicago*, 181
Territorial courts, 23, 26
Thornberry, Homer, 65n
Thornhill v. *Alabama*, 182
Tittle, Charles R., 264n
Todd, A. L., 53n, 64n
Tone, Phillip W., 51n
Tort cases, 116–119
Totenberg, Nina, 87n, 201n, 267n
Trial courts. *See* District courts
Trials, 19–21
Train v. *City of New York*, 268n
Truman, Harry S., 28n, 264, 267, 275

U

Ulmer, S. Sidney, 1n, 2n, 92n, 131n, 133–134, 158n, 159, 161–163, 164n, 167, 172, 175n, 177n, 178n, 187n, 188n, 189n, 190n, 192n, 193–196, 238n, 257n, 284n, 290n
Ungs, Thomas D., 204n
United States Attorneys, 72, 78–84, 90, 122–123, 126, 128
United States v. *Butler*, 156
United States Commissioners, 25
United States v. *Darby*, 242
United States Magistrates, 25, 48n, 104, 122–123
United States v. *Nixon*, 28n, 267n
United States v. *Orito*, 228n
United States ex rel Ross v. *McMann*, 243n
United States v. *South-Eastern Underwriters Association*, 271
United States v. *12 200-Ft. Reels of Super 8mm Film*, 228n

V

Van Buren, Martin, 67
Van Devanter, Willis, 8–9, 186, 247
Varrin, Rene, 93
Victimization, 150n
Vietnam War, 103, 277
Vines, Kenneth N., 2n, 26n, 29n, 68n, 113–114, 120n, 130n, 139n, 176, 196n, 222, 279n, 282n, 284n
Vinson, Fred, 162–163, 180–181
Vinson Court, 179, 183
Virgin Island, courts of, 23, 26

W

Wald, Michael, 240n
Walker, Thomas G., 176, 178n, 190, 284n
Wallace, George, 12, 276
Walsh, Michael H., 92n
Wanner, Craig, 280n

Warren, Bruce L., 70n
Warren, Charles, 248–249
Warren, Earl, 8, 11–15, 67, 135, 162–163, 184–185, 187n, 188–189, 202n, 232–233
Warren Court, 60, 108n, 129, 140–142, 146n, 165n, 212n, 231n, 233, 239, 243, 245, 255, 264, 268, 270, 276–277, 283
Wasby, Stephen L., 15n, 66n, 237n, 245n, 285n, 286n
Watergate, 12n, 13n, 124n, 142n, 227, 275, 278
Way, H. Frank, 161n, 233n
Weber, Max, 18, 42, 45–46, 290, 291n
Wechsler, Herbert, 28n
Weicker, Lowell, 56
Weissman, Edward J. H., 172n, 208n, 210n
Weitzman, Lenore J., 93n, 198n
Wells, Richard S., 88n, 91n, 222
Wenner, Lettie M., 204n
Wenner, Manfred W., 204n
West Coast Hotel v. *Parrish,* 9
West Virginia State Board of Education v. *Barnette,* 246n, 257n
Wettick, R. Stanton, Jr., 240n
Wheeler, Russell, 24n, 135n, 200n, 236n, 281n
Whitcomb, Howard R., 24n, 281n
White, Byron R., 63, 72, 131n, 136n, 162–163, 168–170

Whitebread, Charles H., II, 240n
Whittaker, Charles E., 162–163
Wilkes, Donald E., Jr., 245n
Wilkinson, J. Harvie, 87n
Wilson, James, 67
Wilson, James Q., 122n
Wilson, Woodrow, 64
Wirt, Frederick M., 263n
Withinput, 6, 98–99, 138n, 284
Witt, James W., 241n
Wold, John T., 204n
Wolfe, Arthur C., 277n
Wolfgang, Marvin E., 197n
Women, and judicial selection, 75–76
Women, rights of, 220, 226, 233
Wood, Arthur L., 36n, 89n
Wright, J. Skelly, 37n
Wyzanski, Charles, 54

Y

Yarbrough, Tinsley E., 231n, 233n
Young, James S., 185n
Youngstown Sheet and Tube Co. v. *Sawyer,* 28n, 229, 258, 264, 267, 268n

Z

Zahn v. *International Paper Co.,* 26n
Zavoina, William, 174
Zeisel, Hans, 92n, 93n, 94
Zeitz, Leonard, 241n
Zimmerman, Niel T., 133n
Zorach v. *Clauson,* 246n

82 83 84 85 86   10 9 8 7 6